TIMOTI

COMMON CORE
Mathematics

in a PLC at Work™

GRADES 6-8

Diane J. Briars
Harold Asturias
David Foster
Mardi A. Gale

FOREWORD BY Austin Buffum

A Joint Publication With

NCTM® NATIONAL COUNCIL OF
TEACHERS OF MATHEMATICS

555 North Morton Street
Bloomington, IN 47404

800.733.6786 (toll free) / 812.336.7700
FAX: 812.336.7790

email: info@solution-tree.com
solution-tree.com

Visit **go.solution-tree.com/commoncore** to download the reproducibles in this book.

Printed in the United States of America

16 15 14   5

Library of Congress Cataloging-in-Publication Data

Briars, Diane J., 1951-
   Common core mathematics in a PLC at work. Grades 6-8 / Diane J. Briars, Harold Asturias, David Foster, Mardi A. Gale ; Timothy D. Kanold, series editor.
      pages cm
   Includes bibliographical references and index.
   ISBN 978-1-936764-10-5 (perfect bound) 1. Mathematics--Study and teaching (Middle school)--Standards--United States. 2. Professional learning communities. I. Title.
   QA13.B75 2013
   510.71'273--dc23
                                   2012032775

Solution Tree

Jeffrey C. Jones, CEO
Edmund M. Ackerman, President

Solution Tree Press
President: Douglas M. Rife
Publisher: Robert D. Clouse
Editorial Director: Lesley Bolton
Managing Production Editor: Caroline Wise
Senior Production Editor: Joan Irwin
Copy Editor: Sarah Payne-Mills
Proofreader: Elisabeth Abrams
Text Designer: Amy Shock
Cover Designer: Jenn Taylor

New
Soccer
Techniques,
Tactics & Teamwork

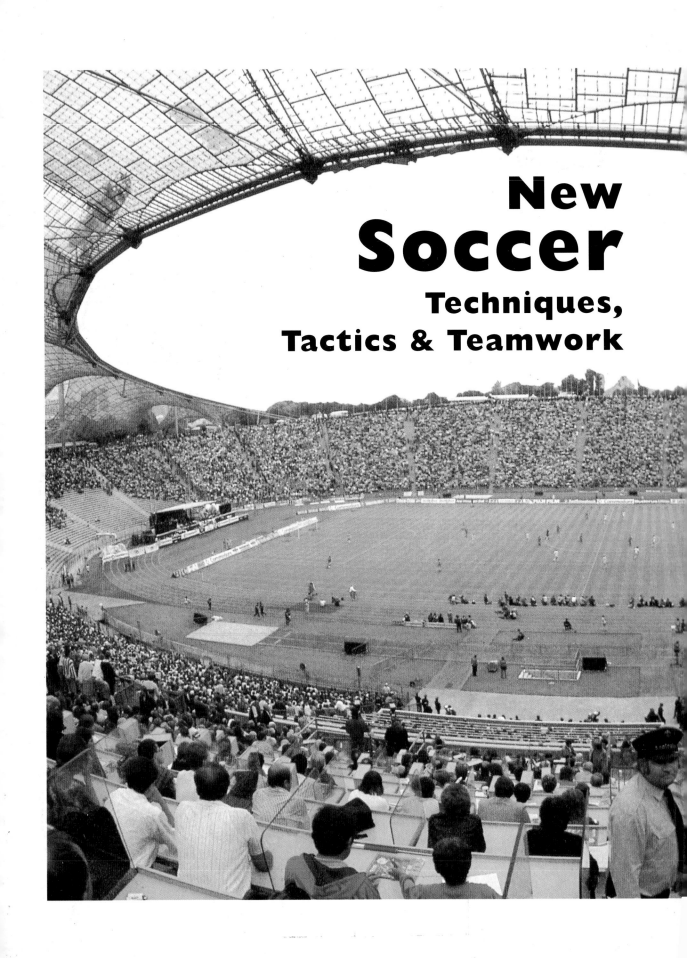

New
Soccer
Techniques,
Tactics & Teamwork

Gerhard Bauer

Introduction by Franz Beckenbauer

Newly Revised & Updated

Sterling Publishing Co., Inc.
New York

Library of Congress Cataloging-in-Publication Data

Bauer, Gerhard, 1940-
  [Lehrbuch Fussball. English]
  New soccer techniques, tactics & teamwork / Gerhard Bauer ;
[translated by Kelly Ramke and Nicole Franke].-- Newly rev. &
updated.
      p. cm.
Includes index.
  ISBN 1-4027-0088-1
  1. Soccer--Training. 2. Soccer--Coaching. I. Title: New soccer
techniques, tactics, and teamwork. II. Title.
  GV943.9.T7 B3713 2002
. 796.334'2--dc21

2002007281

Demonstration of Techniques: Markus Ebner, Max Eckschlager,
Stefan Heigenhauser, Dean Spanring

Photo Credits: Adidas: 149; Baader: 108; Bauer: 49, 52 above, 53
above, 54 UL, 99, 144, 150; bfp-Versand/Lindemann: 146/147;
Birkner: 38, 39, 40, 45, 48, 56 A, 64, 67, 69, 79, 80, 81; Bongarts/L.
Bongarts: 123; Bongarts/Brandt: 88; Bongarts/Dede/Rydlewicz: 36;
Bongarts/Hargreaves: 72; Bongarts/Kienzler: 111; Bongarts/Köpsel:
93; Bongarts/Rentz: 10; Bongarts/Sandten: 77, 121; Bongarts/-
Schneider: 116; B+S Pressefotografie/Beisel: 56 B, 57; Kemmler:
42/43, 46/47, 50/51, 52/53 center, 54/55 UR, LR; Mühlberger: 2/3, 84;
Rauchensteiner: 5, 7, 18, 26/27, 83, 129, 132; Seer: 8; Sinicki: 59, 61

Front cover photo: Hans Rauchensteiner
Jacket design: Joko Sander Werbeagentur, München
Computer graphics: Typodata GmbH, München

Translated by Kelly Ramke and Nicole Franke.
Current English version edited by Nancy Sherman.

Published 2002 by Sterling Publishing Co., Inc.
387 Park Avenue South, New York, NY 10016
Originally published by BLV Verlagsgesellschaft mbH
Under the title *Lehrbuch Fußball*
© 2001 by BLV Verlagsgesellschaft mbH, München
English translation © 2002 by Sterling Publishing Co., Inc.
Distributed in Canada by Sterling Publishing
C/o Canadian Manda Group, One Atlantic Avenue, Suite 105
Toronto, Ontario, Canada M6K 3E7
Distributed in Great Britain and Europe by Chrysalis Books
64 Brewery Road, London N7 9NT, England
Distributed in Australia by Capricorn Link (Australia) Pty. Ltd.
P.O. Box 704, Windsor, NSW 2756 Australia

ISBN 1-4027-0088-1

Contents

Contents

Soccer, a game that continues to fascinate its fans, is considered the number one sport in the world. I was reminded of this fact recently when I looked at the statistical data: every four years, the World Championship Games are watched by 15 billion viewers, a number that nearly defies comprehension.

As a fan and a representative of this sport, I could look at these numbers and lean back, satisfied and relaxed, basking in the glow of being in first place. But this would be the beginning of the end, because sitting still is the equivalent of sliding back. This is nowhere more true than in the game of soccer.

I applaud the publication of a new book on soccer. I think it is justified, since new developments in this game are taking place all the time.

I also think that those who often say that soccer was much better in the past are wrong and unfair. I suggest that those of you who feel this way buy a video of the 1970 World Championship Games in Mexico. When you watch the semifinals, which Germany lost to Italy by a score of three to four, it will renew your appreciation of the drama and excitement that keep soccer alive.

And you will most likely notice something else. In those days, the game was slower and players had much more time. Although the old motto, "Stop—look—play," is no longer applicable, it didn't truly characterize the game even then. But I would still insist that any national championship team today had better play a lot faster. Modern soccer players are not only under time pressure, they are under constant pressure even in open spaces. Thus, occasional technical mistakes can't be avoided.

It is wrong, however (and this brings me back to the point I started to make in the beginning), to believe that the players' technical skills were much better in the past. Nor is this true of their tactical skills. Soccer asks much more of players today.

I have noticed that corner and free kicks are not used nearly as often as they should be. Why that is so, I can't say. This observation, also voiced recently by my colleague Hannes Löhr, is surely another reason why the publication of a soccer book, outlining the process of training and teaching, is very timely. This book attempts to inspire and to give new impetus to daily training sessions with the goal of improving technical and tactical skills, as well as increasing fitness.

I hope you have fun with Gerhard Bauer's book.

Franz Beckenbauer

Preface

Soccer is, and has always been, one of the most appealing sports. This is true not only for the active player, but for the fan who comes to the stadium or watches on TV. In the year 2000, soccer was played every week in Germany by 65,869 senior teams, 100,035 junior teams, and 6,812 women's and girls' teams, all organized by the German Soccer Association (DFB).

Additionally, there are huge numbers of unofficially organized teams and players that meet on a more or less regular basis in their free time for the sheer pleasure of playing the game. As surveys of students have shown, soccer is a favorite in school athletic programs. In spite of this, we must not forget that the competition never goes to sleep.

Besides my full-time activity as the head of soccer education for gym teachers and certified sport scientists at the Technical University of Munich, I was for many years on the board and held the presidency of the BDFL (Association of German Soccer Teachers).

In my capacity as head of the Association of German Soccer Teachers, I am co-responsible for the education of all German "A" license holders and gym teachers. This position gives me the chance to speak with coaches from all sectors of the sport. The one topic discussed most often is the problem of attracting new talent.

In part, this is due to the competition soccer faces from other sports, the changes in the way children spend their free time, and the decline of street soccer. Consequently, it is very difficult to find young people with natural talent. Coaches are truly worried. But keep in mind that problems are here to be solved. Those who are responsible, including the coaches, must look for new and innovative ideas to remedy this situation. Besides intensifying their search for talent and concentrating on appropriate but passionate leadership, the actual training must take into consideration all that we have learned from practical experience and research in sports medicine. From the very start, young players should receive age-appropriate training in accordance with the criteria outlined herein. Exercise programs should be designed to strengthen competitiveness. Only then can we hope to stand up to the challenges of the future.

Everyone involved in the nurturing and training of players and teams (including the players themselves) will find in this book the information and knowledge necessary for a successful training program—for young people as well as for adults. I have included all that I have learned during my many years as a coach in amateur and college soccer and as a college phys. ed. teacher (with an emphasis on soccer). This book will provide the reader with detailed information for a successful training program that optimizes overall performance. The positive response to the previous five editions, which sold out very quickly, makes me hopeful that the sixth edition will achieve this goal as well. I hope it will be helpful to coaches and players at all levels.

I will be very happy, dear reader, if this book increases your enjoyment of the sport, and makes the work of coaches a little easier.

Gerhard Bauer

Gerhard Bauer

The Game's Appeal

The game of soccer has captivated people for centuries, and it continues to grow in popularity all over the world. Its appeal has many different facets. But exactly what is it about soccer that players and fans alike find so compelling?

The Appeal for Players

Soccer and the Need for Physical Activity

When small children kick and run after a ball, they are following their innate desire to move, leap, run, and jump, all a part of healthy physical and mental development.

Their pleasure in playing with a ball grows in direct proportion to their increasing skills. Players of all ages find great satisfaction in being able to move a ball with their feet or their heads. It is intensely gratifying to develop the ability to dribble a ball expertly or to aim a kick accurately.

The Hunting Instinct and Soccer

Hunting has long been essential to human survival. The hunting and fighting instincts are deeply rooted in the psyche. As civilization advances, opportunities to act on these instincts become increasingly limited. Sports, particularly team sports such as soccer, provide an outlet for this innate behavior. The pursuit of the ball, the confrontation and competition between players, the thrill of dangerous moments during the game, the roar of applause after scoring a goal—these are some of today's equivalents to the successful hunt in the distant past.

Soccer and the Impulse to Play

Soccer must be seen first and foremost as a game, at least for young people and amateurs. It is played for the sheer joy of it. It is goal specific and limited by rules and by a clearly defined playing area. The game can be played time and time again, and the outcome is never quite certain.

Everyone plays willingly, even enthusiastically. Concentrating on the game provides a break from everyday concerns. The loss of a game or of points is a short term setback—there will always be another game. Coming and going as they do, game and point losses are not as painful as failing in school or on the job.

The uncertainty of the game's outcome and the crowd's reaction are compelling forces for both players and fans. Up to the very last second of the game, the proverbial Sword of Damocles hangs over every emotionally packed action. Will possession of the ball, an attempt at kicking a goal, or any of the other countless possible combinations work out as anticipated—or not?

Fans and players alike are jerked constantly between hope and despair. Emotions are charged, only to be relieved moments later. In other words, soccer connects with great intensity to the human instincts to play and hunt.

Group Participation and Soccer

Human beings are social animals. A player establishes his place in the hierarchical order of the team. The star and the utility player complement each other. This provides the fans cheering in the stadium a nearly perfect means of satisfying their herd instinct, a legacy from the earliest Homo sapiens.

The Appeal for Fans

Soccer as Theater

The simplicity of the rules allows soccer fans in the stadium to appreciate the technical finesse of the play, the dramatic high points as well as the frustrations and deep disappointments. In essence, the fans are not passive observers but active participants, critically and mentally involved in the action on the field. In addition, fans with playing experience are able to anticipate developments on the field and compare the particular strategy they might have used with the actual play. Though unlike the players on the field, they never experience the consequences of their strategy, they enjoy the vicarious imagining.

Furthermore, fans are an essential part of the overall scenario. They are another separate element, giving noisy approval or disapproval, waving flags and banners, clapping rhythmically and frantically, whistling and hollering. They are an integral part of the whole spectacle.

Soccer as Fertile Ground for Hero Worship

You may understand it well or only register the fact with slight amusement, you may condemn it or be a loyal devotee; but the game of soccer, and professional soccer in particular, gives rise to considerable hero worship and creates an army of unconditionally loyal worshippers.

Fans are fascinated by their hero's accomplishments, cheering him on, often exploding into thunderous applause. They get carried away by the striking display of expert skills. They admire the star's ability to maneuver the ball, his staying power, and the craftiness and cleverness with which he handles his opponents.

The Features of the Game

The game of soccer as a sport spectacle satisfies many drives and instincts.

The object of this adulation is envied, celebrated, and worshipped all at the same time. It is a recognized phenomenon that hero worship thrives in regions that have high unemployment.

Game Characteristics

Like every other game, soccer is distinguished by a special feature: its unique concept. What gives the game its most notable characteristic and the reason it is played so enthusiastically, particularly by young men and women, is the simplicity of this concept: scoring goals without using

The Basis of the Game

Two teams compete, each with 11 players, one of whom is the goalkeeper. The winner is the team that has scored more goals at the end of the set time period. With the exception of the goalkeeper, no player may touch the ball with his hands. Players must kick the ball or hit it with their heads or bodies.

your hands. This is the basic, original idea of soccer. So simple a basis makes it possible for the game to be played with only the most rudimentary of rules. In addition, soccer can

be played almost anywhere. A backyard—even a cement surface—can serve as a playing field. Branches placed on the ground at each end of the playing field can be substituted for the goal. Sidelines can easily be marked with backpacks or even sweaters. The same flexibility holds for the ball. When played for the sheer fun of it, soccer does not require a regulation ball; in a pinch, even a tennis ball will do.

Even for official matches, the rules can be adjusted without losing the original idea of the game. Indoor games, for instance, have different rules. And children under the age of

Structure and Rules of the Game

12 play on smaller fields and on teams of only seven players. In addition, the duration of the game and the size of the ball can be changed without a problem. Whatever the minor adjustments to the game, the basic concept remains essentially unchanged.

Structure of the Game

Every sport has its characteristic structure. Even games that are similar in concept differ considerably in their structure. Soccer bears obvious similarities to handball, volleyball, and basketball, with the following significant differences:

- In soccer, only the goalkeeper may use his hands, and then only when he is in the penalty area.
- In relation to the number of players, the playing field is much larger than for most other sports. The normal size of a soccer field (see diagram on page 13) is 345 feet by 230 feet (105 x 70 m). This is approximately five times the size of a handball court, nine times the size of a basketball court, and roughly 24 times the size of a volleyball court.
- The space that each player covers is also larger. Each soccer player has more than five times as much space as a handball player and almost nine times as much as a basketball player.
- Fewer goals are scored per game in soccer than in most other sports. Usually the final score is very close, heightening the tension for everyone involved.
- Confrontations between opposing players occur frequently. An analysis of games has shown that 250 to 350 confrontations between two opposing players take place during a single game between professional teams. During matches between France and Germany at the 1982 World Championships, some 263

such individual confrontations were tallied, and in 1986, there were 309.
- Goal kicking is preceded by a combination of systematic ball maneuvers that includes the use of the midfield, where both teams fight intensely for control of the ball.
- Contact with the ball is unique in soccer. Only in soccer is the ball received and carried with the foot and the head. Aside from soccer, only football and rugby use the foot for kicking goals.
- The length of time an individual player is in actual possession of the ball is relatively short when measured against the time it takes to play the whole game or the frequency with which a player actually has ball contact. In 1976, Jaschok/Witt timed players' actual ball contact. The study showed the following: Maximum time of contact was 3:50 minutes, the minimum was 20 seconds, and the average was about 2:00 minutes for 50 ball contacts.

Rules of the Game

The FIFA (Fédération Internationale de Football Association) is the international authority that establishes the rules and governs the sport of soccer. These rules are binding for all international competition between male teams. Rules for games played by children and women and those played indoors (and with some limitations for amateur teams) can be amended by the respective state or local authorities.

The rules that are in effect today have a long and turbulent history. The following provides a brief history of the more important developments in the game of soccer.

1846 A team is determined to consist of between 15 and 20 players.

1863 Soccer separates from rugby.

1864 It becomes mandatory to wear shorts that cover the knees and to wear caps with tassels.

1866 The corner kick and free throw are introduced.

1870 The number of players per team is reduced to 11.

1871 The ball may not be stopped with the hands.

1872 Catching the ball with the hands is allowed again, but only for one player: the goalkeeper is born. He may use his hands, but only in the penalty area.

1874 Robert Koch publishes the first book of soccer rules in German. The first German student team is founded in Braunschweig.

1875 The top of the goal is defined by a crossbar, replacing strips of cloth that had been used up until then.

1877 England, where rules had not been used consistently, establishes a uniform structure. Suspension from the game is introduced.

1878 An English referee innovates the game with the signaling whistle as an auxiliary tool to regulate playing.

1880 Following the British example, Germany adopts two 30-minute halves (since changed to two 45-minute halves).

1882 An international authority is established with a board that is responsible for settling all disputes.

1885 Professional soccer is born when England allows players to receive compensation.

1889 The referee, supported by two linesmen, is given unequivocal authority for game decisions. Until then, the game had two observers and one referee. The referee would intervene only when asked to do so by a team's leader.

1892 Betting on the outcome of a game between players and fans is outlawed.

Structure and Rules of the Game

1896   In Germany, the playing field has to be free of trees and bushes. Previously, natural obstacles were occasionally seen.

1900   The German Soccer Club is founded in Leipzig. Other soccer clubs are also established.

1902   England forbids women's soccer.

1903   An 18-yard (16-m) penalty area is established. The goalkeeper is allowed to catch a ball only in this zone.

1904   The International Soccer Association, FIFA, is founded in Paris. The concept of "dangerous play" is defined, and the free throw is introduced. The rule requiring shorts that cover the knees is finally abandoned.

1906   England joins the FIFA. The English rules are accepted internationally.

1907   A player is permitted to be offside in his own territory.

1913   The 9.15-m distance rule is introduced for the free kick.

1921   Goalkeepers are required to wear yellow pullovers during international competition.

1924   Rules for corner kicks are revised. It is now possible to convert a corner kick directly.

1925   New offside rules make the game tactically more offensive. Only two opposing players need to be between the goal line and the attacker at the moment the attacker kicks the ball.

1929   New penalty-kick rules are adopted. The goalkeeper may not move until the kick is completed.

1933   For the British Cup Final, players wear their numbers on the backs of their shirts. This rule is made official in 1939.

1951   By allowing the use of a white ball for night games, soccer enters the television era.

1955   The ban on games played under floodlights is lifted.

1965   England allows the substitution of players in case of injury.

1966   England permits the substitution of two players, regardless of the reason.

1982   The four-step rule for the goalkeeper is adopted.

1985   Additional rules governing the goalkeeper's handling of the ball with his hands are enacted.

1990   The goalkeeper is no longer allowed to accept ball passes by hand that are intentionally kicked back to him.

2000   The goalkeeper is allowed to hold the ball in hand for 6 seconds only. However, he may take as many steps as he wishes to during this period.

The original set of 17 rules established by the FIFA were grouped together as follows:

Requirements for the Game

Rule 1   The field of play
Rule 2   The ball
Rule 3   Number of players
Rule 4   Players' equipment

Guiding and Controlling the Game

Rule 5   The referee
Rule 6   The linesmen
Rule 7   Game duration
Rule 8   Starting the game

Critical Game Situations

Rule 9   The ball in and out of play
Rule 10   Method of scoring
Rule 11   Offside
Rule 12   Fouls and misconduct

Standard Situations

Rule 13   Free kick
Rule 14   Penalty kick
Rule 15   Throw-in
Rule 16   Goal kick
Rule 17   Corner kick

The Duration of Matches According to Gender, Age, and Location

Gender	Individual games outdoors		Competition played indoors			
	Age	Maximum duration	Age	Maximum duration	Overtime	Maximum playing time on any one day
Men	8–10 years 10–12 years 12–14 years 14–16 years over 16 years	2 x 25 min. 2 x 30 min. 2 x 35 min. 2 x 40 min. 2 x 45 min.	under 12 years 12–18 years over 18 years	2 x 5 min. 2 x 10 min. 2 x 15 min.	2 x 3 min. 2 x 3 min. 2 x 5 min.	60 min. 80 min 120 min.
Women	under 12 years 12–14 years 14–16 years over 16 years	2 x 25 min. 2 x 30 min. 2 x 35 min. 2 x 40 min.	under 16 years over 16 years	2 x 5 min. 1 x 10 min.	2 x 3 min. 2 x 3 min.	60 min 80 min

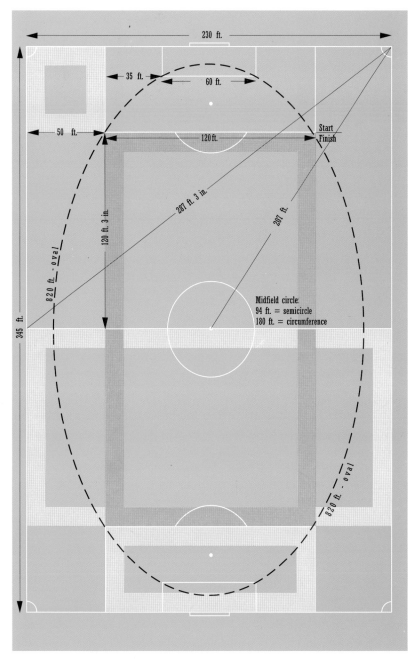

230 ft.

35 ft.

60 ft.

50 ft.

120 ft.

287 ft. 3 in.

120 ft. 3 in.

207 ft.

820 ft. - oval

345 ft.

Start
Finish

Midfield circle:
94 ft. = semicircle
180 ft. = circumference

820 ft. - oval

820 ft. - oval

The standard size playing field is 345 ft x 230 ft (105 m x 70 m), divided into sections of varying dimensions in which specific training can take place. Together with permanent structures such as stairs and barriers, these areas offer a coach many possibilities for organizing and conducting varied training sessions. A skillful organizer can use the different sections of the field for numerous practice and game sessions.

The duration of matches involving men and women of different age levels varies greatly. As this affects the impact level in training, the different playing times are summarized in the table on page 12.

The Team

A big part of soccer's appeal to such enormous numbers of players and spectators is that it is a team sport. The substantial number of players involved and the endless possibilities for offensive and defensive maneuvers enable the players to make the greatest use of their imaginations. The spectators are constantly witness to new and surprising combinations of plays.

Teamwork

The complicated cooperation necessary to a team's success is the result of individual effort, effective interaction between two or more players, and actions involving the entire team as a unit.

Because of the many different types of maneuvers in which players are collectively involved, the effectiveness of a team is always more than the sum of the performances of 11 individual players. The game of a well-coached team often exhibits very special qualities. Often they are influenced by a certain tradition particular to a club. In other words, a certain way of playing the game has been passed down from one generation to the next. In addition, some teams bear the very specific stamp of a successful coach who has a strong personality. The coach's idea of the most successful way of playing soccer becomes the hallmark of the team's play.

The Team

The character of a team will be influenced by the following:
- The particular system being played (see page 137).
- The particular style of offense and defense (see page 143).
- The tactics used routinely by the members of the team (pages 91 and 97).
- The personalities of the different team members and their understanding of the game.

The Team as a Social Group

In psychological terms, the players of a team belong to a subgroup. A subgroup has specific characteristics, structures, and processes that exist among its members, and which distinguish them from those people on the outside. The coach occupies a position somewhat in between. The structure of a subgroup is a hierarchy established among its members, as determined by the relationships between them and their individual performance levels and actions.

A clearly defined hierarchy that is accepted by all members of the group is absolutely essential to a team's success. It eliminates jealousy and fighting for position and imparts the security of having an acknowledged place. A recognized leader can inspire the team in critical situations and raise the team's enthusiasm and overall level of performance.

The following conditions are favorable to the development of a soccer team with a winning attitude and culture:
- The number of members should remain constant during the course of the season, ideally between 18 and 25 (with professionals, 30).
- All members should agree on a clearly defined goal (for example,

to prevent losing their position within a division or to move up in the standings).
- Players should agree on basic rules of conduct (for instance, to be on time for practice sessions and games).
- Players must cultivate and maintain an enthusiastic team spirit.
- Players should identify with, or at least accept, the person in charge (the coach or general manager of the club) or the institution to which they belong.

Team-Building

It is an art to mold 11 individual people into a cohesive and powerful team. It is the job of the coach to establish a lineup based on the talents and strengths of each player. This process starts at the beginning of the season and it may extend over the course of several seasons; creating a solid unit from 11 disparate individuals is the work of time.

Whether putting together a lineup for one game or working on team development over the long run, a coach must consider his players' technical levels, tactical skills and physical fitness. A coach also needs to evaluate his players' temperaments and changing motivations. His players' relative creativity and intuitiveness are other important criteria a coach should consider when he makes decisions.

Soccer is not unlike music. Neither the strings nor the rhythm section alone can convey the full idea of a musical composition. It takes all the individual members of an orchestra working together to produce the sound. Furthermore, orchestras need players of many different kinds of instruments; the one quality it is essential they share is that they are all

expert at playing their respective instruments.

And so it is in soccer: the various strengths and talents of each player are essential to the whole. The tactician needs the fighters; the player developing a play needs the forward; a good offensive player in the midfield needs someone he can count on for protection; a sweeper who is a weak header needs a player who is strong in that department; the somewhat slow-moving player in midfield position must be balanced by a defender who is explosively quick.

A coach needs to keep each player's abilities in mind as he puts his team together. In fact, a keen eye for the strengths and weaknesses of each player is one of the marks of a good coach. The absence of a particular type of player can sometimes make the difference between an average and a successful season.

The following developments are essential to the building of a team:
- Basically, the core of the team should consist of only as many players as necessary. Too little depth often causes problems when one of the regulars gets injured or too many players leave at the same time. On the other hand, having too many players on the bench can give rise to dissatisfaction, jealousy, and discord among players. Ideally, a team should have two substitutes for each position. Since one player is usually capable of playing several positions, a roster of 18 to 25 should be sufficient.

- The age of the players should be balanced. The productive years of a soccer player are between the ages of 20 and 32, with the peak occurring between 24 and 28. A relatively young team often lacks the experience and judgment that make the difference in critical plays and may be short on stability and psychological maturity. However, if the team skews too old, it might lack youth's "fire in the belly" and the willingness to take risks. It takes longer for older players to recuperate. Particularly in professional soccer, older players are often psychologically exhausted and run the risk of burning out.
- Players should complement each other in technical and tactical skills and in physical fitness, as previously mentioned. Also, a team's particular style of play needs to be considered when looking for new players. A team that prefers frontal offense must have exceptional technicians in midfield. On the other hand, such a team needs defenders who operate faster in open space than the opposing forwards. In the reverse, the strikers of a counterattack team need to be exceptional sprinters.
- Players must respect each other as individuals. Sports provides a meaningful demonstration of just how unimportant differences in race and religion are when the members of a group share a common goal. A certain degree of tolerance and life experience is essential for every participant in the game.
- Last, but not least, players must be comfortable within the existing hierarchy of the team. A healthy competition among players can stimulate better performance; intense rivalry for position can handicap performance.

The Lineup

When determining the lineup for a particular match, a coach also needs to consider the following:

- In general, a team successful in previous games should not be changed. (The proverb is, "Don't fix it if it ain't broke.")
- Players who are in a slump should be given a breather. On the other hand, a player should not be taken out of a lineup simply because he is not playing well on a given day. Ruthless substitutions erode morale over the long haul and remove the opportunity of making up for a weak performance.
- The lineup for a specific day may depend on the game tactics to be used against the particular opponent (see page 134).
- The degree of participation and level of performance during training will also influence a lineup. A player who is indifferent during training should be given a swift awakening by the coach so that the morale of the whole team isn't undermined.
- Finally, injury or illness may dictate changes in the lineup.

In the final analysis, only the coach can objectively evaluate all the factors that go into putting together a lineup. He should be the one to make the final decision.

The Player

Even though the team is more than the sum of its players, each individual's performance determines the success or failure of the whole. Not only does the outcome of any single game depend on individual performance, the team itself is shaped by the personalities and performance of its members.

Significance for the Team

Although it cannot be determined precisely to what extent the individual player is responsible for the success or failure of a team, a few ideas are worth considering.

Obviously, a player is most effective when he helps his side score a goal or prevents an opponent from scoring. In a study by Jaschok/Witt of the frequency and duration of individual players' ball contacts (see page 11), it was shown that a player with the shortest ball contact (20 seconds) during the 12 times he had possession of the ball, scored the deciding goal for a 1 to 0 win. This clearly demonstrates that the relation between duration of ball contact and player effectiveness is not direct.

Similarly, quantity (as measured by the distance covered in the course of a game) and quality of play have no direct relation. For example, the value of a player's action is clearly evident when he passes the ball to a teammate who then scores a goal, however much or little ground he covers in the process. Its importance is similar to that of a player who prevents an opposing forward from scoring a goal.

The importance of a positive action (for instance, completing a pass) or a negative action (failing to complete a pass) is also a matter of where and when it takes place. An unsuccessful pass away from the player's own goal is much more serious than losing the ball while dribbling in the opponents' penalty area. In the final analysis, the measure of a player's effectiveness lies in the ratio of his positive to negative actions.

Because the success of a team depends on the effective performance of each of its players, a coach must work with them constantly to

The Player

improve their individual levels of performance and their effective interaction during play. Only thus can the team's overall performance be improved and made reliable in the long run.

Factors Influencing Performance

Many factors can affect the performance of a player day to day. The following are some of the more important ones:
- The player's overall personality and state of mind.
- His natural talent.
- The degree of his technical and tactical skills and his physical fitness.
- His education.
- His life-style and nutrition.
- His relationships with his parents and friends.
- Pressures from school and job.
- The length and quality of his previous experience.

The influence and interaction of these factors is unpredictable. And their effect on performance also cannot be reckoned. A player with only modest talent, for example, can improve his performance a great deal more by rigorous and intense training than can a player who has great talent but little ambition.

Character Traits of a Star Player

In discussions of the future of the sport of soccer, we often hear the complaint that soccer no longer enjoys the presence of such big personalities as Pele, Beckenbauer, Netzer, Uwe Seeler, and Fritz Walter, among others. The problem is cited,

rather superficially, to be the lack of extraordinary skills and talent. Little attention is paid to the fact that it is more than mere talent and skill that go into making a star. Conditioning, technique, and strategy alone, however superb, are not enough to succeed in soccer competition on the international level or to be regarded as a star.

Personalities and, by extension, star players, are shaped as well by the following characteristics:
- Gender and age.
- Physical attributes such as height and build.
- Intellectual abilities and development.
- Strength of motivation.
- Social skills.
- Attitudes and interests.
- Character traits and temperament.

Some of these traits are inborn, of course. But a good number of them can be strengthened by means of an effective training program.

Personal Characteristics
The very most basic are:
- Age.
- Gender.
- Physical traits.

These factors determine the potential to perform. Because they cannot be changed or manipulated, a coach must take them into consideration.

Physical Traits
Physical attributes crucial to athletic performance are:
- Energy.
- Speed.
- Endurance.
- Mobility and flexibility.
- Coordination.

These characteristics, in their many variations and combinations, are subject to the influence of intellect and emotion. Nevertheless, they can be enhanced to some degree by physical training. See the chapter "Condition and Conditioning Training" for a discussion in greater detail (starting on page 65).

Intellectual Abilities
A successful competitor must be armed with the following well-honed critical faculties:
- Perception.
- Concentration.
- Memory.
- Creativity.
- Anticipation (the ability to think ahead).
- Intuition.
- Abstract thinking ability.
- Judgment and knowledge.

More than anything else, these influence the tactical abilities of a player. Their importance and the possibility for their improvement will be discussed in more detail in the chapter on tactics (see page 85).

Strength of Motivation
Some of the factors affecting motivation are:
- The degree of desire to play the game and the need to excel.
- The desire for power or control.
- The need for acceptance.
- Emotions such as fear, anger, and pain.

These personality components influence how a player uses his physical attributes. A skilled and objective coach can do a great deal to bring them out in his team. In tactics and performance, he must recognize the potential effect of motivation on technical and motor abilities, and work to heighten their synergy.

Characteristics and Personality

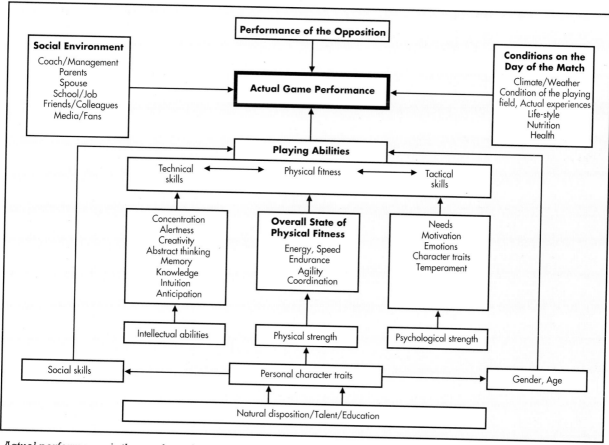

Actual performance is the product of several factors.

Social Skills

In sport, as in life, these will influence success:
- Leadership ability.
- Acceptance of norms and values.
- Loyalty to the team.
- Willingness to act as part of a team.
- Camaraderie.

These attributes develop over time. But they can be deeply influenced by a coach's attitudes and teaching methods.

Emotions and Temperament

The full range of emotions is part of a player's character. His suitability is somewhat dependent on where he falls in the range between:

- Courage and fear.
- Decisiveness and indecisiveness.
- Impulsiveness and caution.
- Aggression and passivity.
- Self-confidence and insecurity.
- Extroversion and introversion.

These traits largely determine a player's potential and performance, as well as the place he occupies in the team's hierarchy. And here, too, a coach's influence is incalculable in nurturing and developing those traits that can improve a player's performance (for more, see page 89).

The personal factors that influence the level of performance of both players and teams have already been discussed in the section "Factors Influencing Performance" (see page 16). These life components can be guided, nurtured, developed, and improved through effective leadership and specific training methods. However, a coach must employ a systematic and consistent approach to training, following a well-conceived overall plan. In order to achieve the desired results, the club management, the coach and the players must work cooperatively, fulfilling their respective responsibilities.

Responsibilities

Club Management

The management is charged with:
- Acquiring and maintaining equipment and facilities necessary for training: the locker room, playing field, workout rooms and equipment, balls, on-site facilities for physical therapy and appropriate emergency medical care, and food and drink for the players.
- Providing appropriate personnel such as players, trainers, physicians, massage therapists, and grounds crew.

Trainer/Coach

The coach is responsible for preparing, conducting, and overseeing the team's training program and schedule, setting program goals, and evaluating the training program's effectiveness.

Players

The degree of cooperation by the players determines the success of the training. The players contribute to the success of the training program by:
- Following an appropriate life-style.
- Establishing their own heightened

performance standards.
- Cooperating during training.
- Taking responsibility for proper cool down (see page 156), and making use of physical therapy, massages, and the sauna.
- Following recommended nutritional guidelines.
- Getting sufficient sleep.

Terms and Principles

"Training" generally refers to those activities designed to improve overall performance. In sports, training usually means preparing for competition. This general definition only describes the purpose of training; it does not address the intended goals, the activities engaged in to achieve them, or the effects of the effort.

A more precise definition of soccer training is: a methodically planned process for achieving athletic perfection. The goal is to achieve optimal performance and readiness of the individual player and the team. Theoretical knowledge (of general and specific training theories, biomechanics, sports medicine, sports sociology and sports psychology) is as important as practical experience. Systematically repeated training results in physical and functional adaptation of the body.

This book has all the relevant information required to establish an effective training program. The emphasis is on technical and tactical skills, physical conditioning, and all-around playing ability.

This chapter introduces the necessary, basic information and discusses training theories. It provides the foundation for the rest of the book. It contains information meant specifi-

cally to deepen understanding of the basics discussed so far.

In practical terms, both approaches to the training process—the general and the specific—are important. The complex effects of training can be properly understood only when both physical and psychological effects are fully considered.

There are three fundamental concepts that form the basis for both the specific and the general approach to training. They are the:
- Teaching Principle (see below).
- Load Principle (see page 30).
- Cyclical Principle (see pages 34 and 35)

Teaching Principles

Principle of Methodical and Systematic Teaching

Training will produce the desired effect long term only when the coach employs methods that complement each other and carries them out systematically over an extended period of time (e.g., gradually increasing the degree of difficulty). The prerequisite is a well-planned training program (see page 24).

Principle of Individuality and Age-Appropriateness

Training differs from player to player and from one developmental stage to the next. Optimal training results can be achieved only when the training goal, the specific exercises, and the method of training are customized to the individual player.

The degree of difficulty of the training program must be adjusted to the mental and physical abilities of the participants.

Principle of Clarity

Technical and tactical principles are picked up and mastered much faster when the desired outcome of the

Training Methods

training session is clearly conveyed. Visual demonstrations in the way of photos from the media, single and multiple slide presentations, and blackboard sketches are helpful in achieving this.

Principle of Awareness

Motivation, concentration, and performance improve when the players understand the purpose and the anticipated effects of an exercise. It is important that players understand the relationship between method and outcome.

Types of Training

When people talk about soccer training, their focus is often on improving performance, and this book is oriented along those lines. But a number of other training methods are available, depending on what a coach wants to accomplish.

Soccer Training in School

In school, soccer training is intended to do more than simply improve a player's performance. It has to take into account many other, overriding responsibilities to its students.

Soccer Training as Part of a Fitness Program

Its main purpose is for the children to have fun. The therapeutic physiological effects of the game are the reason for, not the goal of, training.

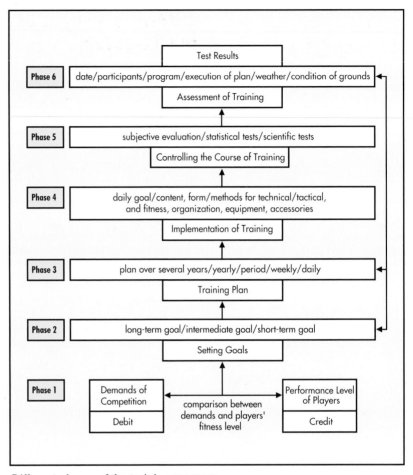

Different phases of the training program.

Soccer Training for Members of a Club

Here, the purpose of training is the improvement of performance. And most training programs are designed to that end.

Regrettably, training for young and amateur players is all too often modeled after training programs for professional players and is taken much too seriously. What is overlooked is the fact that training for professional players is a business: its purpose is to increase their level of performance, which will ensure their income. Training has a totally different meaning for a professional than it does for young and amateur players (notwithstanding the fact that

the latter make up 99.9 percent of all soccer players). For this reason, coaches must put aside their laudable athletic ambitions and develop training methods that retain a sense of fun. The idea is to turn away from grim and stubborn performance pressure and toward healthy ambition. If players are allowed to laugh and have a good time during training sessions, they will be less likely as they mature to retreat from the game of soccer and look for greater pleasure in other kinds of sports.

Performance-oriented training for young players is divided into three levels, depending on age and ability:

- Basic training: 6 to 12 years.
- Intermediate training: 12 to 14 years.
- Advanced and high-performance training: 14 to 18 years.

Perhaps the most important statement in this book is:

Each type and level of training has its specific requirements. The goals, methods, exercises, and game plans of a training session must be chosen accordingly. A responsible coach has the duty to be very careful when he is training children not to use carbon copies of training programs designed for adults.

The differences in age and development are evident in the participants':
- Level of technical and tactical abilities and physical fitness.
- Approach and attitude toward a regular, consistent training program.
- Level of willingness to exert effort during training.
- Physical aptitude (a different "sensitive phase" exists for each level).
- Aptitude for coordinating specific motions and action.
- Speed with which technical expertise is reached.
- Level of intellectual maturity.
- Ability to grasp instructions.
- Ability to convert instructions on strategy into practical game applications.

Appropriate training goals for the different developmental stages of children and young people are summarized on page 23.

Different Phases of the Training Process

In the larger sense, training involves more than just the work on the playing field. Training is a process of many phases that follow each other in a logical order and there is a continuous interaction between them. The different phases are:
- Orientation.
- Establishing goals.
- Planning.
- Implementation.
- Checking progress.
- Evaluation.

Orientation Phase

As has been mentioned earlier, the requirements for competition vary widely and depend on the different performance and developmental stages of the players. Therefore, before converting his abstract ideas about training into a program with specific goals, a coach must evaluate the anticipated demands of a season of competitive games on his players and the team. This is the "debit." A second important step is to evaluate the performance ability and fitness of each individual player.

The soccer played by children and adolescents is vastly different from that played by professional adults. Of course, the same holds true for their technical and tactical abilities and for their physical condition. A coach's objective evaluation of performance for himself, his team, and the club is imperative so as to set realistic goals and develop an appropriate training program. Observation and evaluation of actual games and training sessions (perhaps using video and computer simulations) can provide the coach valuable information for this process.

Establishing Training Goals

To ensure the successful outcome of a training session, it is vital for the objective to be suitable and realistic. Without a clearly formulated objective, a training session amounts to no more than activity therapy, and training can thus be neither planned nor carried out systematically. Whether the objectives are long-term, intermediate, or short-term depends on the following:
- Age and level of development and maturity of the players.
- The players' level of performance.
- Previous training.
- Philosophy and orientation of the coach and the players.
- Number of training periods set aside for practice in the course of the season.
- Day of the week set aside for practice.
- Realistic knowledge of the weaknesses of the players and the team.
- Environmental factors, such as the weather.
- Training facilities and equipment.

Objectives of a Senior Training Program

In the training of senior players, training goals will vary little from one year to the next; rather, they should vary within the season (see page 24). For a season divided into two halves, several weekly subdivisions should be established, including:
- Preparation.
- First round of competition.
- Interim period (winter break).
- Second round of competition.
- Interim period (break without training or practice).

Practical experience shows, and scientific studies have proven, that neither a player nor a team can main-

Phases of the Training Process

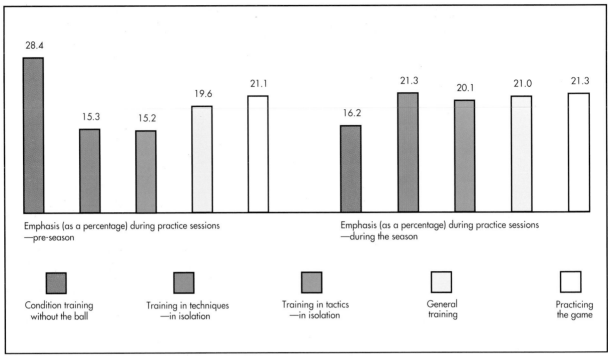

28.4

15.3

15.2

19.6

21.1

16.2

21.3

20.1

21.0

21.3

Emphasis (as a percentage) during practice sessions
—pre-season

Emphasis (as a percentage) during practice sessions
—during the season

Condition training
without the ball

Training in techniques
—in isolation

Training in tactics
—in isolation

General
training

Practicing
the game

The relationship between different phases during practice sessions, according to a survey of 59 coaches.

tain consistently high levels of performance over several seasons.

The performance of a player moves from one distinct level to another and is subject to the biological rhythms and functions of the human body. There is a certain peak level, naturally, but the player will generally be at a point between that and a level somewhat lower, increasing and declining in cycles over time.

The first objective is to select *the specific goal of a training program.* This will determine the relative emphasis on skill and technique, strategy, and physical conditioning. As training goals vary within the phases of a program, so will the emphasis of focus.

The second objective in developing a training program is to establish *the degree of training load,* i.e., the strenuousness of the training routine. A determination of degree of training load should be governed by the principles outlined starting on page 30.

The third objective is to determine *the balance of training focusing on the areas of technique, strategy, and physical conditioning.* (See bar chart illustrating the results of a survey of 59 coaches in all classes.)

Objectives of a Junior Training Program

The objectives of a training program for juniors depend on the developmental stage of the players. Adolescents can have rapid, unpredictable growth spurts. This is a factor a coach must take into consideration when establishing a training program.

Training manuals discuss "sensitive phases." These are the times particularly suited for the development of specific talents, abilities, and skills. If a training program doesn't take advantage of these developmental periods, it is almost impossible to make up for them later—at least this is the general consensus of opinion.

For the same reason, specialization or a soccer-specific training program should not be undertaken too early. Basic early training should give young players opportunities to gain experience in running and movement-related exercises (See the section "Coordination and Coordination Training," starting on page 82).

In addition, long-term training objectives for both junior and senior programs are affected by the division of practice sessions into specific phases. The following tables show training objectives for specific age groups, based on the general knowledge and practical athletic experience usual for each.

Specific goals for teaching technical and tactical skills and for physical conditioning are discussed in greater detail in their respective chapters.

Determining Training Goals

Establishing Age-Appropriate Training Objectives

Objective	6–10 Years	10–12 Years	12–14 Years	14–16 Years	16–18 Years
Sustaining enjoyment in playing and practicing	Enjoying playing with the ball without fear—rolling, jumping, and kicking	Enjoying cooperative play and learning to play, enjoying practice	Enjoying one-on-one competition and competing together to win	Gaining satisfaction and enjoyment from improvement in one's performance and understanding its value to the team	Enjoying performance-oriented practice of tactics, techniques, and conditioning. "Soccer forever!"
Developing overall coordination	Learning to anticipate movement of the ball; motor skills (general)	Improving coordination of ball and body movement; getting a "feel" for the ball	Strengthening overall motor skills and general dexterity, despite rapid growth spurts	Improving body control in one-on-one confrontations; developing toughness in an opponent's attack	Improving agility when under pressure and despite an opponent's attack
Specific technical abilities	Ball control: simple forms of fielding and handling, instep goal kicking	All basic forms of movement and techniques with and without an opponent	Fine-tuning basic form; simulating actual game situations	Position-specific techniques; improving dribbling and tackling in one-on-one situations	Using techniques to accomplish objectives (free kick, corner kick); learning conscious use of techniques when moving fast and when involved in one-on-one confrontations
General and specific conditioning	Running, jumping, leaping, and rolling; endurance and agility during play	Improving quickness and coordination by running, playing rough-and-tumble games, and running relays	Improving endurance and motor skills through extensive running and exercises (gymnastics)	Beginning general and specific muscle training; practice to improve speed and aerobic strength	Training to improve jumping and kicking skills, aerobic endurance, strength of body muscles, and specific speed with and without the ball
Knowledge and implementation of tactical skills	Understanding what "scoring a goal," "avoiding a goal" and "coordinated offense and defense" mean	Playing within a given space and learning to deal with the situations that typically develop there; individual tactics (getting free, coverage)	Improving teamwork (group tactics); practicing the tactically correct reaction to standard situations	Knowledge of tactics used during games; improving individual actions as part of team tactics (offensive, defensive, space coverage)	Independent and responsible execution of tactical maneuvers; application of all personal skills
Knowledge of rules	Knowledge of rudimentary rules: scoring a goal, throw-in, fouls, and misconduct, offside	Adhering to all rules, especially Rule 4 and Rules 8 through 17	Accepting of the ruling of a referee	Readiness to referee a game	Ability to organize and referee games

Teaching self-realization through play

Willingly increasing level of performance during practice as well as during a game	Learning through personal effort to translate various game strategies into action during rough-and-tumble play and running	Converting enjoyment of the game and excess energy into action on the field; after proper instruction, practicing training exercises independently	Overcoming reluctance and (developmentally influenced) negative performances; accepting that the team's success is more important than any one individual's	Striving to raise the personal level of performance by working on tactics, techniques, and fitness (avoiding alcohol, tobacco, etc.)	Combining school and other interests with athletic goals; developing greater motivation
Controlling of effect and aggression	Accepting the fact that losing is part of the game and that "tomorrow is another day"	Learning to experience and control joy, anger, and rage	Developing toughness in one-on-one confrontations; learning to tolerate pain	Learning to handle rivalries and aggression	Developing psychological stability; learning to control competition-induced anxiety and nervousness
			Learning to accept the decision of the referee		
Developing team spirit and socially acceptable conduct	Seeing soccer in terms of teamwork during games and practices	Learning to share tasks with a group or team; establishing friendships	Seeing the team as a group of people with the same goals, interests, and standards; respecting the opponent	Learning to fit into team hierarchy; seeing the team (including the coach) as a group involved in competitive performances	Seeing the team as part of a larger unit (school or club); being loyal to that unit
Learning to organize games and training programs	Learning to follow coach's instructions; fulfill responsibilities	Participating in organizing the training program, setting up groups and handling equipment	Learning to organize training objectives and adjust exercise programs accordingly	Participating in and helping organize practice sessions; train independently; evaluating own progress by checking achievements	Actively participating in and contributing to the success of all team activities; actively contributing to scheduling training and practice sessions

Phases of the Training Process

Training Schedule

A good coach will put in the thought and effort necessary to conceiving and laying out a structured, goal-oriented training program. The result should be formalized in writing.

A written training schedule clearly outlines the structure and objectives of the training program.

This is essential, as the number of training options available and the shifting stresses on the players, both physical and emotional, make it impossible otherwise to keep in mind the program's structure and the desired goals. A number of different schedules are used in soccer training, including the following:

- A schedule which covers several years for the development of a team with young players.
- A yearly training schedule for junior and senior players.
- Various schedules at different periods within the season: the pre-season, competition, interim and transitional periods.
- A weekly practice schedule.
- A daily practice schedule.

The shorter the time period covered by a schedule, the more concise the description of the exercises must be. At the same time, the schedule is more than a mere statement of the objectives and the degree of training load.

A yearly schedule, for example, must include the following:

- Statement of objectives (e.g., moving up in the standings).
- The different training phases of the year.
- The scheduled dates of championship and exhibition games.
- Dates and types of tests and physical examinations.
- In rough form, a statement of specific objectives for techniques, tactics, and physical fitness.

Example of a Training Schedule for a Senior Team for One Year

1. Period: mid-July to mid-August

Type of Training	a) Intensity b) Extent	Training goals	Training exercises
General conditional training; fundamentals of fitness training; repetition of fundamental techniques and tactics	a) 60%–80% b) 80%–100%	**Conditioning** Aerobic endurance, power training; agility **Technique** Repetition of all technical skills; practice sessions for individual players **Tactics** General and individual tactical skills: getting free, coverage, dribbling; basic tactics in standard situations: free kick, corner kick, different combinations, changing positions	Running, jogging, gymnastics Game plays, exercises, individual training with ball, training in specific and specialty skills Individual work on frontal attack, team attack; practical and board exercises

2. Period: mid- to end of August

| Soccer-specific conditioning training; improvement of specific physical conditioning, and technical and tactical skills | a) Increase to 95% b) Reduce to 70% | **Conditioning** Aerobic endurance, general power exercises, special skills

Technique All elements with opponent and increased tempo

Tactics Team training, assigning positions, trying out new game strategies | Extensive interval training, running relay races with and without a ball, abbreviated games, general soccer games (offense/defense)

Complex exercises: one-on-one, short games with special assignments

Game play: offense against defense, practice game with "weaker" opponent; discussions, board exercises |

3. Period: end of August to mid-September

| Soccer-specific reinforcement of complex skills, making them "automatic" | a) 90%–100% b) Reduce from 100% to about 50% | **Conditioning** Highest possible reaction and speed skills; jumping and kicking power

Technique Perfect coordination of technical elements and physical fitness

Tactics Technical and tactical exercises appropriate to a given situation; changing tempo, speed, and positions | Practice all soccer-specific exercises with highest possible speed

Game plays with players assuming different positions, practicing being outnumbered and outnumbering the opposition

Practicing different tactics against weaker opponent |

- The amount of time allotted for each objective.
- The degree of load, particularly the ratio between extent and intensity of training during each period.

The following tables give examples of a one-year schedule for senior players. The basic concept of "training load" in the course of a season is well demonstrated.

In the high performance sport of soccer, high-impact training takes place throughout the year with only very short breaks. Thus, the scheduled training shows more clear differences between the preparation and the competition periods than in those of other serious sports. Three weeks or so of high impact work will be followed by a one-week lower intensity break for recovery. See graphic on pg. 34.

A written schedule for a training program provides a signpost, a general guide or map over the year. However, a coach is not expected to adhere rigidly to such a schedule. Anything can happen, so it is wise to be flexible. In fact, this is another reason why it is helpful to have a general outline that covers an extended period of time. The rationale for dividing a year into different periods is discussed in more detail on page 34.

The suggested schedule outlined on pages 24 through 27 covers one year.

4. Period: mid-September to mid-October

Type of Training	a) Intensity b) Extent	Training goal	Training exercises
Soccer-specific program and additional unrelated exercises	a) 90%–100% b) Increase from 80%–90%	**Conditioning** Increase training load by increasing intensity of exercises **Techniques** Using all technical elements at the highest possible speed in game-like situations against "opponents" **Tactics** Developing "real-game" tactical skills, learning from past competition	Increase in the number and duration of practice sessions, shorten duration of timeouts Basketball, handball, general power training (once a week)

5. Period: mid-October to mid-November

Decrease in intensity to aid recuperation and prevent loss of form	a) Reduce from 100%–70% b) Approximately 50%	**Conditioning** Extended and intermediate endurance, agility training; no speed or power-endurance training **Techniques** Perfect all technical elements using moderate running speed (high number of repetitions) **Tactics** Improve tactics in standard situations	Stretching exercises (gymnastics); endurance training (jogging, soccer-tennis); practice games, increasing the number of players, using a variety of game strategies; no intense one-on-one competition, rather increasing the number of repetitions

6. Period: mid-November to mid-December

Balanced training exercises utilizing many different types of sports to maintain psychological readiness	a) Increase to 80% b) Continue decrease (fewer but more intensive training sessions)	**Conditioning** Work on basic motor skills: increased power, speed, and reaction time **Techniques** Increase in general athletic skills, agility, and dexterity **Tactics** Game comprehension; enjoyment of the game and good humor	Abbreviated rough-and-tumble and soccer games, table tennis, volleyball, basketball, and handball Complex exercises: practicing offense against defense, practice games against weaker opponents

7. Period: mid-December to mid-January: no training

Phases of the Training Process

8. Period: mid-January to end of January

Type of Training	a) Intensity b) Extent	Training goals	Training exercises
General power training (beginning in January), few but very intensive training sessions	a) Increase from 80–100% b) Moderate, approximately 50–70%	**Conditioning** Soccer-specific short endurance training, reaction speed **Techniques** Ball-body coordination, one-on-one competitions **Tactics** Direct pass and double pass alternating with dribbling and combination plays	Intensive interval exercises, including game methods: abbreviated games, one-on-one competition Indoor training with broken plays

9. Period: end of January to mid-February

| For beginning amateur teams, preparation for return matches For advanced amateur teams and professional teams, strengthen form | For beginners a) increase to 100% b) 70–80% For advanced a) decrease to 80% b) increase to 90% | **Conditioning** Basic speed, jumping and kicking power, action and reaction training; training in the beginning: high intensity and longer timeouts; followed by lower-intensity and shorter timeouts **Techniques** Long passes, long kicks (ground with snow cover), driving the ball with speedo **Tactics** Utilizing space, changing sides, changing tempo, alternating between offensive and defensive plays | In contrast to Period 7, increased number of training sessions and increased duration of individual sessions, followed by extensive interval training Complex exercises: practice games, eight-on-eight, using the whole field; game using four goals alternating between three teams |

10. Period: mid-February to mid-April

| Intense training sessions, going through micro-cycles to maintain good form for the final "push" | a) 80% b) 40–50% | **Conditioning** Train to increase endurance (aerobic, anaerobic), later add power endurance, improve basic motor skills, speed, and strength in general **Techniques** As close to "real game" situations as possible: all elements of complex techniques **Tactics** Observing tactical skills of individual players during game practice and work to improve them in training | First extensive and then intensive interval training; increase number of game plays; increased discussions with individual players to raise level of motivation for the final "push" |

Today, coaches often plan the goals, the content and the intensity of the training program with the team captain.

11. Period: mid-April to mid-May			
Type of Training	a) Intensity b) Extent	Training goals	Training exercises
This will depend to a great extent on the standing of the team. If in the middle of the pack, goal-specific training of individual players	a) Approximately 70% b) Approximately 50%	**Conditioning** Reducing the intensity in order to maintain good form over time; high duration of training **Techniques** Improvement of technical skills through individual and specialized training **Tactics** Improvement of individual tactical skills, training in fundamental tactical skills (combination drills, double pass, etc.)	Recuperation through aerobic exercises (distance running); gymnastics (exercising with a partner), rough-and-tumble games, soccer-tennis, abbreviated games in a small group with relatively low intensity (three-on-one, four-on-two, etc.) Establish training programs for individual players and initiate individual exercise sessions
12. Period: mid-May to June			
Total relaxation, but under no circumstances *total inactivity*	a) Reduce to 50% b) Reduce to 40%	**Conditioning** Recuperation and regeneration **Techniques** Recapture the fun of the game **Tactics** Increase knowledge of tactical skills through literature and the like	General physical checkup by physician; undergoing treatment if necessary (surgery) Alternative athletic activities: hiking, mountain climbing, tennis, table tennis, and on a lower scale, swimming, sauna and massage therapy; ball practice alone to improve technical weaknesses

Implementation of a Training Program

Consider the following carefully when planning a training schedule:
• Actual objectives of the program.
• Training methods.
• Training content (game plays, exercises, complex exercises, training games).
• Organization of training sessions (type of structure, assignments, equipment, and accessories).

Daily Training Objectives

The immediate training objectives depend in part on the previously established long-term and intermediate goals, as well as on information gathered during prior competitions and experience with individual players and with the team as a whole. Unforeseeable, external conditions (such as illness or rain, muddy grounds, and snow) will affect short-term objectives.

One invariable objective in a coach's schedule, however, should be to have a good time. A good coach understands that an attitude open to fun does not diminish his commitment to serious, performance-oriented training sessions.

Training Methods

Today, the three areas of performance—techniques, tactics, and conditioning—are usually taught by using real-game situations in the form of game plays or training games.

This becomes increasingly important because children today don't

Phases of the Training Process

play street soccer very often, in contrast with earlier generations.

Clubs committed to competitive sports have specific methods for training. We distinguish between the following areas of training:
- Technical training (see page 60).
- Tactical training (see page 88).
- Fitness training (see page 68).

For the most part, there is agreement among experts on the best methods for training in fitness and tactics. The area of technical training causes the greatest differences of opinion regarding the effectiveness of methods for the development of overall athletic skill. For a discussion of the pros and cons of the technical methods used most often, see pages 60 through 62.

Types of Training

The type and content of training are dictated by the following:
- The training objectives.
- The anticipated training load.
- The training method chosen.
- The levels of development and performance of the players.
- The interest and motivation of the players.
- The available space and equipment (for instance, the number of soccer balls)

The following sets of exercises are important for soccer training:
- General conditioning without the ball.
- Rough-and-tumble games.
- Individual, self-generated exercises to develop a "feel" for the ball.
- Exercises with a partner, standing and moving.
- Game strategies and combinations.
- Complex exercises.
- Small game plays.
- Training games, 11-on-11.

Individual sets of exercises can be combined, resulting in different physical conditioning. The significance of

Significance of Different Methods for Training Techniques Based on Age and Developmental Level

Age in Years	Developmental or age level				
	6–10	10–12	12–14	14–16	16–18
General conditioning without a ball	–	O	O	OO	OO
Rough-and-tumble games	OO	OO	OO	O	O
Independent exercises to improve ball handling	OOO	OOO	OO	OO	OO
Practicing shots on goal	OOO	OOO	OOO	OOO	OOO
Exercising with a partner, standing and moving	OOO	OO	OO	O	O
Competition exercises, one-on-one exercises	O	OO	OO	OOO	OOO
Strategy games, different combination plays	O	OO	OO	OO	OO
Complex exercises	–	O	OO	OOO	OOO
Small game plays	OOO	OOO	OO	OO	OO
Training games	OOO	OOO	OOO	OO	O

– not important   O important   OO very important   OOO extremely important

individual types of exercises for increasing the level of performance is shown in the table above.

Organizing a Training Schedule

The methods and types of exercises chosen have a significant impact on how training sessions are organized. These choices also determine, in large part, the success of the total training program in achieving the set objectives.

There is a close connection between the training load (which needs to be at a certain minimum level for long-term performance to increase) and the way a training program is organized. A maximum training load can be reached only if the transition from one training phase to another is as smooth as possible. The transition should not unintention-

ally increase the load.

When organizing a schedule, the following aspects should be taken into consideration:
- Dividing the players into specific groups (type of division).
- Assigning playing space to each group.
- Alternating the groups between different types of exercise and from one space to another.
- Duration of individual exercises and of training games.
- Frequency, duration, and type of break.
- Providing the necessary equipment and accessories.
- Using permanent structures (buildings, stairs, barriers, etc.) in a stadium or playing field.

Performance Evaluations

Checking Achievement of Objectives

It is not always easy to determine whether the training has fulfilled its set purpose and the goals of a training program have been reached. Because the levels of soccer performance are so varied, it is possible that while an individual player shows unmistakable improvement, the result can be only marginally documented because overall team performance falls short of expectations.

As difficult as it is to assess the outcome of a training program, it is as easy for a coach to overlook the developing performance of players on the bench. An objective means of measuring performance, employing controls to check specific training goals, can help make a more straight-forward determination. The subjective evaluation of a player's improved performance during training sessions and competition will always be one measure. Less equivocal controls are:
• Objective tests measuring specific motor activities.
• Calibrated scientific assessments of performance.

Subjective Evaluation of Improved Performance by the Coach

Over time, experienced coaches develop a rather good eye for a player's level of technical performance and physical fitness. They usually have sufficient distance from the activity of a given game or training session to analyze a performance fairly objectively. However, this kind of evaluation will always remain subjective and cannot stand up to critical scrutiny. As long as the coach and his team are successful, no specific evaluation is needed. But should failures begin to accumulate, it is important that a coach's methods of performance evaluation be beyond question.

Objective Motor-Activity Tests

Sports science has developed a number of objective methods to test a player's performance level. Two

There are many ways to test technical skills. For comparison purposes, the exercises must be standardized.

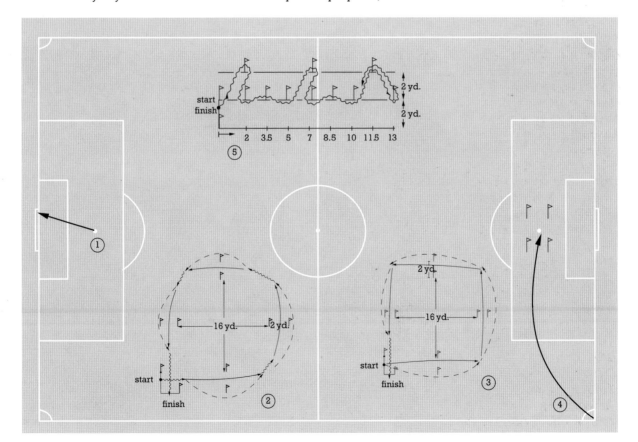

Positions from which to test technical skills:
1. Goalkicking 2. Dribbling-pass test 3. Passing-timing test 4. Goalkicking test from the side 5. Dribbling test

Control of High-Impact Training

such methods are:

- Testing the level of technical skills (see diagram on page 29).
- Testing the level of physical conditioning, as seen in the quality of athletic skills.

Sports science has also developed methods to test the parameters of tactical skills objectively. At this time, however, they do not have great relevance for training purposes. In order for a test to render useful information, it must meet the following criteria:

A test must be *valid*. It must actually measure what it claims to measure. For instance, a slalom course cannot measure dribbling skills, as many other factors come to bear in that activity.

A test must be *reliable*. It must be possible to produce the same result time and again. The method must be clear, the instruments must be accurate, and a standard sequence must be followed.

A test must be *objective*. Instructions for the implementation, analysis, and interpretation of the test must be clearly stated so that the results can be used independently.

Scientific Measurements

Increasingly, professional soccer uses performance-level tests that have been developed by sports medicine. Those best known are:

- Spiro-ergonomic measurements on the treadmill or bicycle, and lactic-acid measurements.
- Lactic-acid test after sprints or after jogging around the field.
- Uric-acid test.
- Computerized power-energy measurements.
- Reaction and speed measurements.

Spiro-ergonomic measurements give information about cardiovascular efficiency (intake and utilization of oxygen). Lactic-acid measurements before and after a workout provide information about aerobic and anaerobic limits (see page 75). Uric-acid measurements after a workout yield information about the degree of fatigue. These measurements make it possible to design and modify subsequent training sessions with the proper physical loads.

Computer-aided energy measurements are able to determine the degree of energy deficit. This is helpful in the case of an injury. By following the curves on a graph, experienced analysts can even detect hidden muscle damage.

Evaluation of a Training Program

A careful analysis of training sessions has several long-term benefits. With a written account, the coach is able to review and establish the following:

- Which players took part in a given training session and how often each player practiced.
- What skills were practiced at what time.
- The extent and intensity of individual training sessions and of the whole season.
- To what degree the long-term training schedule corresponded to the results obtained.
- What kind of weather conditions existed during any given practice session.
- The test results gained during the performance.

A coach can create his own forms for recordkeeping, though it is just as simple to buy forms designed for that purpose at many sports stores.

Guiding the Training Load

Principles of Training Load

Practical experience has established, and training manuals have come to reflect, the connection between **Load, Recuperation,** and **Adaptation,** concerning which the following principles have been formulated:

- A physical load exceeding the absolute threshold of an individual player will deplete substances such as hormones and enzymes in a player's system and, consequently, lead to fatigue (see page 74 concerning the significance of energy availability).
- Depending on the type and amount of load, these substances decrease in different degrees, leading to specific symptoms of fatigue.
- The duration of fatigue depends on the type and degree of fatigue. Even well-trained athletes may show symptoms for up to three days (72 hours) after the event.
- Essential substances depleted during a workout are replaced at an accelerated rate with the intake of nutrition appropriate for an athlete. This biological phenomenon, called *the principle of hyper-compensation*, produces a metabolic adaptation and an accompanying increase in muscle mass.
- According to the *principle of optimum correlation* of stress load to recuperation, the next training session should take place within 12 to 72 hours, at the peak of the hyper-compensation process.
- According to the *principle of varying stress load,* if training sessions with high stress loads are scheduled in rapid succession (for

Duration of Fatigue and Recuperation Depending on the Type of Training Stress Load
(Keul 1978, Kindermann 1978, Martin 1980)

Training Stress Load / Recuperation	For aerobic energy availability (training with low-intensity stress load)	For combined aerobic-anaerobic energy availability (training with average stress load intensity)	For anaerobic energy availability (speed and power exercises, competition)	For anabolic effects (maximum power training)	For effect on the neuromuscular system (speed and technique training, competition)
Ongoing recuperation	With an intensity of 60–70%, recuperation is ongoing				With a short training load (according to the repetition method) and longer timeouts
Quick recuperation (very incomplete)		After approximately 1.5–2 hours	After approximately 2–3 hours		
90–95% recuperation (incomplete with good performance capacity)	After 12 hours with a 75–90% intensity	After approximately 12 hours	After approximately 12–18 hours	After approximately 18 hours	After approximately 18 hours
Total recuperation of the balance between metabolic processes (increased performance capacity)	After 24–26 hours with a 75–90% intensity	After approximately 24–28 hours	After approximately 48–72 hours	After approximately 72–84 hours	After approximately 72 hours

instance, daily exercise sessions), different training objectives should be established for them, which will induce different fatigue processes (e.g., endurance, energy, and central nervous system).

Increasing the level of performance during competition can be achieved only by increasing the physical stress load. According to the *principle of increased stress load,* this can be accomplished by doing the following:
• Establishing a gradual, linear training program for beginners and advanced players.
• Rapid, multi-stage types of performance training.
• Variations of the above.

Components of Stress Load Training

From the prior discussion, it is clear that a training program can be successful only by designing and using a systematic training stress load. The following five so-called "training stress-load components" make up the process.

Stimulus Intensity

The intensity of an individual training stimulus is 100 percent when the stress load is so high that the final repetition of a given activity (such as pressing weights) brings the muscles involved to failure, i.e., they cannot complete another rep. In the case of running, 100 percent intensity is

reached when a player is sprinting at his greatest possible speed. To develop maximum energy and speed, the training stress load must reach maximum intensity (or as close as possible to it). This will be possible only with sufficiently long intervals for recuperation between individual training stimuli.

Stimulus Density

Stimulus density is the relation between stress load and recuperation. The lower the stimulus intensity, the higher the stimulus density. With a low intensity stimulus such as jogging, for instance, training can be almost continuous.

Control of High-Impact Training

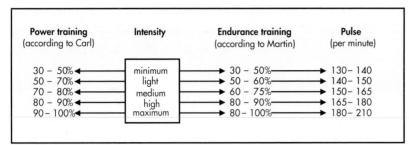

Power training (according to Carl)	Intensity	Endurance training (according to Martin)	Pulse (per minute)
30 – 50%	minimum / light	30 – 50%	130– 140
50 – 70%	light	50 – 60%	140– 150
70 – 80%	medium	60 – 75%	150– 165
80 – 90%	high	80 – 90%	165– 180
90 – 100%	maximum	80 – 100%	180– 210

Ranking the Intensity of a Training Stress Load (including subjective impressions)

Stimulus Duration

The duration of stimulus, or of a series of stimuli (for instance, interval training), is another component. The duration of the stimulus is too long during speed training, for example, if the athlete is unable to perform at maximum intensity throughout the drill or exercise (e.g., a player unable to run at maximum speed in a sprint). Training in that case should be directed toward speed *endurance* rather than maximum speed.

Degree of Stimulus

The overall degree of stimulus combines the duration and the number of stimuli (exercises or repetitions) per training session and is primarily independent of the *intensity* of the individual stimulus. Since there is a maximum training-load limit, the degree and intensity cannot be decreased independently.

Exercise Frequency

From practical experience as well as research in sports science, we know that training is more effective (given the identical training stress load) when it occurs more frequently and less strenuously, as opposed to less frequently and more strenuously. For this reason, it is useful to increase the number of training sessions during

the pre-season period and to make them less strenuous. Even three sessions a day is not too much if the intensity of each individual session is fairly low, and if the objectives and the content are changed regularly.

Physical fitness is improved when there is a balance between length of workout and intensity, and when the training program is spread over several training sessions. This balance plays an important role in the management of the training as a whole and in dividing a training program into several periods.

Methods for Stress-Load Training

Three very different methods for stress-load training are relevant to the management of stress loads. Each one is distinguished by a specific balance between extent, duration, intensity, and frequency. And each method has a different effect on the body.

It is possible to accomplish two essential objectives by a systematic goal-directed application of these methods:
- Skills dependent on physical fitness, energy, speed, and endurance can be developed independently by systematic training (see page 34). Psycho-physiological performance ability can be enhanced. This fact

has important implications for the division of the training program into individual periods (see page 34).

Constant Method (CM)

The three levels in the constant method (CM I–up to 30 minutes, CM II–up to 60 minutes, and CM III–over 60 minutes) can improve almost all aerobic endurance. This is accomplished only if the density of the stress load is high, meaning nonstop training with no timeouts. The duration of the stimuli should be at least 20 minutes. For physically fit athletes, the intensity should be high enough to raise the pulse rate to 160-170 (CM I), 150-160 (CM II), and 140 to 150 (CM III) beats per minute. The constant method is used extensively during the practice season. However, aerobic endurance training must take place on a regular basis during active competition as well, so it is useful to include a training session using the CM method once a week during active competition.

It is very important not to exceed a moderate jogging speed. Experience has shown that coaches and players alike tend to run too fast. This interferes with the desired adaptation process (i.e., an increase in the rate at which carbohydrates and fats are burned). In soccer, the constant training method is used to practice techniques, for example, standard combinations. Game plays with five-on-five or eight-on-eight are ideal because the ball remains in play the whole time. This keeps breaks short and rest periods to a minimum.

Interval Method (IM)

The interval training method uses the systematic alternation between stress and recuperation. Depending on the intensity and duration of the stress load and the intensity of the stimulus

Stress-Load Method: Extent and Ratio of Stress Components; Goals of Fitness Training and Performance Control

Method	Stress load during endurance training	Stress load during power and energy training	Training goal	Performance control
Constant method	E: 70–100% I: 30– 50% B: none PR: 140–160	Not applicable for power training; not effective with low intensity	General long term aerobic endurance	Increasing productivity during pre-season
Examples:	Continuous ball exercises (no breaks), eight-on-eight			
Interval method (extensive)	E: 4–6 series, jogging 4–10 times each, over 50–150 feet (20–50 m) I: 60–70% B: 60–120 seconds PR:160–170/140	E: 4-6 series 10–20 times each I: 40–60% B: 30–90 seconds	Mixed aerobic and anaerobic endurance; maximum energy endurance for increasing energy and power	Maintaining productivity during competition
Examples:	Changing tempo during jogging and training games; three-on-three up to six-on-six or three-plus-three-on two			
Interval method (intensive)	E: 3–5 series of 2–5 runs each I: 80–90% B: 2–4 minutes PR:170–180/120	3–5 series, 6–10 times each I: 55–75% P: 2–5 minutes	Anaerobic endurance and stamina; explosive speed; kicking-shooting power	Rapid increase in productivity
Examples:	Sprints over 15–100 yards (5–30 m); one-on-one; training games one-on-one or two-on-two			
Repetition method	E: 3 series repeated 1–5 times I: 90–100% B: 2–5 minutes PR:180–200/80–100	E: 3–5 series, 1–5 times I: 70–100% B: 3–5 minutes PR:180–220/80	Speed; maximum power	Increasing productivity; maintaining productivity
Examples:	Sprints over 150–300 feet (50–100 m); one-on-one			
Competition method	Training and competition games			Near perfection
E = Extent, I = Intensity, B = Break, PR = Pulse rate during activity/after break				

applied, we distinguish between two types of interval methods:

- The extensive interval method.
- The intensive interval method.

Breaks are relatively short and can be actively used for gymnastics or light ball exercises ("productive breaks"). Circle training, where different types of exercises are carried out consecutively in different areas (circles), lends itself well to the interval method.

During general conditioning training, it is also possible to build physical strength by skillfully combining the exercises with endurance training. In soccer-specific interval-method training, groups of players constantly alternate between workouts and breaks. The primary emphasis is on techniques, tactics, and skills combined with physical conditioning.

Repetition Method

The repetition method also uses constant periods of alternating recuperation and exercise; however, here active periods are conducted at maximum intensity and scheduled timeouts are longer than those in the interval method. Active exercise should be resumed when the pulse rate recovers to approximately 80 beats per minute, e.g., when longer sprints (50–100 m) alternate with longer timeout periods.

Dividing Training Schedules into Periods

Training Methods with Different Intensity Stress Loads

Method suitable for	Examples of training method
Constant method—jogging, low-intensity aerobic-endurance training	Jogging, gymnastics and stretching; techniques and self-generated exercises, running techniques, and combination plays in two or three groups; three-on-one, four-on-two, nine-on-nine
Interval method (extensive)—high intensity, mixed aerobic-endurance training	Runing with changing tempo, circle training, intensive movement gymnastics, one-on-one exercises, technique training at moderate running tempo, double-pass and complex exercises, games with six-on-six to eight-on-eight and with four goals on goal line, attack on defense play when outnumbering or being outnmbered
Interval method (intensive)—high-intensity, anaerobic endurance training	Relay races with and without a ball, running at increasing speed, sprints of 15–150 yards (5–50 m); games of two-on-two up to seven-on-seven and one-plus-one-on-one, one-plus-two-on-two, three-on-two and two-on-two
Repetition method with maximum intensity	Running in hilly terrain, hurdle jumping, working out on stairs and power equipment, jumping down; games of one-on-one until (subjectively) exhausted

Usefulness of Training Methods

The intensity of the stress load is different for each of the above training methods. Also, the effect of the intensity of the different methods (exercises and games) will be different. Therefore, stress-load training can be effective only if the proper training method is chosen. The table on this page lists training methods, grouped according to their different degrees of intensity.

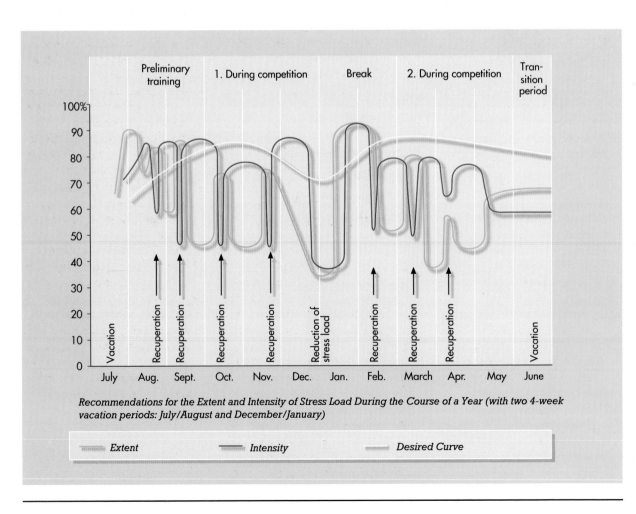

Recommendations for the Extent and Intensity of Stress Load During the Course of a Year (with two 4-week vacation periods: July/August and December/January)

Dividing Training Schedules into Periods

In the section on stress loads, we outlined the principles of the optimal relationship between stress load and recuperation. These hold true as they relate to both individual training periods (that don't follow one another in succession) and to the segments of the training schedule over the whole year. These principles are grounded in the knowledge that the human organism cannot surpass its upper performance limits over an extended period of time without a massive collapse of its physical abilities and some loss of psychological performance readiness.

They also incorporate knowledge of the development, maintenance, and decline of productivity (shown graphically as a sine curve).

As previously mentioned, the division of a "soccer year" into specific periods reflects the application of these principles:

- Pre-season period (four to six weeks).
- First period of competition (about four months)
- Intermediate period (about two months).
- Second period of competition (about four months)
- Post-season period (about four weeks).

Within each period, the extent and intensity of the stress load (and of the total training program) vary greatly.

The overall stress load of the training should be significantly reduced every four weeks during the first half of the year and every three weeks over the second half of the year.

The graph on page 34 gives recommendations for structuring the stress load during the periods of competition and the year as a whole. This allows a recharging of the biological battery and promotes the long-term maintenance of performance level.

Ease up on total stress load by:

- Reducing the extent and, more importantly, the intensity of the stress load.
- Reducing duration of practice.
- Reducing the number of training sessions.
- Shifting training emphasis toward overall conditioning exercises.
- Including alternative athletic activities.
- Increasing use of recuperative therapies (sauna, massage, etc.).

A sound yearly plan divides a long training program into periods of three or four weeks, as discussed on page 24. This kind of planning is recommended in setting objectives for technical and tactical skills.

Interaction of Techniques, Tactics, and Physical Fitness

The basic elements of a player's productivity are his physical fitness and his levels of technical and tactical skill. All other factors discussed so far, particularly those dealing with training, are important only to the extent that they affect these elements.

It is pointless to ask which of the three elements is the most important for a player's performance. It is part of the uniqueness of soccer that weaknesses in one area can be compensated for by strength in others. This holds true at least for the beginning and mid-level player. The higher the level at which a player competes and the stronger the competition, the more difficult it is to compensate for weaknesses in technique, tactics, or fitness. More subtle psychological factors (see "Motivation," page 153) then come increasingly into play. The relative effects of technique, tactics, and fitness are the subject of the following discussion.

Influence of Fitness on Techniques

Basic motor skills, power, endurance, speed, and agility are prerequisites to any kind of human movement. The degree to which they are needed depends on the extent, strenuousness, and duration of the movement. This is especially true for athletes.

Sports-specific techniques also require special fitness-related skills, such as the following:

- Swinging movements of the upper body during a fake require muscle strength and flexibility.
- A flat, hard kick with the arch of the foot requires substantial flexibility (stretching) in the tendons.
- The ability to receive a pass well depends on strength and suppleness in the hips and on good overall coordination.
- A well-developed musculature is imperative for effective jumping for heading or quickly confronting an opponent.

No matter how well grounded in technique, a player cannot perform at a high level in the absence of overall fitness. Once he reaches the stage of fatigue, even technically well-coordinated movements won't be very effective.

Interaction

Influence of Techniques on Fitness

On the other hand, technical skills also influence the physical condition of a player, particularly over the long haul. Well-coordinated technical movements will expend comparably less energy and require less endurance.

This action clearly shows that all game activities depend to a great degree on the technical skills and physical fitness of the player.

Influence of Techniques and Fitness on Tactics

Successful tactical maneuvering (for definition see page 85) requires shrewd and intelligent use of technical skills and physical fitness. This holds true for the tactical executions of individual players, groups of players, and teams alike. A tactical maneuver, for example, involving quick, direct ball control is doomed if players have not mastered the necessary swift, reliable passing technique. Modern tactical variations employed by a team, such as fore-checking (see page 95), require mental alertness and aggressive tackling maneu-

vers, combined with the appropriate techniques. However, exceptional endurance in every player is just as necessary. For the defender in the last defensive line, additional speed is required. Only when all these requirements are met is it possible to employ these tactics successfully.

As these examples demonstrate, the elements of technique, tactics, and fitness are inextricably related in their impact on winning or losing.

Techniques unique to individual types of athletes are important in different ways. In athletic games such as soccer, a well-polished technique gives a player several different means to deal with game situations.

Technical training, according to Grosser/Neumaier includes:
- Instruction in the ideal model of a movement relevant to the given sport.
- The mastery of this ideal movement and its efficient execution.

Often the ideal movement is not possible because of a player's physical makeup or condition (a limited ability, for example, to stretch the ankle or to angle the foot for kicking the ball). The objective in training sessions, however, should always be to reach for the ideal, at least when techniques are practiced in isolation.

Considerable deviation from the ideal movement is not only acceptable; it may be desirable, and even advantageous, in game play. This is certainly true in soccer.

Rapidly moving action during a game demands that a player adjust his approach to a technical action and adapt to the developing situation. For example, a player positioned directly in front of the goal attempts to kick a goal but does not have enough time to carry out the ideal sweeping movement usually prescribed for this situation. This eventuality has consequences for the training process. On the one hand, a player must practice the ideal movement with countless repetitions until it is almost automatic; on the other hand, he must also have the opportunity during training to practice an alternative technique which could be useful in a real game situation.

Soccer-Specific Techniques

When we talk about technique as a means to approach the "job" an athlete does on the playing field, we must ask what tasks the player has to accomplish in the course of a game.

Fundamentally, we have to distinguish between tasks when a player is not in possession of the ball and when he is in possession.

Therefore, we distinguish between:
- Techniques without a ball.
- Techniques with a ball (see overview below).

Receiving and Moving the Ball

Just how far the technical skills of top professional players have evolved over the last few decades is very evident in their play, particularly in their running speed when receiving and moving with the ball. In modern soccer, a player must be prepared for interference, and not only by his direct opponent. Because of the tremendous speed of players on top teams, it is not unusual for them to be challenged by two or even more opponents. Clever ball handling, usually set up by a fake, is one of the most often used means to escape such a situation.

The player receiving the ball combines a body fake with lightning-quick acceleration to rid himself of the opponent(s) (at least for the moment) and open the way for a new tactic.

Implementation

- Receiving a low or high pass from a standing position.
- Moving a low or high pass in the opposite direction from where the ball was played.
- Moving with the ball after a body fake (right) and the run (to the left) or the reverse.

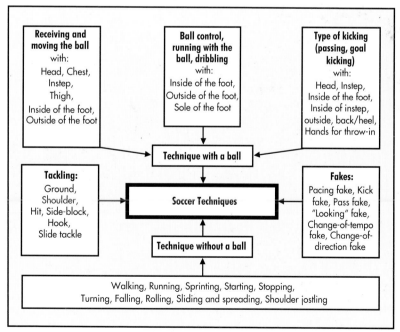

Overview of the technical elements of soccer (see also pages 56 through 57 for goalkeeper techniques)

Soccer-Specific Techniques

- Moving with the ball in the same direction from which it was passed (either a low or high pass).

It is important that midfielders and forwards especially learn very early that, in order to avoid interference from the opposition, a player (who intends to move a pass received in his own territory from a teammate towards the opponents' goal) must be sure to use a body fake to disguise the forward direction of his movement.

Sequence of Movement

Every part of the body (except the hands) can be used for receiving and moving the ball:

- The sole of the foot.
- The inside of the foot.
- The outside of the foot.
- The instep.
- The thigh and shin.
- The stomach.
- The chest.
- The head.

Receiving a ball involves slightly different maneuvers than moving a ball. When receiving, the part of the body that will come in contact is turning towards the ball. The moment the ball makes contact, the body becomes "elastic"—moving with the ball and cushioning its impact. It is important that muscles not tense up. Moving the ball requires the part of the body that has "received" the ball to refrain from pulling back. Rather, contact must be made in such a way that the ball continues to move in the direction the player has chosen, or the surprise will be lost. This is precisely why muscles should not be tense. In addition, tense muscles don't cushion the impact of the ball.

Carrying the ball with the inside of the foot.

Mistakes in Moving the Ball

- The trajectory of the ball has been misread.
  Remedy—Repeated practice of passing from different distances and at different speeds; practice keeping the eyes on the ball all the time it is moving.
- The part of the body that will receive the ball has moved *toward* rather than *with* the ball.
  Remedy—Move foot, thigh, etc., early enough in the direction of the ball; practice without the ball to get a "feeling" for the movement.
- Muscle groups responsible for the necessary movement are too tense (nervousness, etc.).
  Remedy—Consciously practice relaxing by working with smaller, lighter balls.
- A ball "coming in high" is received with the sole, and the tip of the foot is not lifted up high enough.
  Remedy—While standing still, roll a ball back and forth with the sole of the foot.
- A ball "coming in low" is played using the sole, rather than the inside or outside, of the foot.
  Remedy—Inform players of the mistake and practice making the proper reaction "automatic."

Tips for Training

In the past, it was customary to practice control in receiving and moving with the ball from a standing position; now it is recommended that players start practicing "on the move" early, using exercises and game combinations in which a player learns to "bring the ball along" while running. Throughout this practice the player should be challenged by "opponents." In the beginning, this can be done on a loose basis, later on it should be more intensive.

Receiving and Playing the Ball

Carrying the ball with the outside of the foot.

Training in Receiving and Moving the Ball Using Mixed Methods

- Alternate practice of handball and soccer with four goals. The ball is thrown in using hands and moved along with the feet, head, and body.
- Instructions, explanations, and demonstrations of ball-receiving and ball-moving techniques.
- Two players run about 30 feet (10 m) apart. Player A passes or throws the ball to Player B, who receives and moves with the ball, practicing relevant techniques, including body fakes.
- As above; however, the distance between the two players is increased to 60 to 90 feet (20–30 m), and the ball is passed between them with the instep. At first the ball is thrown by hand; later, it is moved along with the instep.
- One goalkeeper with several groups of paired players. Each of the two-player groups moves within a designated space in half of the playing field. The goalkeeper alternately throws and kicks the ball to one of the two-player groups. Both players of that group start toward the ball and quickly try to establish ball control, drive it, and kick a goal.
- Six-on-six games, using the whole playing field and both goals. Use of a "provocation rule" can force passing and receiving for more effective practice, e.g., the ball may not be touched more than three times by a single player during one possession.

Receiving with the chest.

Receiving with the body.

Receiving with the instep.

Soccer-Specific Techniques

Guiding and Driving the Ball

After receiving and driving the ball, but before making a pass or a goal kick, the ball is guided and driven either in various directions or moved with high speed straight ahead. Using fakes, the players are able to create new and surprising game situations with individual tactical maneuvers.

Usefulness

- Moving the ball into a different section of the field to shift the game action.
- Driving the ball away from the opposition.
- Controlling the ball to gain time.
- Controlling the ball to give the team a chance to regroup.
- Driving the ball in one direction, and then unexpectedly changing to a new direction.

Sequence of Movements

The sequence of movements when controlling the ball are so varied and numerous that only the very basic principles can be discussed here.

The difference between controlling and driving the ball depends entirely on the dynamics of the sequence of movements. The player can usually run calmly over the playing field, driving the ball with little interference from his opponents, giving him relatively ample time and space.

In the ideal situation, the ball (in a sense) is "glued" to his foot. The player's body is upright, and he is able to keep track of the movements of the opposition as well as those of his teammates. He is looking ahead, approximately 6 to 10 feet (2–3 m) ahead of the ball. This gives him sufficient peripheral vision to see the ball, his teammates, and the opposition.

The ball can be controlled with the following portions of the foot:

- Inside of the foot.
- Sole of the foot.
- Outside of the foot.
- Instep.
- Heel.

This kind of ball control can be achieved by using either foot and numerous, different combination techniques.

Together with changing directions, doing turns, and rotation maneuvers, the player has a variety of ways to accomplish his task.

Mistakes Made During the Sequence of Movements

- Poor coordination between movements (running, starting, stopping, side to side) and keeping the ball too long.
  Remedy—Pole-running, slalom-style; "fox-hunting" in small groups; running while steadily increasing the speed.
- Driving the ball forward without sufficient "feeling"—the ball is moving too far ahead of the foot.
  Remedy—As above.
- Driving the ball with the inside of the foot or the instep, instead of the outside, while running fast, resulting in needlessly diminished speed.
  Remedy—Running while alternating tempo and driving the ball with the outside or inside of the instep.
- Eyes fixed too much on the ball, reducing the player's awareness of what is going on around him
  Remedy—Shadow-running: two players about 50 feet (15 m) apart drive the ball, with Player A duplicating the movements of Player B. Another alternative: the trainer moves the ball about 30 to 50 feet (10–15 m) in front of the players and the latter follow his changes of direction.

Moving the ball with the inside, sole, outside, and instep.

Dribbling and Faking

Training Tips

Concentrate on using both legs during practice and on moving without fixing the eyes on the ball. According to an established pattern of systematic movements, the ball is driven alternately with the instep, the inside, and the outside of both feet. This is followed by using varying techniques appropriate for a given situation, first against one or two opponents, and then by an abbreviated game play.

As soon as a player can use both legs equally well and has a good feel for the size and movement of the ball, he can almost blindly control the ball. This enables him to look around and take advantage of the best passing opportunity. He can also detect the intentions of the opposition, enabling him to take the necessary counter-measures.

It is important that coordination during running and driving the ball be developed by practicing with increasing speed. Players will develop assertiveness in competition only if they have practiced driving the ball in all directions in brief, disconnected movements with abrupt stops and turns.

Examples of dribbling are given in the next section.

Dribbling and Faking

Often the words "dribbling" and "ball control" are used interchangeably. The basic techniques used to dribble and control a ball are in fact identical. However, it has become customary in soccer to speak of "dribbling" only when a player who has ball possession is being attacked by an opponent. In order to get away from the attacker, the player is forced to camouflage his intended moves. This is accomplished by use of one of the most valuable techniques at his disposal: the fake. With a fake, a player can appear to be going in one direction, only to break suddenly (and for the opponent, totally unexpectedly) in the opposite direction. By accelerating rapidly, he is able to get safely away from his attacker. Dribbling is one of the most important technical skills a player has, particularly in professional soccer, where a player in possession of the ball is usually pressured by several opponents at the same time.

Through well-coordinated fake movements, a player can shake off his attackers, move to a safer space, or remain in possession of the ball just a bit longer. Dribbling, like no other technique, points up the connection between technical agility and physical fitness. Without agility and flexibility, and without enough speed of acceleration, even the most sure-footed player won't be able to extract himself from a tight situation.

Also, the connection between dribbling technique and tactical judgment is very evident. The type and objective of dribbling depends on its tactical possibilities and intentions.

Usefulness

- Breaking through the defense in the direction of the goal.
- Self-defense—moving in the direction of the midfield in order to gain space.
- Luring the opposition to a particular area in order to make room for passing.
- Taking an opponent's attention away from a teammate and then passing to that teammate.

Sequence of Movements

The possibilities for controlling a ball have already been discussed (see page 40). Combining these methods creates countless possibilities for dribbling. It is impossible to list all of them here. When dribbling, a player will intuitively use the best method in the given situation.

Besides the many different combinations of steps, variations in dribbling are greatest in the kinds of fakes a player employs. The most often used are:
- Body and foot fakes.
- Shooting and passing fakes.
- Change-of-tempo fakes.
- "Looking" fakes.

Body and Foot Fake

A player shifting his body or foot position indicates the direction in which he wants to run. If the opponent reacts and turns in that direction, the player interrupts the initial movement and continues in the opposite direction.

Shooting and Passing Fake

Here, a player pretends that he is about to kick or pass the ball, creating a dangerous situation for the opposition. If the opposition reacts and tries to block the ball, the dribbler changes his action with a cut movement (if possible with the "wrong" foot) and goes past the opponent(s). The so-called "wrong" foot is the foot the player stands on, to which he has briefly shifted his weight.

Change of Direction Fake

Here, a player running with the ball suddenly and randomly changes direction several times in a row. This maneuver allows him to get past his opponent and to reach the goal. In this case, speed is less important than a good "feel" for the ball.

Change of Tempo Fake

Here, the player slows down and forces the opponent to do the same. At just the right moment, he accelerates very suddenly, leaving the oppo-

Soccer Specific Techniques

1   2   3

Maneuver with feet without crossing over the ball.

Stopping and starting. The ball is driven with the inside of the foot.

1   2

1   2   3

1   2   3

4

5

6

Fake kick and pushing the ball behind the pivot leg.

3

4

While driving the ball forward, faking a stopping movement (with the sole) and then once more driving the ball (called "Leo" or "locomotive").

4

5

6

4

5

6

Soccer-Specific Techniques

nent behind. Since the opponent has his back to his own goal, he must first make a 90- or 180-degree turn—one reason why this fake works surprisingly well. In contrast to the direction fake, the tempo fake is better suited for players with less developed technique; however, they do need to be good sprinters.

"Looking" Fake

This technique resides in the repertoire of every top soccer player, although most players at this level are clever enough that they seldom fall for the trick. Outmaneuvering top opponents requires an atypical, carefully designed fake. One possibility is to pretend to start an action by looking in a particular direction and then suddenly start dribbling for a breakthrough.

Mistakes in the Sequence of Movements

Players usually make the same mistakes as discussed in the section on ball control (see page 40). These mistakes result in the following:

- The fake chosen does not suit the player's style, his technical skills, or his physical condition.
Remedy—More practice, using different fakes in training games (see above).
- The fake is carried out halfheartedly and without enough confidence. Often a player allows too little time for the fake movements because he does not really believe that they will work. Actually, it is just such telltale hesitation that renders a fake unconvincing and useless. Remedy—Make the player aware of the effect of his actions; have him observe a player with good faking skills; have him play defense to see that opponents really do fall for a calm, well-delivered fake; use them variably in training games.

- The player is not driving the ball hard enough in the new direction and is unable to put enough distance between himself and the opponent.
Remedy—When faking, position the pivot leg for the next step. Remember that only after the *first step away* from the opponent has dribbling been successful.

Training Tips

Successful dribbling is possible only once a player has developed a certain feel for the ball, which is the result of constant practice. Moreover, this skill is crucial, as dribbling always occurs in the course of a one-on-one confrontation, and it requires not only ball sense but courageous body action. Training to achieve lightning-fast reactions to an opponent's defensive moves can be done only in actual one-on-one confrontations. Thus, constant repetition of the complex sequence of movements involved in dribbling and the actual experience of dribbling in confrontations during exercise games are essential.

Methods for Practicing Ball Control, Driving, and Dribbling

- Players move with their foot on the ball around randomly arranged poles.
- As the player moves the ball, the coach calls commands indicating how the ball is to be driven, alternating the inside of the right and left legs with the outside of the left and right legs.
- Players running parallel to each other pass the ball back and forth. The coach runs ahead of them, constantly changing direction from left to right, backward and forward, to practice "looking" fakes. Players must mirror the coach's movements.

Speed should increase throughout the exercise.
- Player A (with the ball) runs in front of Player B. A changes direction and tempo suddenly and B must copy A's movements.
- Run sprints through randomly arranged stakes and relay races.

Tackling

Taking Possession of the Ball

In the same way that offensive players have to develop clever ways to control the ball and to dribble, defending players have to learn to regain possession of the ball using different techniques.

> Methods of taking possession of a ball are generally called tackling.

Tackling is possible only in the presence of a number of favorable factors:
- A player must be motivated, decisive, and ready, and have sufficient concentration to make the risky maneuver confidently.
- A player must be able to recognize the proper moment: he must not attack too early or too late when attempting to take the ball away from the opponent.
- Depending on the positions of the dribbler and the opponent, the proper tackling technique must be chosen.
- A player must be in the physical condition specifically required for the chosen tackling technique (for instance, good agility in the hips for the hook and the slide tackles).
- A player should be able to anticipate the dribbling action of the opponent.
- Tackling is not a mere act of aggression; it should be motivated only by the desire to win. After the tackle, a player should be able to initiate a

new attack. Which tackling technique will have the best chance of success will depend most of all on the position of the two opponents. Do they face each other? Are they next to each other? Behind each other?

The following is a list of different tackling techniques:
- Ground tackle.
- Shoulder tackle.
- Head-on tackle.
- Side tackle.
- Hook tackle.
- Slide tackle.

Ground Tackle

Position of the Two Players
The players are moving directly toward each other. The defending player uses his whole body to tackle the opponent, who has the ball.

Sequence of Movements
The defensive player blocks the ball by applying steady and even pressure to it with the inside of the leg. All the muscles of that leg are tensed, which also serves to protect his knees.

Mistakes
- The defender kicks the ball with the inside of his foot or the instep, instead of blocking the opponent and taking the ball from between his legs. Experience has shown that the ball will move in the direction opposite the tackling player.
Remedy—Two-player practice while standing, using reduced power. Player A hits the ball with the instep; player B blocks it with the inside of his foot.

Using a ground tackle, the player blocks the ball with the inside of his foot.

Head-on Tackle

Position of the Two Players
The tackling player is standing between "man and goal," behind the opponent. In this way, he secures his own goal and has the opponent *and* the goal in his sight.

Sequence of Movements
A tackler, lying in wait, is positioned somewhat diagonally behind the opponent. He starts running with short, quick steps in the direction of the oncoming ball, past the opponent. As soon as the ball is close (both players must be positioned in close proximity), the tackler uses his body to gain a better position from which he can guide the ball (with the inside of his foot) away from the opponent.

Mistakes
- The defending player is too far behind the opponent, obstructing his own view of the oncoming ball. This position also requires that he go around the opponent before proceeding forward.
Remedy—Constant repetition of one-plus-one-on-one practice in passing, starting, and tackling.

Soccer-Specific Techniques

1

2

3

Shoulder Tackle

Position of the Two Players

The players are running next to each other, touching at the shoulders, moving toward the oncoming ball. Both try to gain possession of the ball.

Sequence of Movements

During competition, players can, generally speaking, make contact with an opponent's shoulder, if they keep their elbows close to the body. However, they can do this only when the ball is in close proximity. With a fair, but powerful, use of the body, the player attempts to gain a better position to guide the ball (with the inside of his foot) away from the opponent.

Mistakes

• Making contact with the opponent's shoulder too early and not keeping the elbows close enough to the body. These are rule violations (pushing).
Remedy—Practice shoulder contact movements without a ball; then with a ball, but with less force.

• Shoulder tackle made at the wrong time (e.g., when the opponent's pivot leg is alongside the player), allowing the opponent to balance himself on the other leg.
Remedy—Instruction and practice.

Side Tackle

Position of the Two Players

The players are alongside each other. The dribbler is in possession of the ball. He tries to kick a pass or a goal.

Sequence of Movements

A tackler runs alongside and as close as possible to the opponent, who is dribbling. When the opponent is about to pass or kick the ball, the player attempts to block the ball with either the inside or the outside of the foot, depending on the order of steps he takes. Likewise with the ground-and-hook tackle (see page 48), the ball is not only pushed away with the offensive form of tackling but is blocked with one part of the foot in such a way that it remains in the possession of the tackling player.

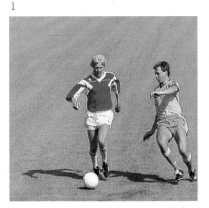

1

2

3

4

5

6

Here, again, it is important that the muscles be contracted.

Mistakes

- The tackle begins too far away from the dribbling player, creating a kicking angle that lets the ball pass by the tackler's leg.
Remedy—Encourage the player to make body contact (touching the opponent's shoulder).

Slide Tackle

Position of the Two Players

The dribbler has escaped the tackler, who remains at his heels.

Mistakes

- The player lowers his center of gravity too little.

- The distance to the ball is too great.
- The sliding movement is carried out with upper body erect.
- The tucking movement at the end of the slide tackle, which lowers the risk of injury, is not carried out.
- The player does not tackle with the favorable leg that is turned away from the opponent, but with the closer leg and thus, touches the opponent before the ball (foul play).

Hook Tackle

Position of the Two Players

As with ground tackling, the players face each other.

Sequence of Movements

In low side-tackle position, the tackler, in a wait-and-see fashion,

After a shoulder tackle (with elbows close to the body), both players fight for ball possession.

moves at an angle towards the dribbling opponent. When the opponent leads the ball to the side, the player tries to move the ball out of the reach of the opponent with a split-like hook movement.

Mistakes

- The player does not bend down far enough before he attempts to tackle and his body weight shifts too far to one side.

Using a slide tackle, a player shifts his weight after he gets set and pushes off the inside leg, sliding with this leg in the direction of the ball.

4

5

6

Soccer-Specific Techniques

Examples of Training for the Hook and Slide Tackles

- Leg stretching exercises (hurdle-jumping body position, leg splits) to stretch thigh and pelvic muscles.
- At the coach's command, leg-split exercises while running slowly, alternating between the right and the left leg, followed by body rolling.
- As above, the player is dribbling, and immediately before going into a leg split, the ball is pushed straight ahead about 3 to 6 feet (1–2 m).
- Player A slowly moves with the ball; player B runs alongside. When A pushes the ball 3 to 6 feet (1–2 m) ahead, B goes after the ball, hooking his leg, and trying to push the ball to the side or trying to block the ball with his body.
- Goal-kicking practice with one-on-one up to six-on-six; passing, however, only after dribbling.

From the very first, all exercises for tackling should be practiced with both the right and left legs.

Different Types of Kicking for Passing and Shooting

There are different techniques for kicking the ball. And indeed, kicking techniques are very important in a soccer game. Accurate passes and accurate shots on goal require very specific techniques.

The different types of kicks are:
- Straight-ahead instep kick.
- Inside-the-instep kick.
- Outside-of-the-foot kick.
- Heading.

The ground-and-hook tackle: as in slide tackling, the player hooks the ball from a low position.

Variations of the straight-ahead instep kick:
- Hip-pivoting kick.
- Overhead kick.
- Lateral-instep kick.

Whenever a player finds himself in an unfavorable position, or when he wants to surprise the opponent(s) with a pass or kick, he can use kicks that are not necessarily mentioned in training manuals, such as:
- The back-heel kick.
- Kicking with the tips of the toes.

Whenever strategy requires, the ball can be pushed with the knee. When in the air, it can be pushed or "kicked" with the back of the head. Very important goals have been scored with these rather unorthodox methods, such as Uve Seeler's back-of-the-head kick during the 1970 World Championship Games in Mexico.

The fact that a game situation forces a player to use unusual kicking techniques does not mean that those used customarily are any less important. Particularly in professional soccer, a player must be in absolute command of exceptional kicking techniques. Only then will he be able to succeed in making tight passes and precise shots on goal, all the while running at top speed over great distances. Mistakes in passing almost always mean loss of ball possession, especially when in his own half of the playing field or in front of his own goal. The opposition will always profit from mistakes of this kind.

For this reason, it is imperative that the greatest possible skill be acquired in kicking and passing. Fundamental mistakes affecting the sequence in the movements of the ball might go "unpunished" during the early years of play; unchecked, they will permanently hinder the development of a player's athletic performance, and they are almost

Different Kicks for Passing and Shooting

always impossible to correct. This is why it is so important to correct a beginner's mistakes early and effectively. Special attention must be paid to this phase in training. With kicking and passing skills, more than with any others, it is essential to recognize mistakes and the reasons for them. The necessary correction depends on what kind of mistake is being made. A coach needs special training in detecting and recognizing faulty techniques. See page 62 for further discussion.

All kicking techniques have similarly arranged, definite patterns. Scientific observation enables us to break down the sequence of movements in kicking into three phases. Each of these phases has a special function; it is imperative to know and understand these phases in order to master their movements and to correct mistakes in performing them. The coach must have a clear understanding of the individual movements that involve arms, body, and feet.

The main phases are the:

Approach phase—The leg or head moves in the direction opposite to that in which the ball is to be kicked.

Main phase—The surface of the body meets the ball.

Ending phase—The kicking leg follows through.

A player has many different kicking techniques at his disposal. Which one he finds most appropriate for a given situation will depend on the technical level the player has achieved and which part of the anatomy he intends to use for kicking. For instance, it is easier to kick with the inside of the foot than it is with the instep, but the ball can be hit harder and farther with the instep technique than with

the technique that uses the inside of the foot. The sequence of the movements is important for a successful kicking technique. Also important are the synchronized movements of the pivoting leg, the body, and the arms. These topics are covered in more detail in "Correcting Technical Mistakes" on page 62.

Instep Kick

Kicking straight ahead with the instep is the most powerful kick, as it carries the ball the farthest. It is *the* classic technique for kicking a goal. When the amount of force is carefully adjusted, it can also be used for short passes. The instep kick technique is better than any other to produce the desired height of a pass, which is controlled by the positioning of the kicking foot. The determining factors are the position of the kicking leg and the pivot leg.

Sequence of Movements

Approach—Straight ahead to the goal.

Pivot leg—Ankle, knee, and hip are lowered.

Free leg—Starting from the hip, then the knee, and finally the ankle joint, the leg moves back in the approach phase. In the main phase it moves forward toward the ball with a whip-like acceleration from the knee joint. In the ending phase it follows through.

Free foot—Flexing the ankle joint, the foot is supported by tightened muscles.

Kicking surface—The instep.

Foot position for an instep kick.

Effectiveness—Instep Kick

Pass too short	xx
Pass too long	xxx
Pass too low	xxx
Pass too high	xx
Effective passing	x
Powerful goal kick	xxx
Precision goal kick	xx
Direct pass	x

Upper body—Bent over the pivot leg and the ball.

Arms—The arm opposite the free leg moves in step, first back and then forward.

Soccer-Specific Techniques

1

2

3

A running, straight-ahead instep kick.

Mistakes

- Direction of approach and kicking motion not aimed at the goal.
- Pivot leg behind the ball.
- Free leg not bent far enough.
- Free foot not flexed enough.
- Poor kicking surface—instep does not hit the center of the ball.
- Upper body leaning too far back.

Training Suggestions for Instep Kicking, Simulating Real Game Situation

- Soccer-tennis in small groups of one-on-one up to three-on-three, with head-high net; depending on

the players' level of skill, receiving the ball or direct passing; "provocation rule," i.e., the ball can be kicked only with the instep.

- "Ball-driving" game with instep technique; using long instep kicks on a narrow section of the field, two groups of players try to push each other out-of-bounds; receiving passes with either foot or hands; throw-in at the point where ball control was regained or where the ball left the field (on the long side).
- Goal-kicking game using one-on-one: players stand about 30 feet (10 m) away from the goal alternating

A hip-turn kick, a demanding variation of the instep kick.

1

2

3

Different Kicks for Passing and Shooting

between playing attacker and goalie; first, the ball is thrown in the air by hand, later drop-kicked, and then played from the ground.

• As above, but distance from the goal increased to 60 feet (20 m), the defender throws the ball 10 feet (3 m) in the air in the direction of the opponent's goal, running after the ball and shooting with the instep.

• As above, but with four players and one ball, the defender has one player passing the ball from the side and a short distance; the oncoming ball is kicked either after

one bounce or it is volleyed; later played against opponents.

• Training game with different "provocation rules."

Special Feature of the "Hip-Turn Kick"

This and the overhead-volley kick are variations of the instep kick. They are intended to allow a high incoming ball to be played before the opponent can reach the ball.

Sequence of Movements

Pivot leg—Turned toward the goal while kicking the ball.
Free leg—Swings up hip-high in an arch towards the ball.
Upper body—Bending almost horizontally over the pivot leg.

Soccer-Specific Techniques

The overhead-volley kick, the most spectacular type of instep kick.

Uniqueness of the Overhead-Volley Kick

The overhead-volley kick can be accomplished with or without a scissors movement. With the scissors movement, the player jumps off the kicking leg. The other leg becomes the swinging leg, its action supported by the jump-off leg. The jump-kick leg is forcefully pulled up, past the swinging leg, where it meets the ball at the instep.

Foot position for the inside-instep kick.

Inside-Instep Kick

Even better than the above maneuver is the inside-instep kick, because this technique gives the ball a spin in flight. This phenomenon, known in physics as the "magnus effect," puts a spin on the ball, which creates unequal air pressure around it, moving the ball in an arch-like curve through the air. With the help of this technique it is possible to score (for instance, using a free kick) by

Effectiveness—Inside-Instep Kick

Pass too short	x
Pass too long	xxx
Pass too flat	x
Pass too high	xxx
Pass with spin	xxx
Goal kick too powerful	xx
Goal-kick accuracy	xxx
Direct pass	xx

shooting the ball around the wall, just inside the goal post.

Sequence of Movements

Approach—In an angle in the direction of the goal.
Pivot leg—"Springy" bend at hip, knee, and ankle.
Pivot foot—About 2 to 3 feet (1 m) behind the ball.
Free leg—In the approach phase, leg swings back from the hip and knee, and forward against the ball in the main phase; throughout the main and the ending phases, the leg is rotated at the hip and knee; in the last phase, the leg comes to rest at an angle in front of the pivot leg.
Free foot—Moderately bent at the ankle and rotated to the outside.
Kicking surface—Inside of the instep.

Different Kicks for Passing and Shooting

Upper body—Over and in line with the pivot leg.
Arms—Bent at the elbows for balance.

Mistakes

• Approach to the ball too direct.
• Pivot leg too close to the ball.
• Free foot not rotated to the outside. (In all of the cases above, the ball has a strong spin.)
• Free-leg movement from knee joint instead of hip produces weak kick.
• Kicking foot not fixed.
• Upper body leaning too far back.

Outside-Instep Kick

This technique could be called the witches' trick among the kicking techniques, because with this kick a player can solve almost all tactical situations: short, deceptive passes, long passes, kicking with spin, and

Effectiveness—Outside-Instep Kick

Short pass	xxx
Long pass	xxx
Low pass	xxx
High pass	xx
Passing with spin	xxx
Strong goal kick	xxx
Accurate goal kick	xxx
Direct pass	xxx

kicking to a teammate who is positioned behind an opponent, even if he seems to be positively out of reach.

Sequence of Movements

Approach—Straight or slightly angled, depending on the intended spin effect.
Pivot leg—Next to the ball, approximately 2 feet (1 meter) away.
Pivot foot—"Springy" bend at the ankle, knee and hip.
Free leg—Swinging straight back

from the knee and hip in the approach phase; forward with steadily increasing inside rotation in the main phase; just before ball contact, increasing whip-like action from the knee; decreasing pendulum swinging motion and increasing bend at hip and knee.
Free foot—Moderate, inside flex at the ankle in fixed position.
Kicking surface—Outside of instep.
Upper body—Bent forward over the ball.
Arms—Held at the side, bent at the elbows for balance.

Mistakes

• Pivot leg too close to the ball.
• Free leg has insufficient swinging motion; rotating motion to the inside.
• Free foot has insufficient inside rotation.
• Ball hit too close to the center instead of on the side.
• Upper body leaning too far back.

Foot position for the outside-instep kick.

Soccer-Specific Techniques

Inside Kick

This is the most frequently used kick in soccer. The technique allows the player to kick accurately. It is particularly well-suited for combination plays. From a short distance, goal kicking with the inside is more successful than instep kicking. The disadvantage is less power behind the kick; therefore, inside kicks are more suited for short and medium distances.

The kicking position of the foot for the inside kick.

Sequence of Movements

Approach—Straight ahead in the direction of the goal.

Pivot leg—"Springy" bend at the ankle, knee, and hip.

Pivot foot—Next to the ball, a one- to two-foot width away from the ball.

Free leg—Swinging back from the hip in approach phase, forward in the direction of the ball in main phase, with increasing outside rotation.

Free foot—Rotated to the outside at about a 90-degree angle to the pivot leg; tips of toes pulled up so that the sole is parallel to the ground, ankle fixed by tensing muscles.

Kicking surface—The inside of the foot at the arch.

Upper body—Leaning over the pivot leg and ball.

Arms—Bent at the elbows and away from the body for balance.

Mistakes

- Toes not pointing in right direction.
- Insufficient outside rotation of the free leg at the hip; insufficiently tensed hip and knee.
- Toes not pulled up sufficiently; ankle not tensed.
- Ball surface is hit too close to the heel or the toes.
- Upper body leaning too far back.

Heading

The heading technique allows a player to reach a high pass, which otherwise could be played only by running backwards. Which one of several players reaches a high-bouncing ball first depends on the timing of his approach and his jumping power.

As in the case with the instep kick, heading techniques also have several variations:

- Header from a standing position—straight ahead.
- Header from a standing position—with a turn in the torso/upper body.
- Header from a jump—straight ahead.
- Header from a jump—with a turn in the torso/upper body.
- Diving header.

Effectiveness—Inside Kick

Long pass	xxx
Short pass	x
Low pass	xxx
High pass	xx
Pass with spin	xx
Strong goal kick	x
Accurate goal kick	xxx
Direct pass	xxx

1   2

Different Kicks for Passing and Shooting

3

4

A diving header.

When heading from a jump, it is best to jump off one leg, since the energy from the momentum of the approach thus transfers into greater jumping height.

In addition, when heading from a jump and turning, it is best to jump with the leg that is closer to the ball. The other leg, the swinging leg, must not only swing upwards, but in the direction of the ball, increasing the rotation of the hip.

Effectiveness—Heading

Short pass	xxx
Long pass	xx
Low pass	x
High pass	xxx
Pass with spin	x
Strong pass	xx
Pass accuracy	xxx
Direct pass	xxx

The following discussion refers to headers from a one-leg jump-off without a turn.

Sequence of Movements
Approach—Straight ahead to the ball and the goal; jumping off from the leg more appropriate in the situation.
Jump-off leg—Arches backward after the jump.
Swinging leg—Swinging forward, high up, bending at hip and knee.
Upper body—Arching backward; the momentum of reaching back in a snapping motion propels the upper body forward; the energy generated puts power behind the header.
Neck and head—Head and neck muscles are tensed by pulling the chin down to the chest during the upper body's rearward motion; eyes are on the ball.

Kicking surface—The forehead; under no circumstances, the temples.

Mistakes
- Jumping off with both legs instead of one.
- Jump-off leg not arched back immediately; allowing no counterbalance.
- Too little power behind the motion of the swinging leg.
- Upper body does not reach back far enough.
- Head and neck are not tensed, resulting in neck injuries.
- Eyes are closed.

A jumping header, straight ahead, while running.

3

4

5

6

Soccer-Specific Techniques

Training Tips for Kicking Methods

The variety of individual kicking techniques discussed in this chapter and the method of the instep kick should make clear the importance of kicking practice.

In addition, the following general concepts are important in the course of training:

- For ground kicks, the use of *both legs* must be mastered by every player; practicing with the weaker leg also strengthens the "good" leg.
- When practicing, concentrate first on consistency and precision, then on power.
- Kicking power is less a function of muscle strength than a very well coordinated use of power; therefore, emphasis must be on relaxed, smooth, whipping movements during kicking exercises.
- Long passes and precise shooting require ample space for the free leg and opposite arm in the approach phase.
- Insufficient space is the most frequent cause of mistakes. However, consider these other causes: insufficient flexibility in the ankle of the jumping leg (instep kick); insufficient rotation of the ankle (inside kick); insufficient flexibility for leg-splits (hip-turning kick). Stretching exercises offer the only remedy for these problems.
- Good timing is a fundamental requirement for converting flanks; a player can acquire the necessary "anticipating" skills only by playing as many flanks as possible in training. PRACTICE! PRACTICE! PRACTICE!
- The training schedule must alternate different activities: short and long ball practice, balls high and low in the air; balls from straight ahead and from an angle.
- Never start goal-shooting practice without such adequate prior warm-up as shooting from every angle and distance, using every appropriate technique (for instance, from short distances with inside or outside kicks), or shooting and kicking under time pressure without creating complex game situations (however, not exclusively). Do not schedule goal-kicking practice for beginners who are fatigued.

Very Important—Goal kicking livens up every practice session, and therefore, must be part of the training.

The technique of fielding low passes.

Goalkeeping Techniques

The goalkeeper occupies a special position in soccer. He is allowed to use his hands within the penalty area. A list of techniques specific to this position includes:

- Fielding low and high incoming balls.
- Fist-punching high balls.
- Deflecting a ball away from the foot of a dribbling opponent.
- Throwing and punting the ball as offensive actions.

The photos here and on the following pages provide excellent insight into the somewhat complicated motions of the goalkeeper.

Deflecting a ball away from the foot.

The basic position of the goalkeeper and the catching of medium-high passes.

Fielding high incoming passes by jumping off with one leg.

Diving for low incoming passes with and without preceding scissors-step motion.

Technique Training

Technique Training

Training in techniques is a large part of overall soccer training. It should be *the* preparation for competition and should, therefore, reflect as much as possible the "real thing." For this reason, and when time is limited (at least in training programs for young and amateur players), techniques are taught in conjunction with tactical actions and the improvement of physical fitness.

When we talk about technical training, we are talking about the science of movement, and attempting to effect a positive change in movement and behavior.

In this sense, technical training can be defined as: acquiring, improving, stabilizing, and making automatic the various applications of soccer-specific techniques.

Teaching and Learning Phase

So technical training is understood to be the acquiring and making consistent and automatic the needed skills for soccer. This is basically the learning of motor skills.

However, the development of any motor skill, in the strictest sense, does not necessarily happen in a linear, or step-by-step, fashion. Thus, players at a particular level acquire abilities that are later on refined, improved on, and made reliable and consistent.

Development of the motor skills necessary for sports-specific performance can better be seen as a series of spirals (turning a player from beginner to professional). Each individual spiral represents a different level of performance. On each level,

a player acquires additional techniques. Only the quality of these skills is raised from one level to the next. Over time, the exercises become more complex, the tempo is increased, and the confrontation between players becomes more intense (see page 61).

Newly acquired techniques must be practiced constantly when training young players, long before the techniques have become fluid or automatic. It does not matter that the skills are not yet elegant or honed; they are in the process of becoming. Soccer can be played even if technical skills are still in the infant stage; they just need to be continually improved. A training program for beginners in which practice takes precedence over playing on the field, serves neither to improve technical skills nor to enhance the young athletes' enthusiasm for the game.

Goals of Technical Training

As mentioned earlier, training objectives must correspond to the different levels of age, development, and learning of those being trained.

Goals for a training program for young people depend on the ages and developmental levels of the players involved. Another criterion is the "training age," which, at the same age level, can differ from one club to another and often even within a club (see table page 23).

In a training program for adults, the goals depend largely on the performance class and, therefore, on the frequency of practice sessions. In lower amateur classes in soccer, there often is not enough time for practice, making it difficult to develop the talent present in the ranks of the players. However, here too, it is

important to establish sound training goals and a systematic way to realize them.

Important Points for Technical Training for Young Amateurs
- Continued development of existing individual technical skills and talent, e.g., good heading skills, dribbling, kicking, shooting, passing, etc.
- Correction of obvious technical weaknesses that hinder further development, e.g., poor ball reception, problems due to weak leg(s), weak foot position for instep kicks.
- Scoring goals with head and foot kicks, dribbling from different distances and angles.
- Strengthening the special skills a player needs for his position.
- Development of special techniques for standard procedures such as corner kicks, free kicks, and penalty kicks.

Important Points for the Technical Training of Professionals
In addition to the goals listed for young and amateur players, the following points are important for professionals:
- Absolute ball control when running and sprinting.
- Continued development of all techniques to improve strength in one-on-one confrontations, specifically, learning new fakes.
- Continued development of techniques that a player does not necessarily need often in the particular position he holds (developing into an all-around player).

Training Principles

The following general principles govern the process of learning and practicing athletic techniques:

- The learning process can be successful only when the player has a clear understanding of the motion or movement he is to learn. Therefore, it is essential when teaching beginners to demonstrate in person or show by some other means (e.g., photos or slides) what it is they must learn.
- Some techniques require specific physical abilities beforehand. If the ability is not there and is not developed in the course of learning a technique, it must be acquired by doing other specific exercises.
- Mistakes in the sequence of movements that become habitual are corrected only with great difficulty. Therefore, in a training program for beginners, all mistakes must be caught and remedied very early; relearning is very time consuming.
- Whenever one physical ability improves (say, sprinting), it is necessary to adapt the other interactive technical abilities to the new level of performance.
- Children learn new techniques quickly, but they also forget quickly. This makes necessary the frequent, steady repetition of newly acquired skills.
- Fatigue interferes with coordination and concentration, making it difficult to learn new movements. Accordingly, new techniques should be taught at the beginning of a session, immediately after the warm-up.

Specific Principles

- Professional players must be able to perform equally well with both legs. Therefore, from the very beginning, practice with both legs should be a standard part of training.
- Techniques should be performed "heads-up." Constantly keeping an eye on the ball must become automatic.
- Techniques should be practiced with a gradual increase in tempo. Quick leg work while standing and while running must be a constant part of the training program.

Children react to technical training with enthusiasm. Playing ball is fun!

Technique Training

Methods, Exercises, and Games for Technical Training

Technical training has two basic components:
1. Game plays, which allow a player to acquire, strengthen, and make automatic ball-control skills (inductive learning).
2. Exercise, which helps a player consciously learn to use the individual elements of the technique (deductive learning).

Learning takes place by two entirely different methods:
1. Learning of individual elements by themselves.
2. Learning a number of technical elements in complex interactions.

Consequently, a coach can choose among the following:
- The game method.
- The simple exercise method.
- The complex exercise method.
- Combinations of two or more of the above.

The Game Method

The game method teaches complex playing skills using real game situations and different types of strategy. This teaches technical skills automatically.

Here, teaching takes place through the play method, which is known in sports didactics as the "holistic method." This method is less "teacher intensive" than that organized around an exercise session. The assumption is that, in the course of a game, a player learns technical and tactical skills through experience (inductive learning), and thus learns and improves them automatically.

Examples of Game Plays

There is a great variety of small game plays that lead to the "big game." The following describes a selection of typical plays.

Game Without a Goal and with Unrestricted Space

- Competition (one-on-one up to eight-on-eight) with different tasks, e.g., controlling the ball with a group; passing the ball from player A to player B to player C, etc.; combination play with double pass; plays with one or two ball contacts per player; playing using only the right or left leg for passing; passing only after one dribble; etc.
- Catch-ball with two-on-one, three-on-one, four-on-two, six-on-two.
- Game in which one team outnumbers the other (say, 6 against 4 or 7 against 5) with a "handicap" for the outnumbering team, e.g., limited number of ball contacts or playing with the weaker leg.

Games with a Goal, Within Lines, or Random Goals

- Goal-shooting games, goal-scoring competitions between two or four players, respectively, from about 30 to 60 feet (10–20 m).
- Game plays with one-on-one up to eight-on-eight with two, four, or six small goals.
- The same between two touchlines. Here one goal or point is scored whenever a player dribbles across the opponent's line.
- Game plays with neutral players throwing the ball in, e.g., one neutral player for both five-on-fives. Passes caught by the neutral players count as a score or point.
- Soccer-tennis games. The height of the net and size of the playing field determine the degree of difficulty.

Small, competitive games, called *circular group games*, have been developed by Bruggemann/Albrecht with three unusual rules.

The game "one and two-on-two with a goal," for example, is played on the regular field with the penalty area extended to midfield. The following rules are observed:

1. The **provocation rule** might be that goals can be scored only by dribbling or by trying to pass from outside the penalty zone. This rule "provokes" players to use very specific technical-tactical skills.

2. The **continuation rule** might be that after gaining ball possession, the player must first pass the ball back to a neutral player positioned in the center circle before the team in possession of the ball is allowed a goal kick.

3. The **correction rule** might be that goals attempted from outside the penalty area can only be made by a direct kick after a back pass.

Technique Training Methods

The Simple Exercise Method

Technical and tactical elements that are important for the comprehensive performance of the game are practiced in isolated form through continuous repetition.

The "simple exercise method" is traditionally used as a special form of the "partial method." This method of teaching, consisting of simple exercises, is very teacher-intensive (deductive learning method). Here, "simple" means that the actions are not yet part of complex game strategies, and players are not yet getting sidetracked into more complex actions. Soccer training today makes increasing use of practicing only one part of the overall game action, such as the hip-turn kick. This method is particularly useful for teaching or strengthening new skills when there is little time available for training.

Clearly, though, a soccer training program with too much emphasis on this method is probably neither effective nor much fun for participants, especially beginners.

Exercise Games

There are a good number of games from which to choose:
- Individual exercises with the ball to improve "feeling" for the ball, such as dribbling, running a slalom course, running in a designated circle; ball-control practice alternating the inside and outside of the foot and alternating the left and right foot.
- Exercises in groups of two to six players, standing and running.
- Heading exercises on the wall.
- Running relay races.
- Combination plays in groups of two or three players with a prearranged running route. Regularly increasing difficulty is achieved with different

levels of exercise, such as:
a. Exercises while standing (seldom used today).
b. Running exercises (jogging, running, sprinting).
c. Exercises against an opponent (an imagined opponent, a half-active opponent, and then an active opponent).

For children, one-on-one exercises have all the elements of a game.

The Complex Exercise Method

Here, specific plays are taken from real game situations and practiced through constant repetition.

Techniques and tactics are used as they would be in a real game. Repetition is the teaching tool. The goal and the effectiveness of the method make this the intermediate step between simple exercises and the game method, described earlier.

Examples of Exercises
- Starting from the sides at midfield, a left- or right-winger and a center forward, opposed by one or two players, drive the ball in the direction of the goal line, concluding the exercise with a pass to a center forward.
- While running, a forward passes to a center forward. This player then passes to a third player in midfield (either by kicking or using a header) who has moved up, and who attempts a shot on goal from the second line. Both forwards may be pressured by players from the opposition.

The *degree of difficulty* of this method can be increased by the following, systematically employed steps:
- Exercises according to specific game strategies with "half-active" opponents.
- Exercises according to varied game strategies that are used with "half-active" opponents.
- Solving game situations using all techniques practiced so far.

Basically, the number of participants can be increased so that the offense is outnumbered by the defense, the two sides have an equal number of players, and the offense outnumbers the defense.

Technique Training

Advantages and Disadvantages of the Methods

The advantages and disadvantages of the methods listed here have long been subjects of debate, and remain so. Each one of the three methods has specific advantages and disadvantages. However, all of them have their place in a modern training program. In fact, it is difficult to imagine a program without them. Some determinants for the most appropriate method are:

- The goal set for daily training.
- The amount of time available for training.
- The amount of equipment and the number of balls on hand.
- The age and developmental level of the players.
- The athletic performance level of the players.

- Training readiness.

In the table below is a comparison of the advantages and disadvantages of the different methods Depending on the specific training situation, a coach may want to put more emphasis on one method than another.

In schools today, the game-play method is often used exclusively, since experts believe that a process-oriented teaching approach is the best for the overriding objectives (such as socialization and affective learning) of this play. Teaching of these behaviors is easier by this means than by methods that train skills in isolation.

However, if time is limited and a coach needs to address a specific technique, isolated exercises are the best choice.

For senior players and for more advanced young ones, the complex method is particularly useful because it trains all performance-related aspects at once and as close as possible to the real situation. When training junior players, it is best to alternate between playing, exercising, and a second round of playing.

Mixed Method

When contrasting all three training methods, it is clear that no one method alone is ideal for all situations. Basically, using a mix of all three methods in the course of an individual training session (especially when used over several consecutive sessions) will have the greatest benefit. As mentioned above for training junior players, the "whole-part-whole" method is an ideal solu-

The simple exercise, game and complex exercise methods are the three most important training procedures for the development of technical skills and tactical actions; with the mixed procedure they are combined in such a way that their advantages are used and their disadvantages are avoided.

	Simple Exercise Method	**Game Method**	**Complex Exercise Method**
	Suitable for beginners and advanced players	Suitable for beginners, advanced, and professional players	Suitable for professional players
Main purpose	Development of an exact basis in technique, precision and execution of the technique	Joy in playing the game! Skillful choice of technical maneuvers and easy adapation of individual elements to the game situation	Complex development of technique, tactic and condition; developing approaches to close game situations in competition
Advantages	1. Greater training effect within a short period. 2. Familiarity and execution of motions. 3. Beginners start from the bottom, no technical prerequisites necessary. 4. Precise line-up forms allow great overview for trainer. 5. In cramped surroundings, more players can train. 6. Allows greater flexibility in organization of training.	1. The game is fun—also suitable in schools. 2. Ideal for youngsters of all ages. 3. Ball and body technique adapt to the game situation. 4. Reaction, will power, and correct behavior in the game improve. 5. Less coach intensive. The trainer can observe more carefully or take over the special training. 6. Tactics will be improved.	1. Technique, tactics and conditioning are improved at the same time and in focus. 2. Through a great effect in hand-eye coordination, better training results in a shorter time. 3. High impact in intervals. 4. Appropriate for circle training. 5. With the exercises for techniques and tactics, understanding, reacting, and decision-making within set boundaries are improved.
Disadvantages	1. Technique is practiced without bearing on real game situations. 2. So everything looks somehow different in the game. Enables greater objectivity. 3. Training can easily become routine and boring (particularly with bad trainers). 4. Youngsters lose sense of fun very fast. 5. Basically, physical condition is not improved.	1. Exact execution of technique gets lost in the enthusiasm of the game. 2. Early mistakes easily become habit. 3. Less effective hand-eye coordination because it takes too long, therefore too short breaks. 4. More time necessary for the learning of new techniques. 5. Beginners might be unable to cope with complexity of tasks. 6. Conditional effectiveness can only be estimated.	1. Same disadvantages as with the Simple Exercise Method. 2. With these forms hardly any exercises known for duels. 3. Outcome largely dependent on players' motivation and ambition. 4. Trainer must constantly observe, measure time, etc. Very coach intensive. 5. Too little attention may be given to technique.

Correcting Technical Mistakes

tion; this involves alternating between game plays, exercise, and game plays again. The advantages of each method are thus maximized, and the disadvantages minimized. At the same time, the player first learns the importance of individual techniques while playing the game. This serves as motivation for the second step: the separate training of individual elements. This method's effectiveness (the whole point of training) becomes clear when a player can check his skills in a game-play situation within a single training session and measure how much they have improved.

Correcting Technical Mistakes

In the course of the training program, a player is bound to make mistakes in the sequence of movements. If these mistakes are not recognized and corrected immediately, they will become ingrained, which is a great disadvantage for the development of the player. Even later, when a player has already learned the basics, mistakes may appear that have to be corrected.

Sadly, many coaches fail to develop a good eye or the skill necessary to recognize the reasons for the mistakes. Thus, they tend not to intervene systematically to remedy them with the proper exercises.

Technique will be inadequate when the sequence of movements deviates significantly from the ideal in the following areas:

- Improper spatial position and timing of simultaneous and consecutive movements of arms, legs, upper body, and head. (See discussion of the Sequence of Movements under "Kicking," pages 49-54.)
- Energy not used economically (often seen in nervous players).
- Poorly coordinated movements.

- Strength, tempo, and range of motions not appropriate for a particular action.
- Sequence of movements not sufficiently consistent and precise.

A coach needs a great deal of experience to recognize the many possibilities for mistakes. He must be as committed to gaining this experience as he expects his players to be to learning how to avoid mistakes.

Reasons for Mistakes

The reasons for mistakes are beyond counting. They may be as simple as that a player is not very talented or that the training period has not been sufficient to allow him to develop the necessary technical skill. Some other frequent causes of mistakes are:

- Insufficient motivation, as well as the factors it affects: concentration and attentiveness.
- An unclear understanding of (or even totally misunderstanding) the sequence of movements.
- General or specific physical shortcomings.
- Wrong teaching methods, unreasonable demands, or unrealistic expectations.
- Fear of injuries or failure.
- Insufficiently healed injuries interfering with performance.
- Poorly developed "feeling for movement" (the body's periphery gives faulty feedback to the central nervous system and the player perceives movements differently from the way they are actually carried out).
- Inappropriate transfer of movements from other sports (e.g., the use of both feet when heading, as in volleyball).

The numberless possibilities for mistakes and the reasons for them make it extremely difficult to determine the appropriate remedies. The process is further complicated by the

fact that, although some mistakes may appear identical, the reasons for them can be very different. As an example, a player's weak heading skills might be the result of insufficient jumping power or of a fear of injury.

Corrective Measures

Corrective measures must be carefully chosen to address the specific reason for a faulty movement. Whatever the reason, repeated demonstration and clarification of the *proper* movement is always a good first step. If technique is still faulty, try:

- Demonstrating and explaining the *wrong* movement, so that the player becomes conscious of his mistake.
- Simplifying exercise and game methods.
- Assigning specific tasks, e.g., kick only low passes. This is an instep-kick exercise that leads to better foot and upper body positioning.
- Actively guiding the body into the proper position. The coach might keep a player's upper body straight during a hip-turn kick.
- Reducing fear through exercises and game playing with a lighter ball (for instance, during heading practice).

Physical Fitness and Fitness Training

The Latin phrase, *conditio sine qua non,* expresses perfectly the reality regarding physical fitness: it is the one requirement "without which not," i.e., the one thing most fundamental to athletic performance. We have already discussed the interdependent relationship between techniques, tactics, and physical fitness (see page 35). To reiterate, physical abilities and, specifically, their availability during competition, depend on a number of different factors.

Factors of Physical Conditioning

In sports training literature, the concept of "conditioning" has a range of meanings.

In a broader sense, conditioning refers to the physical and psychological qualities necessary for athletic performance. (See an outline of them in the table on page 17). These numerous qualities and skills are interactive and interdependent, and their mutual effects will be especially crucial during athletic activity. When dribbling or shooting a goal, for example, the physical effects of the player's prevailing mental attitude (motivation, concentration, etc.) are immense and immeasurable, needless to say. Every coach knows that even though his team seems to be in

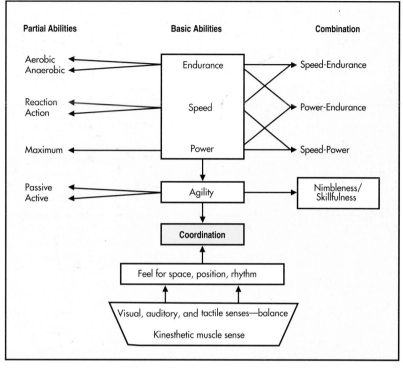

The basic physical abilities (in the narrow sense), their different components, their functional connection, and the types of combinations resulting from those abilities.

top physical condition, any number of emotional states can interfere with their ability to perform well.

In a narrower sense, fitness in sports performance and training refers chiefly to the physical aspects, such as motor skills, coordination, endurance, power, speed, and agility.

In sports-science literature, the factors of fitness—power, speed, endurance, and agility—are also defined as motor activities of the muscular and nervous systems, requiring physical conditioning and skill.

Even if the best description of physical condition generally pertains to the interconnectedness of its many elements, the following observation is made from the second, narrower interpretation.

The specific condition of a soccer player is a combination of power *and* endurance, power *and* agility, power *and* speed (see table at left).

Factors Influencing Physical Conditioning

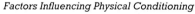
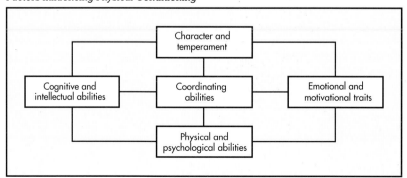

Power and Power Training

Power and Power Training

> In sports, power is defined as the ability to overcome or counteract resistance through muscle activity.

Here, resistance is the gravity and inertia of his own body that the player must overcome.

The muscular system operates through the use of different kinds of muscle contractions. We differentiate between three:
- Dynamic accelerating (jumping).
- Dynamic bending (landing).
- Static holding and moving (for instance, during one-on-one confrontations).

A Slight Digression

The Muscle System

At the same time, the human body has three different kinds of muscle:
- Smooth muscle, which makes up the internal organs and is controlled by the autonomic nervous system.
- The cardiac, or heart, muscle, which has its own control system.
- Skeletal muscle, which is controlled by the central nervous system, as has already been mentioned.

We further distinguish between two main types of skeletal muscle, depending on their structure and function:
- The white, fast muscle fiber (fast twitch = f.t. fiber), which is primarily involved in quick, power-intensive movements.
- The brown, slow muscle fiber (slow twitch = s.t. fiber), which is active during muscle activities of less intensity but longer duration.

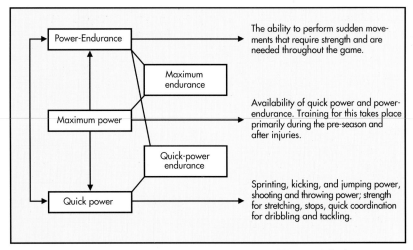

The basic motor skills of power and strength, sub-skills, and their importance for the performance skills of a player.

Quality of Power-Strength

Depending on the degree of resistance the muscular system must overcome, the length of time the system is able to do so, and the speed with which muscles contract while countering the resistance, it is different qualities of muscle power-strength to which we refer (see table above).

These power-strength qualities are not all equally important for soccer players. Since the physiology of muscle and nerve functions differ from one individual to another, it is important to choose the proper training method for the development of power-strength in a given player.

Power Strength

> Maximum power strength represents the highest level of power a player can generate through his own willpower.

This quality depends on the type of muscle fiber an individual has and on his inter-muscle coordination. The thicker the individual muscle fibers, the more of them that have been trained to contract, and the more efficiently they contract, the greater the athlete's strength.

The output of the muscle can be dynamic as well as static. Accordingly, training can consist of isometric, as well as isotonic, muscle contractions (isotonic or isometric training, respectively).

Note: Sufficient maximum power strength is fundamental for optimal development of quickness and endurance.

Quick Power

> Quick power is the ability of the muscular system to overcome resistance with quick, explosive contractions of the muscle fibers.

The level of this ability can be a limiting factor in the performance of a player. The extent to which quickness can be generated is also influenced by the player's strength. This in turn has consequences for the training of quickness.

Significance for the Player

Power Energy (Power Endurance)

> This is the ability to sustain powerful movements or actions over an extended period of time without experiencing obvious fatigue.

During game plays, continuous strength performance remains at low to moderate levels. This is instrumental to developing endurance.

Aerobic endurance is a major determinant of this power quality (see page 75) because of the fast re-synthesizing process of phosphate, the energy-producing mineral.

The Significance for the Player

Without sufficient endurance in the leg and body muscles, a player cannot satisfy the high demands of a dynamic sport. Without a well-developed capacity for power energy (endurance), he will be highly susceptible to injury. A player needs quick power energy to be able to make fast starts and stops, and for dribbling, tackling, shooting goals, and heading. He also needs it in different forms, such as shooting power and jumping power.

A player must have maximum power endurance in the stretching muscles of the legs and the body as a basis for overall quickness. This is the best guarantee against injury when making quick, powerful movements.

Vaulting.

Chest bouncing.

Pulling against resistance.

Shoulder tackling while jumping.

Alternating rolling and jumping.

Power and Power Training

Today, appropriate, systematic, and proper training, guided by experts and relatively risk free, can be done in fitness clubs in order to achieve maximum power strength. Perhaps fitness clubs, which have become ubiquitous, can reduce the aversion to such training, and even increase participation through the opportunities they offer.

In soccer training, maximum power endurance is usually being built during the preseason, between seasons, and after injuries. For rehabilitation after injuries—in addition to physical therapy—isometric exercises and exercises on isokinetic power equipment are remarkably effective. One-sided muscle deficits can be successfully treated with those exercises, and the danger of a player's re-injuring himself can be avoided.

Power Training

Power training must be preceded by a sufficient warm-up. Muscles must be allowed to stretch and loosen up between exercises. The individual power training is as follows:

Power Strength Training

First Phase—
Muscle-Development Training
This training increases the size of all white muscle fibers.

Training Method:
Extensive Interval Training
Intensity   50–70%
Series   3–5
Repetitions   many
Length of breaks   1–2 minutes
Tempo   slow to medium

Second Phase—
Coordination Training
Here, the muscle learns voluntarily to contract as many fibers as possible at one time. A muscle contraction in a well-trained athlete will involve up to 85 percent of the muscle fibers at the same time. The inter-muscular coordination of a less athletically inclined person is much weaker.

Training Method:
Intensive Interval Training (or Training by the Repetition Method)
Intensity   75–100%
Series   5–8
Repetitions   3
Length of breaks   2 minutes
Tempo   quick

With the Repetition Method, intensity comes close to 100%; the breaks in the series are clearly extended to achieve balance. For most of the exercises, the player's own body weight is insufficient for optimal training. Thus, it generally entails training with a partner or with additional weight, in the form of dumbbells, a sandbag, a medicine ball, or weight machines.

Types of Training

- Intensive exercise on weight equipment (leg presses, etc.) for the muscle groups that move the ankle, knee, and body.
- Knee bends with dumbbells (bending up to 60 degrees).
- Exercises with a partner on the back (climbing stairs, etc).
- Jumping off steps, the edge of a box, or a low table and immediately jumping up (high jump) after the landing (polymetric training); also, with weights (using a weight vest or sandbag for additional weight), trying to reach the greatest possible height when jumping.
- Brisk bending and stretching of one leg (also done with added weights).

Quick Power Training

For a boost in maximum power during the season (after deliberate training during the pre-season), players do not need to do general training exercises without a ball. Except for the active season, quick power training can be incorporated into exercises geared toward the overall development of the players (see below). Game-specific training (such as game plays in small groups) serves simultaneously to improve intra- and inter-muscular coordination and special quick power.

Training Methods

Similar to conditioning training for power strength, but with an intensity of 50–70% and explosive quickness of movement.

Exercises for Overall Development

- All soccer-specific game plays: one-on-one up to eight-on-eight.
- All running and rough-and-tumble games.
- All running and jumping exercises where the body's own weight is used for quick power movements (jumping up and down, jumping and running forward, jumping or running uphill [or stairs], zigzag jumping [jumping on one leg]).
- All exercises involving pushing and kicking the ball with the forehead; exercises with a suspended ball.
- Push-pull exercises with a partner.
- Hurdle jumping over partners.

Specific Exercises for the Body

- Rigorously played rough-and-tumble games.
- Sit-ups from a reclining position on the floor or on a slanted board.
- Stretched out on the floor, using the abdominal muscles to lift the legs and upper body simultaneously.
- Throwing exercises with a medicine ball.
- Exercises with a partner involving lifting, carrying, pushing, and pulling.

Strengthening knee bends.

Leg lifts to strengthen the stomach muscles.

Knee stretches.

Crunches. Lifting the upper body to strengthen stomach muscles.

Horizontal jump rope to strengthen abdominals.

Lateral push-ups to strengthen transverse and rectis abdominals.

Speed and Speed Training

Power Energy Endurance Training

Essentially, endurance is a function of maximum power strength and aerobic stamina. It is not necessary to do separate endurance training when occasional training sessions for power strength and soccer-specific endurance are scheduled. However, if maximum training is not scheduled at least every three weeks, reminders should be set up and the following training methods should be included in regular training sessions.

Training Methods

The same extensive interval method that was recommended for power strength training can be used (see page 68). Specially organized circle games are very effective.

Types of Training

Most of the exercises listed under training for power strength and quick power can also be used here. In comparison to the quick-power training, load intensity is somewhat reduced (a lighter medicine ball is used, for instance), and the duration of the load is increased. On the contrary, the duration for the load intensity should be increased. The tempo should not be reduced, since that would have a negative effect on the quick-power performance.

Additional Exercises

- Running 150 to 300 feet (50–100 m) in relay races or carrying a partner on the back.
- As above, only two or three players carry one (Roman chariot race).
- Four-on-four "horseman-soccer" using a small-size goal. Each team consists of two players—one is the rider; the other is the horse. Duration of play is two minutes; after two minutes, the players change positions.

- Medicine ball with a heavy strap (or in a net with a long strap) is swung with both arms around the body; upper body moves in a wide circle (see photo page 80).

Speed and Speed Training

The speed of a soccer player is much more complex than, for instance, the speed of an athlete running the 100-meter dash.

> Speed in soccer is a combination of several individual skills that can best be defined as:
> 1. The ability to recognize a game situation and its possibilities as quickly as possible = speed of recognition.
> 2. The ability to anticipate the development in a game situation, particularly the behavior of the opponent directly involved, as quickly as possible = speed of anticipation.
> 3. The ability to react quickly to unforeseen situations during the game = reaction speed.
> 4. The ability to rapidly change direction when running fast without a ball = speed of changing directions.
> 5. The ability to carry out game-specific actions with the ball under time pressure = action speed.

Implications for the Player

The qualities listed above are of paramount importance for today's soccer player. All phases of modern soccer have become faster, and much more dynamic and athletic. A player can perform effectively under these new conditions only if his thought processes, reactions, and actions are likewise more flexible and quick. The table on page 71 compares the different qualities of speed with a few typical game situations in which they would be used.

Speed of Recognition

A player is bombarded with a constant stream of visual and auditory stimuli. He must selectively consider those that are relevant to a given game situation. Instant recognition requires the following:
- High motivation.
- Years of experience.
- Freedom from fear and stress.
- A combination of general and specific attentiveness.

Speed of Anticipation

The ability to anticipate developing game actions is closely tied to the player's experience. Older players (e.g., the sweeper), with superior speed of anticipation, are able to compete successfully with younger players, even though younger players can react faster.

Speed of Reaction

Whenever a goalkeeper reacts to a sudden shot on goal, or a defender to an opponent's dribbling action, anticipation plays only a secondary role. In such cases, the speed of reaction is the decisive factor.

Reaction time is the time it takes for a stimulus (for instance, the kick of the ball toward the goal) to translate into the first visible reaction of the muscular system. Reaction time depends on:
- The type of stimulus (auditory, visual, or tactile). A player must react rapidly to visual stimuli; for

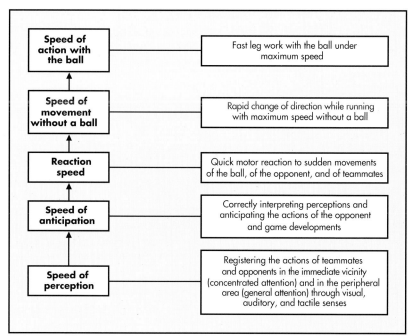

Speed of action with the ball	Fast leg work with the ball under maximum speed
Speed of movement without a ball	Rapid change of direction while running with maximum speed without a ball
Reaction speed	Quick motor reaction to sudden movements of the ball, of the opponent, and of teammates
Speed of anticipation	Correctly interpreting perceptions and anticipating the actions of the opponent and game developments
Speed of perception	Registering the actions of teammates and opponents in the immediate vicinity (concentrated attention) and in the peripheral area (general attention) through visual, auditory, and tactile senses

Characteristics influencing speed and their importance for the performance level of a player.

that reason, the coach should not use a whistle when practicing reaction speed.

- The type of reaction necessary (simple reaction, chosen from several possible stimuli, and reaction to complex stimuli).
- Choosing an action depends on the player's skill level and experience.

Speed of Direction Change (without the ball)

Here, the initial speed and acceleration are most important. A player's progress is often interrupted by stops and changes of direction as he adjusts his own actions to those of the opponents. This kind of speed is influenced by the following:

- The ability of the leg muscles to stretch instantly and powerfully, which is based in turn on maximum power availability.
- Quick, well-coordinated leg and foot work.

- All-around good coordination.
- The skill to coordinate actions automatically.

Action Speed (with the ball)

Winning a game always depends on the speed with which players receive and drive the ball, their ability to keep possession of the ball under pressure from the opponent while running at high speed, and their ability to drive and dribble and to make accurate shots on goal.

Even though these skills are built on speed without a ball, they are intimately related to the ball sense and technical skills a player possesses. Many players are simply "too fast" for systematic game strategies. They have yet to match their technical skills to their innate speed skills.

The training of game-specific action speed is designed most of all to achieve optimum coordination between speed of movement and

technical motor action. This is accomplished by combining high-speed running during techniques and tactics exercises with games using "provocation rules."

Speed Training

Most of the qualities that make a player "fast" are game specific. Therefore, training is successful only when using game plays and exercises with a ball. However, the power of leg and body muscles often limits acceleration speed, and likewise, good acceleration skills can interfere with fast foot work. For that reason (at least for performance-oriented soccer training), it is necessary to add systematic sprint training with the ball to the training that develops power energy.

Consider the following general and soccer-specific principles:

General Principles

- Speed training without intensive warm-up is poison. It causes injury.
- Speed training is useless when a player is tired. At best, it increases speed endurance; usually, it decreases speed.
- Training intensity must be kept at a maximum or high level; otherwise, it benefits only endurance and does not increase speed. This is particularly important when breaks are short.
- The training must be short, and the intensity low. When running 100 to 150 foot (30–50 m) sprints, breaks should be at least three minutes long. They can be used for light exercises with a ball or for relaxation and stretching exercises.
- Moderate sprints in slightly hilly terrain are good for improving foot work (developmentally at its peak between the ages of 13 and 15).

Speed and Speed Training

- Sprinting in moderately elevated terrain with additional weights is recommended to improve speed power.

  Factors influencing speed are different and can be adjusted to each developmental stage (sensitive phase). Results will vary. Foot work can be improved especially, for instance, between the ages of five and seven. Also, reaction speed can be improved considerably around the age of 10, but less so when a player is six or seven years old. Muscle mass, however, will not increase until puberty.

Specific Training Principles

- Speed of perception depends to a great degree on psychological factors. In part these factors are determined by heredity, but they can be positively influenced by a systematic training approach (i.e., by creating an optimum level of motivation, reduction of fear, etc.).
- During competition, a player is constantly challenged to react selectively to visual stimuli; it makes sense to conduct game-specific reaction-speed training in the form of small game plays.
- General and specific speed coordination can be improved by playing rough-and-tumble games.

Types of Training

- All suitable game plays with relevant game rules.
- All technical training at high and maximum tempo.
- All forms of exercise that improve maximum power strength and quick power of leg and body muscles.
- Sprints with and without a ball over 15 to 100 feet (5–30 m) and from different positions (standing, lying flat on the back, or on the stomach); additional exercises can be included in these sprints, such as half turns of the body, full turns, simulated head kicks, fakes, etc. In general, sprints should not cover more than 100 feet (30 m); ideal are:
- Sprints of 15 feet (5 m) and 50 feet (16 m).
- Slalom runs where the distance between poles is 5 to 30 feet (2–10 m).
- Relay competitions.

The competitive nature of soccer demands the utmost speed from players.

Endurance and Endurance Training

- Running and rough-and-tumble games.
- In groups of two, shadow games with changing speeds.
- Relaxed running with increasing and varying speeds.

Endurance and Endurance Training

Soccer games played by adult teams have two 45-minute periods, in which top players may cover a distance of up to nine miles (14 km) (see table, page 76). These two facts alone show how important endurance is for the effectiveness of a soccer player.

> In athletics, endurance is defined as the physical and psychological strength to overcome fatigue following prolonged strain, and to recover performance rapidly.

Endurance for training purposes, as far as motor activities are concerned, has further subdivisions. One is a division into time periods:

- Short-term endurance—45 to 120 seconds.
- Medium-term endurance—2 to 8 minutes.
- Long-term endurance—over 8 minutes.

Long-term endurance is further divided (see page 74), taking into account different requirements in energy availability:

- Long-term endurance I—up to 30 minutes.
- Long-term endurance II—30 to 90 minutes.
- Long-term endurance III—over 90 minutes.

Because of the involvement of different parts of the muscular system, we distinguish between:

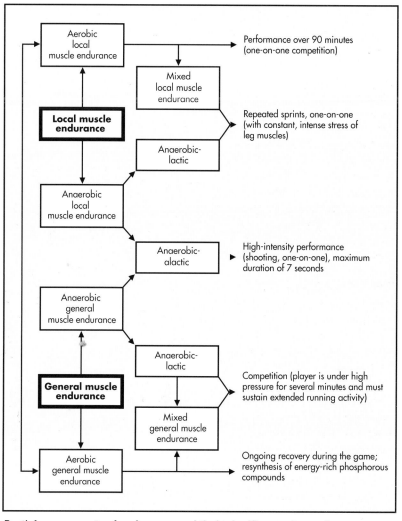

Partial components of endurance and their significance for performance levels.

- Individual or local muscle endurance.
- General muscle endurance.
  Approximately one-sixth to one-seventh of the total muscle mass is involved; together, the muscles of both legs make up about one-sixth of the total muscle mass.
  Depending on the type of energy required, we distinguish between:
- Aerobic endurance.
- Anaerobic endurance.
- General or mixed aerobic endurance.

Further divisions reflect the different kinds of work that muscles perform:
- Dynamic endurance.
- Static endurance.

The table above outlines the complex relationships among the varieties of endurance.

Of the many components of endurance, only a few are important for soccer.

Endurance and Endurance Training

Importance for the Player

The distances and intensities of running required in professional soccer are listed in the table on page 76. A player (depending on his position and performance class) covers about 10 miles (14 km) in the course of one game. He runs in relatively short (1–10 second) bursts, followed by longer "breaks." While walking and/or jogging, lactic acid, which accumulates over time, is largely broken down by the aerobic process.

According to Liesen (1983), during the course of a game the average accumulation of lactic acid is approximately 4 to 7 mMol per quart of blood. This is low when compared to intensive training of anaerobic medium-period endurance (for which 20 mMol per quart of blood has been measured). Given these measurements as a guide, a soccer player in top condition should have, at a minimum, the following specific endurance capabilities:

- General endurance, because he uses one-sixth of the total muscle mass in running.
- Dynamic endurance, because only dynamic muscle activity takes place during a game.
- Extremely rapid short-term endurance with maximum power-energy output and speed, up to 10 seconds.
- Aerobic long-term endurance based on a well-functioning physiological process (metabolism), in which glycogen, and to some extent fat, are broken down.

Also needed, although to a much lesser extent, is anaerobic endurance. Long-term anaerobic endurance capability is important because it is responsible for the process that makes energy available by resynthesizing energy-rich phosphorus compounds.

Type of Energy-rich Substances in Muscle Fibers and Their Importance for Athletic Performance (compiled from information supplied by Weineck, 1988)

	Availability in the body in large calories (Kcal)	Maximum time	Rate of movement: possible speed of muscle contraction	Comment
Adenosine triphosphate (ATP)	1.2	0–2 seconds	approximately 100%	only sufficient for 2–3 muscle contractions
Phospho-creatine acid	3.6	2–20 seconds	approximately 90%	up to 7 seconds, exclusively responsible for ATP resynthesis
Breakdown of glucose	1,200	7–10 seconds	approximately 50%	after 7 seconds' lactic-acid buildup, reaching maximum buildup at 40–70 seconds
Anaerobic glucose breakdown	5,024	7–10 seconds	approximately 25%	for soccer players, very important for resynthesis of ATP
Aerobic breakdown of fat	50,000–209,340	60 seconds up to several hours	approximately 12%	delivers approximately 30% energy during rest

As an Aside

In professional soccer during the '70s, anaerobic short- and medium-term endurance training was much favored. The interval method, using repeated running exercises with and without a ball, was employed particularly during the pre-season and in the middle of the season. This highly intensive training method created considerable stress with the lengthy repetition of training stimuli. The result of such stress is an increase in lactic acid buildup, followed by impaired coordination and the loss of important vitamins (B, C, and E) and minerals (calcium, potassium, and magnesium), causing the disturbance of enzyme functioning for several days.

Today, we know that anaerobic training does not contribute to an improvement in soccer-specific endurance; rather it decreases existing aerobic endurance.

Highly intensive interval training should be included in the training program only occasionally (approximately every 14 days) during the competitive season.

Factors Influencing Aerobic Long-Term Endurance

A host of different requirements have to be met before aerobic endurance is achieved. Some of these factors are:

- Sufficient glycogen level. Glycogen is stored directly in the muscle fiber and in the liver. Training can increase the amount of glycogen stored in the liver.

- Sufficient level of enzyme activity, which guides the breakdown of glycogen and fat. This enzyme activity (metabolism) benefits from an effective training program.
- Improvement of the cardiovascular system (increasing the size and efficiency of the heart muscle and the number of capillary blood vessels in the muscles). Endurance training can almost double the oxygen-exchange surface.
- Blood and red blood cells in sufficient quantity to transport oxygen and remove accumulation of lactic acid.
- Improvement of the intake and use of oxygen. Endurance training can particularly benefit the latter.

Endurance Training

Depending on the type used, endurance training can create very different levels of stress for a player. The overall stress load to which players will be exposed can be controlled by a coach's choice of methods and objectives when he puts together the yearly training schedule. Proper choices, therefore, are the basis for the division of training into separate periods (see page 34). As always, it is important to adhere to fundamental principles and to use the proper exercises for a given method.

Principles of Training

- Basic aerobic endurance is best achieved with prolonged exercise periods with pulse rates from 140 to 170 beats per minute; in professional soccer, this is also the case with the intensive interval method (see page 32).
- Anaerobic short- and medium-duration periods are combined with the intensive interval method; this

method is adapted by using soccer-specific game plays.
- Intensive (aerobic) and special stress-load training require good, basic endurance, which should be addressed first during pre- and mid-season training sessions.
- Endurance training for beginners and children should be low in intensity and should be conducted according to the long-term training method.
- Aerobic long-term endurance training with pulse rates of approximately 140 beats per minute and anaerobic limits with lactic-acid levels of approximately 2 mMol/L are regenerative. These can be very important in the case of over-training.
- Nourishment rich in carbohydrates and a life-style appropriate for athletes (sufficient sleep, use of sauna, massage, etc.) will enhance the effects of training.

Aerobic Endurance Training

- Jogging with steady tempo and low intensity, pulse rates of 140 to 150 beats per minute (aerobic limit), duration of 30 to 45 minutes.
- As above with increased intensity, pulse rates between 150 to 170 beats per minute (anaerobic limit), duration of 20 to 30 minutes.
- As above with alternating tempo, varying pulse rates.
- Timed running around a track 12 by 150 feet (4 × 50 m); time instructions given at every corner.
- All game plays, five-on-five up to eight-on-eight.
- Technical training without breaks (i.e., constantly passing balls over 150 to 200 feet [30–40 m] while running).

Running Program According to Liesen

Professor Liesen, the medical adviser for Germany's national soccer team, recommends the following tempo-changing programs for improving aerobic endurance and speed:

1. Start with approximately five to eight minutes of relaxed trotting with stretching and loosening-up exercises.
2. Change to jogging for approximately 10 minutes.
3. Gymnastics, loosening-up, and stretching exercises (particularly for the legs), six to eight stretches per muscle group is sufficient.
4. Relaxed trotting with three to five increases of 60 to 120 feet (20–40 m) each; at least 100 yards (300 m) slow jogging between every increase.
5. Approximately five sprints over 30 to 60 feet (10–20 m) or ten sprints over 15 to 30 yards (5–10 m) with maximum intensity (from different starting positions); slow jogging for 70 yards (200 m) after every sprint.
6. Above is followed by three to five minutes of relaxed jogging.
7. Running five sets of hurdles consisting of 10 hurdles each at maximum intensity; slow jogging for 100 yards (300 m) between each hurdle.
8. Approximately 10 minutes' aerobic jogging with special emphasis on deep, rhythmic breathing; players must still be able to talk while jogging.
9. Slow jogging for at least five minutes.

Endurance and Endurance Training

Age-dependent Training of Fitness Skills (Male Youth)

Fitness skills	6-10 yrs	10-12 yrs	12-14 yrs	14-16 yrs	16-18 yrs	18+ yrs
Maximum power				O	OO	OOO
Speed			O	OO	OOO	→
Endurance				O	OO	OOO
Aerobic endurance		O	OO	OO	OOO	→
Anaerobic endurance				O	OO	OOO
Anticipated speed			O	OO	OO	OOO
Reaction speed	O	OO	O	OO	OOO	→
Speed without ball	O	OO	OO	OOO		→
Speed with ball		O	OO	OO	OOO	→
Agility	OOO	OOO	OO	OO	OO	→
Coordination	O	OO	OO	OOO	OOO	→

O   Start of a goal-oriented training with low stress load and playful training methods.

OO Performance training with increased stress load and varied, general, and specific training methods.

OOO Performance training with high stress load and general and special training methods during the pre-season and during the competition season.

Anaerobic Endurance Training

Here, the exercises recommended for power energy and power speed are also well applied, following the extensive and intensive interval method. Anaerobic endurance is achieved through game plays using only a few participants (i.e., one-on-one, two-on-two, one-on-two); also highly intensive, complex exercises and relay races with and without a ball.

High-performance soccer. Results of game analysis (supported by videotapes) by Waldemar Winkler (UEFA Cup Games HSV Hamburg against Inter Milano, 1984). The results are approximately 30 to 40 percent higher than comparable studies conducted by Winkler in 1981, and 280 percent higher than those by PALFAI in 1962. Since 1962, the average increase in performance is approximately 10 percent per year.

Players (Club)		Halves	Running Distance in Yards/Meters				
			Walking	Jogging	Running fast	Running very fast	Totals
Altobelli (Inter Milano)		1st 2nd	1170/1896 m 1972/2070 m	1706/1560 m 1569/1435 m	1115/1024 m 883/807 m	601/550 m 793/725 m	5501/5030 m 5508/5037 m
Rummenigge (Inter Milano)		1st 2nd	2187/2288 m 2380/2177 m	1149/1051 m 1155/1056 m	470/430 m 503/460 m	420/384 m 284/260 m	4541/4153 m 4323/3953 m
Wuttke (HSV)		1st 2nd	2287/2091 m 2099/1920 m	2083/1905 m 2118/1937 m	932/852 m 610/558 m	544/497 m 618/565 m	5846/5345 m 5445/4980 m
van Heesen (HSV)		1st 2nd	869/795 m 865/791 m	4969/4544 m 4579/4187 m	1469/1343 m 1652/1511 m	544/497 m 598/547 m	7850/7179 m 7695/7036 m
Brady (Inter Milano)	(substituted for after 56 minutes)	1st	1657/1515 m	3162/2891 m	1303/1192 m	488/446 m	6610/6044 m
Magath (HSV)	(substituted for after 70 minutes)	1st	984/900 m	3892/3559 m	1877/1716 m	713/652 m	7466/6827m

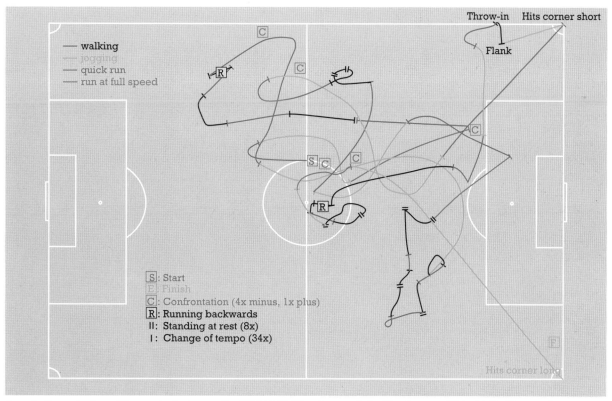

walking
jogging
quick run
run at full speed

Throw-in   Hits corner short
Flank

C
C
R
C
S C
C
R
F
Hits corner long

S: Start
E: Finish
C: Confrontation (4x minus, 1x plus)
R: Running backwards
II: Standing at rest (8x)
I: Change of tempo (34x)

In only five minutes of the game between the TSV 1860 München and the Hamburger SV in 2000, Thomas Hassler covered the described 897 yd (820 m) distance.

Today, sprint tests with light barrier measurements belong in a modern training program.

Flexibility and Flexibility Training

Flexibility and Flexibility Training

The importance of agility in individual athletic performance has already been discussed. In addition, agility affects such aspects of technique as power, stamina and speed, and it is vital for well-coordinated complex movements.

> Flexibility is a player's ability to use one or more joints to perform sweeping movements, either alone or with the support of outside forces.

The term "flexibility" also implies both agility and suppleness. In practical terms, we distinguish between two types of flexibility:
- Active flexibility.
- Passive flexibility.

Active Flexibility—The greatest, widest possible movement of a joint that a player can accomplish through his own effort with the (abductor or adductor) muscles of that joint.

Passive Flexibility—The greatest, widest possible movement of a joint that a player can accomplish with the help of outside forces (a partner, a ball, etc.) by contracting the opposite (respectively, adductor or abductor) muscle of that joint. Passive agility is always greater than active; for that reason, it is important to do not only stretching exercises, but those that strengthen the muscles as well.

As an Aside

Biological Prerequisites

Flexibility training can be conducted effectively only if the basic anatomical and physiological prerequisites for flexibility are in place, or at least in the developing stages. The following factors influence flexibility:

Structure of the Joint

The inherent structure of a joint determines its ability to move and the way in which it moves. Soccer training cannot change this structure.

Muscle Mass

Well-developed muscles are not detrimental to good flexibility, as long as training to build muscle is combined with flexibility training.

Muscle Tone

Muscle tone (the degree to which a muscle can be contracted) has a great influence on flexibility. Muscle tone is guided by muscle spindles (running parallel to the muscle fibers) via the central nervous system. A muscle tightens or tenses up due to:
- Fatigue.
- Prolonged rest (sleep).
- Psychological excitement (for instance, prior to the start of a game).

Elasticity of a Muscle

The elasticity of a muscle depends on the degree of stretch resistance that the structure of the muscle and the attached tissues allows. For example, the stretch resistance of muscle is reduced by 20 percent if the temperature increases by only 3 degrees Fahrenheit (2 degrees Celsius).

Elasticity of Tendons and Ligaments

The movement of a joint is limited by muscles as well as by ligaments and tendons. As with muscle fibers, these tissues have different degrees of elasticity, which can be improved with proper training.

Influence of Temperature

As has already been mentioned, muscle flexibility increases when the body temperature increases. This can be accomplished by:
- Active warm-ups
- Massages.
- An increase in the outside temperature (taking a hot bath).
- Warm clothing.

Importance for the Player

A soccer player needs good, basic flexibility in the shoulder and hip joints, as well as in the spinal column. However, depending on the techniques used, he must be particularly flexible in specific joints.

Flexibility and the Instep Kick

A ball can be kicked hard and low at the same time, only if the player has good flexibility in his ankle joint. If the ankle joint is not flexible enough (see illustration on page 79), the ball will always move in an upward curve, and shots on goal that travel 50 to 60 feet (16–20 m) will sail over the goal.

Flexibility and the Hip-Turn Kick

A hip-turn kick requires pronounced passive and active flexibility. To enable the high extension of the leg, the inner thigh muscles (the abductors) must be strengthened. At the same time, the elasticity of these muscles can be greatly improved by stretching exercises (see photos on page 81).

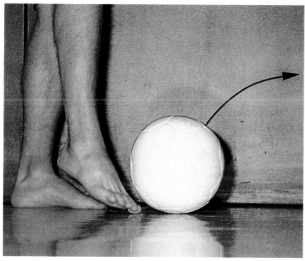

The position of the pivot leg and the way the foot is held will determine the direction of the flight of the ball.

Flexibility and Tackling

When compared to other soccer-specific techniques, hook and slide tackling are difficult movements. A player can perform these well only if his hip joints have the necessary flexibility. Find relevant exercises discussed and illustrated on pages 80 and 81.

Flexibility and Dribbling

A soccer player who can't perform quick pendulum-like movements of the upper body is said to be "stiff in the hips." This statement is only partially correct. The ability to move the upper body in this manner is determined by the condition of the stomach and back muscles (abdominal and latissimus groups). So-called "stiff-hip" players can overcome poor flexibility with specific power training of the relevant muscle groups.

Flexibility Training

Loss of flexibility is age-related and starts early—at about the age of 12. Training, therefore, should take place regularly, daily if possible. Since flexi-

bility exercises are comparably easy, players should do them regularly at home. About 10 standard exercises, taking about 15 to 20 minutes, are all that is needed. We distinguish between three different methods:

Active Flexibility Exercises

Here, the player exercises with swinging, bouncing movements, moving as far as the joints will permit. Even though muscles, tendons, and ligaments are not stretched equally here as they are with the stretching method (see static flexibility exercises, next column), this method has enormous advantages: it strengthens the muscles that move joints, increasing active elasticity.

In addition, these exercises teach muscles to contract before they are overstretched (or pulled). This reflexive action is extremely important in soccer because of the many abrupt changes in direction.

Passive Flexibility Exercises

In this case, specific muscle groups are stretched much farther (with outside support, such as a partner) than is possible with active exercises.

The disadvantage is that the muscles involved are not strengthened. In addition, there is greater danger of injury if the partner does not have enough feeling for the stretching movement the player is performing.

Static Flexibility Exercises—Stretching

This method has now found general acceptance in soccer training. This is to be applauded, because proper stretching exercises are the best way to increase flexibility of the muscles and joints. We will discuss here only two of the six best-known stretching exercises.

Stretching

These are stretching exercises in their original form. They are performed with slow, deliberate movements that momentarily extend the joints, and hold them in that position for up to ten seconds. The player should "listen" to the muscles, "feel" the way the tension in the muscles lessens, and consciously relax into the stretch.

Flexibility and Flexibility Training

Stretching and strengthening the torso muscles.

Stretching the calf muscles.

Stretching Position

Just as important as the movement itself is the position in which the stretching is done. The muscle that is to be stretched should not contract at the same time; it should be free to relax. For instance, attempting to stretch the back muscle of the thigh by bending forward is not efficient because this large muscle group is also carrying the weight of the upper body. The exercise may cause pain, but the gain is minimal, as the fixed muscle is not entirely free to stretch.

Tightening—Relaxing—Stretching

In this method, the muscle to be stretched is first isometrically tightened for a maximum time of 10 to 30 seconds, followed by 2 to 3 seconds of total relaxing, and then stretched again for another 20 to 30 seconds. The muscles will relax better after they've had a chance to contract. The second stretching action is then much more effective.

Stretching the hip extensor muscles.

Stretching the knee muscles.

Stretching the leg, torso and back muscles.

Stretching the hip extensor and knee-bending muscles.

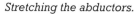

Active stretching of the abductors.

Active stretching of the hip muscles.

Stretching the abductors.

Flexibility Training Program to Do at Home

1. Stretch the musculature of the hip in the supine position (see photo opposite page).
2. Stretch the muscles of the hip joint and knee (quadriceps), from a standing or kneeling position.
3. Stretch the knee-bending muscles and the calf muscles (see photo on page 80, top and middle).
4. Stretch the gluteal and back muscles by stretching in a sitting position.
5. Stretch the abductor muscles while standing (see photo opposite page).
6. Stretch the gluteal, hip-bending, and knee-stretching muscles in cross-legged position.
7. Stretch the intercostal muscles and the upper spine (see photo on page 80, top left).
8. Stretch the hip-joint stretching (flexor) muscles while simultaneously strengthening the hip-joint bending (extensor) muscles with vigorous jumping; stretch the legs up and out, alternating between the left and right legs.
9. Stretch the abductor muscles while simultaneously strengthening them by jumping and stretching the legs up and sideways, alternating between the left and right legs (see middle photo at right).
10. Do jumping jacks with alternate leg splits, scissors crossing, and knee bends.

Coordination and Coordination Training

Coordination and Coordination Training

Throughout this book and particularly during the discussion of techniques and technical training, we have stressed the importance of well-developed, all-around coordination.

Coordination is the ability of a player to handle soccer-specific as well as general situations confidently, economically, and speedily. Thus, we distinguish between specific and general coordination.

Well-coordinated movements require good interaction between the nervous and muscular systems. This leads to fluid, harmonious movement that uses energy economically.

Factors Influencing Coordination and Their Meaning for the Player

General coordination allows a player to deal effectively with unusual situations that develop suddenly. For instance, after being fouled by an opponent, the player can roll rather than fall, and thereby avoid an injury. With well-developed specific coordination skills, he can continue to dribble, even when pressured by two or more opponents, by combining quick leg work, clever fakes, sudden turns, and changes of direction.

All of the following factors contribute to the smooth, well-adapted movements that make for good coordination.

Orientation Skills (sense of direction)

This skill is particularly important for the goalkeeper in such instances as when he needs to catch the ball and is being pressured from the side, or when he needs to return to the goal area and the narrow penalty area is crowded with opponents and with his own teammates.

Sense of Timing

To be able to head or kick an incoming pass, a player must be able to judge the distance, speed, and flight path of the ball. Players with little experience have problems judging the flight path of a ball that has been kicked with spin. They are often unable to coordinate their reactions and movements. Good timing develops only if a player has been given enough opportunities during training to practice judging a ball's movements. Countless other situations call for good timing as well, such as when a pass is not kicked directly to a teammate but into an "empty" space. A player in this situation has to judge the sprinting speed of the receiver, the speed of the ball and the space available before the ball reaches the goal line.

Combination Skills

The mark of an elegant soccer player is the ability to combine different techniques with fluid motion. These skills are in constant demand when faking, starting, falling and starting again, darting sideways, and making other similar moves. In each of these movements, the ball is handled differently. Thus the importance of combination skills becomes clear.

Power, Speed, Reaction, and Endurance

We have already said that basic motor skills are fundamental to well-coordinated movement. For a sequence of movements to be carried out effectively in a given situation, a complex of motor skills, physiological function and coordination training must come together.

Coordination Training

To a certain degree, coordination skills develop automatically in the course of playing the game. At the same time, however, specific training in general coordination skills should be conducted for all age groups.

General Coordination Skills

A player with a good repertoire of general movement skills will usually have good coordination. The ability to learn new techniques depends to a great degree on general coordination skills. Children, for instance, should have the opportunity to gain experience in many different sequences of movements during the course of specific soccer training. Here, the following training activities are useful:
- All running and rough-and-tumble games
- Basketball, handball, volleyball, and hockey games, in addition to soccer practice games.
- Exercises taken from gymnastics (e.g., rolling in different directions) can be incorporated as part of the indoor training during winter.
- Exercises on the trampoline (also during winter training indoors).

Specific Coordination Skills

Several different methods and means are available for teaching specific coordination skills.

Methodical Steps

- Ball-handling practice with random speed changes.
- Taking shots on goal with passes from the front, sides, and back, kicking with the leg that is stepping forward and keeping the other leg in the back.
- Practicing fakes to the "chocolate side" and in the other direction.
- Enlarging and reducing the game space during game plays.
- Changing the relative dimensions of the game space, for instance, from 60 by 125 feet to 100 by 60 feet (20 × 45 to 30 × 20 m).
- Playing on snow and ice.

Combining Techniques

- Driving the ball in uninterrupted movements in different directions.
- Punching the ball into the air, rolling forward, and catching the ball at the completion of the roll, either in the air or at the moment when it hits the ground; keeping control of the ball while running.
- Running fast while carrying two balls at the same time; a slalom run through poles.

Practicing Under Time Pressure and Pressure from the Opposition

- Practicing all one-on-one exercises.
- Driving the ball during relay competitions.
- Dribbling while being pressured by one or more players.

A player's coordination skills are developed through the complex and subtle choices of movement that he must make when leaping to head a high ball.

Variations

- Carrying the ball without looking at it.
- In shots-on-goal practice, the coach calls the kicking technique immediately before ball contact is made.
- During shots-on-goal practice, immediately before the ball is kicked, the goalkeeper randomly vacates a corner; or the coach, standing behind the goal, gives a hand signal, informing the player into which corner the ball is to be kicked.

Practicing with Additional Game Pressure

- Ball-juggling during "active" breaks in interval training—concentration and precision are important here.
- One-on-two play, dribbling toward the goal, kicking a goal—again, emphasizing concentration and precision.
- Catching a hard-kicked pass and driving the ball with a fluid motion at maximum speed.

Tactics and Tactical Training

In addition to techniques and physical fitness, tactics play an important role in achieving success in competition. Tactical planning and actions are fundamentally oriented towards the end result, which means that tactics are implemented to score goals, to prevent goals from being scored and to win the game in the end, as well as to achieve the highest possible standing in the division at the end of the season.

In general, tactics are defined as the systematic, success-oriented implementation of actions by individual players, groups of players, and teams—taking into account the level of performance skills of the team, that of the opposition, and any situation on the field. The term "tactics" in soccer, as well as in other sports, means different things:

- Tactics of planning, preparing, and organizing a competitive game.
- Tactics as the availability of experience in and knowledge of game situations, and the use of technical, physical, and psychological methods for managing those situations.
- Tactics as a plan for specific actions.
- Tactics as a practical deployment of an action.

Depending on a given situation, tactical maneuvers can be carried out by an individual player, a group of players, or by the entire team.

The graphic on page 86 gives an overview of the many tactical maneuvers available to the team. We distinguish between:

- Team tactics (see page 91).
- Group tactics (see page 97).
- Individual tactics (see page 109).
- Game tactics (see page 119).

- Tactics for standard situations (see page 124) and
- Tactics for a given day (see page 134).

Tactical maneuvers in a game situation depend primarily on whether the team has possession of the ball or must first gain possession of it. Thus, we distinguish between:

- Offensive tactics and
- Defensive tactics.

Since all tactical maneuvers take place within a specific game plan, these are discussed later (see page 137).

Tactical Tasks of Players and Management

According to the expanded meaning of the term "tactics," responsibility for the success of the team rests not only on its players and coach, but also on its management. The following discussion outlines the areas of responsibility for the people involved in planning and preparing for competition: the owner, the board, the manager, the physician, the masseur, the coach, and the players.

Owner, Board, Manager, Physician, Masseur, and Coach

- Travel plans (including hotel reservations) for out-of-town games.
- Arrangements for training camps.
- Arrangements for food and drink for the day before the match and the day of the match.
- Provisions for extreme weather conditions (cold: tights, gloves, headbands; heat: special liquids, ice bags, etc.).
- Choice of uniform (adjusted to given situations; e.g., light-colored game uniforms for night games).
- Proper preparation for games taking place in another country

(e.g., proper immunization, arrivals scheduled to guarantee sufficient time for acclimatization, sufficient amounts of germ-free water, etc.).

Additional Responsibilities of the Coach

- Analysis of the opposing team (lineup, game strategy, playing methods, strengths and weaknesses of individual players).
- Designing game tactics for the specific opposition and environmental conditions.
- Establishing the lineup according to game tactics.
- Evaluating the condition of players and preparing them accordingly (calming down or pepping up).
- Choosing the proper equipment (shoes, types of cleats).
- Overseeing warm-ups.
- Providing drinks for the break (tea, electrolyte-replacements).

Additional Responsibilities of Players

- Analyzing the probable strengths and weaknesses of the opponent.
- Mental preparation for the match and the opponent.
- Testing the condition of the playing field and deciding on proper shoes.
- Attitude adjustments before the game.

Influences on Tactics

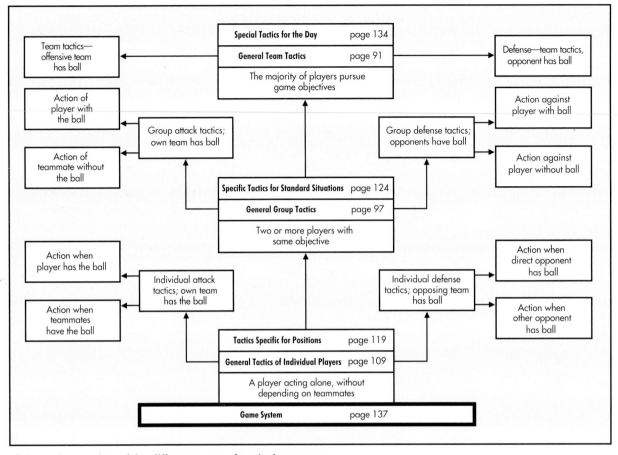

Schematic overview of the different types of tactical maneuver.

Influences on Tactics

Planning and preparing for a match, the choice of game tactics, and the actual play of the game are influenced by several different factors.

Tactical maneuvers of the whole team will be affected by:

- The team's long-term strategy and its present standing in the division.
- The actual objective of the game being played, i.e., win, win by a large margin, draw, or even lose by only one point (in the case of Cup Ties).
- The actual condition of the team (i.e., the psychological and physical condition, the lineup, etc.).

- The opponents and their condition (i.e., place in the division, lineup, strategy, tactics, strengths and weaknesses, and personalities of the individual players).
- The type of match (i.e., training game, exhibition match, championship game, etc.).
- Day and time of the game (whether daylight, Wednesday-Friday schedule, night game under lights).
- Where the game is played (whether at home, away, in another country, under unusual weather conditions, on a field that is used for training only).
- The expectations of the spectators.
- The way a particular referee handles the rules of the game.

In addition to the factors that influ-

ence all players generally, each individual player will choose his own, unique tactics, considering such things as:

- His personal goal, such as making up for a prior poor performance, securing his place on the team, impressing the coach from the opposing team with a spectacular performance (trade!), impressing the fans, the press, etc.
- His own physical condition that day.
- The strengths and weaknesses of his direct opponent.

Further discussion of these issues can be found in the section on "Tactics for the Day"(see page 134).

Sequence of a Tactical Maneuver

Tactical Maneuvering—Tactical Skills

For the spectator, a tactical maneuver may appear to take only seconds, perhaps even only fractions of a second, because he notices only the short, visible part of the action. This visible phase, however, is preceded by a number of other phases that a player must complete perfectly if the outcome of that phase visible to the fan is to be successful. In order to do this, other skills besides techniques and physical fitness are necessary.

Sequence of a Tactical Maneuver

Tactical actions can be performed by individual players, groups of players, or the whole team. The complexity of the action demands mental, psycho-logical, and physical commitment from players. The table below explains the different phases:

Phase 1—Assumes any number of game situations. Here, for instance, a midfielder just received the ball.

Phase 2—A player needs good sensory capabilities, such as peripheral vision, tactile senses, muscle sense, equilibrium, and a sense of space and position. To utilize these skills fully, a player must have motivation and concentration.

Phases 3 and 4—A player needs intelligence in the form of knowledge, lucid memory of events occurring on the field, creativity, foresight, and the ability to make quick mental adjustments.

Phase 5—Intention becomes concrete action, and the established game plan takes shape. For this, the player needs self-assurance, calmness, consistency, assertiveness, the ability to function under stress and remain undisturbed when interfered with, courage, determination, and the willingness to take risks and make decisions.

Phase 6—It is here that the mental and psychological processes result in visible motor actions. Technical skills, fitness, and coordination determine the quality of the action. But such emotional qualities as self-control, stamina, and courage greatly affect the action's outcome.

Phases 7a and 7b—Here again, mental skills are implemented in analyzing, understanding, and remembering the action's cause and effect. Unless a player has the ability to do this fairly objectively, this phase will not be very successful.

Schematic Model of the Sequence of Tactical Actions, with Practical Examples of the Phases

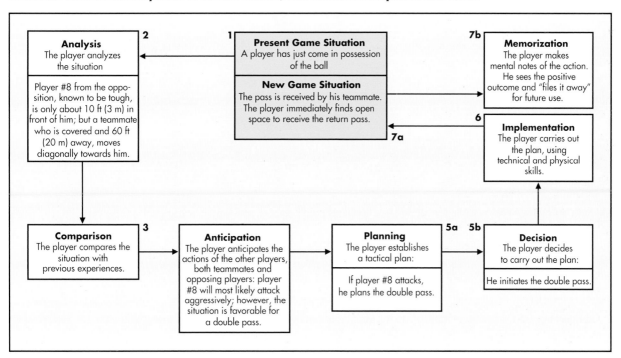

Tactical Training

Tactical Ability

Tactical ability is subject to the influences of the following:

Motivational Factors
Need, motivation, emotion, interest, attitude.

Sensory Factors
Peripheral vision, focused vision, spatial-related auditory sense, tactile sense, equilibrium.

Intellectual Abilities
Knowledge (of rules, typical game situations, and tactics that have proven successful), ability to concentrate and keep track of game events, ability to think and plan ahead, creativity.

Character and Temperament
Forcefulness, willingness to endure, self-assurance, courage, willingness to take risks, conscientiousness, ability to act and achieve, optimism.

Tactical Training

The tactical ability of an individual player, and thus of the entire team, rests on a number of very different basic qualities. For their differences alone, these qualities cannot be strengthened by a single method. Basically, they are:
- The development of motivational and emotional abilities.
- The development of intellectual abilities.
- The development of practical ability and fitness, as well as other factors involved in taking practical action.

The following examples are meant as suggestions for the deliberate training of tactical skills by coaches and players alike. The discussion is not comprehensive.

The coach already provides simple brief instruction to young players in proper tactical action.

Improving Motivation

Needs, motives, emotions, interests, and attitudes are different for each player and can be assessed only by way of one-to-one discussions. General appeals, such as those made during halftime or at players' meetings, are only supplements. Players must be educated as to the connection between motivation and tactical ability. True motivation is usually achieved with a few, pointed remarks. Often, however, motivation is ruined by too many instructions or by instructions that are too complicated.

Also, fatigue has a negative influence on the ability to concentrate. Therefore, a proper balance between practice and rest during training, and a proper lifestyle are prerequisites if the following are to be effective.

The level of a team's motivation is proof of a coach's quality.

Improving Sensory Abilities

Anyone who has had a chance to watch a game played by deaf players will appreciate the importance of *all* the senses' performing effectively.

Although the degree to which a player is able to use his senses is influenced by heredity, in the context of this discussion, we believe that improvements are possible. Other requisites for an effective training program are lifestyle (sufficient sleep, no alcohol or nicotine, etc.) and an adherence to the principle of optimum balance between stress load and recuperation.

Peripheral vision is reduced when training sessions are held on a field or based solely on abbreviated game plays. To be able to sense the opponent's position and to anticipate his attack effectively, tactile senses should be trained by organizing game plays in a smaller space, preferably where one side outnumbers the other.

The ability to assess a game situation quickly can be improved by employing "provocation" rules (e.g., contact with the ball is allowed only twice).

Kinesthetic senses, for instance, are improved when the coach demands self-correction from a player. This forces a player to pay more attention and to become more aware of the movement of his muscles.

Improving Intellectual Abilities

Improving *concentration attention* must be an ongoing part of a training program. For example, ball-juggling practice should follow an exhausting exercise or training session. The game plays already mentioned, where only limited ball contact is allowed, also help to improve these skills.

By introducing varieties of game plays and exercises, a player is constantly asked to think, to adjust, and to relearn. Improved concentration is the reward, and it will have a positive effect on the player's performance during competition.

Mental training (visualization) and personal observation and insight will further improve concentration skills.

On one hand, *training for tactical knowledge* is the task of the coach; on the other hand, every player is responsible for generating his own means of improving this skill. Many possibilities are available. Individual as well as group discussions using a blackboard can be helpful; the coach might analyze videos and films for the group. Players themselves can conduct a kind of "observation" training where particular situations are analyzed (e.g., actions taken by midfielders, behavior during one-on-one confrontations, use of space, switching positions and responsibilities, switching from offense to defense, or standard game situations). As previously mentioned, a player can practice mental training in the form of visualization. In his mind, the player goes through one-on-one, double passing, and standard strategies. Memorization will not improve simply by playing and repeating plays. To become an above-average player, he must go over the game and its specific situations in his mind after the game, "see" the way particular actions developed, and how they proceeded. He must analyze cause and effect, other players' reactions, and his own performance with critical distance. Praise and reprimands from the coach will strengthen the experience if they are given objectively.

Improving Character Traits and Temperamental Behavior

For many tactical strategies, character traits such as courage, willingness to take risks and responsibility, calmness, and self-confidence are immensely important.

A coach should be a strong example.

Note: An anxious coach will have anxious players; a coach who is not afraid to take risks has players who love to take risks.

It is important to help a player trust his own performance and his ability to perform. Vital to this process is the one-on-one discussion. The coach might want to encourage the player to take the risks necessary for the successful completion of a task (dribbling, long passes, etc.). At the same time, the coach needs to assure the player and his teammates that even if a risky play does not work out, their willingness to try is still viewed in a positive light.

The necessary *sense of responsibility* can be instilled by giving players a say in and responsibility for matters affecting the game. The coach must assign specific responsibilities to each player.

Certain emotions, the need to compensate, egotism, and fatigue can all run counter to responsible behavior. A coach should address these negative tendencies early on.

Tactical Training

Calmness and composure are particularly important during decisive games. Positive comments called in by the coach during such games are very effective in buoying the team's effort. Critical comments during the game and during halftime are usually counterproductive; if necessary, however, they should be objective and given in the form of suggestions. Fear of a possible loss, or even a loss in the standings, should be discussed *before* the game. The possibility of losing is usually not all that dramatic (certainly not in youth and amateur leagues).

Calmness and composure don't have to be abandoned in the course of a game that the team is losing. Armed with inner confidence, a player will be able to overcome pregame stress. One-on-one talks with a player are very helpful here.

Assigning concrete and specific tasks will help remove fear. A player will know that he is not alone with the responsibility assigned to him when his coach reminds him of the importance of teamwork. Furthermore, sufficient warm-up, stretching exercises, and massages will help achieve overall relaxation.

It is clear that individual attention from the coach can have a positive effect on a player's performance in many ways. One-on-one talks are among the most important morale-building measures a coach has at his disposal.

Practice of Complex Tactical Skills

The actual training of complex tactical skills has many technical components. The following methods are useful:
- Standard combinations.
- Double passing, wall play.
- Complex exercises.
- Game play, one-plus-two-on-two.
- Game practice on small and regulation-size fields.
- Exhibition games.
- Point games.

Which of these methods is best? That will depend primarily on the performance level of the players. Complex exercises and small game plays are best for strong players.

Since these players already have a large tactical repertoire, it is sufficient to correct mistakes during breaks.

However, beginners and young players can acquire proper tactical skills (i.e., combinations) only with methodical, step-by-step instructions. The following steps are necessary:

1. Learning and practicing the technical elements that are necessary for tactical maneuvers.
2. Introduction of combinations through demonstrations, instructions, and explanations.
3. Practicing combinations, first without an opponent, later with an opponent (active and semi-active).
4. Introducing and practicing a variation of combination plays or a second variation of the same combination.
5. Alternating practice of two or more basic forms or variations with an active opponent (opponent does not know which variation has been chosen).
6. Trying out different forms of combination plays as part of conducting complex exercises during small game plays.
7. Using a combination play during training games.
8. Application of tactics in competitive games.

The coach must constantly remind players to make conscious use of the newly acquired tactical skills during competitive games, since they will be inclined to use only those skills that they have already mastered.

Team Tactics

> Team tactics are defined as the purposeful, planned offensive and defensive actions of all the players on a team.

Actions that are carried out by an individual and a group together are part of a more complex structure. Team tactics include the following:
Offensive Tactics—own team is in possession of the ball
- Alternating tempo and rhythm of the action.
- Manipulating the space.
- Alternating technical methods.
- Playing for time.
- Counterattack.
- Frontal attack.
Defensive Tactics—opponents are in possession of the ball
- Playing for time (see page 94).
- Covering opponent, space, and mixed coverage (see page 92).
- Fore-checking in the opponent's half of the field (see page 95).
- Falling back to your own half of the field (see page 95).

Alternating Tempo and Rhythm of the Game

Successful teams will use both technical and tactical methods in a constantly changing pattern during the course of a game. This makes it difficult for the opponents to stick to their strategy.

Well-planned changes of tempo and rhythm are the mark of a top team. Teams that are constantly attacking with fast passes often don't have enough strength left at the end of the game to withstand the pressure

of an aggressive opponent. The opposition will have no problem adjusting its own strategy accordingly; they will wait patiently for the right time to attack. On the other hand, an opponent might be caught by surprise when, after having passed the ball back and forth for some length of time, a dribbling player suddenly breaks through. By the way, this strategy is characteristic of high-class teams with great techniques; for example, the FC Bavaria has been following this strategy for many years.

Manipulation of Space

Inexperienced teams usually start their offense in that part of the field where they took possession of the ball. It is inevitable that they will run into a tightly organized opposition because their attack begins in the midst of the greatest number of opponents. Changing sides should take place only in midfield when it is safe to do so, because a square pass in front of one's own goal is the most deadly sin in soccer—it always brings the opposition in possession of the ball and in shooting position.

Alternating Technical Methods

Alternating the tempo and rhythm of the game is usually connected to a change in techniques. The action of a team that always uses the same technique is predictable, and makes the team easy to defeat. Therefore, a team's game strategy should always alternate between:
- Short and long passes.
- Combination plays and dribbling.
- Shooting from the second line, double-pass combinations into the

penalty area of the opposition, etc.

By practicing complex game strategies which already contain these elements in a mixed form (see page 101), players learn to make the deliberate changes from one technique to another.

Playing for Time

When a team is leading, or if it is outnumbered due to an injury or a penalty, and the game is almost over, the team will stall or play for time to prevent the opposition from scoring. In addition, the counterattack (see next subject) and strong combination plays in midfield or in the opponent's half of the field are particularly successful. It is important that the play not be taken to the opponent's goal. The team simply passes the ball back and forth in a way that appears to be totally unplanned and random. However, it is important that the players remain attentive and alert. As many players as is practical should participate in the combination plays, which means they must be constantly moving about and ready to receive the ball at any time. If players lose concentration and become inattentive during the playing-for-time maneuver, they leave themselves wide open to a counterattack by the opposition.

Counterattack and Frontal Attack

When a team has gained possession of the ball, the attack on the opponent's goal can take two different forms:

Counterattack—Here, the strategy is to reach the opponent's half of the field with long diagonal or through

Team Tactics

passes, or by fast dribbling through the midfield. Especially effective is a counterattack that not only sets the action in motion but gets the ball into the opponent's half of the field at the same time.

Frontal Attack—Here, the attack is carried out much more slowly. Midfield is not the place for long, risky passes; rather, players should use the safe relay method, covering short distances with each pass. For the frontal attack, many more offensive players have to be involved than for a counterattack. Defenders, midfielders, and forwards are in much closer contact during a frontal attack than a counterattack. Advantages and disadvantages of each are shown in the table on this page.

Coverage of the Opponent and Space

The tactics of covering a player, a space, and a combination of the two has significance for group tactics. The principles of these tactics are also valid when every player of the team is involved in covering his respective opponent.

Covering a player means that after the team has lost possession of the ball, each player must proceed immediately toward his respective opponent. The closer the opponent is to reaching the goal with the ball, the tighter the coverage must be. If only one player switches to defense, the whole defensive strategy is in jeopardy, since something like a chain reaction is set in motion, wherein a player thinks he is not responsible for covering just his own opponent, but also for covering his "neighbor's" opponent.

When *covering space* after losing the ball, every player involved in the offensive actions should immediately proceed back to his own zone. Midfield players and forwards who have moved diagonally out of their zones during offensive actions can move straight back (after checking with their "neighbors," who are changing defensive positions), and temporarily cover the zone of a different opponent. The plain space coverage is today played with a line of 3 or 4 defenders as a last bulwark before the goal.

For *combination coverage*, in addition to covering the center forward positions, players often have to cover another specific, individual opponent, as dictated by the particular situation. Players taking over this coverage play only a limited role in their team's offensive actions. In this way, if their team should lose possession of the ball, they can immediately switch back to one-on-one coverage of their respective opponent.

A Comparison of Counterattacks and Frontal Attacks

	Counterattack	Frontal Attack
Objectives, Tasks	Quick change from defense to offense	Reliable and ball-controlled combination play
Requirements	Basic defense	Basic offense
	Strong defense, good goalkeeper	Quick defenders with great technique, responsibly-minded defenders
	Forwards who enjoy running and are strong in conditioning and attack	Close cooperation among all players on the team
	Backfield players with good technique for long passes	Possibly three center forward positions
Advantages	Lots of room for own quick-footed forward	Ball control through reliable passes
	Opponent is tricked into making mistakes due to own defensive action	Because of this—more fun!
	Own offense possible due to good defense, chance to surprise opponent	Play-for-time possible, advantage in connection with fore-checking
Disadvantages	Forwards are on their own	Space for forwards is limited
	Little cooperation between team players	Danger: counterattack by the opponents
	Risky through passes, easy for opponent to catch	Reduces chances to reach opponent's goal

Team Tactics

Comparison of One-on-One and Space Coverage

	One-on-one	Covering space
Objectives, Tasks	Every player covers his respective opponent Impediment and disturbance even before receiving ball	Every player covers the opponent in *his* zone (zone coverage) Ball-oriented coverage of opponent
Requirements	Disciplined coverage by all defenders and midfielders Good tackling and endurance, courage, fighting strength, aggressiveness	Accepting or turning over coverage of opponent Attack of ball carrier by several players at once Every player moves toward the ball
Advantages	Clearly defined tasks; no question of responsibility Concentrating on *one* opponent Vulnerable opponent Opponent has his back to his own goal	Economical movement, saves energy Same starting position for all players for own offensive action Method gives better mutual support than one-on-one coverage Consequently, better chance for wall and double pass
Disadvantages	Opponent determines the "march route" Therefore, interruption of defensive plan because of position changes Vulnerable to quick opposing forwards	Space is only a mental concept Susceptible to dribbling at the border line of zones Susceptible when game action switches to the opposite side Changing opponents Opponents not challenged when regaining ball

Playing for Time by Destroying the Opposition's Game Plan

Another form of playing for time at the end of a game is to destroy the game plan of the opposition. This method is used when a team wants to preserve a narrow lead, save the day with a tie, or has little energy left to mount a counterattack. Here, a team will try to disrupt the flow of the opponents' game. Often, the methods used to accomplish the task are not very attractive. In the so-called "kick and rush" method, the ball is all too often moved across the field in the direction of the opponents' goal without any real plan; a more considered approach would be to use diagonal passes in the direction of the corner flag on the opposite side of the field. Teammates following the action thus have the best chance of catching up with the ball.

Another way of destroying the opponents' game is to use an offside kick, or even to kick the ball beyond the goal line. In both cases, it is hoped that during the seconds it takes to get the ball back into play, the defense will have regrouped. Generally, this type of play is not recommended. In modern soccer, where we talk about planned tactical strategies, there is little justification for it. A designed plan (see page 91) could achieve the same effect. However, soccer also claims that the end justifies the means (providing the players remain within the rules). In special situations, it is acceptable to use the "destructive" game plan.

Fore-checking

This team tactic, originally used in ice hockey, has today become a standard in the repertoire of every well-trained soccer team. The objective of this aggressive defense is to regain the ball as fast as possible, independent of the half of the field in which the ball is played. Usually, the ball carrier is pressed (see page 105) by two or more players, while the rest provide coverage of the space in the vicinity of the ball. This tactic works only if the defenders also move to midfield, creating close contact with players in every position.

Falling Back

The extreme opposite of fore-checking is "falling back." With this tactic, the ball carrier from the opposing team is attacked with a stalling technique to give as many teammates as possible time to get back and guard their own goal. Then, a solid defense, several lines deep, is organized. Because of this tight defense, the ball carrier is forced to the touch line or has to use square passes in front of the defensive line.

Fore-checking and falling back are defensive strategies that have their advantages and disadvantages. They are compared in the table on this page.

The better of these two methods for any given team always depends on the team's ability.

Comparison of Fore-checking (Pressing) and Falling Back

	Defense with fore-checking already in the opponent's half (pressing)	Defense by falling back to one's own goal
Objectives, Tasks	Rapidly regaining the ball immediately after loss, possibly while still in opponents' zone	Securing own goal immediately after opponent gains the ball
Requirements	Basic aggressive-defensive position of all players; Attacking opposing ball carrier with several payers (pressing); Close spatial contact among defense, midfield, and forwards; Quick defense as a weapon against opponents' counterattack	Basic aggressive-defensive position of midfield players and defenders; Pretending attacks on opposing ball carrier; Counterattack from own defense; Reliable goalkeeper familiar with penalty area
Advantages	Quickly regaining possession of the ball; opposition cannot "steal" time; Short running distances when switching to defense; Effective against weak opponent; Good for team that uses frontal attack	Counterattack from opposition is easier to handle; Tightened space of opposing forwards; Very effective when space coverage is used; Good position for starting offense
Disadvantages	Susceptible to counterattack by opponent; Own forward constantly under pressure	Opposition in midfield keeps ball unhindered; Opposition dictates game rhythm

Team Tactics

The drama of the game is most apparent in tackling.

Group Tactics

> Group tactics are defined as purposeful, planned, offensive and defensive cooperative actions for the purpose of managing game situations.

Aside from the methods and skills employed by the individual player and by the team as a whole, there is another class, called group tactics. In the course of a game, the following groups of players will often plan and cooperate:
- Goalie/sweeper/defender.
- Sweeper/midfielder/defender.
- Defender/midfielder.
- Midfielder/midfielder.
- Midfielder/forward.
- Forward/forward.

The type of action taken in response to a given situation depends on the positions of the respective players, the game strategy, team tactics, and the type of game the opposition is playing. Group cooperation makes possible the following actions.

Offensive Tactics:
Action of the Player with the Ball

- Initiate standard combination with short passes.
- Initiate double pass with a direct or delayed pass.
- Turn ball over.
- Fake kick, then dribble.
- Initiate side and wing change with long pass.

Action of Teammates

- Be available to participate in standard combinations.
- Be available for double pass.
- Be ready to receive the ball.

- Change position on the field, wide as well as deep.
- Entice opponent to leave the area he is covering.
- Run behind the opponent.

Action of Players in the Group

- Wing play.
- Shift action to another area.
- Play against numerous defenders.
- Overcome offside trap.

Defensive Tactics:
Against Ball-carrying Opponent

- Tackle, protect the goal.
- Accept and pass on coverage of an opponent.
- Tackle by pressing with two or more teammates.
- Delay tackling.
- Safeguard goalkeeper on both sides, ready for second shot on goal.

Against Opponent Without the Ball

- Interrupt opponents when they change positions.
- Prevent double pass by covering space.
- Shift position in the direction of the ball.

Against the Whole Opposing Group

- Space coverage.
- Mixed coverage.
- Set offside trap.

In order to make it more clear, the list is divided into group-tactic tasks, individual tasks (i.e., action of the player with the ball), and actions against an individual player (i.e., actions against the ball-carrying opponent). Some of these actions have previously been covered under "individual tactics" (such as passing

and shaking off coverage by an opponent).

Below is offered a more detailed explanation of the cooperation between individual players in the overall tactical strategy of the group.

Offensive Group Tactics

Change of Position

Changing a player's position always changes the task associated with that particular position. In modern soccer, the following positions are exchanged:
- Across the width of the field (i.e., between forward striker or midfield players).
- Along the length or depth of the field (i.e., between midfield players and strikers or between defenders and midfield players; see photo).

Exchanging positions has the following advantages for the team in possession of the ball:
- Changing positions creates, briefly at least, two open areas from which passes can be kicked (providing the defensive player goes with the player who is changing).
- Opposing defenders are lured into new positions and may thus be confronted by tasks with which they are not familiar.
- The defensive strategy is at least temporarily disrupted, and the opposition is forced to regroup.
- Defending players have to shift their concentration to the change in action; thus, their attention to the opposing player they are covering is momentarily diverted.

Group Tactics

Short Pass Combination

For simple combination passes of 15 to 50 feet (5–15 m), players have a number of different tactics available. Since these combinations occur with great frequency, they have come to be known as *standard combinations*. They can involve two or three players. The drawings on pages 100 and 101 show the most important two- and three-player combinations.

Wall Pass and Double Pass

Both the wall pass and the double pass are more advanced forms of the standard combinations; they are meant to counter tight one-on-one coverage. They allow a forward to defend himself successfully against tight coverage and aggressive interference during a pass reception. The terms "wall pass" and "double pass" are often used interchangeably. Nevertheless, the following technical distinction is made:

- Wall pass is a combination with two passes.
- Double pass is a combination with three passes.

The photos on the opposite page show the sequence of action of a double pass (as defined above).

The basic form of the wall pass can be varied in many ways. In one variation, the second pass can be delayed, keeping the opposing player in the dark. Will the player go toward the goal himself or will he pass again? A particularly effective variation of the double pass is when the last pass is not kicked to the player who started the action, but to a third player (see photo opposite page).

Two players change positions: across the width of the field (above) and the length of the field (below).

1

2

3

4

5

Group Tactics

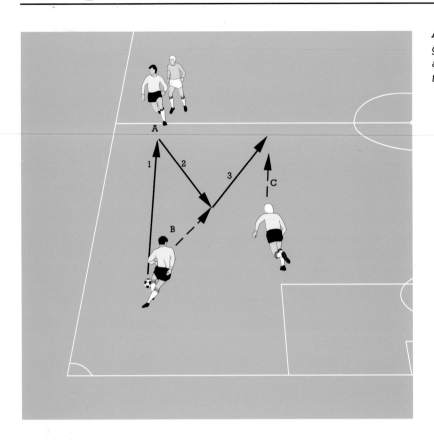

A double pass, in which the last pass goes to a third player, creating an additional element of surprise for the opposition.

Running Behind

The so-called "running behind" tactic is a very effective variation in modern soccer. Here, the player who just kicked the pass changes space by going both deeper and wider. The second player, delaying his return pass, uses deceptive moves to kick the ball to his teammate.

"Running behind" is a tactic often used in modern soccer both on the wings and the midfield.

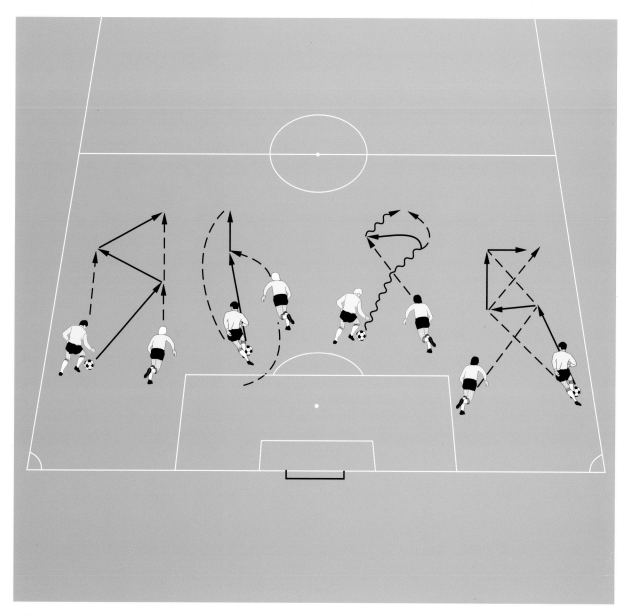

Expansive Combination

Expansive combinations are particularly useful in quickly covering great distances to the opponents' goal. This tactic must be practiced routinely until the moves become automatic, as it is likely to lead to mistakes. The drawing shows a number of suitable combinations for groups of two and three.

Typical standard combinations for groups of two are also used for training technical skills. They can be combined in various forms.

Group Tactics

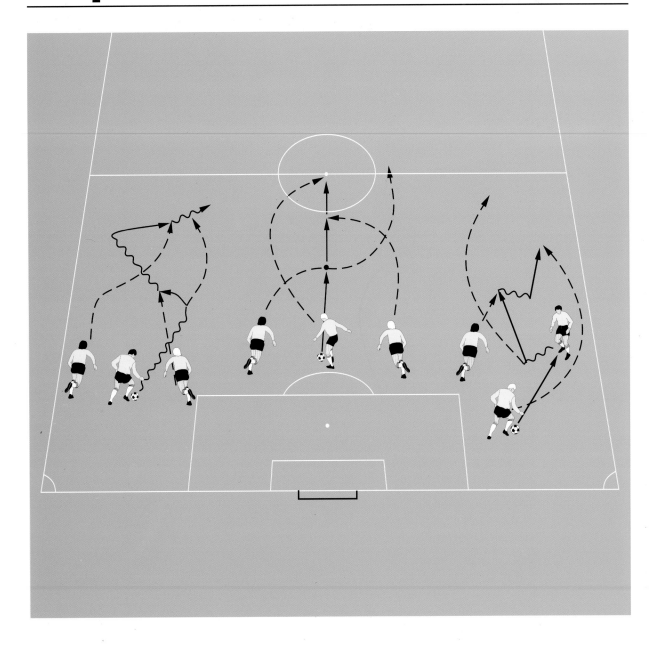

Practicing standard combinations for groups of three helps players develop a "feel" for action without the ball, for passing into open space, and for the many different ways of using open space.

Plays from Sides to Side

In modern soccer, the space in front of the goal is guarded by a mighty "wall" of several layers of defenders. Attacks from either the left or right side are, therefore, very dangerous. The objective of this kind of attack is to drive the ball through the less densely covered space and make a sharp pass to the advancing forward behind the backs of the opponents.

Since the sweeper or inside defender often has to leave his central position to support the defense, there is usually a teammate in the middle who is free to receive the pass.

Every basic form of open-space combination has several variations. These enrich the tactical wing strategy.

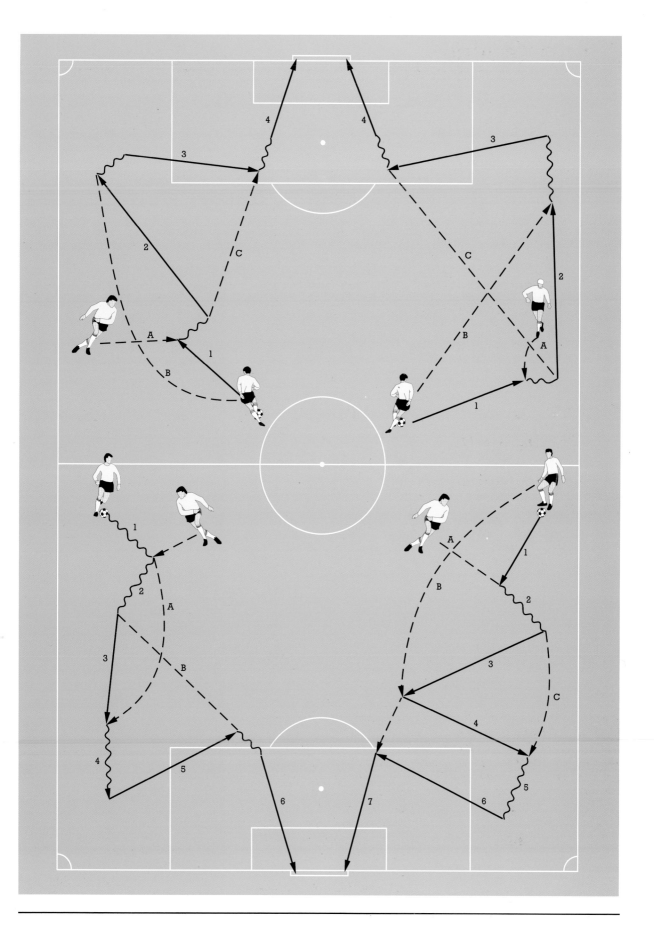

Group Defense Tactics

Changing the Field of Action and Switching Sides

Today, it is common for two or more players to begin to attack the ball-carrying offensive player in midfield. The rationale is to disrupt the ball carrier and keep him from shooting a pass. The obvious result is that the defense creates a player deficit on the opposite side of the field, in spite of the fact that five or even six players operate in midfield. The pressure on the ball carrier can be relieved by using the back pass. The receiving player in the back should follow with a diagonal flank pass, shifting the game action to the other side of the field. Often the shift from one side to the other is repeated several times within one offensive action. When the opposition gets tired from trying to catch up (and not until then), the tactic is changed, often with a through pass kicked toward the penalty area of the opposing team. This game tactic should not be used excessively, however, as each use allows time for the opponent to reorder and reposition his defense.

The possibility for using the many variations of combination plays is much greater in a three-player group.

The picture at right shows the safeguarding of a team player through a sweeper who is in a slightly diagonal position behind him. The sweeper positions himself slightly to the side of the open space.

Beating the Offside Trap

The offside trap is a very effective modern defensive tactic for groups and for the team (see page 108). There are three basic countermeasures against the offside trap:
- High, square passes behind the forward-moving defense line. Since the ball is in the air for a relatively long time, out of reach of the opposition, midfielders have a good chance to take possession of it.
- Break-through dribbling from the rear. A midfielder, moved into the field of action by a back pass, attempts to break through with fast, explosive dribbling.
- Wall and double passes in a tight space. A wall pass, particularly in the variant of a delayed kick, to the center forward has the best chance for success.

Defensive Group Tactics

Safeguarding the Player Who Is on the Attack

The aggressive attack on a ball-carrying opponent, in midfield as well in the defensive line, can be carried out aggressively and without risk only if the attacker has at least one teammate for backup. This situation is typical for the combination sweeper/center forward, and the type of midfield action known as "pressing." It is important that:
- The player safeguarding the teammate in the back keep a distance of 6 to 10 feet (2–3 m).
- The two players involved make sure that the space to the left and right of the ball-carrying opponent is covered.

The attacking player should safeguard the space toward the middle, while the other player falls back somewhat to safeguard the outside.

Group Tactics

Turning Over Coverage of an Opponent

Basically, turning over coverage to a teammate takes place when an opponent leaves the zone in which he was being covered. The switch takes place between zones. This is always a risky maneuver. Today, players often agree not to transfer coverage when in, or directly in front of, the dangerous penalty area. Instead, they stay with the opponent for whom they are responsible. Coverage of the opponent must be turned over even if the player has outplayed his assigned cover. It is important that the player who was outplayed move back behind his teammate (who has taken over coverage) as quickly as possible, in order to support him in the one-on-one confrontation.

For teams that use team coverage, the coverage of an opponent who is about to break through is primarily the responsibility of the sweeper. He should not move too fast or get too far ahead, otherwise he loses contact with the rest of the defensive line. It is enough to prevent the opponent, who is 60 to 75 feet (20–25 m) in front of the goal, from scoring. The opponent can initiate aggressive action only if he can be supported by his teammates.

Forming a Pattern of Midfield and Defensive Players

For the group-tactic strategy discussed above, it is important that the individual players moving in the direction of the ball maintain a pattern deep enough that they cover each other (i.e., line up in deep formation). In this way, the ball carrier is constantly prevented from dribbling through.

Shifting Position in the Direction of the Ball

Old soccer aphorisms advised greater coverage "to the opponent with the ball" and that "you have to have more players close to the ball than the opponent." These have filtered down in modern soccer to the simple phrase, *"ball-oriented coverage of the opponent."* This is why several players at once apply pressure on the ball-carrying opponent. This can be accomplished only when every player participates in the defensive move toward the ball. The drawing below shows the accordion-like movement of the players.

After a pass, players shift their position in the direction of the ball; the opponents closest to the ball are covered more tightly.

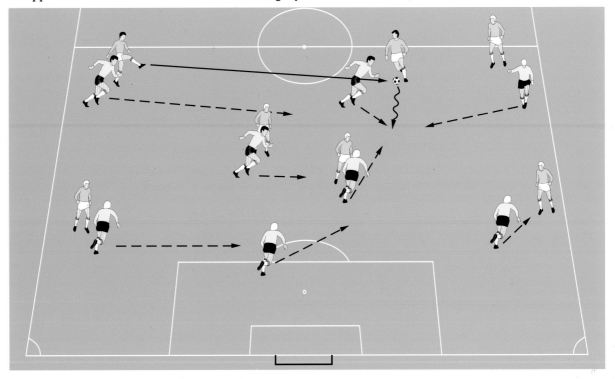

Coverage of Space

The fundamental difference between the coverage of a single opponent and the coverage of space is discussed under individual tactics (starting on page 109). While one-on-one coverage can be carried out successfully by one player, space coverage is generally successful only as a group or team tactic. Every player is responsible for defending a particular space (zone). He has to attack every opponent, with or without the ball, who enters this zone. If the opponent moves to another zone, the teammate assigned to that zone automatically takes over the coverage. Both methods, one-on-one and space coverage, have special advantages and disadvantages and make specific demands on the team that uses them. See the chart on page 94 for a comparison of one-on-one and space coverage defense tactics.

The drawing shows one of many possible ways of dividing defensive space into zones (example of a 3-5-2 system).

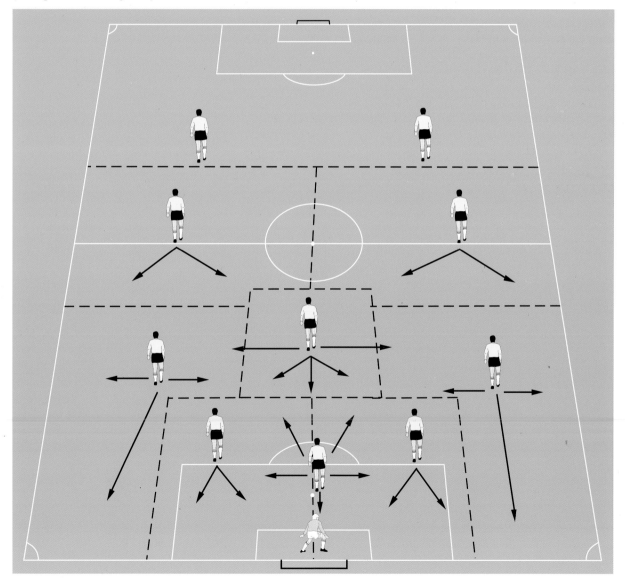

Group Tactics

Mixed Coverage

The space coverage "euphoria" of the early 1980s has abated, to be followed primarily by a more balanced use of mixed coverage. It makes use of the advantages of both tactics and aims to minimize the disadvantages. Here, the players in the center forward position are covered one-on-one, at least while the action is in the middle of the opposition's half of the field. In the remaining areas, players use space coverage. In theory, this sounds rather simple; however, in practice it is something else. Forwards are constantly on the move, and the space they leave must be covered immediately. This requires a great deal of running on the part of the midfield and defensive players, as well as great mental flexibility. The alternating spaces that are covered must be protected by both the sweeper and the forwards.

Preparing the Offside Trap

Aggressively preparing an offside trap, a tactic that involves every defensive player, has become one of the most effective defensive tactics used today. Unlike what was used in the past, the signal for the advance of the defensive players does not come from a player (e.g., the sweeper). Rather, it is the way in which a typical game situation develops that signals an aggressive, joint move to the midline. The result is that the offside line automatically moves forward several yards. The opposing forwards are forced to react, meaning they have to retreat. This, in turn, stops any offensive move, and combinations have to be developed all over again by using back passes.

The following situations have a good chance of success when preparing an offside trap:

- When the goalie or a defender returns the ball back into the game via a corner or free kick.
- When a free kick from midfield is cleared and returned to the game.
- When an opposing player in possession of the ball is pressed in the midfield and tries to protect the ball by using a back pass.

In every case, the defense moves forward aggressively. For this risky maneuver, it is important that a few midfielders safeguard the action by moving in scissors-like fashion toward the advancing defense in the direction of their own goal.

The player wearing dark clothes in the right hand corner has run into the offside trap of the red team. The passing of player No. 18 happens too late.

Individual Tactics

Individual tactics are generally defined as purposeful, planned, coordinated offensive and defensive actions a player performs to manage typical game situations, independent of any specific responsibilities related to his position.

The following offensive and defensive actions are performed by an individual player:

Player in Possession of the Ball

- Receiving and moving with the ball.
- Passing.
- Flanking.
- Shot on goal from short and long distances.
- Dribbling to protect ball possession.
- Dribbling for breaking through.

Teammate in Possession of the Ball

- Getting free.
- Being available for a pass.

Opposing Player in Possession of the Ball

- Tackling—taking away the ball
- Retreating or delaying.
- Pressuring to the sideline.
- Protecting the goal.
- Coaxing passes toward opponent in vulnerable position.

Opponent Not in Possession of the Ball

- One-on-one coverage.
- Space coverage.
- Coaxing away to prevent pass

reception and to intercept passes (see above).
- Interference during ball reception.

Although many of the individual tactical maneuvers were discussed in the chapter on techniques, the chief concern there was the motor skills involved in them. Here, we will take a closer look at the tactical skills involved in employing those techniques.

Individual Offensive Tactics

Receiving and Moving with the Ball

Receiving and driving the ball should always be preceded by a fake. The ball should always be moved into spaces from which effective action can be taken (e.g., a shot on goal, a pass, etc.). Faking and moving with the ball can be accomplished effectively only if the player is able to assess correctly his own position, those of his teammates, and those of the opposition *immediately before he takes possession of the ball.*

When receiving the ball, the player must keep in mind the motto, "Body between opponent and ball." This makes it all the more important for the receiver to have mastered ball control with both legs.

Passing

The success of the whole combination play hinges on the quality of the pass. A pass can be high or flat, hard or soft, with or without spin, and made with or without an obvious swinging motion of the leg(s), which announces the direction or type of kick. With so many considerations to make, it is clear that, from a tactical point of view, the nature of the pass depends on the particular game situation.

The following fundamental rules must be observed for passing:

- Timing, direction, and flight path are determined not by the player who kicks the pass, but by the player who is free to receive it. The player who has ball possession must read the movements of his teammates in order to know when and where to direct the pass.
- A variety of passes and combination plays should be employed throughout the game. Repeated use of the same combinations makes it easy for the opposition to anticipate and develop tactical countermoves. It is much more difficult to develop countermoves when there is a constant change from through to square passes, forward to back passes, long to short passes, and passes kicked directly to a teammate or to an open space. The surprise keeps the opponent off balance.
- Weather and field conditions play a vital role in passing. In heavy mud or deep snow, it is better to kick passes high and wide. On the other hand, smooth, wet grass calls for short, direct passes.
- A pass should be directed to the side of a teammate that is away from the opponent.
- A pass kicked to the forward for a shot on goal should be directed to a player's strong (kicking) foot.

Flanks

Flanks are passes to a receiver that are directed high above the heads of the opponents. Unfortunately, they are all too often kicked "blindly" into the dangerous space in front of the opposition's goal.

Basically, the rules here are the same as for other passes, though a few additional points are well noted:

- Flanks with spin are difficult to receive. At the same time, they are

Individual Tactics

more difficult for an opponent to anticipate. With practice, flanks with spin can become very important tactical weapons.

- Corner kicks in the form of flanks kicked with spin toward or away from the goal cause considerable embarrassment for the goalie.

- A shift of game action in midfield should be accomplished exclusively with flanks. This might prevent an interception, if the flank has not been kicked cleanly.

- Flanks directed toward the opposing goal should be short and kicked hard, over the heads of the players. A method once very popular, that of high-arching passes that drop vertically at the end of the flight, has lost its real effectiveness against forwards and goalies today.

Shots on Goal from Short or Long Distances

Shots on goal from far away create excitement for players and fans alike. These are the shots most likely to be kicked during training. In reality, however, most of the scoring is done from a very short distance—within the penalty area. (During the 1996 European Championships, more than 80% of the 64 goals were scored from short distances.)

Shots on goal can be made effectively by heading, with the instep or the outside of the instep, and with the inside, tip, or heel of the foot. The success of a shot depends more on how accurately the ball is kicked than on how hard it is kicked. In addition to technical skills, the player must possess intuition, good nerves, and lots of tactical routine. From a tactical point view, the following are recommended for shots on goal:

- Shots on goal from a short distance —up to approximately 35 feet (11 m)—should be direct, and aimed precisely into the *corner* of the goal

box. Aim close beside the goalpost, *not* the goalkeeper!

- Shots on goal from farther away should be kicked sharply and powerfully, and directed to the right or left *half* of the goal. Aim at the space between the goalie and the goalpost.

- Shots on goal from a short distance are much more dangerous for the goalie when they come suddenly. For this reason, do not announce your intention with an obvious swing of the kicking leg. Short passes should direct shots on goal, leaving out the "middle man."

- Each goalie has a weak side (usually the left). Shots on goal to that side obviously have a better chance of success.

- Fake the direction and timing of the kick for shots on goal that immediately follow dribbling. The "hidden" kick has a greater chance for success. In this action, the player kicks often while turning, before stopping the dribbling action. The result is that the goalie cannot observe the action or the direction of the shot.

- When shooting in the manner described above, the position and motions of the goalie have to be considered. Shots from a narrow angle should be low and with spin. These should be aimed at the long corner.

- If the goalie is relatively far in front of the goal box, he can be "faked out" by hooking the ball.

- Faking before kicking causes miscalculations on the part of the goalie. The ball can be kicked past him, for instance, by using the "wrong" foot.

- On smooth, wet grass, low passes, or so-called "bouncing balls," are particularly difficult to calculate.

Exercises for Practicing Shots on Goal from Short Distances

- Aim shots toward the goal while running in the penalty area, alternating angles and distances to the goal. The coach stands behind the goal and signals into which corner he wants the shot to go.

- As above, but choose techniques relevant to the objectives: dribbling, lifting, sharp kicks. The goalie is instructed to change his position in front of and in the goal box.

- As above, but with additional tasks, such as passes that immediately follow a goal. These passes alternate between low and high kicks over short and long distances.

- Game plays of two-on-one, two-on-two, and three-on-three toward the goal. Also, simulate "passing after shots on goal" by using a neutral player for shooting a flank from the side. Two-on-two and three-on-three can be played, switching tasks after the loss of the ball.

- Additional types of plays: one-plus-one on one-plus-one using two small goals; goalie plus two-on-two using small size goals; goalie plus three-on-three with two neutral players (in the backfield and on the side toward the goal) changing tasks after the loss of the ball; arbitrary teams on two goals in half of the playing field with a variety of "provocation rules" (e.g., taboo zones on the sides for the defense, one-time-only ball contact, scoring only with direct shot on goal, scoring only with heading, etc.).

Dribbling to Keep Possession of the Ball

The following situations call for dribbling to keep possession of the ball:

- The ball carrier momentarily does not have a receiver because his teammates are all covered or are too far away.

- The intended receiver has moved into offside, and passing has to be delayed (by dribbling) until he is out of the offside position.
- The ball carrier's own team is under heavy pressure; dribbling without apparent purpose in midfield—or even better, in the opposition's half—can relieve some of the pressure.

Some basic tactical principles for dribbling in order to keep possession of the ball are discussed in the next chapter.

Break-through Dribbling

Break-through dribbling is used in the following situations:
- Counterattack from midfield or defensive move from open space into opponent's territory.
- Countering an opponent's offside trap.
- Taking the risk of dribbling in the opposition's penalty area in order to tempt an opponent to commit a foul and, thereby, gain a penalty kick for the team.

All three methods of dribbling demand that players keep several points in mind:
- Avoid starting to dribble from a standing position; always start from a running position.
- Always start dribbling with a fake.
- In principle, the player should always observe his opponent while dribbling.

Tactical Basics

The following apply for both forms:
- A pass is always faster than the fastest player with the ball. Therefore, the ball should generally not be dribbled when one's own teammate is better positioned toward the opponent's goal.
- At the beginning of the game, it is best to do very little dribbling for a number of reasons: first, because the opposing defender is particularly aggressive at the beginning of the game, and second, the dribbling player has yet to find his

Decisiveness and determination are clearly evident from head to toe in the dribbling player.

Individual Tactics

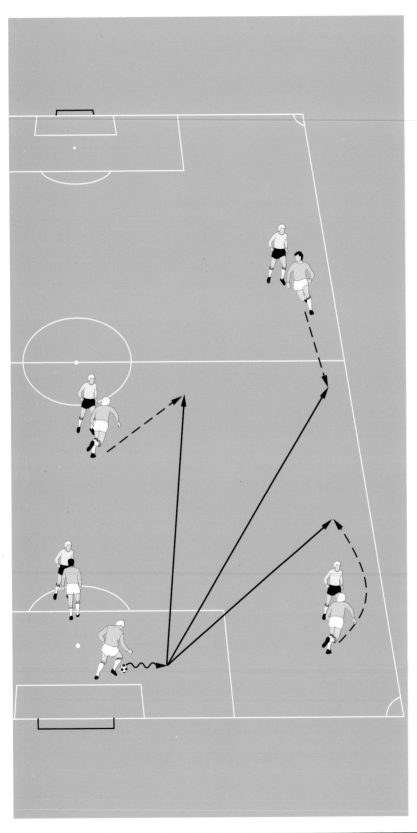

rhythm. Players who lose several tackles at the beginning do not regain their usual performance level for the remainder of the game.

- Be sure not to dribble toward an opponent but into the free spaces to the left and right of him.
- It is always best to dribble while running rather than while standing.
- Always start to dribble with a fake.
- Start the fake at the right moment and from the right distance: too often, a fake is attempted too late and too close to the opponent.
- If the dribbling should prepare a shift of game through a long pass, then the dribbling should be performed counter-directionally. In this way, the opponent is lured out of the later area of action.
- Generally, one should not lose sight of the opponent while dribbling. This makes it possible to react to his defensive action and to change the direction of dribbling.

Getting Free and Being Available

In general, a player gets free in order to become available to receive a pass. But there are other reasons for getting free, such as:

- To exchange positions with a team-mate (wide change).
- To make room for a teammate for break-through dribbling (deep change).
- To lure a player away from a one-on-one coverage, creating a hole in the defense of the opposition.
- To fake a particular combination and facilitate the surprise action of a teammate.

In running to get free, a player should be mindful of these elements:

Getting free within one's own defensive zone.

Timing

Running should commence at the moment a teammate has given the signal (by eye contact) that he is ready to pass. If a player starts too soon, he may be covered again before the pass has been kicked; if too late, the opposing player will have the advantage when he tackles. Proper timing is particularly important when playing direct combinations. For newly formed teams or new groups or pairs (e.g., midfielder passing/forward getting free and receiving), it can often take weeks or months to fine tune the critical aspects of time and space. For the same reason, it takes time to integrate a new player into the team. Therefore, training should commence early in the formation or transition of any group or team.

Form

Getting free is accomplished with a sudden start, or better yet, with fake steps to the right for a start to the left, and vice versa. The player should attempt to run behind his opponent so that the opponent cannot observe him and the ball at the same time.

Direction

This is an especially difficult question because there are so many effective moves for each of the countless possible game situations. Sepp Herberger gave somewhat contradictory advice some 50 years ago when he said, "Go to the man with the ball," and, at the same time, "A player must be able to stay away." Nevertheless, this is still true today. The following basic rules make getting free more interesting, and more difficult for the opponent to read.

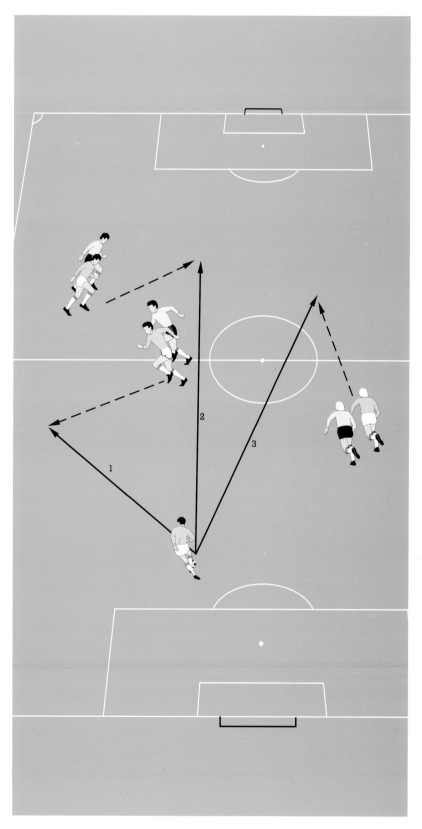

Getting free by running a diagonal pattern.

Individual Tactics

- When in his own half of the field, a player makes himself available by running toward the sideline.
- In midfield, the player runs a diagonal pattern, trying to get behind the opponent.
- The movement of the center forward hinges on the position of the sweeper or the next player closest to the goal. Also, keep an eye on the distance to the offside limit. The forward often has to run at right angles or diagonally back to his own midfield area to get free.
- If several players are running to get free at the same time, action should be coordinated in such a way that the ball carrier is able to pass in any direction. This tactic, however, requires tactical discipline and a high degree of readiness to act in the free-running players. Above all they must accept that only one player can be played at. No free-running player is allowed to object if the ball is not passed to him.

Here is the ideal situation: the player in possession of the ball has the option of passing in any direction, and a change of game position is also possible (see page 97).

The forward can run either wide or deep to get free.

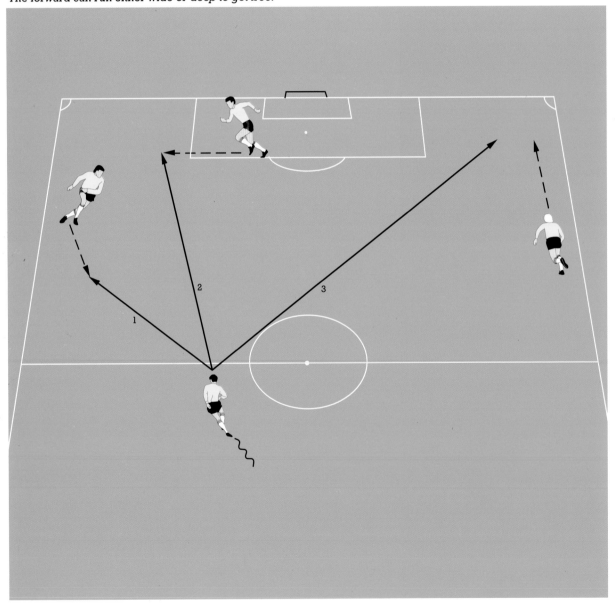

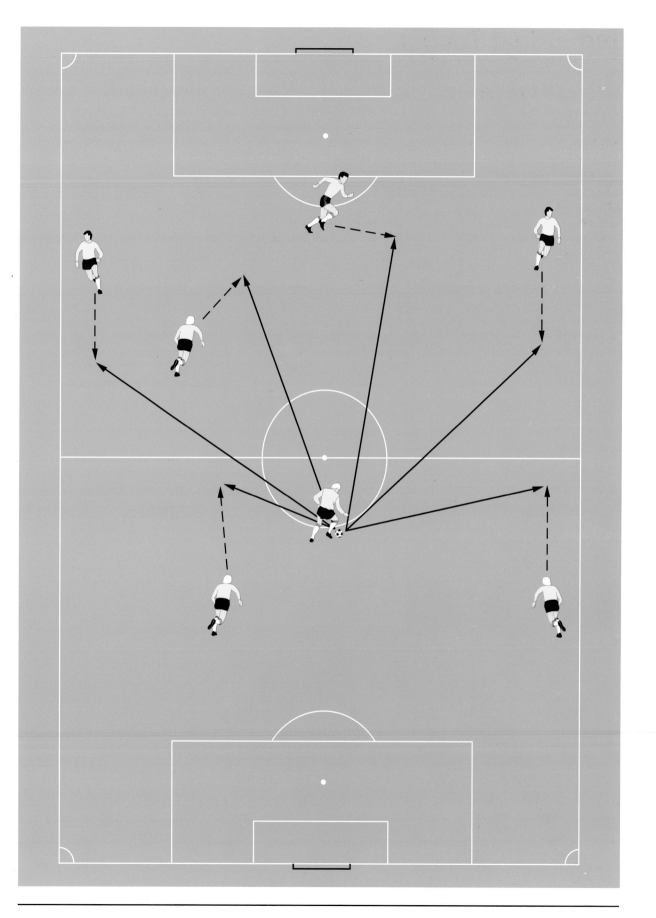

Individual Tactics

Individual Defensive Tactics

Tackling

A player well trained in tactics does not tackle at the *first* possible moment, but at the *best* possible moment. The following "moments" are the best to try to take the ball away from the opponent:

- The very moment when the opponent is trying to receive the ball. The player covering the intended receiver jumps decisively in front of him, either taking control of the ball or kicking the ball away from the opponent.
- The moment the receiver is trying to take possession and move away with the ball. At this point, he is standing on one leg and is totally engaged in starting to pass, leaving him little opportunity to defend himself against the opponent's imminent attack.
- When the opponent is already in possession of the ball. Wait for the

moment when he briefly lets the ball bounce off his foot.

This last situation described is not quite as favorable. It calls for the defensive player to turn the situation to his advantage by using additional tactics. It is important that he:

- Match the tempo of the opponent 6 to 10 feet (2–3 m) away from him.
- Not approach the opponent from the front but from the side. In this way, he totally blocks the opponent's move to one side and pushes him in the direction of his own stronger leg.
- Lure the opponent into a miscalculation with a fake, creating a favorable situation for either a hook or a slide tackle.

It is important that a hook or a slide tackle be considered only when the player is totally sure of success. If not, the dribbler will be difficult to catch, since the tackler must get back on his feet again before he can pursue the opponent.

Moving Back and Delaying

If a team is outnumbered by the opposition as the members move from midfield in the direction of the goal, the attack on the ball-carrying player must be delayed. While one player continues to engage the ball carrier, the rest of the defense covers the opposing players until reinforcements arrive from midfield and the numerical balance is reestablished.

Defenders should always attack in such a way that a pass to the opposing forward is blocked, as his position creates the greatest danger (usually the center forward). While the defender is moving back, he does not let up on his attack on the ball carrier, preventing him from making a successful pass.

Dribbling and tackling are basic elements of the game, just as are the shooting of goals and the defense of the goal. It is the very contrast in the basic elements of the game that excites player and spectator alike.

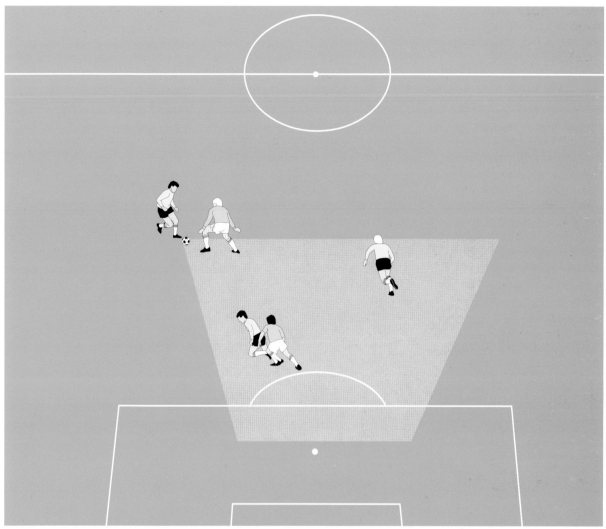

*If the opposition outnumbers the defense, the attack must be delayed;
at the same time, the pass to an opponent is blocked.*

Pushing to the Side

This tactic was mentioned earlier, in the chapter on tackling (see page 46). If a defender in midfield sees no chance to tackle the ball-carrying opponent successfully, he should at least try to prevent the dribbler from breaking through in the direction of the goal. By this means, the opponent is given room on the side of his strong kicking leg, while he is steadily pushed in the direction of the sideline.

Protecting the Goal

If a player in possession of the ball is dangerously close to the goal, it is always more important to block a possible shot on goal than to try to gain ball possession, which might be faster, but is very risky. In this case, the defender moves between the ball and the player in such a way that he blocks the stronger kicking leg of the opponent. He is then forced to dribble with his weaker leg or to kick a square or a back pass. This gives other teammates an opportunity to regain ball control.

Individual Tactics

Protection Against Dangerous Passes

What we have discussed above is also true in protecting against dangerous passes. For instance, when an opponent has gained ball control in his own half of the field, he will quickly switch from defense to offense. He will usually have only one or two (and for the opponent, very dangerous) options for passing. The attacking player should position himself at least in such a way that the opponent is unable to make an accurate pass. An aggressive attack to regain the ball can be made only when the particularly dangerous opponent is covered again.

One-on-One Coverage

One-on-one coverage is also called opponent-centered coverage. Usually a defender concentrates on one particular player. He can cover him either closely (press-cover) or lightly—6 to 10 feet (3–5 m) away.

Close coverage means actual body contact. It is more difficult for the offensive player to lose the defender when only a narrow space remains between the two players. Basically, a defender should choose a position that enables him to:
- Stand between the opponent and his own goal.
- Keep his eyes on both the opponent and the ball.
- Stand on the side that is closer to the ball, diagonally behind the opponent.

Covering In-between Space

An individual player takes over space coverage only when his teammates are outnumbered. Here, a player positions himself between two opponents, keeping his eyes on both. The opponent who is closest to the ball and the goal must be covered tightly. If the ball is passed to one of the two opponents, the one who is the likely receiver is attacked with one-on-one coverage.

The position of the defenders in one-on-one coverage depends on the game situation and where the ball is. The sweeper stands on the side closest to the ball in the back. In case the game is played with a line of defense instead of sweepers, then the last player also advances up to the penalty area.

Game Positions and Tactics

All the previously described tasks that are the responsibility of the individual player and the tactics available to him to manage specific game situations can generally be applied to all players, regardless of their position. Depending on his specific position, each player also has other tasks to perform and special tactics he can put to use.

Available defensive and offensive tactics depend largely on the tactical abilities of the individuals, the group, and the team as a whole. The tactical methods specific to any one position influence all the others. Therefore, if a coach stresses group and team tactics at the expense of individual tactics, his team is doomed.

Tactics and the Goalkeeper

The tactics used by a goalie are markedly different from those of any other player. One look at the rules of the game makes it clear that the goalie occupies a special position on the team, with tactics designed specifically for his position. Among others, the following aspects distinguish the tactics of a goalkeeper:

- How he positions himself in the box and in front of the goal.
- His basic position during shots on goal.
- Catching and/or punching.
- Handling the ball from a dribbling forward.
- Handling offensive action.
- Handling defensive action.
- How he handles the penalty kick.
- Building a "wall" against a free kick.

Position in and in Front of the Goal Box

The goalkeeper's position is influenced by his ability to orient himself not only in the box but also in the penalty area. Because the action in the game is ever changing, a goalkeeper is always on the move, following the ball. When moving out of the box, he has to defend the empty goal box behind him (when the ball is coming toward the center of the goal), the space to the right (when attacked from the right), and the space to the left (when the attack comes from the left, as perceived by the goalie). He must always get back to the center of the goal. Since he is concentrating on the ball, he must orient himself spatially in the box and the penalty area when retreating. To help do this, many goalkeepers draw an additional vertical line through the middle of the goal box toward the playing field (which is unlawful).

Standard situations, like free kicks and corner kicks, are particularly difficult for the goalie when the penalty area is crowded. Often he has only fractions of a second to make the decision to leave the box.

Basic Position for Shots on Goal

Some goalkeepers belong to the category of "fliers," those who try to compensate for their lack of positioning skill with spectacular show. A good goalie has the intuition always to be in the right place at the right time, i.e., he is always in the position from which he has the best possible chance for an effective defense.

Distance of the Ball from the Goal

Here are the basic rules:
- If the ball is in the opposition's half of the field, the goalie steps up to the edge of the penalty area, in order to catch a possible through

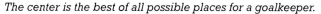

The center is the best of all possible places for a goalkeeper.

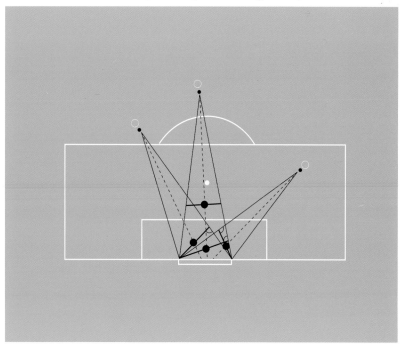

Game Positions and Tactics

ball. This is particularly important for teams that play with 3 or 4 defense players, i.e., without a sweeper.

- If the ball is in his half of the field, up to about 75 feet (25 m) in front of the goal, he remains on the line so as not to be surprised by wide passes with descending curves.
- If an opponent approaches with the ball and reaches the penalty area, the goalie runs toward him in such a way that he shortens the angle of approach.

The Angle of the Ball's Flight Path and the Direction from Which the Opponent Approaches the Goal

Note: In all actions, the goalkeeper should shift his weight forward onto the balls of his feet and be ready for action with his arms spread. It is from this position that he is able to react most quickly. He should avoid standing back on his heels and leaning backward.

The rules are as follows:

- If the opponent approaches the goal, and the space in which he can effectively make his shot on goal is a section with a 45-degree spread, the goalie takes a position as shown in the drawing on page 119.
- If the opponent approaches at a sharp angle, the goalie moves slightly back in the direction of the goal line at an angle about half the above number. From this position, he is better able to control balls with spin that are kicked into the long corner. This position is also better for incoming flanks and back passes.

The Position of His Own Defensive Player

The following basic rules apply:

- As long as a teammate is engaged in a one-on-one with a ball-carrying opponent, the goalie remains in his basic position in the goal box.
- If a teammate is covering part of the goal, the goalie can move toward the "unprotected" area of the goal, safeguarding that space.

Catching and Punching

When the opposition attacks from the side with corner kicks and flanks, the goalie often has to decide with lightning speed whether to catch or to punch the high, incoming ball. The following basic rules apply:

- Balls that can be handled confidently and securely should be caught by the goalkeeper and not deflected away.
- When the ground and the ball are wet, or when in doubt, punching is preferred to catching.
- Since the reach for catching balls with one arm is greater than with both, balls that can barely be reached should be punched; this also applies to shots on goal that can be deflected on the line.
- Balls that are kicked into the penalty area from the right should be punched away from the penalty area to the left side with the right hand, and vice versa. A variation of punching with the fist is to use the flat of the hand. This extends the goalie's reach, allowing him to push a high pass over the horizontal board or a low pass into a corner around the goalpost.

Leaping

As has already been mentioned, a goalkeeper is rather seldom forced to leap, if he knows how to position himself properly. Should it be necessary, the leap can be preceded by a

short step. A leap to the right begins by moving the left leg in front of the right pivot leg in the direction of the leap. One step with the right leg begins the jumping move.

Goalkeeper and Penalty Kicks

The referee's whistle is the signal for the goalie to start his tactical maneuver. On principle, the goalie should never get involved in the discussion over the decision itself. The calmer he remains, the more he will impress the player who makes the shot. When playing in league soccer, where the player making the penalty kick is well known, it is good for the goalie to keep written notes about past penalty kicks.

For the shot itself, the goalie must concentrate only on the ball and the foot of the shooter. They will give him information about the corner chosen for the shot. The shooter will try using fakes to confuse the goalie; likewise, the goalie tries to deceive the shooter with fake movements of his upper body and by swinging his arms back and forth. Statistics show that goalkeepers who anticipate the corner of the shot and leap in that direction shortly before the shot is made have the best chance for defense. However, leaping too early gives an advantage to the penalty shooter when he carries out the penalty kick with a delayed run-up.

The "Wall" as Defense Against a Free Kick

A well-positioned "wall" can greatly decrease the danger of a free kick. Opinions concerning who should position the wall are divided. One gives authority to the player who stands immediately behind the ball and can look over it in the direction of the goalpost on the near side. Most goalkeepers want to arrange the wall

Tactics of the Goalkeeper

themselves. To do so, however, they must leave the prime space in the center of the box, which may give the opposition a chance to score when the free kick is executed quickly.

The directions from the goalie must be loud, clear, and distinct. It is best to use the names of the respective players who are posted at the outside of the wall. The names must be called out in a calm voice. Basically, the wall is posted approximately 2 feet (1/2 m) beyond the direct line between the ball and the goalpost.

The Goalkeeper and Defense

Usually the goalie is regarded as the key person on a team. He should take advantage of this role and direct the defense from the rear. If he pays close attention, he is better able than anyone else to detect gaps in the defensive coverage of an individual player, a group, or the opposing team. If the goalkeeper and the defense communicate well, all that is needed is to call out the name of the individual whose coverage is not adequate. The defense can then reinforce it immediately.

The Goalkeeper and Offense

The goalie should be the number one offensive player on the team. Depending on the game situation, he has a number of means for introducing new offenses through aimed actions:

- Through a fast and deep pass to one of the players in his own half of the field.
- Through aimed kick-outs deep into the opponent's half of the field.
- Through a short pass to a defender who then controls the ball in a combination play from the backfield.

The creation of the "wall" for the free kick requires hard, courageous players.

Game Positions and Tactics

Tactics of the Sweeper

Besides the game with a line of defense with 3 or 4 players, games today are played with a sweeper, i.e., with a "free man" in the defense. The sweeper has the following tasks:

Directing the Defense

Because of his position on the field, the sweeper has a good view of the developments of a game; from this vantage he can guide the movements and actions of his teammates.

Safeguarding the Front Line

This tactic was mentioned earlier, in the section on group tactics (see page 105). The sweeper usually moves with the ball. If one of his teammates is trying to regain ball possession with a one-on-one, the sweeper is able to provide cover. The distance between the sweeper and the opponent narrows as the opponent approaches the goal. Ideally, he will be no more than 6 to 10 feet (2–3 m) behind the defender.

Safeguarding Open Space and Lanes

Passes are not only kicked to covered forwards, but also into open lanes and spaces. Since the sweeper does not have an opponent for whom he is directly responsible, he is free to cover open spaces and is, therefore, an ideal receiver. Experienced sweepers deliberately leave lanes open in order to facilitate (or to provoke) a pass to the open space. With experience and a good eye, he is usually able to intercept the pass.

Passing as a Signal to Initiate Offense

Owing to his position on the field, the sweeper often has the best chance to initiate offensive action without interference. Time and again, he receives short passes from his teammates. Depending on the situation, he uses them for short or long offensive passes.

Joining the Offensive Line

The modern sweeper actively participates in the offensive action. Sometimes he does this to bring an element of surprise into the game, sometimes when his team is trailing and cannot afford the luxury of an uninvolved defense player in an intensely offensive game. Since he does not have a designated opponent, he is able to move far into the territory of the opposition before he is attacked. Ideally, the penetration into the opposition's territory should be on the side where the opposing forward is restricted in his actions (because he is covering his opponent) or where the opposition has obvious weaknesses.

Sometimes, the sweeper is part of the four-man defensive line as a second inside defender. Oftentimes, the two inside defenders switch back and forth in their tasks of covering open space. This makes sense only in a four-man defensive line. In a 3-5-2 system, among other things, the sweeper must alternate between the open spaces on the left and right of both defenders.

Tactics of the Defenders

The action of a defender in one-on-one coverage or space coverage depends on the team's tactics (see page 94). There is a marked difference between the tactics of the inside defender and the outside defender. The inside defender primarily attacks the center forward in the middle of the field in front of his own goal. This function is so vital that he will seldom get involved in his team's offensive actions or take over other defensive tasks.

The outside defender, on the other hand, will switch from his designated position in the direction of the goal if the ball is played on the opposite side of the field, so that he can support the sweeper in covering the vulnerable space in front of the goal. He will only cover his direct opponent close to the sidelines, for when the ball returns to his side by means of a flank, he will have enough time to fight the opponent in a tight one-on-one coverage.

Modern outside defenders often get involved in the offensive game of their teams along the sidelines much earlier than in the past. This is particularly effective when the opposition plays with only three defenders (using the 3-5-2 system), or if the defender's own outside forward (through a change in midfield) lures the opposing defender to the sideline. The attack of the defender can take place either as a counterattack or as a frontal attack.

Basically, the defender should finish his attack with positive actions (flanks or shots on goal) and not get involved in a risky dribbling action that might cost him the ball, for this often leads to dangerous counterattacks.

Tactics of the Midfielders

To a certain degree, every midfielder has offensive and defensive tasks to fulfill. These players are responsible for switching quickly from offense to defense and from defense to offense.

In addition, they are involved in the shifting action from one side of the field to the other. Changing the rhythm of the game is also their responsibility (see page 91). Teams playing with four or more midfielders often pair them up. Only one of the two pairs may get involved at any one time in an offensive action.

Action zones for midfielders can vary widely, as has already been mentioned. (See some examples in the illustration on page 139.) During fast counterattacks, midfielders should follow diagonal running patterns. Usually these players should move at the edges of the defensive zones—an elegant way of avoiding the attacks of opposing players. Continuously running diagonal patterns makes it difficult for the opposing sweeper to maintain position and game strategy. The midfielder today must have the skills of a forward. He will be expected to:

- Move the ball in dynamic fashion into the territory of the opposition.
- Cover long distances in open space to reach the sides (wings).
- From that position, use flanks and back passes to the defense line.
- With long passes from the second line, force a defensively oriented opposition to attack prematurely.

A shot on goal is the spice of the game. Intuition, tactical skill, and ingenuity come together in the attempt to score.

Tactics of the Center Forward

Today's center forwards are left to their own devices again and again, while being outnumbered by the opposing defense. Most of the time they are brought into the action because of a through pass. They must hold their own against a great number of defensive players or control the ball until midfield players can move up for support. In either case, the task can be accomplished only if they have great technical skills and can control the ball with *both* legs. They can evade direct, tight coverage by changing positions and pulling to the outside. To counter the disadvantage of being outnumbered, one of the two center forwards can

move in the direction of the sweeper. In this way, a forward ties up both the defender and the sweeper in a small space. This tactic clears space for a breakaway by the midfielder, who is moving upfield.

Teams that play with two center forwards can create havoc in the defense with the following tactics:

Position Change of Center Forwards
—The teammates can change places from left to right or right to left, immediately initiating a combination play.

Position Change in Open Space
—Here, one player starts to move at an angle toward the rear; the other player moves at a forward angle so that the teammate playing the ball has the opportunity to pass either wide or short.

Giving Over and Luring Away
—In a small space immediately in front of the goal, the dribbling center forward can give the ball over to the teammate next to him, at the same time luring away an attacking opponent.

Position Change for Receiving a Flank
—To prepare for flanks, the center forwards run diagonally across the field, crossing each other as each heads for one of the goalposts. Short passes are handled by the player at the short side of the goal, long passes by the other player.

Tactics in Standard Situations

Tactics in a Standard Situation

At the European championship 2000, 26 percent of all goals scored were the result of standard situations. This means that, statistically, approximately every fourth goal in soccer is scored after a corner kick, a free kick or a penalty kick. For this reason, standard situations deserve intense study and practice during training.

Teams that use their technical skills and physical strength effectively in standard situations (e.g., throw-in far into the penalty area) will enjoy many advantages.

At their most basic, standard situations are divided into the following:
• The tactics of the attacker in possession of the ball (offense).
• The tactics of the defending team (defense).

Offensive players have the tactical advantage because they can bring the ball into play without being pressured by the opposition and without any immediate time pressure. Sadly, this advantage is all too often overlooked.

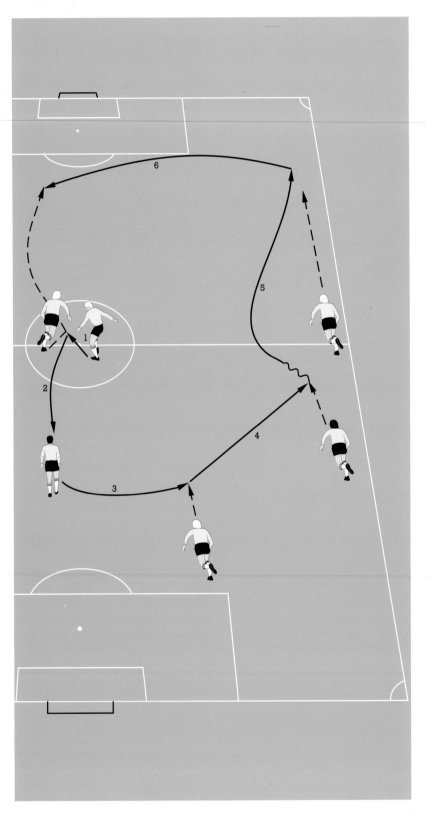

The kickoff at the start of the first half serves to keep control of the ball.

Tactics for Kickoff

Offensive Kickoff Tactics

The foremost consideration for the team that is kicking off is whether the kickoff is at the start of the game or period, or after the opposition has scored. At the *beginning of a period* and after the first ball has been kicked forward (as required by the rules), the ball should be passed back immediately. Driving the ball to the opposition's half is not good tactics because of the great number of players there. The back pass lures the opposition out of its half of the field, shifting the balance to its disadvantage. In addition, the back pass gives teammates the opportunity to lose their initial nervousness by getting involved in unpressured combination plays.

For psychological reasons, the kickoff *after a successful score by the opposition* is another thing entirely. The opposition is ecstatic. The players are so caught up in the excitement that they don't concentrate on the kickoff. The "buzz" hasn't quite worn off when the kickoff takes place, and the defensive players are not yet in their proper positions. In such a situation, the kickoff should be a counterattack. The ball is driven with quick through passes into the open space where the opposition has not yet taken up coverage. A precision flank kicked to the forward, sprinting after tempo dribbling has moved the ball to the sideline, is particularly effective.

The surprise counterattack kickoff after a successful score by the opposition.

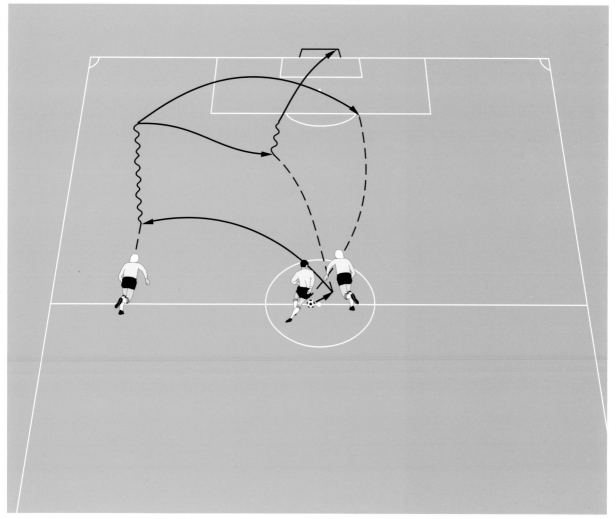

Tactics in Standard Situations

Defensive Kickoff Tactics

The variations discussed so far make it clear how important it is that every player concentrate on the defense when the opposition kicks off. The defensive team should not give away its tactical advantage (the concentration of manpower in its half of the field) and move too many players forward too quickly. It is sufficient to move two or three players into the territory of the opposition and start pressing the man who has the ball.

Both center forwards (positioned at the kickoff circle center line while the midline position kicks off) have a good chance to intercept the back pass. They must sprint aggressively into enemy territory while the kickoff is carried out. The opposition seldom counts on such actions. The surprise often causes them to lose the ball after the first few contacts.

A tactic for quick recovery of the ball after the opposition's kickoff: both center forwards immediately start toward the opposition's half of the field in order to intercept the back pass.

Four different options for corner kicks.

Tactics for the Corner Kick

Offensive Tactics and Corner Kicks

The offensive tactics used in a corner kick and the position of the attacking players must take into account:

- The strengths and skills of the players (e.g., a strong corner kicker, expert shooters from the second line, an expert dribbler).
- The strengths and skills of the opposition (e.g., a goalkeeper with good ball control in the penalty area, tall players with good heading skills).
- The weather (sun, wind, ground conditions).

Basically, the offensive strategy for corner kicks is governed by the following:

- The more players there are in the goal area, the more difficult it is for the goalkeeper to field the ball outside the goal box. For this reason, it is prudent to have at least two attackers in this area to act as troublemakers, even if they don't have good heading skills.
- Corner kicks that spin toward the goal or away from it are difficult for the goalie to judge.
- Sharp, straight corner kicks are more difficult to handle by the defense than balls that are curving.
- The opposition adapts quickly and easily to corner kicks that are always made using the same tactic, so use variations.

- The corner kicker should signal his teammates to make them aware of the type of kick he intends to make. Following are a few variations that have proven to be effective.

Long Corner Kick

This ball, kicked with spin, moves away from the goal toward the goal-post at the far end, between the penalty area and the goal area. This is especially recommended if the opposition is good at intercepting flanks and if the team has some header specialists.

Corner Kick to the Near Corner of the Goal Area

Here, the ball is kicked sharply to the inside at head level. This method is

Tactics in Standard Situations

recommended if the opposition as a whole is stronger at heading and if the variation is slipped in only once in a while as a surprise. During the carry-out, a teammate runs to the point agreed upon at the goal area; from there he can extend the ball with a header backwards or convert it himself.

Short Corner Kick
The ball is passed to a teammate positioned only a short distance away. The teammate should move as quickly as possible along the goal line into the penalty area. When this maneuver is used, it is important to

This is the basic defensive position of a team.

make sure that the opposition (after the first pass) is not given a chance to set an offside trap. This method has the advantage over other corner-kick methods that the team keeps ball possession. The short corner kick is also recommended if the team has a good dribbler who can drive the ball decisively into the opposition's penalty area.

Corner Kick as Back Pass
Here, the ball is moved back, deep into midfield, where the team can control ball possession, or the action can be concluded by an expert attempting a shot on goal from the second line. This method is particularly good in the last moments of a game, when the team has a narrow

lead. Controlling the ball in midfield, as well as shooting from the second line, gains valuable time and might save the game.

Corner Kick and Defensive Tactics
The defensive team can make up for the attacker's tactical advantage by the following actions:

Safeguarding the Goal Area and the Goalkeeper
This is accomplished with one or two defenders. One is positioned directly in the goal area near or next to the goalpost (so as not to obstruct the goalie's view); the second defender is positioned at the goalpost at the far end. If the goalie has to leave the box

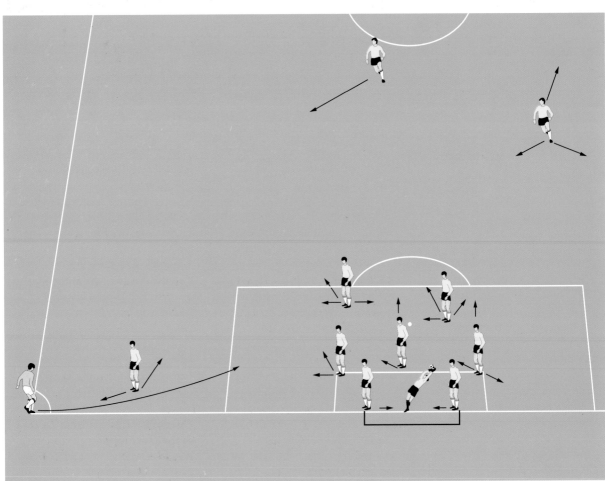

Tactics for the Corner Kick

Because the chance for success is so great, the corner kick always creates maximum tension for both players and fans.

to intercept a flank, both defenders move to the middle of the goal area, protecting both halves.

Safeguarding the Goal

Experience has shown that in corner-kick action, most scoring is the result of headers by players positioned just inside or outside the goal line.

Therefore, the front of the goal line should be guarded by three defensive players. If the corner kick comes into the goal area, these players can cover the goalie; if the ball comes into the penalty area in front of the line, the defenders have a good chance to move the ball to midfield.

Preventing Corner Kicks

Often a defensive player moves within 30 feet (9 m) of the corner-kick area so as to prevent the shooter from kicking accurately and to interfere with a possible short corner kick.

Guarding Strong Opposing Headers

Strong headers of the opposing team are usually discovered early in the game. When, in the course of a corner-kick action, tall defensive players leave their positions and move forward, trouble is brewing. These players must be covered by teammates who are equally strong headers. But they must not be deceived by fake kicking motions prior to the corner kick, which might lead to a bungled response. When-

ever the opponent jumps in the air for a header, the defending player must follow his movements, even if there is no chance of reaching the ball. This is the only way to thwart dangerous headers.

Constructing an Offside Trap

A successful defense of the first corner kick does not mean that all danger has passed. If the ball has been kicked out of the penalty area to the feet of an opponent, it is imperative that this opponent be attacked immediately by two defensive players simultaneously. This attack is the signal for the whole team to move forward with lightning speed because it moves the offside line away from the dangerous goal area.

Tactics in Standard Situations

Good coordination of players allows a team to use many different methods for the throw-in. Here are four examples.

Initiating Counterattacks

The opponent usually gives up his regular defensive positions during corner kicks. The opposition has only a few players in its half of the field. This is an ideal situation in which to initiate assault-like counterattacks. The attack can be started by the goalie after he has fielded the ball. A punt deep into the enemy's territory is particularly good. A well-aimed throw to either of the two players who are waiting at the left and right corners of the penalty area can also initiate a quick attack. The midfield players also try to start quick counterattacks.

Basic Position of Defending Players

The type of corner kick the opposition has planned is usually not known. Therefore, the defending team must choose positions from which every defensive tactic discussed so far can be carried out successfully (compare drawing, page 128).

Tactics for a Throw-In

Offensive Tactics

The throw-in and the combination play have the same requirements:
- One or two players get free at the same time.
- The free players, who have

switched positions, open space for each other by taking their direct cover with them into another zone (see drawing above).
- The players who are free determine the type, time, and direction of the throw-in.
- In contrast to regular combination plays, the offside rule is suspended during a throw-in. This allows the players who are free to run behind the opposing defense. It also avoids a concentration of opposing defenders around the throw-in.
- The direction of the throw-in depends on where it starts. In general, we distinguish between four different situations:

Throw-in Deep in the Team's Own Territory

In order to avoid square passes in front of the team's own goal, the throw-in should always be made forward along the sidelines (see drawing on page 130). Under no circumstances should a square pass move the ball into the middle of the team's own territory.

Midfield Throw-in—Opponent Attacking

The sweeper gets free by running in the direction of the player throwing the ball; a midfielder starts to run behind the waiting players' backs into the free space (see drawing).

Midfield Throw-in—Opponent Defending

The midfielder, positioned across the field from the opponent throwing the ball, begins to move forward, taking his cover with him. Defenders or midfield players, coming from behind, get free by running into the free space (see drawing).

Throw-in in Front of the Opponent's Goal

Because of the suspension of the offside rule during throw-ins, the sweepers are able to move all the way into the goal area. Immediately before the throw-in, midfield players run toward the penalty area. The ball is thrown in the direction of the penalty area. At the same time, the midfielders move forward and try to intercept the throw-in.

Throw-in and Defensive Tactics

Defensive players move according to the same guidelines discussed earlier for combination plays. This means that the defenders are tightly covered in the immediate area of the ball; their movements are followed with one-on-one coverage. It is important too, that the offenders, who are farther away, be unable to move freely behind the last defenders.

Tactics for the Free Kick

Free Kick and Offensive Tactics

According to the rules, free kicks can be kicked *directly* or *indirectly.*

For free kicks *in midfield,* a team should make good use of the basic tactical advantage, possession of the ball. To do so, the team keeps control of the ball in its own territory by kicking short, sure, quick passes back and forth. Owing to the danger of losing the ball, through passes are seldom called for.

Many different methods are available for free kicks *close to the goal of the opposition.* A free kick can be executed quickly, surprising the opponent, but only after the referee has returned the ball. If a quick free kick is not possible, the kick should be carefully planned. The following options are available:

Direct Shot on Goal

Each team has players who are able to turn their shooting strength into dangerous free-kick weapons. Well-aimed balls that are kicked sharply with spin (around the "wall" or over the wall into either of the corners of the goal) are particularly dangerous for the goalkeeper, since it is difficult to anticipate the direction of the ball.

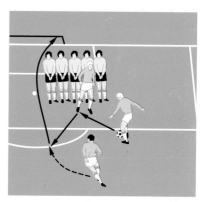

Well-trained teams have a large repertoire of methods for free kicks. Here are four examples.

Tactics in Standard Situations

Indirect Shot on Goal

Three attackers are needed to accomplish the indirect free kick: one player for the free kick and two other players, one to his left and one to his right. This basic strategy can be varied in many ways. It is an easy method to deceive the opposition. Some examples of the carry-out are shown on page 131. Regardless of which variation is used, a few players should be positioned to the left and right of the opponent's wall so as to obstruct the goalie's view even more.

Free Kick and Defensive Tactics

Free kicks by the opposition can be successfully defended if every member of the team is involved and has a clearly defined role. Players should take their positions as quickly as possible and with absolute calmness. During training, the sequence of movements must be planned and the strategy practiced until they are nearly automatic.

- Although the player closest to the ball is no longer allowed to position himself in front of it in order to prevent a fast carry out, he should nevertheless design his retreat for the building of the "wall" in such a way that he moves between the ball and the goal. Only thus can he prevent a quick, direct free kick. At the same time, the "wall" is assembled with the assigned players. The tallest players are posted at the corners.
- The goalkeeper or one of the players (usually the one positioned behind the ball) gives clear, concise instructions.
- The rest of the players assume coverage of the space to the right and left of the wall.

In case of an indirect free kick, the wall should move forward to shorten the angle (after the first contact with the ball), or dissolve, allowing the players to switch to one-on-one coverage.

Note: The players in the "wall" must stand firm with eyes open!

Defense of Free Kicks from a Narrow Angle

Free kicks that are carried out between the penalty area and the sidelines are particularly dangerous because they can be aimed at the area immediately in front of the goal. For this reason, a wall of at least three defenders is recommended. The formation of the rest of the players is the same as for the basic corner kick (see drawing).

Positioning the Offside Trap and Initiating Counterattacks

For the offside trap and the fast initiating of counterattacks, the same tactical basics apply with the free kick for the opposing team as for the corner kick. In this regard, see pages 129 and 130.

With a high carry out of the free kick, the players in the "wall" jump high in the air in order to block the ball.

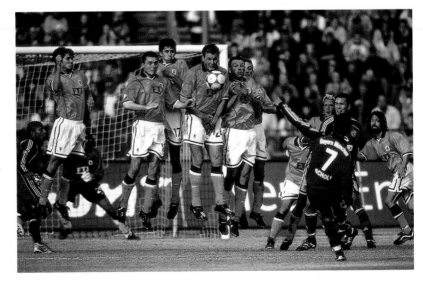

Tactics for the Penalty Kick

Tactics for the Penalty Kick

Penalty Kick—Offensive and Defensive Tactics

A penalty kick is awarded when a foul (that would otherwise result in a free kick) is committed within the penalty area. Indirect penalty kicks are possible, but seldom awarded. In an indirect penalty kick, the ball must be played forward.

The offside rule is in effect during the penalty kick. Therefore, the offensive player may not be closer to the opposition's goal line than the last defending opponent. This is the only position from which players can reach for a ball that is bouncing off a goalpost or is punched out by the goalkeeper without running into an offside situation.

A basic, logical formation for offensive and defensive players is shown in the drawing below. Players of both teams line up along the penalty area so that the bouncing ball can be handled equally well by defenders and attackers.

Training for Standard Situations

The above discussion makes it clear that standard situations give a team numerous possibilities for intelligent tactical maneuvers.

Combining theory with systematic, practical exercises of game situations will improve the tactical skills of individual players and the team as a whole. This holds true for both defensive and offensive players.

Many coaches shy away from practicing standard situations because they believe that players do not get enough physical conditioning in the process. This is only partly true. Training for standard situations can be planned separately, before or after regular practice sessions.

Because of the lighter training load, such training can be scheduled more frequently after the second half of the competitive period. Since games become more important in the second half of the season, tactical skills for standard situations become especially important.

The basic formation of attackers and defenders for a penalty kick.

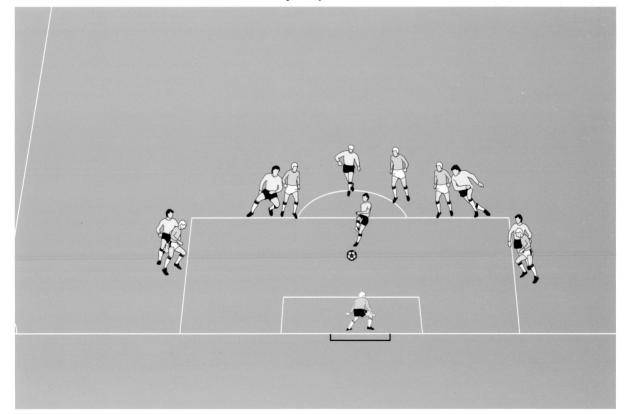

Tactics for the Game Day

Tactics for the Day

The tactics employed by individual players, groups of players and the team need to be adjusted according to the specific conditions of the day.

The tactical components used by the team and the individual players were generally reviewed on page 86. Here, we examine a few aspects in more detail.

Long-term Goal and Standings

The long-term goal for the team is defined by management (in the case of professional teams), the coach, and the team. The actual tactical maneuvers to be used will vary according to the team's standing in the division and overall team objectives. For instance, if a young team plans to advance to a higher standing in its respective division during the next two or three years, and if the team wishes to move up a place in the league standings toward the end of the current season, it will play with a tactical line of approach, perhaps even risking some defeats in the interest of better long term progress.

Actual Objectives for the Day

For amateur teams and teams with young players, the objective of every game ought to be to win—by as wide a margin as possible. With that team objective, tactics are clearly defined.

From European championship games, we know that for professional soccer teams, even a narrow loss (in point games) is sufficient for the team's advancement. In this case, defensive tactics are the choice. Defensive specialists will see more action, the game system will be different, and the defenders must play a much more disciplined defense.

Actual Condition of the Team

The actual performance level of the team is always in flux. Players are injured, suspended, or in a personal slump; new players have to be integrated into the team; a winning or losing streak has lifted or depressed morale, and conflicts within the team can undermine willingness to cooperate and perform.

These factors must be recognized by the coach and the lineup (see also page 15), and the choice of tactics must reflect them.

The Opposing Team

There are very few games in which a team is so superior that its members can honestly say, "What do we care about the opponent? They have to play our game!" It is *always* important to find out as much as possible about the opposition. They, too, can have a bad day for the same reasons mentioned above. It is difficult to plan ahead for such a situation. However, many factors that can influence a game are often known or can be anticipated. These can and should affect the tactics the team decides to use.

Through close observation, a good coach will gather important information early in the game. This information can be passed on to his players in the form of tips and calls during the game or at halftime. A preliminary analysis of the opposition should note the following important points:

- The lineup.
- The game system.
- Group and team tactics.
- Players particularly strong or weak in technique and tactics.
- Specific variations of standard situations.
- Overall physical condition of individual players.

Type of Game

Although soccer players play to win, the type of game a team is playing (training, friendship, point or championship) will influence how a win, a tie, or a loss is evaluated. A loss in a point game can be made up in the next game; in a championship game, a loss means the team is out. Clearly, these factors influence the choice of tactics.

Training and friendship games are good times for experimenting with different methods and lineups, as the final score is not especially important.

Day and Time of the Game

Teams playing a Friday-Wednesday-Friday schedule often try to reserve the necessary energy for the next match by playing a calm, ball-controlling game. Teams with good technical skills have an advantage in such a situation.

Games played under the lights, as compared to day games, require different considerations. For instance:

- Players who wear glasses are at a disadvantage, and this will have consequences for the lineup.
- Dark uniforms are difficult to see. If need be, the team has to replace their favorite team jerseys or shorts with a more easily visible uniform.
- Because of the lights, balls kicked high in the air are difficult for all players to judge, but especially so for the opposing goalkeeper. Take advantage of this—attack from the wings and with flanks!

Direct Opponents

Location of the Game

Tactics are often different for games played at home than for those played away from home. Location can even influence the game system. Many teams play more defensively when on the road than they do in front of their own fans. Sometimes, at an away game, a coach hopes that the opposition, in the euphoria of playing in front of its fans, will get a little careless. This makes counterattacking much easier.

Also, games played in other countries, particularly those with an unfamiliar climate, require special tactics and considerations. This holds true as well for pre-game preparations (overnight accommodations, nutrition, fluids necessary for the climate, and medical care, such as inoculations).

Other Conditions

Conditions change from day to day and from game to game. Tactics may have to be adjusted with the following in mind:

- Climate and weather.
- Playing field and ground conditions.
- Fans.
- Referee.

Climate and Weather

Very high temperatures require special preparation (proper fluids) and influence the choice of tactics (e.g., using combinations that force the opposition to do most of the running).

During the winter months, the choice of proper clothing is important (gloves and tights). Actual weather conditions, such as rain, the angle of the sun, and wind direction and velocity, play an important role. It makes sense to choose the half in which the team can play with the wind and sun at its back, even though those conditions may change during the course of the game. When playing against the wind, it is a good idea to use low passes and to drive the ball forward with safe combination plays.

Condition of the Playing Field

Dimensions of playing fields vary greatly, especially in amateur and youth leagues. The same is true of the condition of the ground (grass, ash, artificial grass, snow, and mud). These conditions are different from field to field; they can differ even within a field. It is vital to consider them when choosing shoes. Ground conditions will also influence the way the game is played. Wet grass, for example, calls for short passes and accurate kicking; in muddy conditions or deep snow, however, passes must be high and wide.

Expectations of the Fans

Fans in different places have different expectations and reactions. Professional players accordingly adjust the type of game they play.

The Referee

Despite the fact that all referees receive the same training, their interpretation of rules is not the same every time. This is particularly true of Rule #12. Smart players adjust their behavior on the field and their one-on-one confrontations accordingly.

Personal Goals

A solid performance for the good of the team is not the sole motivation for some players. Some want to achieve personal glory; others may want to secure a permanent position on the team, to impress a new coach or a scout, or to atone for a poor performance in the past. Usually, such ambitions have the opposite effect. The team motto should be, "Keep it simple; do what is possible; avoid foolish risks."

The Immediate Opponent

A quick, highly competitive opponent has to be handled with different technical and tactical methods than an opponent whose primary skills are technical. The latter is usually sensitive and less aggressive in one-on-one confrontations. In addition, his passes may not be very fast.

Many players use very distinct techniques and tactics; they may favor particular faking methods, or they may have only one strong leg. A good player should adjust his tactics accordingly during a game, as these things are revealed. Of course, it is a great advantage to know these things about an opponent beforehand.

The offensive player can also adjust to the particularly hard play of a defensive player. The direct double pass is a good tactic to use against a defender who uses tight coverage during ball reception.

Mechanics of the Game

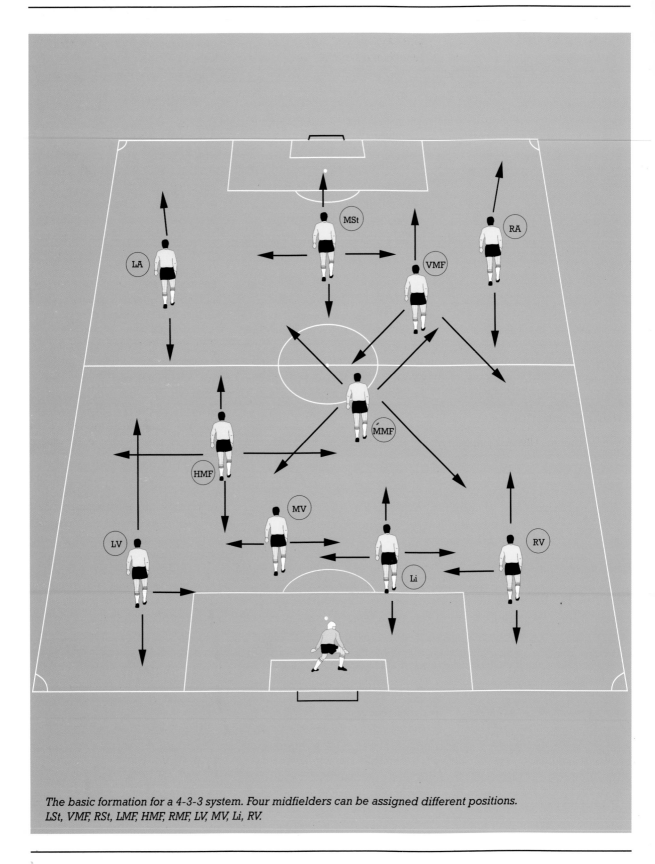

The basic formation for a 4-3-3 system. Four midfielders can be assigned different positions. LSt, VMF, RSt, LMF, HMF, RMF, LV, MV, Li, RV.

System of Play

A system of play is the framework for tactical plans and actions. It can, however, also be part of the tactics themselves, such as when, for tactical reasons, a change in a particular game system takes place, whether planned or not.

> A system of play is the basic format that assigns distinct spaces on the playing field to each player for offensive and defensive movements, and defines the tasks connected with those positions.

Teams that play modern soccer usually are not too closely tied to these spaces; as a matter of fact, in some circumstances players are even required to switch into spaces not assigned to them. It is important to note that switching spaces does not alter the basic system originally in place. A change to another system occurs only when one player takes over the position of another player.

The drawings on pages 136, 138, 139, 141, and 142 show the basic positions and the spaces preferred for offensive and defensive actions in the systems played most commonly today. The systems are: the 4-3-3 system (page 136); the 4-4-2 system (pages 138 and 139); the 3-5-2 system (page 141); and the 4-5-1 system (page 142).

Characteristics of Modern Systems

Modern systems should have the following characteristics:
- Players divided evenly over the field of play.
- Responsibilities divided evenly among the players.
- Strong defense of the goal.
- The ability to have the greatest possible number of players in the vicinity of the ball.
- The ability to change quickly from offense to defense.
- The participation of every player in offensive and defensive tasks.
- The ability to switch positions and tasks across the width and length of the field.
- Room for different opinions about the game and variations of group tactics.

Which system makes the most sense for a given game depends on the tactics chosen for the game, which players are available, how well the available players work together, and the physical condition of the players.

Special Characteristics of the Individual Systems

The 4-3-3 System

In the 4-3-3 system, players are spread out over the field in a very balanced way. In this sense, it is similar to the W-M formation, which is no longer used. This system has advantages for teams that do not have a great deal of tactical experience. It is, therefore, well suited for teams with young players.

In contrast to the systems we will discuss next, the 4-3-3 system has three forward positions. This has advantages and disadvantages. The

advantage is that both wing positions are in place; this makes it easier for teams with less experience in tactics to play the wing and switch sides.

However, by establishing definite positions for three forwards, the team loses some of the flexibility necessary to vary game tactics in midfield, where, for instance, the midfielders alternately move into the center forward position. Furthermore, it is easy for the opposition to see that the team is using the 4-3-3 system. And finally, the 4-3-3 system, with only three players in midfield, does not lend itself well to modern team and group tactics, such as space coverage and pressing.

The 4-4-2 System

In the 4-4-2 system, the midfield is strengthened by one more player. This basic formation is more defensively oriented than the 4-3-3 system with its three forward positions.

Formation of the four midfielders can take the shape of a rectangle lying on its side or standing on one of its corners. The midfield player in front is expected to be the attacker in the open spaces on the left and right sides of the center forward.

This system is particularly suited for teams with good tactical skills and players who are able to switch back and forth between midfield and forward positions. The considerable distances they have to cover, however, require exceptional endurance and speed.

Both forwards can function as outside and middle forward, or they can serve as a double point in front of the opponent's goal. In the latter case, the two wing positions are not covered, so that there is space for quick counterattacks by the defense from those positions or from the space in the midfield to the sides.

The positions of the midfielders are

Mechanics of the Game

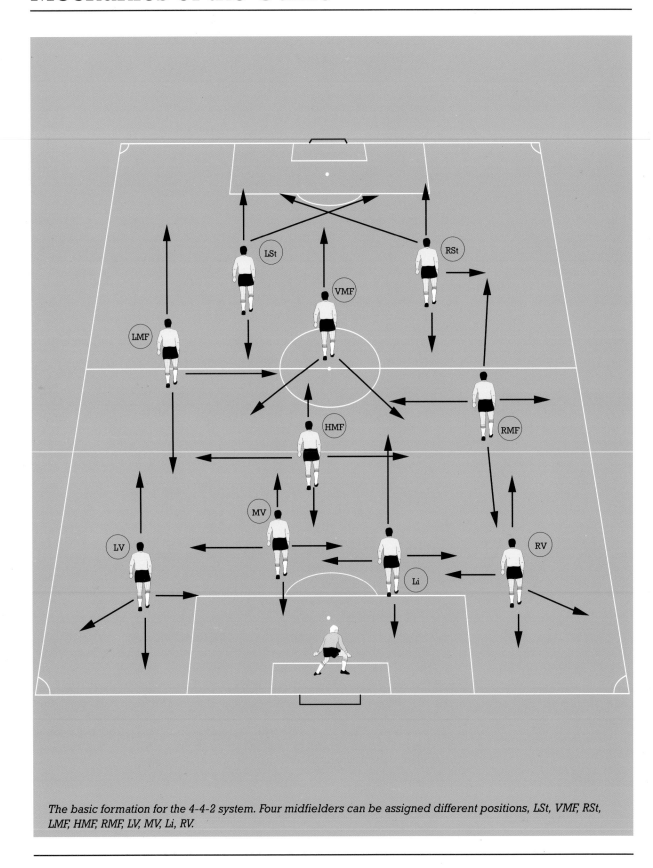

The basic formation for the 4-4-2 system. Four midfielders can be assigned different positions, LSt, VMF, RSt, LMF, HMF, RMF, LV, MV, Li, RV.

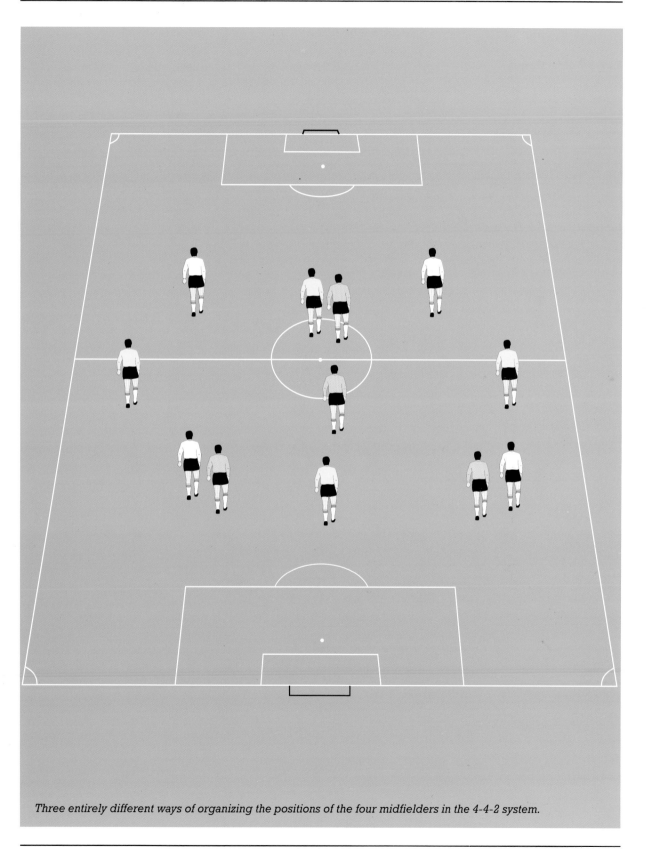

Three entirely different ways of organizing the positions of the four midfielders in the 4-4-2 system.

Mechanics of the Game

shown in the drawing on page 138.

The 3-5-2 System

This system evolved from the 4-4-2 system. Since many teams today operate with only two center forward players, the trainers regard it as a personal luxury to cover the last defensive barrier with four defensive players. Two well-trained defensive players are perfectly capable of covering the two opposing center forwards one-on-one, if a free player (the sweeper) is safeguarding the open space in the rear.

Because of the tight, five-player formation in midfield, it is possible to use space coverage to safeguard the areas left and right of the centrally positioned defender. The large number of players in midfield makes it possible to use today's modern team tactics, such as fore-checking and pressing, ensuring a livelier and more attractive game.

The 4-5-1 System

The 4-5-1 system is a variation of the 3-5-2 system, which becomes an extreme form when the number of defensive players (at the expense of the center forward) is raised from three to four.

This system is used when teams need to reinforce the defense of the goal because they are playing a much stronger opponent. With this system, however, one of the basic demands of the modern systems of play—that the players be divided evenly over the field—is not met. The biggest burden falls on the forward, since he is totally on his own. Two or three defenders are covering him, and he is seldom available to field a pass.

The 3-4-3 System

A few years ago, a trainer of teams with high performance technique, who wanted to offer fans a more attractive style of offensive soccer, initiated a change of trend in the mechanics of the game. As opposed to an earlier trend, which saw more and more players retreat from the center forward into the defense and the midfield, we now see more and more teams playing again with three regular sweepers, one mid-field sweeper, and two outside sweepers. In the 3-4-3 system, three real center forwards act behind four midfield players. They can be positioned in different ways, as with the 4-4-2 system (see page 139).

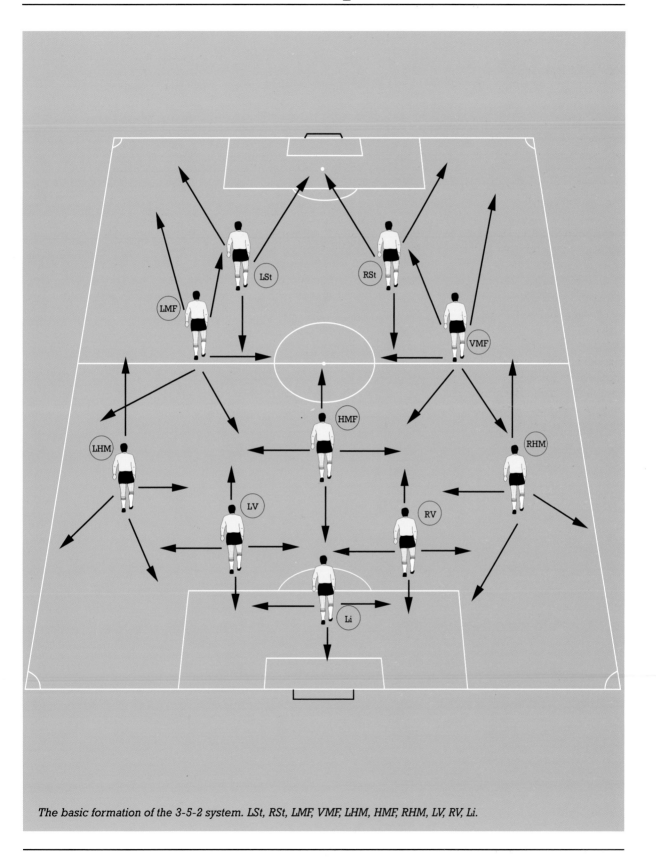

The basic formation of the 3-5-2 system. LSt, RSt, LMF, VMF, LHM, HMF, RHM, LV, RV, Li.

Mechanics of the Game

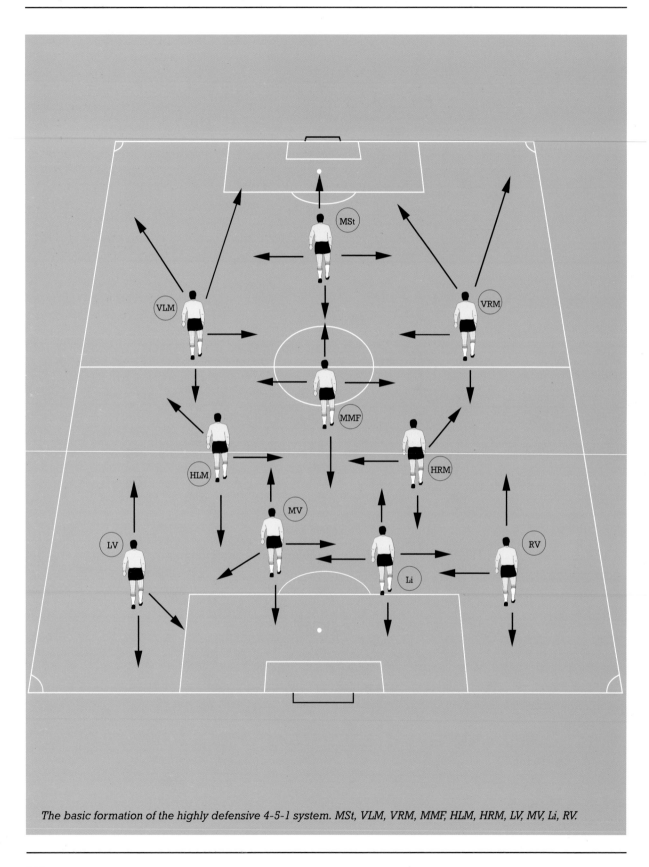

The basic formation of the highly defensive 4-5-1 system. MSt, VLM, VRM, MMF, HLM, HRM, LV, MV, Li, RV.

Style

Soccer teams each develop their own distinctive style, based on the club's tradition, the coach's philosophy, and the players.

> The special character that a team's playing exhibits is shaped by the personalities of the players and the coach, and is known as its style.

Even before the turn of the century, many teams were known for their particular styles of play. We still talk about some of them:

- The English kick-and-rush style.
- The Scottish low-pass style.
- Schalker-Kreisel (the circle/rotary style of the German club Schalke).
- Czechoslovakian alley-way style.
- Austrian slicing style.

Top national and international teams distinguish themselves by the style of soccer they play. Many *South American teams,* notably those from Brazil, are characterized by their short passes. Their style is rich in technique and full of tricks. The ball is moved around a great deal. Instead of moving the ball toward the opponents' goal the shortest way possible, the ball is passed back and forth, diagonally and across, in what becomes one long relay pass. The players express their playfulness and show off their technical skill at the same time. Suddenly, the game explodes with a through pass deep into enemy territory.

For years now, the *German and Dutch national teams* have operated with forced fore-checking and cleverly designed offside traps. The opponent in possession of the ball is aggressively attacked in his own territory. Pressure is often applied by two or even three players. In order to prevent the opponents from launching a counterattack behind the back of the forward-moving team, the defenders arrange an aggressive offside trap.

The finals for the European Cup in 1993 were a classic example of this game tactic, which was practiced rather seldom at the time.

Ever since the world championship games in 1982, the *Russian national team* has demonstrated an exceedingly fast game, often using direct passes across wide spaces. Almost every player moves with the attack and then retreats when the opposing team is on the offensive.

British teams still practice a highly aggressive soccer style. Toughness and aggressiveness dominate in one-on-one confrontations. The tempo remains brisk throughout the game, or as long as the players' energy holds out. Changes of tempo and rhythm, used effectively by other national teams, are rare for British teams.

Training Equipment

All you really need to "play" soccer is a piece of grass and a ball. Presumably, this minimum need for equipment is one of the reasons why soccer is played all over the world. Lack of equipment never interferes with enjoyment of the game.

It is likewise possible for teams to train with only a minimum of equipment. However, any training program oriented toward high performance and very differentiated skills calls for modern equipment. A team that is well equipped enjoys a more varied exercise program, permitting better training. In addition, the greater variety of exercises makes training less monotonous and more fun.

Large Equipment

- Shooting walls (permanent and movable, with and without target markings) to practice kicking, passing and driving skills, and for reaction training (see photo opposite page).
- Suspended "Walker" ball (see photo, page 146).
  Suspension balls are good for practicing heading techniques, and for building jumping strength in complex situations. Most of all, they are perfect for players practicing on their own. The Walker model is best for simulating the motion of a ball in flight.
- Movable goals in different sizes.
  By varying the number, position, and size of the goals, it is possible to use small game plays in many different ways and to adjust the training goals according to a given performance level for each player.

Small Equipment

- Soccer balls that are appropriate for different surfaces.
  Most soccer balls have the same size and weight, but their material and color make them appear different. For indoor soccer practice, it is best to use balls made of unlaminated leather or velour. Balls used on grass and hard surfaces also made of leather, but their surface may be laminated to give them different degrees of resistance. Some of them are even made entirely of synthetic materials. For women and young players, lighter and smaller balls (for instance, size four instead of five) are recommended.
- Medicine balls.
  Medicine balls come in different weights and sizes. They are particularly suited for special conditioning training. They allow players to engage in more playful endurance and strength training.
- Identification shirts.
  Most of the popular neon-hued team shirts are light, perspiration-repellent, hygienic, and quick to dry. They are big, well-fitting, and easily worn over a sweat suit. Their chief purpose, of course, is to help identify different training groups.
- Identification poles and cones.
  Well-planned training sessions constantly change zones, goals, and locations. Plastic marking poles are useful in almost every type of ground condition.
- Hurdles.
  Easy to transport and quickly adjustable for height, hurdles are a valuable aid in developing jumping strength. They are also very helpful for fitness training (hurdle races and relay races).
- Practice "dummies."
  These are life-size figures made out of wood or plastic that can be carried or wheeled around. They are helpful for practicing corner kicks and free kicks. Using them, a player can practice these skills by himself.
- Power (weight training) equipment and dumbbells.
  The equipment for general power (strength) training is too expensive for most teams. It is available in fitness clubs and gyms that provide qualified instructors. Sometimes, it is possible to contract with them to allow use by players. Power equipment is recommended for rehabilitation training after injuries.
  For specific power training, a club should nevertheless invest in some smaller items. The following equipment has proven to be effective.
- Light weights (dumbbells).
- Ankle weights.
- Weighted shoes.
- Sandbags.
- Jumping ropes.
  With this minimal equipment, a coach can put together a power (strength) training program that is both effective and fun for the players.

Equipment and Accessories

Weighted vest for the improvement of jumping and sprinting strength.

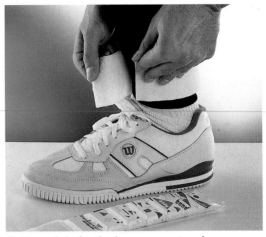

Ankle weight for the improvement and strengthening of the leg muscles.

Coordination training with hurdles.

Small markers as orientation and boundary guides.

The "dummy" as a training partner.

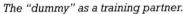

A suspended ball, the Walker model, helps "to give you a leg up."

There are various types of shooting walls…

…here in easily transportable miniature form.

Miniature goals for training in kicking and passing.

Slalom posts give your training the right swing.

Equipment for coordination and balance training after injuries.

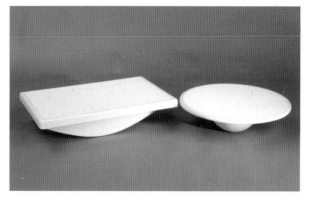

Accessories

Accessories

In addition to the training equipment discussed above, coaches and players need personal accessories for training and competition.

Accessories for the Player

- Shorts, T-shirt, socks.
- Sweat suit.
- Studded shoes and tools.
- Cleats.
- Shoes for play on hard ground and indoors.
- Shin guards.
- Athletic supporter.
- Elastic bandages and tape.
- Arm band for the captain of the team.
- Goalkeeper's cap.
- Bag for personal gear.
- Washcloth and hand towel.

Clothing worn for training and competition is usually supplied for the team. Obviously, the material should be adapted to the climate. Tricots are a good choice because of their combination of man-made fibers and old-fashioned cotton and wool. The outside of the material draws perspiration away, preventing the player from catching cold. On particularly cold days, the player can protect himself with additional underwear (tights). The color of the clothing should be chosen carefully; it should stand out against both the opponent's uniforms and the background. Green T-shirts and shorts are as bad when playing on grass as is dark clothing when playing under the lights. Clothing in fabric with a wild pattern is not suitable for the same reason.

Each player should choose his own soccer shoes. Of course, a coach can give professional advice.

Today, shoes with short rubber or plastic cleats are used almost exclusively because they put much less stress on the ankle and knee joints. With the new arrangement of these cleats, the same shoes can also be worn for competition. Children and young players should not wear anything else for competition or for training.

Senior players, however, do still use deeply cleated shoes for extra-secure grip when playing in long grass and in snow. More expensive shoes have titanium added to the cleat material for better traction. These shoes are strongly recommended for hard surfaces, artificial surfaces, and most of all for indoors. Normal soccer shoes are not well suited for these types of surfaces. Quick changes in direction are difficult and can permanently damage the ankle and knee joints.

Many accessories are available to protect against injuries. Knee and shin protection is mandatory for many professional players. What is good for professionals is also good for young and amateur players. An athletic supporter provides effective protection and is strongly recommended. Elastic bandages and tapes offer good support after injuries. And last, but not least, a well-equipped bag with items for personal hygiene is a must for every player.

Shoes with studs for grass.

Different Kinds of Soccer Shoes

Shoes with plastic or rubber cleats for hard surfaces and artificial grass.

Equipment

Accessories for the Coach

- Whistle.
- Tactical game board (see below).
- Training log.
- Tape recorder.
- First aid kit.
- Thermos bottle for ice water.
- Supply of cleats.

The coach must be well equipped for the varied tasks of training and competition. More than coaching responsibilities await the coach of young and amateur teams. Often he is masseur, counselor, and "medicine man" to the team—and often all at the same time.

For most coaches, the referee's whistle is standard equipment. Some coaches, however, have stopped using a whistle. They feel the whistle lends too militaristic an aspect to the commands. Very few coaches have a tactical game board, a training log, or a tape recorder. The tactical board (now available in a relatively small format that can be folded) is a very useful training tool. Before a game, it can be used to demonstrate important tactical choices; during a game (at halftime), it is useful for conveying information visually. The training log is a perfect means to record important data from training sessions and competition. Over time, this data becomes a valuable aid in long-term planning. It also helps to control and evaluate all training and game decisions. The tape recorder (one that fits in the palm of the hand) allows the coach to record important observations during the game. Unrecorded observations tend to get lost in the excitement of the game. If a coach is also the "medicine man," he will want to have a first-aid kit on hand, as well as a supply of cleats.

A thermos bottle filled with ice and water is strongly recommended for first-aid after injuries, such as bruises and pulled ligaments or muscles. The immediate application of ice greatly reduces the amount of bleeding into the tissue. This, in turn, reduces healing time. Ice *spray*, on the other hand, does not have nearly the same effect as ice water because it affects only the surface; in fact, it has been shown to increase bleeding deeper within the tissue.

The tactical game board is a valuable tool for the coach. He can demonstrate objectives and tasks before a training session or a game. He can also illustrate mistakes that were made during a game.

Sport-Specific Nutrition

The higher the performance level advances in soccer, the more important become certain aspects that were earlier considered only secondary in serious sport.

By now, it is well established that without proper, balanced nutrition and adequate hydration specifically adapted to the sport of soccer and to the energy consumed during play, outstanding performance is not possible.

The provision of sufficient nutrition and fluids must be guaranteed both before the competition and after.

At the professional level, many clubs employ full-time nutritionists or have a chef who travels with them when they are on the road.

For athletes, proper nutrition means eating properly before, during, and after competition. Sadly, most people know very little about what constitutes proper nutrition. In fact, the human organism is really not very different from an engine. A sophisticated engine needs superior fuel and oil in order to function at its peak.

This is also true for a player. The higher the demand for superior performance in training and competition, the higher the nutritional intake must be.

Proper nutrition requires sufficient amounts of the following:
- Nutritional value.
- Essential minerals.
- Vitamins.
- Liquids.

At the yearly conference of the Association of German Soccer Teachers (1989), Max Inzinger, the nutritional counselor of the FIFA, outlined the basic requirements for proper nutrition. What follow are Inzinger's recommendations.

Nutrition that is deficient in essential elements can have dire physiological and psychological consequences for an athlete, including:
- Lack of concentration.
- General fatigue.
- Lack of energy.
- Muscle cramps.
- Blackouts.
- Visual problems.
- Shortness of breath.

What follow are the basic requirements for proper nutritional and liquid intake:
- Proper caloric intake must be established individually for every player.
- Carbohydrate storage must be sufficient.
- Increased demand for vitamins must be taken into account.
- Availability of electrolytes and minerals must be assured.
- Body fluids must be balanced through proper fluid intake.

Individual Caloric Needs

The amount of energy an individual needs depends on the person's constitution, the amount of daily pressure, and the frequency of his or her training. According to Inzinger, the daily caloric intake is calculated with the following formula:

Body size × a value number = energy needs

A player who is six feet (180 c) tall and is in training between one and two hours daily (not counting any other activities) needs a daily caloric intake of 3960 calories. The individual value number is calculated according to the following table:

Value number	Training frequency
18	1–2 times weekly
20	3–4 times weekly
22	1–2 hours daily
24	3–4 hours daily
28	5–6 hours daily

Proper Eating Habits

The old saying "A student with a full belly can't study" holds true for an athlete as well. According to the findings of nutritional scientists, there are several reasons why it is better to change from eating a few large meals to eating frequent smaller meals.

Inzinger recommends the following meal schedule:

7:00 AM:	Breakfast 20 percent of the daily calories
9:00 AM:	First snack 10 percent of the daily calories
10:30 AM:	Second snack 5 percent of the daily calories
12:00 noon:	Lunch 20 percent of the daily calories
2:00 PM:	Third snack 10 percent of the daily calories
5:00 PM:	Fourth snack 5 percent of the daily calories
7:00 PM:	Dinner 20 percent of the daily calories
9:00 PM:	Late snack 10 percent of the daily calories

Preparation for Competition

Nutrition Rich in Carbohydrates

Ideally, every meal should consist mainly of those foods that are needed before and after different kinds of activities. For intellectually active people, protein is essential, whereas, for physically active people—and especially for athletes—carbohydrates are vital.

The total nutritional needs for a soccer player involved in competition and training can be broken down as follows:

- Carbohydrates   60 percent
- Fat   25 percent
- Protein   15 percent

In general, a player should consume one ounce of carbohydrates for every eight pounds (7 g for every kg) of body weight.

The amount of protein needs to be increased whenever a training schedule is heavy and after an injury. In order for the body to have the optimum amount of carbohydrates available at the time of a match, some nutritional scientists recommend "carbohydrate (carbo) loading."

- Two days before a game, eat food low in carbohydrates.
- The day before and the day of a game, eat carbohydrate-rich foods.

By reducing the intake of carbohydrates two days before a game, the body goes into carbohydrate deficit. The body adjusts with a kind of hyper-compensation reaction.

Carbohydrates are found in many different foods. The time it takes to convert carbohydrates (sugar metabolism) to energy differs for specific athletic performances and depends on the type of carbohydrates consumed. For example:

- Whole-wheat bread   60–240 minutes
- Fruits and vegetables   60–100 minutes
- Bread and baked goods   40–60 minutes
- Sweets and sweet drinks   15–40 minutes
- Glucose   10–20 minutes

It makes sense to adjust a player's food intake so that he will have a large supply of carbohydrates at the appropriate time. Approximately two hours before the game, the player should eat whole-wheat products. Later, small amounts of dry, baked goods should be consumed. Later still, the player needs something sweet to drink.

Importance of Vitamins

Vitamins are the catalysts that create energy through metabolism. According to Inzinger, an athlete's need for vitamins is three to four times as high as it is for normally active people. The following vitamins are of special importance:

- Vitamins A, B1, B2, B6, and B12.
- Vitamin C.
- Vitamin D.

High amounts of these vitamins can be found in:

- Whole-wheat products.
- Potatoes.
- Brown rice.
- Fresh fruit.
- Fresh vegetables.

White bread, white rice, and cooked fruits and vegetables have a much lower vitamin content.

Essential Minerals

Of the numerous minerals essential to the human body, the following are of particular importance for the athlete:

- Potassium.
- Sodium.
- Calcium.
- Magnesium.
- Iron.
- Iodine.

According to Max Inzinger, two-thirds of all athletes suffer from magnesium deficiency. Normal nutrition needs to be supplemented with magnesium. This is particularly important because our food contains only very small amounts of this essential mineral. During times of intense athletic activity, it is recommended that players also take potassium, iron, and iodine supplements.

Replacing Body Fluids

In the course of a hard-fought competition in high temperatures, a player can lose up to three quarts (3l) of fluid. This loss must be replaced quickly. Because essential minerals are also lost in increased perspiration, water alone is not sufficient.

It is essential to replace fluids and electrolytes during the game (at half-times), as well as after the game. It is important to use the proper fluids and to give them at the right time.

Proper Fluids

Proper fluids are those with the appropriate amounts of sugar and essential minerals. Very sweet fruit juices and sodas with a high sugar content are generally not recommended. Instead, use mineral water with a low sodium content and a high magnesium content.

Isotonic drinks may be used if the sodium content is low and the content of calcium, potassium, and magnesium is high.

Whenever players prepare their own drinks from mineral powder, they must follow the directions carefully. High doses of electrolytes can cause counter reactions and increased water loss. Actually, players can mix themselves a very good drink by combining fruit juices, tea, and mineral water.

Proper Intake of Liquids

The way the drink is taken is as important as the type of drink used:

- Immediately before, during, and after the game, it is essential that drinks be taken in small sips, not gulped. However, large quantities of liquid can be taken two hours before and after the game.
- Thirst should be quenched with warm or lukewarm drinks rather than very cold drinks. Cold drinks inhibit hunger because they remain in the stomach longer than warmer liquids. The result is that a player will not eat the quantity of food he needs after the game.
- Finally, there is nothing wrong with a glass of beer after the game. This can be taken with, or better yet, after a meal.

Motivation of the Player

The impact of motivation on the level of performance has already been discussed (in the chapter on tactical skills). A player who is overly motivated will be nervous and uptight. However, he can also be insufficiently motivated, which will lead to a lack of interest and a poor performance. Neither of these levels of motivation are conducive to good, competitive performances. In general, we distinguish between:

- Self-motivation.
- Motivation from the outside (the coach, teammates, friends, etc.).

How motivation influences performance becomes clear when we look at the process of motivation.

The Motivational Process

Human beings are motivated to action (and to athletic performance) for many different reasons:

- **Elementary** needs such as the desire to move, the need to play, the ambition to perform well, the need for recognition.
- **Individual** motives.

For human beings, motivation as an impulse usually develops over time through education and other external influences. One legitimate motivation in professional sports is the expectation of financial reward. Another, less effective factor is fear, which, sadly, often plays a large role. Fear can keep a player from attempting risky tackles and from diving for passes.

Many conflicting motives and needs influence a player's level of motivation. Sometimes, motives and needs are not apparent until external situations and conditions are favorable. A player may be unaware of some of his motives, or he may not know

the reasons for them and need to do some work in order to understand them. At times, the coach or his teammates may have to assist him with this.

For instance, a coach might have to curb a new player's overly aggressive actions on the field. The new player might be trying to win a permanent position on the team. During the same game, it might be necessary for the coach to push an older player, who has been with the team for a long time and has lost some of his motivation.

Accordingly the process of motivation can de defined as follows:

> A player's motives and needs as incentives for action are made conscious and expressed, and then guided to bring them into harmony with the demands of a given day.

Performance-enhancing Motives and Needs

The following are motives and needs that can positively influence the level of performance in sports:

Needs

- To be active and moving.
- To expend excess energy.
- To obtain self-fulfillment.
- To dissipate aggressive tendencies.
- To enjoy the play instinct.
- To be active.
- To take risks.
- To use the hunting instinct.
- To satisfy curiosity.
- To take advantage of the adventure instinct.

Preparation for Competition

Motives

- Ambition.
- Outside recognition.
- Love of performing in front of an audience.
- To gain social standing.
- Sociability.
- To conquer a lack of self-confidence.
- Love of travel.

Overall, motives and needs are guided by two basic factors:

- The hope of success.
- The fear of failure.

Experience has shown that soccer players are more motivated by their hope for success than by their fear of failure. The anticipation of a win, the celebration that usually follows, and the possibility of the team's moving up in the standings is a better basis for motivating players than pointing out the consequences of failure.

Setting Attractive Goals

The effect of motivation on players depends to a great degree on how attractive the goal is. It is not easy to motivate players when the only result of winning a game is that the team moves one point closer to the team ahead of them. A significant jump in the standings, however, provides a much greater spike in the level of motivation. Furthermore, a coach can influence his players by his own attitude and by the way he values the outcome of the team's efforts. If necessary, the coach must adjust his presentation of the goal in order to maximize its motivational impact on individual players and the team. To reach the desired goal, he might use a number of approaches: "A tie is OK"; or "Only a big win can be considered a success"; or "Let's treat the fans to a beautiful game."

Interim Stages of Motivation

An essential aspect of motivation is the chance players have of achieving a desired goal. Keep in mind, though, that objectives that seem too easy or too difficult to accomplish are often approached with either overconfidence and carelessness or with hesitancy and too little confidence. Experience has shown that dividing a goal into several sub-goals works the best.

It is the responsibility of the coach to state a goal in such a way that the players come to believe (without becoming arrogant) that they have a chance to be successful. In his efforts to define a particular sub-goal, the coach must be careful not to lose credibility. Players are sensitive and easily able to detect oversimplification and exaggeration. Motivation using either of these tactics will fall on deaf ears. Clearly, it is not a simple thing to motivate a team. Any such attempt must consider each player's individual level of motivation and the actual demands being made on the player and the team as a whole.

Mental Training

In the beginning, we talked about the importance of self-motivation as a stimulus for a player's performance.

Mental training is important for self-motivation. Visualization techniques can be very helpful. For this kind of training, a player must relax himself psychologically and physically. This relaxed state allows him to be receptive to self-generated or outside affirmations ("You *are* successful") and to visual images (seeing himself dribbling successfully or going through the motions of a perfect combination play). We know, for instance, that Paul Breitner uses this technique to prepare himself mentally for an important game. The necessary state of relaxation can be achieved only in a calm, quiet atmosphere. In such a state, a player is able to:

- Run through technical and tactical tasks.
- Devise special strategies for handling a particular opponent.
- Reduce imagined fears.
- Develop self-confidence through self-hypnosis.

Surely, mental training is not for every player, and not only because life in the locker room is so hectic. Most players are not open to such subtle techniques.

They lack the knowledge and the ability to reach the necessary state of relaxation through mental training or other new forms of active self-influence. For those players who are interested, however, and for those who find it difficult to prepare themselves psychologically for a game, mental training is highly recommended. The coach may want to seek the advice of a sports psychologist in this.

Warm-up and Cool-down

Overcoming Pre-game Stress

Soccer has its share of "World Champion Training" teams that fall apart under the pressure of competition. But aside from those instances, many experienced players suffer pre-game stress before important games. Their stress is usually caused by fear of failure, which can be hard to put into words. Occasionally, a player has very legitimate worries, such as fearing an opponent who is well known for his toughness, or concerns about re-injuring himself. Other stress is often caused by an exaggerated expectation on the part of fans, created by the media. Many other factors can contribute to the level of stress, such as a strange environment, particularly ecstatic fans, extreme weather conditions, etc.

The effects of stress are as different as they are numerous. They range from physiological changes that can be measured objectively, such as changes in pulse rate, reaction time, and muscle tone, to psychological effects, such as changes in personal habits. It is common to see an increase in the level of adrenaline during periods of stress. Although adrenaline is necessary for high levels of psychological and physical performance, it will actually decrease the level of performance if the body releases too much of it.

What can a coach and his players do to maintain the proper level of adrenaline? Psychologists recommend special relaxation methods, such as self-hypnosis, progressive muscle relaxation, and biofeedback. However, for soccer, these methods have not been very effective.

The following methods have proven more successful:
- Providing players with objective information about the opposing team and their specific opponent.
- Giving each player precise and clear instructions about the tactical tasks for which he is responsible.
- Explaining the risks a player is expected to take and informing him about what support he can expect.
- Creating a realistic understanding of the demands upon the players that might be distorted by outside influences.
- Appealing to teamwork ("One for all and all for one").
- Assigning the tasks that lie ahead for every player.
- Decreasing fears an individual player might have.
- Providing adequate time for extensive warm-up training.

Warm-up and Cool-down

The warm-up takes place immediately before a game; the cool-down, immediately after. Both measures are of vital importance for activating high levels of performance. There are several aspects to warming up:
- Mental warm-ups (see above).
- Passive warm-ups (i.e., with warm bath and massage).
- Active warm-ups of the body for physical activity.
  We will discuss only the last.

Importance of Warm-up Training

Before starting to train or exercise, and before every game, a player should go through a purposeful, systematic warm-up. The importance of this is widely acknowledged. A warm-up is the best prevention against injuries and it maximizes the effect of training and the success of performance during a game. Unfortunately, this is still not taken seriously enough by many players. All too often, the result is a micro-injury— small tears in the muscle fibers, often imperceptible at the time. Over the span of weeks and months, these small injuries can add up to serious muscle damage.

A systematic warm-up routine that slowly increases in intensity will warm up the muscles by about 4 degrees Fahrenheit (2 degrees Celsius) and increase flexibility by 20 percent. This considerably reduces the chance of injury and speeds up reaction time. Furthermore, stress can impede the protective mechanisms of the muscle system. In competition, a player must be ready to deliver 100 percent in terms of energy and speed from the very outset. For all these reasons, a proper warm-up is imperative.

For the reasons above, the value of a good warm-up cannot be overstated. Other of its many benefits include the following:

- A proper warm-up allows the circulatory system slowly and safely to prepare the body for the increase in physical stress load that lies ahead. The process is similar to warming up the engine before taking a car on the road.

Preparation for Competition

- Metabolic processes essential for high levels of physical activity are slowly primed, making energy available by means of an increased metabolic rate, delaying the letdown, and saving important carbohydrate reserves for the extra energy required at the end of a game.
- It reduces excess adrenaline, which in turn decreases pre-game jitters (see above).
- A good warm-up routine, including stretching exercises, relieves tightness in muscles (from a previous training session or following a long trip to the stadium).
- Work with the ball increases ball-handling and soccer-specific technical agility. This is especially important for young and amateur players, who usually train only twice a week. Every player knows the importance of the first pass in a game. This makes good ball handling all the more crucial in the first few minutes of a game.
- During the warm-up, a player has the chance to get to know the field of play. This is immeasurably important in "away" games. Players get a feel for the unfamiliar stadium or field and its individual character.
- Soccer is a team sport and warm-up training as a group promotes the players' sense of belonging, of being part of a team.

Structure of Warm-up Training

Depending on the players' age and level of training, and the outside temperature, a warm-up period should last at least 15 to 30 minutes. The better the level of training, the older the players, and the lower the temperature, the longer the warm-up should be. It goes without saying that systematic warm-up before a game should not be suspended, even when the outside temperature is high.

A well-planned warm-up routine should incorporate the following basic elements:
- Five to ten minutes of slow jogging.
- Five to ten minutes of passive stretching.
- Five minutes of work with the ball, going over all the important techniques.
- Two minutes of 100-foot (30-m) runs, steadily increasing in speed until the maximum is reached.
- Five minutes of work with the ball, practicing position-specific techniques.
- Approximately 10 short sprints, stops, and changes of direction, all with maximum speed.

After the warm-up, every player should show visible signs of perspiration. Often players will change their shirts before going on the field. This is a good time for the coach to say a few words of encouragement.

Importance of Cool-down

It was West Germany's Sepp Herberger who said, "After the game equals before the game." In other words, what is proper to do before a game is also proper after a game. Although he was referring at the time more to the inner, mental attitude of the players, this idea is equally valid for the physical aspect. So today's player has the additional task after the game to go through a cool-down.

Track and field athletes, whose success depends entirely on their individual personal fitness and not on the performance of teammates, have long understood the importance of cooling down. For these athletes, the warm-up and the cool-down usually take much longer than the actual competition. Many performance-oriented soccer teams have also come by now to understand the value of a good cool-down period. They do not wait until the next training day. Instead, they include a 15-minute cool-down period in their overall program. This may involve warm baths, massages, and an actual recuperation program.

The same basic program is important for young players and amateur teams. They should schedule a cool-down period after every game, particularly during a championship series. Players who have a cool-down period will be in much better shape for the next game than will opponents who do not.

What is the rationale, and what are the positive effects of such a cool-down? And what form should it take? Uric acid measurements have shown that the level of fatigue the day after a game is much lower for players who have undergone a cool-down period following the game. This follow-up exercise increases the amount of uric acid released by the body. Uric acid is a by-product of metabolism, accumulating in the body as a result of physical activity. It is a measure of the body's level of fatigue and of the time needed for recuperation.

Structure of a Cool-down Program

- Time — At least 10 to 15 minutes
- Tempo — Slow jog
- Pulse rate — Approximately 130 beats per minute

Additionally, a warm bath and a massage can be helpful. Running should be followed by loosening and stretching exercises.

> ### *Closing Wishes from the Author*
>
> The discussion of the cooling down concept has brought us full circle. After studying the information contained between the covers of this book, it is up to you to transfer all your newfound knowledge to your daily training sessions.
>
> I hope you have great fun, but more than that, even greater success!
>
> Yours!
> Gerhard Bauer

Index

Index

Index

Acknowledgments

To Lynn—thank you for your friendship; professional collaboration; insights about mathematics teaching, learning, and assessing; and support.

—Diane J. Briars

To Chérie, the greatest teacher I have ever known: thanks for your support.

—David Foster

To my loving, unconditionally supportive David, who always encourages me to stretch and grow.

—Mardi A. Gale

My heartfelt thanks to Diane, Harold, David, and Mardi for their dedicated, creative, and tireless effort to turn the idea of this book into a collaborative reality. They are each champions for the cause of improving 6–8 mathematics education as a major aspect of their life's work.

Special thanks to Solution Tree—Jeff, Douglas, Lesley, Joan, and Sarah—for their time, tireless effort, commitment, and belief in the importance of this work for the mathematics community.

Sincere thanks to the National Council of Teachers of Mathematics and the Educational Materials Committee for their support of this series and their leadership in the mathematics education of teachers and students.

Finally, thanks to all of the authors and reviewers for this series. Many of their great ideas surface across the books and serve to bring coherence to the Common Core mathematics message.

—Timothy D. Kanold

Solution Tree Press would like to thank the following reviewers:

Scott Adamson
Professor, Mathematics Division
Chandler-Gilbert Community College
Chandler, Arizona

Laurie Boswell
Head of School and Grades 6–8
Mathematics Teacher
The Riverside School
Lyndonville, Vermont

Laura Godfrey
Instruction Resource Teacher of
Mathematics
Madison Metropolitan School District
Madison, Wisconsin

Eric P. Johnson
Director of K–12 Mathematics and
Instructional Technology
Clark County School District
Las Vegas, Nevada

Jessica McIntyre
Principal
Aptakisic Junior High School
Buffalo Grove, Illinois

Gretchen Muller
Mathematics Professional Expert
Alameda County Office of Education
Hayward, California

Kit Norris
Lead Consultant
E²-PLC Consulting Group
Southborough, Massachusetts

Sarah Schuhl
PLC Associate and Mathematics
Instructional Coach
Gresham, Oregon

Visit **go.solution-tree.com/commoncore** to download the
reproducibles in this book.

Table of Contents

About the Series Editor

Timothy D. Kanold, PhD, is a mathematics educator, author, and consultant. He is former director of mathematics and science and superintendent of Adlai E. Stevenson High School District 125, a model professional learning community district in Lincolnshire, Illinois.

Dr. Kanold is committed to equity and excellence for students, faculty, and school administrators. He conducts highly motivational professional development leadership seminars worldwide with a focus on turning school vision into realized action that creates greater equity for students through the effective delivery of professional learning communities for faculty and administrators.

He is a past president of the National Council of Supervisors of Mathematics and coauthor of several best-selling mathematics textbooks over several decades. He has served on writing commissions for the National Council of Teachers of Mathematics. He has authored numerous articles and chapters on school mathematics, leadership, and development for education publications.

In 2010, Dr. Kanold received the prestigious international Damen Award for outstanding contributions to the leadership field of education from Loyola University Chicago. He also received the Outstanding Administrator Award from the Illinois State Board of Education in 1994 and the Presidential Award for Excellence in Mathematics and Science Teaching in 1986. He now serves as an adjunct faculty member for the graduate school at Loyola University Chicago.

Dr. Kanold earned a bachelor's degree in education and a master's degree in mathematics from Illinois State University. He completed a master's in educational administration at the University of Illinois and received a doctorate in educational leadership and counseling psychology from Loyola University Chicago.

To learn more about Dr. Kanold's work, visit his blog Turning Vision Into Action at http://tkanold.blogspot.com, or follow @tkanold on Twitter.

To book Dr. Kanold for professional development, contact pd@solution-tree.com.

About the Authors

Diane J. Briars, PhD, is a mathematics education consultant and is the senior developer and research associate for the Algebra Intensification Project, a National Science Foundation–supported design-based research project to support underprepared algebra students. Previously, she served for twenty years as mathematics director for the Pittsburgh Public Schools. Under her leadership, Pittsburgh schools made significant progress in increasing student achievement through standards-based curricula, instruction, and assessment. Dr. Briars was a member of the writing team for the *Curriculum and Evaluation Standards* and the *Assessment Standards for School Mathematics*.

Dr. Briars is also involved in national initiatives in mathematics education. She has served as a member of many committees, including the National Commission on Mathematics and Science Teaching for the 21st Century headed by Senator John Glenn. She is a former president of the National Council of Supervisors of Mathematics and board member for the National Council of Teachers of Mathematics, and she has served in leadership roles for other organizations, including the College Board. She earned a PhD in mathematics education and her master's and bachelor's degrees in mathematics from Northwestern University, and she did postdoctoral study in the psychology department of Carnegie-Mellon University. She began her career as a secondary mathematics teacher.

Harold Asturias, PhD, served as the director of the New Standards Portfolio Assessment Project and the Mathematics Unit for New Standards—a project to develop national standards and assessments. In that capacity, he was part of a team of experts whose efforts, involving many states and over a thousand teachers, resulted in the successful production of two assessment systems: the New Standards Portfolio and the Reference Examination. In addition, he was part of the team that produced the New Standards Performance Standards and was a member of the writing group for the National Council of Teachers of Mathematics (NCTM) Assessment Standards for School Mathematics. Asturias has also served on the board of TODOS: Mathematics for ALL, an NCTM affiliate whose mission is to advocate for an equitable and high quality mathematics education for all students—in particular, Hispanic/Latino students. At the state level, he has served as president of the California Mathematics Council.

Asturias earned a professional medical doctor degree and surgeon degree from the Universidad de San Carlos de Guatemala in Central America and a degree in elementary teacher credentials with emphasis on bilingual education, Spanish, from the California State University School of Education in Los Angeles.

David Foster is the executive director of the Silicon Valley Mathematics Initiative (SVMI) comprised of seventy-six member districts in the greater San Francisco Bay Area. Besides the intensive work in California, SVMI consults across the country, including New York, Illinois, Massachusetts, Ohio, Tennessee, and Georgia. SVMI is affiliated with programs at University of California, Berkeley, Stanford University, and San Jose State University. Foster established SVMI in 1996 working as mathematics director for the Robert N. Noyce Foundation. He has consulted with the Partnership for Assessment of Readiness for College and Careers and develops exemplars for the Smarter Balanced Assessment Consortium. He was a regional director for the Middle Grade Mathematics Renaissance of the California State Systemic Initiative and also taught mathematics and computer science at middle school, high school, and community college for eighteen years. He works part time for San Jose State University and is codirector of the Santa Clara Valley Mathematics Project. He is also co-chair of the advisory committee of the Mathematics Assessment Resource Service/Balanced Assessment and is a consultant to the Urban Mathematics Leadership Network that works with the twenty-five largest school districts in the United States. Foster is the primary author of *Interactive Mathematics: Activities and Investigations*.

Mardi A. Gale is a senior research associate at WestEd and has been involved in public education as either a teacher or a professional development facilitator for over thirty years. She was one of the original seven regional directors for the state of California for the Mathematics Renaissance K–12 program, an initiative funded by the National Science Foundation. In this capacity, she worked with vertical slices (K–12) of schools in developing a coherent, articulated mathematics program across elementary and secondary grades. After having taught in classrooms of all levels and serving as Beverly Hills Unified School District's mathematics specialist and a mentor teacher, Gale also worked as a consultant and staff developer for the Los Angeles County Office of Education. Gale has participated in many facets of cutting-edge assessment, both in California and nationally. In addition, she has written mathematics curriculum appropriate for middle school. Presently Gale is a primary curriculum developer for WestEd's Algebraic Interventions for Measured Achievement and is the director of professional development for the project. In addition, she is a senior staff member on the Institute of Education Sciences–funded project Making Middle School Mathematics Accessible to ALL Students, and she is responsible for facilitating piloting and professional development. Gale is also a coauthor of the source book, *Making Mathematics Accessible to English Learners: A Guidebook for Teachers.*

To book Diane J. Briars, Harold Asturias, David Foster, or Mardi A. Gale for professional development, contact pd@solution-tree.com.

Foreword

In *Common Core Mathematics in a PLC at Work™, Grades 6–8*, series editor Tim Kanold and authors Diane J. Briars, Harold Asturias, David Foster, and Mardi A. Gale provide the information and tools necessary to move educators from Common Core State Standards (CCSS) awareness to implementation—from *knowing* to *doing*. As this book advises, the best way to move this implementation effort forward is through the Professional Learning Communities at Work™ (PLC) model, in which teachers share their craft, knowledge, and wisdom; create new and more equitable learning experiences for students; and learn together how to meet the challenges of implementing the CCSS expectations for middle school students.

PLCs offer an approach to mathematics professional development that runs contrary to what many middle school math teachers have experienced. I know PLCs offer something very different than what I experienced as a middle school math teacher in the early 1980s. I worked in complete isolation from my other eight colleagues except for the one glorious day of collegial staff development we shared each year, only to return to our classrooms for the following 180 days of isolated instruction. Of course, we now know that effective staff development is embedded within the day-to-day practices of teaching and learning, and that adult learning is best sustained when it is facilitated through thirty to one hundred hours of collaborative time with colleagues in a six- to twelve-month period (Darling-Hammond, Wei, Andree, Richardson, & Orphanos, 2009). This support is precisely what PLCs offer when done well, as in the PLC at Work model.

PLCs also help teacher teams address one of the most critical issues surrounding middle school mathematics instruction—equity. Ensuring that *all* students have the opportunities and the timely support needed to achieve at high levels is an ongoing challenge of middle school teachers in general and of middle school math teachers in particular. Equity is achieved when teachers, through their collaborative efforts, have similar expectations for all students and work together to see that *all* students are successful. They develop a sense of collective responsibility for all students and move away from the ideology of "my room, my kids." This book paints a vivid picture of that kind of powerful collaboration and provides both the information and tools needed to help teams make the *learning for all* mantra a reality rather than a clichéd chant.

I join many of my highly esteemed colleagues who have already pointed out that, while the CCSS are a step in the right direction, the simple act of adopting a new curriculum will not, on its own, improve student learning or provide the kind of equity schools desire. Over my forty years in education, I have noticed a strong tendency on the part of U.S. educators to look for that one silver-bullet solution to the challenge of providing high levels of achievement for all students. I was often amused in California by how much attention was focused on the selection of the "right" reading series; as if we could help all students learn to read if we only selected the right books. I see some of this thinking finding its way into the conversations surrounding CCSS. Do we really believe that if we simply adopt the "right" set of standards that all students will learn at high levels?

Fortunately, this book makes an extremely valuable contribution toward this point by framing the discussion of CCSS around first- and second-order change. Goodman (1995) discusses *change without difference*, and identifies top-down, technical responses as first-order changes. These include, but are not limited to: changes in school and administrative structures, bell schedules, and class sizes. Over the years, teachers have been trained in a plethora of specific instructional strategies, such as writing standards or learning targets on the board, managing cooperative learning groups, and asking higher-order thinking questions—all are well intended, but are random acts of improvement. These efforts are usually met with teacher skepticism, subversion, and questions like "Why are we doing this?" As Fouts (2003) notes:

> There is evidence that one of the reasons schools remain unchanged is that the reforms or changes have been superficial in nature and/or arbitrary in their adoption. Teachers and schools often went through the motions of adopting the new practices, but the changes were neither deep nor long-lasting. In other words, the outward manifestations of the changes were present, but the ideas or philosophy behind the changes were either not understood, misunderstood, or rejected. Consequently, any substantive change in the classroom experience or school culture failed to take root. The illusion of change is created through a variety of activities, but the qualitative experience for students in the classroom remains unchanged when the ideas driving daily practice remain unchanged. (p. 12)

So, the question is simply this: will the CCSS be implemented as first-order change and, thus, end up on the pyre of well-intended attempts to improve learning for all students? This book, indeed this series of books, provides a compelling case to move forward with CCSS as not simply a new set of standards, but as the kind of second-order change that will be required in order for this educational reform to be accomplished and sustained over the long term.

—Austin Buffum

References

Darling-Hammond, L., Wei, R. C., Andree, A., Richardson, N., & Orphanos, S. (2009). *Professional learning in the learning profession: A status report on teacher development in the United States and abroad.* Dallas, TX: National Staff Development Council.

Fouts, J. T. (2003). *A decade of reform: A summary of research findings on classroom, school, and district effectiveness in Washington State.* Seattle: Washington School Research Center, Seattle Pacific University.

Goodman, J. (1995). Change without difference: School restructuring in historical perspective. *Harvard Educational Review, 2,* 1–5.

Introduction

These Standards are not intended to be new names for old ways of doing business. They are a call to take the next step. It is time for states to work together to build on lessons learned from two decades of standards based reforms. It is time to recognize that standards are not just promises to our children, but promises we intend to keep.

—National Governors Association Center for Best Practices (NGA) & Council of Chief State School Officers (CCSSO)

One of the greatest equity considerations for mathematics instruction, and instruction in general in most school districts, is that it is too inconsistent from classroom to classroom, school to school, and district to district (Morris & Hiebert, 2011). Often, equity and achievement gaps are thought of only in terms of differential performance of different racial, ethnic, or gender groups. However, equity is much more than that. At its core, in a professional learning community, equity is ensuring that all students have the opportunity to learn mathematics at a high level and to access the subsequent support needed to ensure success in that learning.

How much mathematics a middle school student in the United States learns, and how deeply he or she learns it, is largely determined by the school the student attends and, even more significantly, the teacher to whom the student is randomly (usually) assigned within that school. Hill, Rowan, and Ball (2005) indicate there is a variability of 15 percent in teaching from classroom to classroom in the same school. The inconsistencies middle school teachers develop in their professional development practice—often random and in isolation from other teachers—create great inequities in students' mathematics instructional and assessment learning experiences that ultimately and significantly contribute to the year-by-year achievement gap in your school (Ferrini-Mundy, Graham, Johnson, & Mills, 1998). This issue is especially true in a vertically connected curriculum like mathematics.

The hope and promise of *Common Core Mathematics in a PLC at Work™, Grades 6–8* is to provide the guidance and teacher focus needed to continue work outside of existing paradigms regarding mathematics teaching and learning. The resources in this book will enable you to focus your time and energy on issues and actions that will lead to addressing the Common Core State Standards (CCSS) for mathematics challenge: *All students successfully learning rigorous standards for college- or career-preparatory mathematics.*

And it is not easy. As a middle school grades 6–8 teacher you have perhaps the most difficult job at moving student learning in mathematics forward, but you can do it. This book is designed to provide you with the ongoing professional development focus necessary to do so with confidence.

Most of what you will read and use in this book, as well as this series, has been part of the national discussion on mathematics reform and improvement since the National Council of Teachers of Mathematics (NCTM) release of the *Curriculum and Evaluation Standards for School Mathematics* in 1989. In 2000, NCTM refocused the U.S. vision for K–12 mathematics teaching, learning, and assessing in the *Principles and Standards for School Mathematics* (PSSM) and the National Research Council (NRC) followed by providing supportive research in the groundbreaking book *Adding It Up* (NRC, 2001). NCTM (2006) followed with *Curriculum Focal Points for Prekindergarten through Grade 8 Mathematics: A Quest for Coherence.* (See appendix E at **go.solution-tree.com /commoncore** for a full description of changes in mathematics standards from 1989 to 2012.)

Your ability to fully implement previous mathematics teaching and learning frameworks and standards was limited by the very system of states' standards and their corresponding *assessments* that caused resistance to teaching the deeper, richer mathematics curriculum described in national and state standards documents. This resistance was due in part to the assessment of state standards. Even when states' standards included higher expectations, such as problem solving and reasoning, state testing typically reflected only the lower-cognitive procedural knowledge aspects of the states' standards. In many school districts, it often felt like a race to get through the grade-level or course curriculum before April of each school year as the *wytiwyg* phenomenon—what you test is what you get—kicked in.

For the most part, therefore, significant improvement in student learning of middle school mathematics has been *happenstance*. If a student happened to attend the right school with the right conditions, with the right teacher, with the right program, and with the right processes for learning mathematics in place, then he or she might have a chance for a great mathematics learning experience.

Since 1989, mathematics teaching and learning in the United States have been mostly characterized by *pockets of excellence* that reflect the national recommendations for improved student learning in mathematics. The lack of coherent and sustained change toward effective practice has been partially caused by a general attempt to make only modest changes to existing practices. In this context, professional development opportunities were often limited or, in some cases, nonexistent. This situation is defined as *first-order change*—change that produces marginal disturbance to existing knowledge, skills, and practices favored by faculty and school leaders who are closest to the action.

The CCSS expectations for teaching and learning and the new consortia assessments usher in an opportunity for unprecedented *second-order change*. In contrast to first-order change, second-order change requires working outside the existing system by embracing new paradigms for how you think and practice (Waters, Marzano, & McNulty, 2003). Furthermore, the Education Trust (Ushomirsky & Hall, 2010), in *Stuck Schools*:

A Framework for Identifying Schools Where Students Need Change—Now, indicates that in an environment where funds and capacity are limited at best, educators and policymakers need to establish clear priorities. The CCSS will be your catalyst for providing the support you need, as a middle school teacher or teacher leader, to effect real change in a meaningful way.

In this book for middle school teachers and teacher leaders, the five chapters focus on five fundamental areas required to prepare every teacher for successful implementation of CCSS for mathematics leading to the general improvement of teaching and learning for all students. These areas provide the framework within which second-order change for improved student achievement can be successfully achieved. The five critical areas are the following.

1. **Collaboration:** The CCSS require a shift in the grain size of change beyond the individual isolated teacher or leader. It is the grade-level or course-based collaborative learning team (collaborative team), within a Professional Learning Community (PLC) at Work culture that will develop your expanded knowledge capacity necessary to bring coherence to the implementation of the CCSS for mathematics. The grain size of change now lies within the power and the voice of your horizontal or vertical collaborative team driving the PLC process in your middle school. Chapter 1 describes how to become part of a high-performing collaborative team.

2. **Instruction:** The CCSS require a shift to daily lesson designs that include plans for the Standards for Mathematical Practice that focus on the process of learning and developing deep understanding of the content standards. This change requires teaching for procedural fluency *and* student understanding of the grade-level Common Core standards. One should not exist without the other. This will require your collaborative team commitment to the use of student-engaged learning around common high-cognitive-demand mathematical tasks in every classroom as part of every unit or chapter. Incorporating the CCSS Mathematical Practices into your daily instruction and unit design is the focus of chapter 2.

3. **Content:** The CCSS require a content shift to less (fewer standards) is more (deeper rigor with understanding) at each grade level. This emphasis will require new levels of knowledge and skill development for every mathematics teacher to understand what the CCSS expect students to learn at each grade level or within each course, blended with how students are expected to learn it. What are the mathematical knowledge, skills, understandings, and habits of mind that should be the result of each unit of mathematics instruction? A middle school mathematics program committed to helping all students learn ensures greater clarity and low teacher-to-teacher variance on the questions, What should students learn? How should they learn it? These questions, related to the mathematics content domains and content standard clusters, are addressed in chapter 3.

4. **Assessment:** The CCSS require a shift to assessments that are a *means* within the teaching-assessing-learning cycle and not used as an *end* to that cycle on a unit-by-unit basis. Assessments must reflect the rigor of the standards and model the expectations for and benefits of formative assessment practices around all forms of assessment, including traditional instruments, such as tests and quizzes. *How will you know* if each student is learning the essential mathematics skills, concepts, understandings, and dispositions the CCSS deem most essential? *How will you know* if your students are prepared for the rigorous assessments from the two assessment consortia: Partnership for Assessment of Readiness for College and Careers (PARCC) and the SMARTER Balanced Assessment Consortium (SBAC)? The development and use of in-class formative assessment processes and the formative use of high-quality summative assessment instruments are described in chapter 4.

5. **Intervention:** The CCSS require a shift in your team and school response to intervention (RTI). Much like the CCSS vision for teaching and learning, RTI can no longer be invitational. That is, the response to intervention becomes R^2TI—a required response to intervention. Stakeholder implementation of RTI programs includes a process that *requires* students to participate and attend. How will you *respond* and act on evidence (or lack of evidence) of student learning? You'll find answers to the deep challenges of RTI in chapter 5.

Moving beyond familiar practices—second-order change—is never easy. It will require your willingness to break away (or to help a fellow teacher break away) from the past practice of teaching one-standard-a-day mathematics lessons with low-cognitive demand. This change will require all teachers to depart from a past practice that provided few student opportunities for exploring, understanding, and actively engaging and one that used assessment instruments that may or may not have honored a fidelity to accurate and timely formative feedback. Now every teacher will be required to embrace these new paradigms to meet the expectations of the CCSS for mathematics in grades 6–8.

Based on a solid foundation in mathematics education research, *Common Core Mathematics in a PLC at Work, Grades 6–8* is designed to support teachers and all those involved in delivering meaningful mathematics instruction and assessment within these five second-order change areas. It is our hope that the suggestions in these chapters will focus your work on actions that really matter for you and your students. Above all, as you do your work *together* and strive to achieve the PLC at Work school culture through your well-designed grade-level, course-level, or vertical collaborative learning teams, your collective teacher voice, knowledge capacity, and motivation will grow and flourish.

Each chapter's Extending My Understanding section has resources and tools you can use in collaborative teams to make sense of and reflect on the chapter recommendations. As a collaborative team, you can make *great decisions* about teaching, learning, and assessing and how your response to learning will impact student mathematics achievement. As Jim Collins and Morten T. Hansen (2011) indicate in *Great by Choice*, you may not be able to predict the future, but you and your team can create it. Our professional development goal is to help every teacher and teacher leader make great decisions toward a great mathematics future for students—every day.

CHAPTER 1

Using High-Performing Collaborative Teams for Mathematics

The Common Core State Standards provide a consistent, clear under-standing of what students are expected to learn, so that teachers and parents know what they need to do to help them learn. The standards are designed to be robust and relevant to the real world, reflecting the knowledge and skills that our young people need for success in college and careers. With American students fully prepared for the future, our communities will be best positioned to compete successfully in the global economy.

—NGA & CCSSO

Students arrive at middle school with many challenges, and grades 6–8 teachers are expected to ensure all students achieve proficiency in the rigorous Standards for mathematics content as well as the Standards for Mathematical Practice described in the CCSS. How can you successfully help your middle school students achieve these expectations?

One of the characteristics of high-performing and high-impact schools that are successfully closing achievement gaps is their focus on teacher collaboration as a key to improving instruction and reaching all students (Education Trust, 2005; Kersaint, 2007). A collaborative culture is one of the best ways for teachers to acquire both the instructional knowledge and skills required to meet this challenge, as well as the energy and support necessary to reach all students (Leithwood & Seashore Louis, 1998). Seeley (2009) characterizes this challenge by noting, "Alone we can accomplish great things. . . . But together, with creativity, wisdom, energy, and, most of all commitment, there is no end to what we might do" (pp. 225–226).

A core premise of this book is that *professional learning communities* provide the best collaborative environment necessary for you to share your creativity and wisdom, create more equitable learning experiences for all grade-level students, and harness the energy and persistence necessary to meet your students' needs, as well as the challenges of understanding and implementing of the CCSS expectations for grades 6–8.

Research affirms the value of your collaboration with others and its positive impact on student achievement (Learning Forward, 2011). Many professional organizations include teacher collaboration as an essential part of professional growth and responsibility (Learning Forward, 2011; National Board of Professional Teaching Standards, 2010;

National Council of Supervisors of Mathematics, 2007). Whether you are a veteran or novice mathematics teacher, your participation in a collaborative team benefits student learning.

Just as students in groups need direction and support to work together well, middle school teachers in collaborative teams also need direction and support to effectively collaborate. This chapter defines and details how to operate successfully as you make the paradigm shift from working as an individual in relative isolation to working within a highly effective collaborative team. Whether you are part of a new team, or a veteran team with deep experience in the PLC process, this chapter enables you to identify the current stage of your collaboration and the types of work and discussions in those stages and provides several critical collaborative protocols through which you can measure your team's continued progress.

Professional Development Paradigm Shift

The Common Core State Standards for mathematics (NGA & CCSSO, 2010a) are a significant advance over previous mathematics standards in terms of their requirements for students, teachers, and organization and structure and their treatment of particular mathematical content. These advances include:

- Emphasis on developing students' conceptual understanding as well as procedural skills

- Fewer topics taught with greater depth at each grade level, providing more focus and coherence within and across the grades

- Increased rigor of content and assessment of content knowledge combined with increased emphasis on applications

- Focus on the progression of standards across grades, reflecting, to the extent possible, how students learn necessary content

- Inclusion of habits of mind—the Standards for Mathematical Practice—that students are to develop in addition to content expectations

As described in chapters 2, 3, and 4, implementing the CCSS in grades 6–8 will require reasonable but significant changes in your mathematics curriculum, instruction, and assessment. To successfully meet those changes, you will need to be engaged in significant, ongoing professional learning with your colleagues.

The fundamental purpose of professional development is the continuous improvement of professional practice (Corcoran, Shields, & Zucker, 1998). Typically, professional development consists of events—experts lead one-day presentations, courses, conferences, or webinars—that you might engage in periodically. While such events can be valuable and instructive, especially as ways to gain initial understanding of the CCSS, they are far from sufficient to support ongoing reflection about and changes in your instruction and assessment.

What is needed is ongoing, sustained professional learning with colleagues—that is, engaging colleagues in a collaborative learning team as part of a larger professional learning community. Linda Darling-Hammond (2010) summarizes effective professional development, as follows:

> Effective professional development is sustained, ongoing, content-focused, and embedded in professional learning communities where teachers work over time on problems of practice with other teachers in their subject area or school. Furthermore, it focuses on concrete tasks of teaching, assessment, observation, and reflection, looking at how students learn specific content in particular contexts. . . . It is often useful for teachers to be put in the position of studying the very material that they intend to teach to their own students. (pp. 226–227)

In other words, effective mathematics professional development is in many ways the opposite of much of the professional development that you might experience—it is sustained and embedded within professional learning communities and focused on the actual tasks of teaching using the materials teachers use with students. What is meant by *sustained*? It means *effective professional development*—programs that have demonstrated positive and significant effects on student achievement with between thirty and one hundred hours of contact time for teacher collaboration over the course of six to twelve months (Darling-Hammond, Wei, Andree, Richardson, & Orphanos, 2009; Garet et al., 2010). This high-quality professional development often involves collaborative teacher study in a structured way of the very curriculum that is being taught as well as students' acquisition of that curriculum. Embedded in your instructional practice at the lesson level, this approach ultimately leads to your deeper understanding and thus wider adoption of the curricular and instructional innovations sought (Cohen & Hill, 2001; Hiebert, Gallimore, & Stigler, 2002; Penuel, Fishman, Yamaguchi, & Gallagher, 2007; Wayne, Yoon, Zhu, Cronen, & Garet, 2008). These are precisely the components that must be included in professional development efforts for middle school mathematics teachers to enable them to meet successfully the implementation challenges of the CCSS.

Your collaborative effort is part of the necessary professional development paradigm shift required to effectively address *equity*, a critical aspect of middle school mathematics instruction. Equity—ensuring that all students have the opportunities and supports they need to achieve at high levels—is one of your greatest challenges as a grades 6–8 teacher. Too often, grades 6–8 teachers work as independent contractors, developing lesson plans, assessments, and intervention strategies alone, without consultation with colleagues. This lack of collaborative effort creates inequities in students' mathematics instructional experiences and is a contributing factor to achievement gaps. Equity is mostly about consistency in providing high-quality learning opportunities across classrooms. In order to improve mathematics education within schools across the United States, this inconsistency in quality of instruction due to teacher isolation must be overcome (Kanold, 2006). How can this be done? By engaging in a collaborative learning team as the engine that drives the professional learning community process in your school, middle school mathematics teachers can strive to overcome disparities in student achievement. Your collaborative teams provide the supportive environment necessary to share your creativity and wisdom and to harness the energy and persistence necessary to meet the demands of students' needs and the challenges that arise from Common Core expectations.

Teacher Collaboration in a Professional Learning Community

Although great teaching does not look the same in every classroom, the Common Core standards expect you and your colleagues to commit to high-quality instruction and assessment processes as an essential element of successful student learning. Implementing the CCSS with fidelity requires you to not just teach mathematics content but to teach students processes and proficiencies for ways of thinking and doing mathematics—a habit of mind, so to speak. In the CCSS, these learning processes are revealed through the eight Standards for Mathematical Practice (see chapter 2) and the Standards for Mathematical Content (see chapter 3). Your participation and engagement in effective collaborative team discussions on a unit-by-unit basis allow for the creation and implementation of a rigorous and coherent mathematics curriculum and prevent ineffective instructional practices. Implementing the CCSS for mathematics means you and your colleagues working together in collaborative teams must "balance personal goals with collective goals, acquire resources for [your] work, and share those resources to support the work of others" (Garmston & Wellman, 2009, p. 33).

Professional learning communities have become ubiquitous in education, and you may equate PLCs with teacher collaboration. At the same time, various definitions and understandings regarding a PLC *culture* abound. In this book, we use the work of DuFour, DuFour, and Eaker's (2008) *Revisiting Professional Learning Communities at Work* and DuFour, DuFour, Eaker, and Many's (2010) *Learning by Doing* to define the conditions for collaborative mathematics learning teams in an authentic PLC culture. For our purposes, we will refer to grade-level or course-level groups of teachers working together in a PLC culture and process as *collaborative teams*.

DuFour et al. (2008) define a PLC as

> educators committed to working collaboratively in ongoing processes of collective inquiry and action research to achieve better results for the students they serve. Professional learning communities operate under the assumption that the key to improved learning for students is continuous, job-embedded learning for educators. (p. 14)

Typically, schools or districts commit to operating as a PLC with various collaborative learning teams (like grade-level teachers or mathematics teachers) operating interdependently within it to accomplish the larger PLC goals. Becoming a collaborative learning team (collaborative team) is more than meeting regularly to discuss instruction with your collaborative team members. The defining feature of a learning community is "a focus on and commitment to the learning of each student" (DuFour et al., 2008, p. 15). DuFour et al. (2008) identify six characteristics of effective PLCs.

1. PLCs have shared mission (purpose), vision (clear direction), values (collective commitments), and goals (indicators, timelines, and targets)—all focused on student learning.

2. There is a collaborative culture with a focus on learning. However, collaboration is a means to an end, not an end in itself. According to DuFour et al. (2008),

"*Collaboration* is a systematic process in which teachers work together, interdependently, to analyze and *impact* professional practice in order to improve results for their students, their teams, and their school" (p. 16).

3. Collaborative teams engage in collective inquiry into "1) best practices about teaching and learning, 2) a candid clarification of their current practices, and 3) an honest assessment of their students' current levels of learning" (DuFour et al., 2008, p. 16).

4. PLCs are action oriented; they learn by doing. In other words, team members not only read, analyze, and plan but also act on their plans, then learn from the results of their actions.

5. They are committed to continuous improvement. The goal is to create conditions for perpetual learning by engaging in an ongoing improvement cycle of gathering evidence of student learning; developing and selecting strategies to address learning needs; implementing the strategies and analyzing their effectiveness; and then applying new knowledge in the next cycle.

6. Collaborative team members are results oriented. All teachers' efforts "must be assessed on the basis of results rather than intentions" (DuFour et al., 2008, p. 17).

In short, a PLC process involves a shift from a culture of isolated, independent professional practice focused on the achievement of students in your class to one of collaborative, interdependent practice with shared accountability for the learning of all students—even those that you do not teach personally. No longer is the focus on *my* students or *your* students, rather it centers on *our* students in the grade level or in the course.

Considering the unprecedented clarity of the CCSS for mathematics, DuFour et al. (2010) verify why is it essential to take action in your collaborative team to develop a shared understanding of the content and the assessment of what is to be taught, because doing so:

- Promotes clarity among your colleagues

- Ensures consistent curricular priorities among teachers

- Is critical to the development of common pacing required for highly effective common assessments

- Ensures that the curriculum is viable—that it can be taught in the allotted time

- Creates ownership among all teachers required to teach and assess the intended curriculum

Teacher Collaboration Versus Cooperation or Coordination

Although teacher collaboration is an essential aspect of a PLC, what is often considered *collaboration* is actually cooperation or coordination. Cooperation is about being a team player. One potential danger of cooperation is the exclusion of a diversity of team member ideas. Consider a scenario in which your team members share ideas and lesson plans about how they each teach a learning target about defining and interpreting integer exponents to eighth-grade students. In this case, teachers share resources to cooperate, although each teacher retains his or her own authority to teach and assess the learning target as he or she best understands it.

Coordination, on the other hand, requires the teacher team to do more planning and communicating than cooperation does. Efficiency regarding the management aspects of the course tends to drive teachers to coordinate. For example, an eighth-grade team may coordinate a schedule so all teachers have access to the computer lab to explore geometric transformations during the geometry unit, or it might divide up different content standards from a particular CCSS content standard cluster in order to create end-of-unit assessments for the team. Note that coordination can serve purposes of efficiency but does little to push inquiry and discussion of the daily instruction and assessment in the classroom—the true purpose and high-leverage work of middle school collaborative teams in a PLC.

Whereas *cooperating* and *coordinating* are about individuals on the teacher team making decisions, *collaborating* is about creating interdependence with your colleagues as you work beyond consensus building. When your team is collaborating effectively, members are creating new structures and ways of working that are focused on academic success for all students, not just the students in their own classes. Graham and Ferriter (2008) offer a useful framework that details seven stages of development of collaborative teams. The level at which teams fall within Graham and Ferriter's framework is directly correlated to the level by which team members effectively collaborate. Table 1.1 highlights these seven stages.

Teams that are at the first three stages of collaborative team development are trying to understand what they are supposed to do and accomplish as a team. Consider the following scenario. The seventh-grade team begins meeting weekly at the beginning of the year with little direction as to the purpose of meeting (stage one). Shortly, the team begins to share how each teacher approached proportional reasoning—7.RP (see appendix C, page 194)—in his or her respective classrooms (stage two). By the end of the semester, your seventh-grade collaborative team begins to discuss the homework problems that best represented what students should know and be able to do as they work with the constant of proportionality in tables and graphs—7.RP.2b (see appendix C, page 195)—and who would compile the assignment sheet for this standard to be distributed to students (stage three). At this stage, the seventh-grade teachers are *cooperating* as they begin to share their own classroom practices and delegate team responsibilities.

Teams in stages four and five are coordinating around common planning of instruction, developing common assessment instruments and tasks, and analyzing student-learning results. Consider this scenario. An eighth-grade team comes together to develop a common quiz (stage four) to assess students' ability to use data from a random sample to draw inferences about populations—8.SP (see appendix D, page 206). The following year, the eighth-grade team also creates common assessment instruments for all course

Table 1.1: The Seven Stages of Teacher Collaboration Diagnostic Tool

Stage	Questions That Define This Stage
Stage one: Filling the time	What exactly are we supposed to do as a team? Why are we meeting?
Stage two: Sharing personal practice	What is everyone doing in his or her classroom for instruction, lesson planning, and assessment during this unit?
Stage three: Planning, planning, planning	What should we be teaching during this unit, and how do we lighten the load for each other?
Stage four: Developing common assessments	How will we know if students learned the standards? What does mastery look like for the standards in this unit?
Stage five: Analyzing student learning	Are students learning what they are supposed to be learning? Do we agree on student evidence of learning during this unit?
Stage six: Adapting instruction to student needs	How can we adjust instruction to help those students struggling and those exceeding expectations?
Stage seven: Reflecting on instruction	Which lesson-design practices are most effective with our students?

Source: Adapted from Graham & Ferriter, 2008.

Visit **go.solution-tree.com/commoncore** for a reproducible version of this table.

units or chapters and uses collaborative team time to analyze and compare results, in order to determine how all eighth-grade students are performing on the learning standards for the course and subsequently take action on that learning (stage five).

In the final two stages, teams begin deep collaboration as members take collective responsibility for the learning of all students, differentiating instruction and designing assessments based on student needs by reflecting on the question, Which of our instructional and assessment practices are most effective with our students? After analyzing the data from the unit common assessment instrument (test), the eighth-grade team has identified a small group of students struggling to apply some of the Pythagorean relationships (8.G, see appendix D, page 205). The team develops a differentiated lesson to extend the knowledge and reasoning of students who have mastered the learning target and provide targeted support for struggling learners (stage six). The eighth-grade team will be at a stage seven when it regularly makes adjustments to instruction based on learner needs and discusses the instructional strategies that have the greatest impact on student learning.

Using table 1.1 to diagnose and assess your collaborative team's development supplies crucial data for the appropriate supports, resources, and professional development action. At what stage do your collaborative teams operate? Are teachers cooperating, coordinating, or collaborating? When your collaborative team works together, are discussions focused on sharing each teacher's lessons or activities without inquiry into assessing student learning? Are meetings centered on when the unit test will be given in class without questioning how teachers are connecting larger concepts throughout the unit? You can use the descriptors in table 1.1 to determine your current team's stage of development.

There are several high-leverage actions (see page 20) that describe the work of a high-functioning collaborative team that has been working together for several years. If your team is just getting started, or is not engaged in any of these actions currently, do not try to implement all of these actions simultaneously. Each activity requires considerable effort and commitment. Less is more. Focus on a few actions for the year and work to implement them well.

Collaborative Practices

The goal of teacher collaboration is deep, widespread knowledge of subject-area content and consistent implementation of best-practice instruction for that content. The structure designed for collaborative efforts is critical for success. Five aspects of collaborative practice are the following:

1. Collaborative team participants

2. Collaborative team commitments

3. Collaborative team leaders

4. Collaborative team agendas and meeting minutes

5. Collaborative team time

In order to do the work of the team described in table 1.1 and to move effectively and efficiently to the more advanced stages of team collaboration, it is important that your team responds to each of these five collaboration factors.

Collaborative Team Participants

Individual team members' needs, interests, and expertise will often affect the flow and the work of your team. Collaborative team members may also vary according to the needs of your school or district. Typically, middle or junior high school collaborative teams are comprised of all teachers of a particular grade level or course, including teachers for students with special needs or English learners (ELs) who are supporting mathematics instruction. Your collaborative teams might also benefit from other faculty and staff members participating on your team, including faculty members from other departments and school support personnel, such as counselors or paraprofessional tutors.

Team members need only have a common curricular, instructional, and assessment focus about which to collaborate. While there is no ideal or magic number of teachers on a collaborative team, experience seems to suggest that teams much larger than seven or eight can be challenging (Horn, 2010). When your team is too large, discussions become unwieldy and a few extroverted teachers can hijack participation, limiting other team members' voices. It is possible for larger teams to engage in productive dialogue; however, a higher level of facilitation will be required. Your middle school mathematics department should also consider individual compatibility when making recommendations for assignments to grade-level collaborative teams. The ability to work with colleagues who understand how to share information and work with a positive attitude on various team projects is important. One way to nurture this expectation for becoming an effective team member is through the development of clear team commitments and behaviors.

Collaborative Team Commitments

The purpose of collective team commitments is to create a respectful, open environment that encourages diversity of ideas and invites criticism combined with close inspection of practices and procedures. Various protocols are available to assist your teams in establishing actions to which team members agree to adhere. The process need not be arduous, complicated, or time consuming. The protocol in figure 1.1 is one model that your team can use to establish and review collective commitments throughout the year.

Setting Team Collective Commitments

Because we need our best from one another in working as a team, it is essential that we set collective commitments for our work cultures. Collective commitments are values and beliefs that will describe how we choose to treat each other and how we can expect to be treated.

As we set three to four collective commitments for ourselves, please note that establishing these does not mean that we are not already good people who work together productively. Having collective commitments simply reminds us to be highly conscious about our actions and what we can expect from each other as we engage in conversations about our challenging work.

Step one: Write three or four "We will" statements that you think will have the most positive influence on our group as we collaborate on significant issues about teaching and learning. Perhaps reflect on past actions or behaviors that have made teams less than productive. These are only a jumpstart for your thinking.

Step two: Partner with another colleague to talk about your choices and the reasons for your selection. Together decide on three or four commitments from your combined lists.

Step three: Move as a pair to partner with two to four other colleagues to talk about your choices and the reasons for your selection. Together decide on three or four commitments from your combined lists.

Step four: Make a group decision. Prepare to share your choices with the whole group.

Step five: Adopt collective commitments by consensus. Invite clarification and advocacy for particular commitments. Give all participants four votes for norm selection. It is wise not to have more than three or four.

Source: Adapted from P. Luidens, personal communication, January 27 and April 9, 2010.

Figure 1.1: Setting middle school teacher team collective commitments protocol.

Visit **go.solution-tree.com/commoncore** for a reproducible version of this figure.

Your middle or junior high school collaborative team should keep collective commitments focused on behaviors and practices that will support the collaborative work of your team. Some teams find it useful to post their norms in a conspicuous place as a reminder to each other. Other collaborative teams might choose to highlight a commitment at each meeting as a reminder of the commitments of the team. For great advice and insight into collaborative team protocols, go to www.allthingsplc.info under Tools & Resources for additional ideas. Visit **go.solution-tree.com/commoncore** for links to additional resources.

As an example, members of a seventh-grade collaborative team decided their collective commitments would be to: (1) listen to understand, (2) challenge ideas, and (3) keep the focus on teaching and learning. Although the team included most of the same people as the previous year, team members reflected on the previous year and observed that sometimes one or two individuals passionate about their ideas often hijacked the discussions without hearing others' ideas. The collective commitments reflect the collaborative team's dedication to hearing all ideas and respectfully challenging each other.

Each team member has the responsibility to hold one another accountable for the agreed-on team commitments in a form of lateral or peer-to-peer accountability and collaboration. To address team members for not adhering to the norms is a permissible and expected aspect of the team culture. Your collaborative team might find it useful to establish a collective commitment that addresses what happens when a commitment is not honored. The purpose of the collective commitments is to raise the level of professionalism and liberate your team to openly, safely, and respectfully discuss the work at hand. As your collaborative teams grow and develop or change membership, collective commitments will likely change. Regardless of whether your collaborative team members change, you should revisit your collective commitments a minimum of once each school year, usually at the start of the year.

Collaborative Team Leaders

Just as effective professional development doesn't happen without planning and facilitation, collaborative team meetings also need intentional forethought and someone from your team to lead the group. The role of team leader or meeting facilitator might rotate or be delegated to one individual. On one hand, one person assigned team leader for the entire school year might bring continuity to team discussions and functions. (A team leader may have other responsibilities related to the work of the team in addition to leading team meetings.) On the other hand, perhaps rotating the role of team leader or meeting facilitator gives more teachers the opportunity to take ownership and develop in their ability to facilitate discussions. To make the most of the collaborative meetings, the team leader's role should involve intentionally maximizing your group's ability to collaborate by inviting diversity of thought and challenging ideas and practices. An effective collaborative team always knows who is driving the meeting. An effective middle or junior high school mathematics team leader will encourage all members to participate and ask questions of each other to push for clarity and understanding. An effective team leader will also summarize team questions, understandings, decisions, and actionable items in a timely fashion.

Collaborative Team Agendas and Meeting Minutes

Designing time for mathematics collaborative teams is a considerable commitment of resources in people, money, and time. The payoff occurs when collaboration around teaching and learning mathematics results in professional growth and increased student achievement. Agendas and meeting minutes are tools that lend themselves to more efficient use of time. The team leader is responsible for seeking input from team members, determining the agenda, and making the agenda public to the team a few days prior to the meeting. Agendas acknowledge that time is valuable and are essential to successful meetings (Garmston & Wellman, 2009). An agenda need not be complicated or long. Figure 1.2 provides a sample agenda from a seventh-grade collaborative team.

Tuesday, October 16

- Share and analyze results from the ratio and proportional reasoning test.
  - How did our students do overall?
  - Were the results what we expected?
  - Did anyone's students do much better? What might they have done differently than the rest of us?
- Review learning targets for the geometry unit.
  - Do our learning targets capture the key content concepts?
  - Do the learning targets together represent a balance of higher-level reasoning and procedural fluencies?
- Bring your best ideas for reinforcing proportional reasoning in this unit.
  - What have you tried in the past that seems to have worked?
  - Are there ideas, problems, strategies that you have tried that didn't work?
  - What task or problem might we use to help students understand scale drawings?

Figure 1.2: Sample team-meeting agenda.

Visit **go.solution-tree.com/commoncore** for a reproducible version of this figure.

Meeting minutes are beneficial and do not need to be overly detailed. Minutes serve many useful purposes. First, minutes for each meeting capture the actions and decisions that the team has made. Teams have found it useful to go back to minutes earlier in the year or even to the previous year to recall discussions related to the ordering of content or why they decided to use a particular instructional approach for a concept. Minutes also capture who is responsible for various action steps, such as creating a scoring rubric and key for a quiz or test, or arranging for copies of artifacts for all team members.

Notice that the minutes in figure 1.2 are quick bullet points that communicate the focus of the meeting so team members can come prepared with ideas, data, or other possible resources for the next meeting. Also note that the team leader provides guiding questions for team members to reflect on prior to the meeting. He or she primes the pump of expectations, so to speak. Team members can give prior thought and consideration to the topics, thus making the meeting more productive.

If you are like most middle school teachers, you serve on multiple teams—both your mathematics teams and a grade-level team—creating a challenge to attend all team meetings. The minutes are also an efficient way to communicate to others what transpired at the meeting. So if you are unable to attend a meeting, you can use the minutes as a resource to see what was discussed and decided. Much like students absent from class, if you are absent from the meeting, you are still expected to know and carry out the team's decisions. Technology is an effective means by which to make minutes public to others. For example, teams can post minutes in an email, to a wiki, to a team blog, or on a team website.

The minutes also provide one form of communication to the mathematics department chairperson, school principal, or other relevant school leaders. The minutes allow school leaders to provide targeted guidance, direction, or resources to support the work of your collaborative team. Figure 1.3 provides an example of a sixth-grade team's meeting minutes that were posted electronically. Notice how the meeting blends a balance of team procedural issues (when to give the formative cumulative exam based on the calendar) with team instructional issues (students' struggle and teacher review of student work).

- We debriefed the high-cognitive-demand Mixing Juice task, discussed how each teacher introduced it, discussed students' struggles, and reviewed our collective student work. We also updated teacher notes about student solutions, how to score the solutions, and discussed practices to introduce when students don't produce the solution.

- After today's meeting, we are thinking about doing a variation of Julie's social-emotional learning activity after the first quiz, which we'll discuss at the next meeting.

- We discussed how to deal with the shortened first-term grading period. We are thinking we should stay with the plan of giving the formative cumulative exam on the Monday after the grading period ends.

- We decided that we would only spend two class periods on the end-of-unit project—one to get students started and the other to review completed projects—and have students complete the rest outside class. Alison is ordering project supplies. We made a schedule of teachers and classrooms that would be available before and after school for students who want to work on projects at school.

Figure 1.3: Sample team-meeting minutes.

Visit **go.solution-tree.com/commoncore** for a reproducible version of this figure.

Laying the groundwork for collaboration by articulating both the expectations of how your collaborative team members work together (toward constructive discussions and decision making) and the logistics of announcing and capturing your team discussions is essential. Attention to these fundamental team-management issues supports deeper and more meaningful discussions that will impact student learning of mathematics. Once expectations have been articulated about collaboration, your collaborative teams can engage in meaningful discussions around mathematics teaching and learning.

Collaborative Team Time

Clearly, for collaborative teams to work effectively, you need adequate time for collaboration. The research indicates that significant achievement gains are only achieved when grade-level or course-based teams of teachers are provided with sufficient and consistent time to collaborate (Saunders, Goldenberg, & Gallimore, 2009).

The world's highest-performing countries in mathematics allow significant time for mathematics teachers to collaborate and learn from one another (Barber & Mourshed, 2007; Stigler & Hiebert, 1999). This requires that school districts shift their priorities to support regular collaborative professional development opportunities in the form of grade-level or course-based teacher collaborative team time (Hiebert & Stigler, 2004). Finding adequate team time is clearly one of the challenges educators face in implementing PLCs. But, it can be done.

How much time? As a grades 6–8 teacher you should have dedicated periods of grade-level, course-based, or cross-grade-level teacher collaborative team time every week, with at least sixty to ninety minutes of meeting time. This time needs to be embedded within your professional workday; that is, it should not be scheduled every Tuesday after school once a week (Buffum et al., 2009).

Figure 1.4 provides a few ideas to make your collaborative team professional development time a priority (Bowgren & Sever, 2010; Loucks-Horsley, Stiles, Mundry, Love, & Hewson, 2009).

---

1. Provide common time by scheduling most, if not all, team members the same planning period during the day.

2. Create an altered schedule for early-release or late-arrival students on an ongoing basis, if feasible to your community.

3. Use substitute teachers to roll through the day, releasing different collaborative teams for two to three hours at a time.

4. Occasionally release teachers from teaching duties or other nonteaching duties in order to collaborate with colleagues.

5. Restructure time by permanently altering teacher responsibilities, the teaching schedule, the school day, or the school calendar.

6. Purchase teacher time by providing monetary compensation for after-school, weekend, or summer work.

Figure 1.4: Options for scheduling teacher collaboration time.

Visit **go.solution-tree.com/commoncore** for a reproducible version of this figure.

Typically, schedules in middle schools have built-in time for interdisciplinary team meetings. A core premise of the original middle school concept was that each teacher is part of an interdisciplinary team—mathematics; English, reading, and language arts; science; and social studies teachers—that is responsible for teaching the same group of students. Ideally, the interdisciplinary team operates as a collaborative team. Both discipline-specific and interdisciplinary collaborative teams can operate within a middle or junior high school: the teams' goals and work are different but complementary. One focuses on discipline-specific teaching and learning; the other focuses more on student support, often the social and emotional needs of students. The challenge is scheduling the team meeting time so that both collaborative teams can work effectively.

The High-Leverage Work of Mathematics Collaborative Teams in a PLC

Your collaboration with colleagues is about "purposeful peer interaction" (Fullan, 2008, p. 41). Purposeful peer interaction begins as you use a common vocabulary for your team discussions. It is an important factor contributing to your focused interactions with colleagues. The vocabulary and format of the CCSS grades 6–8 may be somewhat different from what you are accustomed to using. Figure 1.5 defines key terms used in the CCSS and identifies the domains that are presented in grades 6–8 (see appendices B, C, and D for complete listings of these content standards).

Standards define what students should understand and be able to do.

Content standard clusters summarize groups of related standards. Note that standards from different clusters may sometimes be closely related because mathematics is a connected subject.

Domains are larger groups of related standards. Standards from different domains may sometimes be closely related. The domains for grades 6–8 are Ratios and Proportional Relationships (grades 6 and 7), the Number System, Expressions and Equations, Functions (grade 8), Geometry, and Statistics and Probability.

Source: Adapted from NGA & CCSSO, 2010a, pp. 44–45.
Figure 1.5: How to read the CCSS for mathematics.

Visit **go.solution-tree.com/commoncore** for a reproducible version of this figure.

The focus and coherence of the CCSS for grades 6–8 mathematics (see appendices B, C, and D for each grade level respectively) and the careful attention paid to standards progressions mean that some of the topics you traditionally taught in certain grades have been moved to other grades, and some topics have simply been eliminated from the middle school curriculum. For example, Numbers and Operations with fractions and its attendant standards are mostly completed by the end of fifth grade as standards for Ratios and Proportional Reasoning begin. The purpose of this more focused curriculum is to provide you more time to teach fewer critical topics in greater depth. (See chapter 3 for a discussion of specific changes.)

You need to spend time in your grade-level, course-level, or cross-grade-level (vertical) collaborative team reviewing and reaching agreement on the scope and sequence you will use to ensure alignment of the mathematics content with your district's expectations as well as the CCSS. You should also spend some collaborative team time in vertical team discussions. For example, if you are a seventh-grade teacher, you should meet with sixth- and eighth-grade teachers to ensure appropriate articulation across grade levels.

Overall, the work of your collaborative team should focus on reaching agreement and taking action in five fundamental areas.

1. **Content, teaching, and learning:** The team must agree on the mathematics (content) students should learn, the mathematical tasks they should experience, and the instructional strategies to ensure student engagement and acquisition of conceptual understanding, procedural fluency, problem solving, and reasoning capabilities. (See chapters 2 and 3.)

2. **Summative assessment instruments:** The team must agree on the development and use of common and coherent unit or chapter summative assessment instruments to determine if students have learned the agreed-on curriculum and how to respond when students either don't learn or do learn that curriculum. (See chapter 4.)

3. **Formative assessment processes:** The team must agree on the development and use of a common formative assessment and feedback process to monitor students' learning. (See chapters 4 and 5.)

4. **Support and intervention:** The team must agree on appropriate mathematics intervention, instruction, and intentional student support based on the results of formative classroom assessments, including results on summative assessment instruments. (See chapters 4 and 5.)

5. **SMART goals:** The team must agree on SMART (strategic and specific, measurable, attainable, results oriented, and time bound) goal targets and disaggregation of data to monitor progress of all students (Kanold, 2011; O'Neill & Conzemius, 2005). (See chapters 4 and 5.)

Your collaborative team can use these areas to provide direction and consolidate planning for instruction and assessment. Figure 1.6 describes high-leverage, high-inquiry collaborative team tasks for your team's meaningful collaboration.

Collaborative Teacher Team Agreements for Teaching and Learning

1. The team designs and develops agreed-on prior knowledge skills to be assessed and taught during each lesson of the unit or chapter.

2. The team designs and implements agreed-on lesson-design elements that ensure students actively engage with the mathematics. Students experience some aspect of the CCSS Mathematical Practices (such as Construct viable arguments and critique the reasoning of others or Attend to precision) with the language embedded in the daily lessons of every unit or chapter.

3. The team designs and implements agreed-on lesson-design elements that allow for student-led summaries and demonstrations of learning the daily lesson.

4. The team designs and implements agreed-on lesson-design elements that include the strategic use of tools—including technology—for developing student understanding.

Figure 1.6: High-leverage activities of grades 6–8 grade-level and course-level collaborative teams. continued →

Collaborative Team Agreements for Assessment Instruments and Tools

1. The team designs and implements agreed-on common assessment instruments based on high-quality exam designs. The collaborative team designs all unit exams, unit quizzes, final exams, writing assignments, and projects for the course.

2. The team designs and implements agreed-on common assessment instrument scoring rubrics for each assessment in advance of the exam.

3. The team designs and implements agreed-on common scoring and grading feedback (level of specificity to the feedback) of the assessment instruments. Two or more team members together grade a small sample of student work to check on consistency in scoring and grading feedback.

Collaborative Team Agreements for Formative Assessment Feedback

1. The team designs and implements agreed-on adjustments to instruction and intentional student support based on the results of both formative daily classroom assessments and the results of student performance on unit or chapter assessment instruments, such as quizzes and tests.

2. The team designs and implements agreed-on levels of rigor for daily in-class prompts and common high-cognitive-demand tasks used to assess student understanding of various mathematical concepts and skills. This also applies to team agreement to minimize the variance in rigor and task selection for homework assignments and expectations for makeup work. This applies to depth, quality, and timeliness of teacher descriptive formative feedback on all student work.

3. The team designs and implements agreed-on methods to teach students to self-assess and set goals. Self-assessment includes students using teacher feedback, feedback from other students, or their own monitoring and self-assessment to identify what they need to work on and to set goals for future learning.

Visit **go.solution-tree.com/commoncore** for a reproducible version of this figure.

You can use figure 1.6 as a diagnostic tool to measure the focus of the work and energy of your team. Do you have low implementation or high implementation for each of the high-leverage actions? Meaningful implementation of the CCSS will require time—time to digest the CCSS for mathematics for grades 6–8; time to create a focused and coherent curriculum; and time to design instruction and assessments around the high-leverage actions listed in figure 1.6.

Collaborative Protocols

Several protocols combine collaboration with a spotlight on the teaching and learning of mathematics. Five structured protocols can be especially beneficial for you and your team. These protocols provide different settings in which you can collaborate and share reflections and beliefs about teaching and learning.

1. **Lesson study:** Lesson study differs from lesson planning. Lesson study focuses on what teachers want students to learn; lesson planning focuses on what teachers plan to teach. A modified lesson study example is shown in the feature box on

page 24 and can be used to improve the quality of your lessons and instruction as a team.

2. **Peer coaching**: Peer coaching is a kind of partnership in which two or three teachers engage in conversations focused on their reflections and thinking about their instructional practices. The discussions lead to a refinement and formative assessment response to classroom practice. The participants may rotate roles— discussion leader, mentor, or advocate. Teachers who engage in peer coaching are willing to reveal strengths and weaknesses to each other. Peer coaching creates an environment in which teachers can be secure, connected, and empowered through transparent discussions of each others' practice.

3. **Case study**: Case study can be used to address a wide range of topics or problems the collaborative team encounters. The case study presents a story—one involving issues or conflicts that need to be resolved through analysis of available resources leading to constructive plans to address the problem. Typically, case studies are used to examine complex problems—the school's culture, climate, attendance, achievement, teaching, and learning (Baccellieri, 2010).

4. **Book study**: Book study is a familiar and popular activity for you to engage in conversations with colleagues about professional books. It may be a formalized activity for some collaborative teams; however, book study can emerge in any number of ways—from hearing an author speak at a conference, from a colleague's enthusiastic review of a book, or from the mutual interests of teachers who want to learn more about a topic. Book study promotes conversations among faculty and staff that can lead to the application of new ideas in the classroom and improvement of existing knowledge and skills. Book study is a great way to connect with a personal learning network as you blog, tweet, Skype, or use other forms of communication to connect with colleagues outside of your school.

5. **Collaborative grading**: Collaborative grading occurs as your team reaches stages four and five (see table 1.1, page 13) of team collaboration. In this situation, you and your colleagues design a common unit test together and assign point values with scoring rubrics for each question on the exam. Together you grade and discuss the quality of student responses on the assessment instrument and develop an inter-rater reliability for scoring of the assessment tool. Achieving consistency in grading students' assignments and assessments is an important goal for collaborative teams.

From the point of view of instructional transparency and improvement, lesson study is a particularly powerful collaborative tool that merits close consideration. Lesson study has been shown to be very effective as a collaborative protocol with a high impact on teacher professional learning (Hiebert & Stigler, 1999). A modified lesson study provides a reflective collaborative team activity.

Example of a Lesson-Study Group in Action

Typically, teachers choose a content area that data indicate is problematic for students. Consider a lesson-study group that develops a goal related to the CCSS Mathematical Practices (see appendix A, page 181). The teachers select Mathematical Practice 1 as the goal—students will learn to make sense of problems and persevere in solving them. They share ideas about how to help students achieve this goal through the content of the lesson. The teachers select content from the CCSS domains and content standard clusters that presents a particular challenge to students. In this case, the group chooses "Interpret and compute quotients of fractions, and solve word problems involving division of fractions by fractions" (6.NS.1, see appendix B, page 188). The teachers use various resources to learn more about the content and its connections to other mathematical concepts, as well as information from research about students learning this content. From those resources, the teachers together designed a lesson to address the goal. One team member was asked to teach the lesson and be observed by one or two other members of the team. The teacher who taught the lesson and the observers debriefed the team about their observations and made changes to the lesson design. The revised lesson was taught with a final debriefing of the second instructional episode. By the end of the lesson study, these teachers have increased their knowledge of pedagogy and mathematics content. By contributing to development of the lesson and engaging in discussions of the lesson's strengths and limitations, they have also raised the level of respect and trust among team members. The lessons learned from participating in lesson study extend to the teachers' daily instruction.

Lesson study may seem time and work intensive for a single lesson. Nonetheless, the benefit of lesson study is the teacher professional learning that results from the deep, collaborative discussions about mathematics content, instruction, and student learning. The lesson-design tool in figure 2.16 (page 69) is designed to support your lesson-study work. Also, see the lesson-study references listed in the Extending My Understanding section at the end of this chapter for more information about this powerful activity for stages six and seven (see table 1.1, page 13) collaborative team development.

Looking Ahead

The CCSS for mathematics define what students should know and be able to do to be college and career ready—which now includes mathematics content through second-year algebra, along with proficiency in the Standards for Mathematical Practice (see appendix A, page 181).

Your collaborative team is the key to all students successfully learning the Common Core mathematics standards for grades 6–8 through effective instruction, assessment, and intervention practices. In subsequent chapters, we'll provide tools to assist you and your colleagues' work to make the vision of the Common Core for mathematics a reality for all students.

Highly accomplished middle school mathematics teachers value and practice effective collaboration, which professional organizations have identified as an essential element to teacher professional development (Learning Forward, 2011; National Board for Professional Teaching Standards, 2010). Teacher collaboration is not the icing on top of the proverbial cake. Instead, it is the egg in the batter holding the cake together. Your school is a learning institution responsible for educating students and preparing them for the future. Your school is also a learning institution for the adults. The professional learning of teachers is not solely a prerequisite for improved student achievement. It is a commitment to the investment in the professionals like you, who have the largest impact on students in schools. The process of collaboration capitalizes on the fact that teachers come together with diverse experiences and knowledge to create a whole that is larger than the sum of the parts. Teacher collaboration is *the* solution to your sustained professional learning—the ongoing and never-ending process of growth necessary to meet the classroom demands of the CCSS expectations.

Chapter 1 Extending My Understanding

1. A critical tenet of a mathematics department in a PLC is a shared vision of teaching and learning mathematics.

    ○ Do you have a shared vision of what teaching and learning mathematics looks like? If not, how might you create one?

    ○ Does this vision build on current research in mathematics education?

    ○ Does your vision embrace collaboration as fundamental to professional learning?

2. Graham and Ferriter (2008) identify seven stages of collaborative team development. These stages characterize team development evolving from cooperating to coordinating leading ultimately to a truly collaborative team.

    ○ Using table 1.1 (page 13), at what stage are your teams operating?

    ○ What role might you play in helping your team transition to a more advanced stage?

3. Using figure 1.6 (page 21), identify the high-leverage actions your team currently practices extremely well. What is your current level of implementation on a scale of 0 percent (low) and 100 percent (high)? How might you use this information to identify which actions should be your team's priority during this or the next school year?

4. Implementing the CCSS might seem daunting to some teachers, and as a result, there may be resistance or half-hearted attempts to needed changes in content, instruction, or assessment. Consider leading your collaborative team through a Best Hopes, Worst Fears activity. Give team members two index cards. On one, have them identify their best hopes for implementing the CCSS. On the other card, have team members record their worst fears. Depending on the level of trust and comfort of the team, the team leader might collect the index cards and read the best hopes and worst fears anonymously, or individuals can read

their hopes and fears aloud to the group. The purpose is to uncover concerns that if left covered might undermine collaborative teamwork. Team members should talk about how they can support one another to minimize fears and achieve best hopes.

Online Resources

Visit **go.solution-tree.com/commoncore** for links to these resources. Visit **go.solution -tree.com/plcbooks** for additional resources about professional learning communities.

- *The Five Disciplines of PLC Leaders* (Kanold, 2011; go.solution-tree .com/plcbooks/Reproducibles_5DOPLCL.html): Chapter 3 discusses the commitment to a shared mission and vision by all adults in a school for several tools targeted toward monitoring collaborative actions. These reproducibles engage teachers in professional learning and reflection.

- **AllThingsPLC (www.allthingsplc.info):** Search the Tools & Resources of this website for sample agendas and activities and insights for effective collaborative teamwork.

- **The Educator's PLN—The Personal Learning Network for Educators (http://edupln.ning.com):** This website offers tips, tools, and benefits for starting your own PLN.

- **The Center for Comprehensive School Reform and Improvement (www .centerforcsri.org/plc/websites.html):** This website offers a collection of resources to support an in-depth examination of the work of learning teams.

- **Inside Mathematics (2010a; www.insidemathematics.org/index.php /tools-for-teachers/tools-for-coaches):** This portion of the Inside Mathematics website helps mathematics, teachers, coaches, and specialists support the professional learning teams they lead. Tools to support lesson study and teacher learning, including video vignettes that model coaching conversations, are available.

- **Inside Mathematics (2010b; www.insidemathematics.org/index.php /tools-for-teachers/tools-for-principals-and-administrators):** This portion of the Inside Mathematics website supports school-based administrators and district mathematics supervisors who have the responsibility for establishing the structure and vision for the professional development work of grade-level and cross-grade level learning teams or in a PLC.

- **Learning Forward (2011; www.learningforward.org/standards/standards .cfm):** Learning Forward is an international association of learning educators focused on increasing student achievement through more effective professional learning. This website provides a wealth of resources, including an online annotated bibliography of articles and websites to support the work of professional learning teams.

- **National Council of Supervisors of Mathematics (NCSM; www.math ematicsleadership.org)**: NCSM is an international leader collaborating to achieve excellence and equity in mathematics education at all levels. This portion of the NCSM website provides a variety of resources for mathematics coaches and specialists to support the professional learning teams they lead.

- **The Mathematics Common Core Toolbox (www.ccsstoolbox.com)**: This website provides coherent and research-affirmed protocols and tools to help you in your CCSS collaborative teamwork. The website also provides sample scope and sequence documents and advice for how to prepare for CCSS for mathematics implementation.

- **Chicago Lesson Study Group (www.lessonstudygroup.net/index.php)**: This website provides a forum for teachers to learn about and practice lesson study to steadily improve student learning. To learn more about lesson study or other collaborative protocols, see the following resources.

  ○ *Lesson Study: A Handbook of Teacher-Led Instructional Change* (Lewis, 2002)

  ○ *Powerful Designs for Professional Learning* (Easton, 2008)

  ○ *Leading Lesson Study: A Practical Guide for Teachers and Facilitators* (Stepanek, Appel, Leong, Managan, & Mitchell, 2007)

  ○ *Data-Driven Dialogue: A Facilitator's Guide to Collaborative Inquiry* (Wellman & Lipton, 2004)

- **The National Commission on Teaching and America's Future (NCTAF & WestEd, 2010; www.nctaf.org/wp-content/uploads/STEMTeachersin ProfessionalLearningCommunities.AKnowledgeSynthesis.pdf)**: With the support of the National Science Foundation and in collaboration with WestEd, NCTAF (2010) released *STEM Teachers in Professional Learning Communities: A Knowledge Synthesis*. NCTAF and WestEd conducted a two-year analysis of research studies that document what happens when science, technology, engineering, and mathematics teachers work together in professional learning communities to improve teaching and increase student achievement. This report summarizes that work and provides examples of projects building on that model.

- *Learning by Doing: A Handbook for Professional Learning Communities at Work* **(DuFour et al., 2010; go.solution-tree.com/PLCbooks/Reproducibles _LBD2nd.html)**: This resource and its reproducible materials help educators close the knowing-doing gap as they transform their schools into professional learning communities.

CHAPTER 2

Implementing the Common Core Standards for Mathematical Practice

The Standards for Mathematical Practice describe ways in which developing student practitioners of the discipline of mathematics increasingly ought to engage with the subject matter as they grow in mathematical maturity and expertise throughout the elementary, middle and high school years. Designers of curricula, assessments, and professional development should all attend to the need to connect the mathematical practices to mathematical content in mathematics instruction.

—NGA & CCSSO

The CCSS for mathematics include standards for student proficiency in mathematical practice as well as content standards for developing student understanding. According to the CCSS, "The Standards for *Mathematical Practice* describe varieties of expertise that mathematics educators at all levels should seek to develop in their students" (NGA & CCSSO, 2010a, p. 6). The ultimate goal is to equip your middle school students with expertise that will help them be successful in doing and using mathematics not only in grades 6–8 but in their high school, college, and career work, as well as their personal life. College instructors of entry-level college courses across disciplines rated the Standards for Mathematical Practice of higher value for students to master in order to succeed in their courses than any of the content standard domains. This was true for college instructors in each of the fields of mathematics, language, science, and social science (Conley, Drummond, de Gonzalez, Rooseboom, & Stout, 2011).

The Common Core Standards for Mathematical Practice are built on processes and proficiencies that have long been important in mathematics education. The first of these are NCTM's (2000) process standards—problem solving, reasoning and proof, communication, representation, and connections. The second are the strands of mathematical proficiency described in the National Research Council's (2001) report *Adding It Up*— adaptive reasoning, strategic competence, conceptual understanding, procedural fluency, and productive disposition. These foundational processes are further described and compared to the CCSS Standards for Mathematical Practice in appendix A (page 181).

This chapter provides an analysis of the eight Mathematical Practices. It also describes research-informed instructional practices and lesson-design elements that will help you understand and incorporate the eight Mathematical Practices into your daily classroom instruction. This information is designed to help you and the members of your collaborative middle school teams to answer these questions: (1) How can I design lessons that embed the Mathematical Practices into my daily instruction? and (2) What instructional practices will enable me to create a learning environment that will engage my students in the Mathematical Practices on a regular basis and develop proficiency in these practices to increase their learning?

The Mathematical Practices are not a checklist of teacher to-dos. Rather the standards describe what your students should be doing as they engage in learning the CCSS mathematics content standards. The CCSS explicitly call for "connecting the Standards for Mathematical Practice to the Standards for Mathematical Content" (NGA & CCSSO, 2010a, p. 8) and identify the standards that set expectations for student understanding as potential *points of intersection*. Student conceptual understanding is a foundation for applying the practices, and conversely, the practices are a vehicle for building conceptual understanding. According to the CCSS:

> Expectations that begin with the word "understand" are often especially good opportunities to connect the practices to the content. Students who lack understanding of a topic may rely on procedures too heavily. Without a flexible base from which to work, they may be less likely to consider analogous problems, represent problems coherently, justify conclusions, apply the mathematics to practical situations, use technology mindfully to work with the mathematics, explain the mathematics accurately to other students, step back for an overview, or deviate from a known procedure to find a shortcut. In short, a lack of understanding effectively prevents a student from engaging in the mathematical practices. (NGA & CCSSO, 2010a, p. 8)

You promote conceptual understanding when you explicitly make, or ask students to make, connections among ideas, facts, and procedures (Hiebert & Grouws, 2007). The following four actions help students to make these connections (Kanold, Briars, & Fennell, 2012):

1. Challenging students to think and to make sense of what they are doing to solve mathematics problems

2. Posing questions that stimulate students' thinking, asking them to justify their conclusions, strategies, and procedures

3. Having students evaluate and explain the work of other students, and comparing and contrasting different solution methods for the same problem

4. Asking students to represent the same ideas in multiple ways—using multiple representations, such as symbols, graphics, or manipulatives to demonstrate a concept

An important aspect of implementing the CCSS Mathematical Practices and content expectations for grades 6–8 is developing a collective understanding of the instructional practices and the pedagogical knowledge to enact them in the classroom. If your school or district is not already emphasizing student conceptual understanding as a valuable student outcome and as a way to increase procedural fluency, now is the ideal time to do so. The paradigm shift of teaching fewer standards with greater depth during each year of middle school is designed to support student development of such understanding. You should work with your collaborative team members to design and effectively enact lessons that encourage students to think deeply about the mathematics content and require them to demonstrate understanding of that content as well. This becomes your personal and ongoing collaborative team challenge.

As you focus deliberate attention on the CCSS Mathematical Practices, the challenge is to envision these practices as student outcomes for proficiency as part of instruction. As you collaborate with others around instruction, your dialogue will focus specifically on interpreting and implementing the Mathematical Practices as you design curriculum and instruction around the CCSS content standards that begin with the verb *understand*. The tasks used, the questions asked in the classroom, and the discourse in which students participate will combine to advance students' abilities to engage in the Mathematical Practices. A powerful collaborative team discussion can result by taking each of the eight CCSS Mathematical Practices listed in appendix A (page 181) and working with team members to identify evidence of these various student practices as an outcome of your unit-by-unit lesson design.

The Common Core Standards for Mathematical Practice

The Mathematical Practices describe what your students are *doing* as they engage in learning the CCSS mathematics content standards. How should your students engage with the mathematics standards and interact with their fellow students? By creating a classroom culture that extends beyond typical teacher-centered instruction, you can successfully facilitate students' engagement in mathematics learning that leads to proficiency in the Standards for Mathematical Practice. These standards support and sustain a learning environment in which the content standards are enacted and framed by the specific expertise you help students develop in order to extend their understanding and application of mathematics.

Figure 2.1 (page 32) provides a framework for the eight Mathematical Practices. Mathematical Practices 1 and 6 are viewed as overarching habits of mind, because they are used in almost all mathematics activities. The remaining practices are grouped to highlight close connections between the various Mathematical Practices. This model provides a lens for you to view your collaborative team's curriculum, instruction, and assessment and to identify how team members develop student proficiency in the Mathematical Practices.

To assist your collaborative team in discussing the eight Mathematical Practices, we provide three questions in figure 2.2 (page 32) that you can use on a unit-by-unit basis. In this chapter, we address the first two questions. The third question is left to you and your collaborative team to explore and answer.

Overarching Habits of Mind	Reasoning and Explaining
1. Make sense of problems, and persevere in solving them. 6. Attend to precision.	2. Reason abstractly and quantitatively. 3. Construct viable arguments and critique the reasoning of others.
	Modeling and Using Tools
	4. Model with mathematics. 5. Use appropriate tools strategically.
	Seeing Structure and Generalizing
	7. Look for and make use of structure. 8. Look for and express regularity in repeated reasoning.

Source: Adapted from McCallum, Black, Umland, & Whitesides, n.d. Used with permission.

Figure 2.1: CCSS Mathematical Practices organization model.

1. What is the intent of the Mathematical Practice, and why is it important?
2. What teacher actions develop this Mathematical Practice?
3. What evidence is there that students are demonstrating this Mathematical Practice?

Figure 2.2: Key questions to better understand the CCSS Standards for Mathematical Practice.

The explanations and examples of the Mathematical Practices that follow will help you and your team reflect on your instructional practice and answer the questions in figure 2.2. During your collaborative conversations, you can generate ideas for how to support the Mathematical Practices in your daily lesson and weekly unit design and analyze ways to assess your students' interactions using the practices. As a result of your team discussions and efforts to modify your instruction, you can monitor your progress toward implementing the Common Core mathematics. The Common Core Look-Fors Mathematics app (http://splaysoft.com/CCL4s/Welcome.html) for the iPad or iPhone is an example of one tool you can use to monitor your growth as you transition through implementation of the Common Core State Standards. A tool for teachers and teacher leaders, this app provides for informal peer observation and is a source for data analysis related to instruction that advances student experiences with the Mathematical Practices. The app's *crowd-sourcing* feature allows users to access the online resources that other educators have shared, evaluated, and tagged to the Common Core content standards.

Overarching Habits of Mind

Solving problems is one of the hallmarks of and is the essence of doing mathematics (NCTM, 2000). Mathematical Practices 1 and 6 are fundamental dispositions that are developed in mathematical thinkers early in grade school and reinforced and threaded throughout a student's K–12 mathematical experiences. These two practices connect to your current classroom instruction and general problem-solving efforts. Promoting students' proficiency in these practices becomes an important aspect of your daily lesson design and includes the tasks you choose, the way you lead classroom discourse, and the quality of student work you expect for proficiency.

Mathematical Practice 1: Make Sense of Problems, and Persevere in Solving Them

The first step in exploring CCSS Mathematical Practice 1, "Make sense of problems and persevere in solving them," is to provide a clear definition of what a problem is as it specifically relates to mathematics instruction (NGA & CCSSO, 2010a, p. 6). A *problem* is defined as *a situation*, be it real or contrived, in which a challenge (question or unknown) that requires an appropriate response (such as an answer, solution, explanation, or counterexample) is presented and for which the person facing the challenge does not have a readily accessible appropriate response (Kantowski, 1980). That is:

> To solve a problem is to find a way where no way is known, to find a way out of a difficulty, to find a way around an obstacle, and to attain a desired end that is not immediately attainable, by appropriate means. (Hatfield, Edwards, Bitter, & Morrow, 2008, p. 100)

Students do not always initially see a viable solution pathway and sometimes will need multiple attempts to successfully solve the problem. This inherently means that problems can vary regarding topics, contexts, structure, and so on. Furthermore, it means that teaching problem solving is not about teaching specific problems but about teaching students how to use their knowledge, skills, attitudes, and resources to successfully respond to problems (Pölya, 1957). Thus, as students learn mathematics, they learn to solve problems, and they build new mathematical knowledge by using a variety of tasks, problems, and processes (NCTM, 2000).

What Is the Intent of Mathematical Practice 1, and Why Is It Important?

When your students are engaged in problem solving, it means they are drawing on their understanding of mathematical concepts and procedures, as well as problem-solving strategies and heuristics, to reach a successful response to the problem. This practice describes what proficient solvers do to make sense of and solve problems. It is implicitly organized around Pölya's (1957) four problem-solving phases: (1) understand the problem, (2) make a plan, (3) carry out the plan, and (4) look back.

Understanding the problem involves students being able to explain the meaning of a problem to themselves and others by analyzing givens, constraints, relationships, and goals and representing the problem. In making a plan, students anticipate possible solutions and have a variety of strategies and heuristics that they can apply, such as considering similar problems and trying special cases or similar forms. They are also able to translate among problem representations—equations, verbal descriptions, tables, graphs, and diagrams—and look for patterns and regularities (Van de Walle, 2004).

While carrying out the plan, students continually monitor their progress, asking whether what they are doing and the results they are getting make sense. Finally, once they've found a solution, students look back and check whether their answer makes sense in the context of the original problem. They are also able to compare and contrast their approach with those of other students and extract useful ideas, strategies, and approaches to remember for solving future problems.

While many of these behaviors should be familiar, this practice emphasizes two habits of mind of proficient problem solvers that too often are overlooked: (1) sense making throughout the problem-solving process, and (2) perseverance. Asking "Does this make sense?" is an opening question that proficient solvers ask themselves as they try to understand and present a problem, as they work toward a solution, and when they get their solution. Manifestations of this include thinking "This can't be right" or "There must be an easier way" as one carries out computations or arrives at a solution.

Developing students' perseverance in the problem-solving process and beliefs in their abilities as problem solvers is another notable aspect of this practice. Too often, students believe that if they cannot solve a problem within a few minutes, they are not able to solve it at all. For example, Reys, Lindquist, Lambdin, and Smith (2009) report:

> Children who think they should always be able to solve problems immediately and easily are likely to view as impossible any problem where the solution is not immediately apparent, and they are unlikely to persist in working toward a solution. (p. 110)

Students' beliefs about their intelligence—whether intelligence is a fixed trait (fixed mindset) or one that can grow over time (growth mindset)—also directly influence their motivation to learn mathematics and their willingness to engage and persist in challenge tasks (Dweck, 2006; NCSM, 2010).

What Teacher Actions Develop Mathematical Practice 1?

You, as a middle school teacher, play a critical role in supporting your students' ability to make sense of problems and persevere in solving them. The first of these roles is the presentation of appropriate problems or rich mathematical tasks for students to solve. While it seems that *appropriate* is subjective, figure 2.3 highlights seven questions to discuss within your collaborative team when planning lessons to assess the quality of a problem or mathematical task.

Examining students' interactions with a problem (for example, students' work, discourse, and processes) should provide information about how students' thinking is hindered or evolving by interacting with the problem or task. This list of questions is not exhaustive, but it is a beginning step toward examining problems that will potentially benefit students' mathematical learning.

Successful problem solving does not mean that your students will always conclude with the correct response to a problem but rather that they will undertake a genuine *effort to engage* in the problem-solving process, drawing on resources such as appropriate tools, prior knowledge, discussion with others, and questions to aid in the process.

1. Is the problem interesting to students?

2. Does the problem involve meaningful mathematics?

3. Does the problem provide an opportunity for students to apply and extend mathematics?

4. Is the problem challenging for students?

5. Does the problem support the use of multiple strategies?

6. Does the problem have multiple entry points?

7. Will students' interactions with the problem reveal information about students' mathematics understanding?

Figure 2.3: Seven planning questions that promote CCSS Mathematical Practice 1.

Visit **go.solution-tree.com/commoncore** for a reproducible version of this figure.

You can also help students to understand that the answer is not the final step in problem solving. A great deal of mathematical learning can happen when students are guided to explain and justify processes and check the reasonableness of solutions. In many instances, students can learn about other solutions for the problem and other ways of solving the problem, and they can make mathematical connections to other problems and content.

You are instrumental in developing your students' abilities to make sense of problems and persevere in solving them. The tasks, guidance, and classroom environment all contribute to students' progress in this practice. To learn how to persevere in solving problems, students must be given opportunities to meet challenges but not be overwhelmed by them.

Consider the fencing problem in figure 2.4. While this is a valuable problem to solve in isolation, it is even more valuable as a way to explore the relationship between perimeters and areas of rectangles and as an informal introduction to optimize problems.

Ms. Brown's class will raise rabbits for their spring science fair. They have 24 feet of fencing with which to build a rectangular rabbit pen in which to keep the rabbits.

1. If Ms. Brown's students want their rabbits to have as much room as possible, how long would each of the sides of the pen be?

2. How long would each of the sides of the pen be if they had only 16 feet of fencing?

3. How would you go about determining the pen with the most room for any amount of fencing? Organize your work so that someone else who reads it will understand it.

Source: Adapted from Stein, Smith, Henningsen, & Silver, 2000.

Figure 2.4: Sample geometry problem—Rectangular fencing task.

Visit **go.solution-tree.com/commoncore** for a reproducible version of this figure.

In this problem, notice that students are asked to (1) find the rectangle with the greatest area given 24 feet of fencing, (2) find the rectangle with the greatest area given 16 feet of fencing, and (3) generalize their results to find the rectangle with the greatest area given any amount of fencing. As they work on part one, Will students draw pictures? Will they make tables? Will they do a systematic investigation, proceeding from the rectangle with smallest to largest widths of whole units (for example, width of 1 foot, 2 feet, 3 feet, and so on)? Will they try all possible rectangles, or will they stop when they realize that the area of a 7 × 5 rectangle is the same as that for a 5 × 7 rectangle? Furthermore, will some students exclude the 6 × 6 square from consideration, because the problem calls for a *rectangular* pen, and they think that a square is not a rectangle? Without providing too much of a lead to the solution, what types of advancing or assessing of student thinking questions might you ask students who are stuck? How will you structure your discussion of students' different solutions to maximize the collective learning of the class? These last two questions are key components of your collaborative team lesson planning for using such a task and are discussed further when using the lesson-design template in figure 2.16 (page 69).

Observing students' interactions with a problem (for example, students' work, discourse, and processes) provides information about how their thinking is hindered or evolving by interacting with the problem or task.

Although the list of questions in figure 2.3 is not exhaustive, it is a step toward examining problems or tasks that will potentially benefit students' mathematical learning and develop their perseverance. One way to develop perseverance is to also assign problems of the week as a teacher team activity. Problems that support use of multiple strategies, or have multiple entry points, provide ways for all students to engage in solving the problem. Such problems also are more likely to provide you with information about your students' mathematical understanding, because all students will have some way to attack the problem. Successful problem solving does not mean that your students will always conclude with the correct response to a problem but rather that they will undertake a genuine effort to engage and persevere in the problem-solving process, drawing on resources, such as appropriate tools, prior knowledge, discussion with others, and questions to aid in the process—at a high-cognitive-demand level.

The level of high cognitive demand refers to the type of thinking that tasks require of students. This is different from *level of difficulty* and *level of importance*.

- **Level of difficulty:** Some tasks may be more difficult for some students than others, but that does not mean that the tasks require different types of thinking. For example, both $11/14 \div 7/8$ and $1/2 \div 3/4$ are procedures without connections—lower-cognitive-demand tasks—even though the first task is computationally more challenging than the second. These tasks are *without connections* because the computation is done in isolation, rather than being connected to a context, a different representation, or other problems.

- **Level of importance:** It is important for students to be able to do certain lower-cognitive-demand tasks, such as being able to immediately recall the decimal equivalents for common fractions like ½, ⅓, ¼, ¾, ⅕ (memorization) or knowing a procedure for how to find the decimal equivalents for any fraction (procedures without connections). However, the point is that initially developing students' underlying conceptual understanding through engagement in high-cognitive-demand tasks facilitates students' learning and retention of lower-demand skills.

Stein and Smith (1998) also note certain teacher behaviors contribute to the maintenance or decline of high-cognitive-demand student behavior during a task or problem used in class. Table 2.1 provides an adapted version of these teacher behaviors.

Table 2.1: Factors Associated With the Maintenance or Decline of High-Level-Cognitive Demand

Maintenance of High-Cognitive-Demand Student Behavior	Decline of High-Cognitive-Demand Student Behavior
• Scaffolding of student thinking and reasoning • Pressing for justifications, explanations, or meaning through questions, comments, or feedback • Modeling of high-level performance by teacher or capable students • Selecting tasks that build on students' prior knowledge • Drawing frequent conceptual connections • Providing a means by which students can monitor their own progress • Providing sufficient time to explore	• Routinizing problematic aspects of the task • Failing to hold students accountable for high-level products or processes • Providing insufficient time to wrestle with the demanding aspects of the task or so much time that students drift into off-task behavior • Shifting the emphasis from meaning, concepts, or understanding to the correctness or completeness of the answer • Having classroom management problems • Selecting a task that is inappropriate for a given group of students

Source: Adapted from Stein & Smith, 1998, p. 27.

Visit **go.solution-tree.com/commoncore** for a reproducible version of this table.

A great deal of mathematical learning can happen when students explain and justify processes and check the reasonableness of solutions. In many instances, students can learn about other solutions for the problem and other ways of solving the problem, and they can make mathematical connections to other problems and content. Helping students to persevere in the process and learn to habitually reflect on their solution process (or processes) and ask themselves, "What should I remember about solving this problem that might help me in the future?" is a key step in helping them become proficient problem solvers.

Mathematical Practice 6: Attend to Precision

Inherent in learning mathematics is the need to be precise. Precision is not just about the accuracy of a solution, but also about being precise in the way teachers and students communicate about mathematics. Communication here is broadly defined. It includes oral and written communication, vocabulary, notation, and symbols. Terms used in mathematics have intentional and rich definitions. Notation and symbols have specific meanings and uses. When your communication in the mathematics classroom veers from the correct use of vocabulary, notation, and symbols, you often miss opportunities for learning. Precise use of mathematical vocabulary supports students' development of the critical nuances of mathematical ideas within content-specific terms. Attention to precision is about clear student communication with the teacher and peers, using accurate mathematical vocabulary, and appropriately using labels as the means to support and articulate mathematical reasoning.

What Is the Intent of Mathematical Practice 6, and Why Is It Important?

CCSS Mathematical Practice 6, "Attend to precision," refers to the need for students to communicate and calculate precisely and correctly (NGA & CCSSO, 2010a, p. 7). Middle school students who are proficient in this practice:

- Use careful, accurate vocabulary

- Use symbols, most notably the equal sign, and notation correctly

- Label axes and represent quantities appropriately when constructing graphs

- Include units with quantities as necessary

- Perform calculations carefully and appropriately

- Describe the procedures they used accurately

Precision in vocabulary includes students using mathematics terms correctly in writing and speaking, such as using *rate of change* instead of *goes up by* or *goes down by* when describing changes in quantities and using *scale factor* instead of *what I multiplied by* when describing how they calculate an equivalent ratio. Attending to precision also includes students using clear definitions in communication with others.

What Teacher Actions Develop Mathematical Practice 6?

Students often emulate their teachers when it comes to the use of precision with definitions, general language, and ideas related to mathematics. You need to be sure you are modeling precision in your mathematics instruction. Reaching agreement on language and notation usage is an appropriate use of your time during lesson planning in your collaborative team time.

As an example, precision also includes using notation, symbols, and models. During a unit on probability, middle school students learn new notation and models, such as tree diagrams, to represent probabilities and sample spaces—7.SP.8 (see appendix C, page 199). Figure 2.5 shows a student's attempt to use a tree diagram to solve a probability problem. Although the student drew a tree diagram and correctly used it to solve the problem, the student's work shows a lack of precision in constructing the model, in using notation, and in using symbols.

Stacy is on the girls basketball team and has just been fouled. She gets two free throws. A free throw is worth 1 point, and she is a 50 percent free-throw shooter for the season. What is the probability that she will score 0 points, 1 point, or 2 points during her free throw attempts?

$^{27}/_{50} = 50\%$

Throw One   Throw Two

0 < 0 = 0

1 = 1

1 < 0 = 1

1 = 2

0 points = 25%

1 point = 50%

2 points = 25%

Figure 2.5: Sample probability problem.

First, the student does not use the equal sign (=) correctly. In the tree diagram, instead of making an *outcomes* column to the right of the tree diagram and listing the outcome for each terminal branch, the student uses the equal sign to denote *gives an outcome of*, which results in equations 0 = 1 and 0 = 2. Similarly, in describing the probabilities, the student uses the equal sign to denote the probability instead of using correct probability notation: P(0 points) = 25 percent. Attending to precision means helping students to attend to such details in the use of symbols and notation.

Precision also arises in representing situations with equations and graphs, defining variables, labeling graph axes to clearly identify the quantities represented, and being aware of differences in graphing discrete and continuous quantities. For example, when students create an equation and graph to represent the cost of purchasing team T-shirts, where each shirt costs $10, and there is a $25 setup fee, they should clearly define the independent variable as the number of shirts purchased and the dependent variable as cost in dollars. They should also recognize that the graph should show discrete points or discrete points connected with a dashed trend line rather than a solid line, because the domain of the function is discrete, not continuous.

Additionally, students are expected to be accurate and appropriate with procedures and calculations. Accuracy is self-explanatory, but appropriateness as it relates to precision is a bit more elusive. Part of solving problems provided in context involves determining the level of precision that is necessary. Sometimes an estimate is sufficient. If that is the case, how close of an estimate is warranted or acceptable? The same is true with measurement. The context of the problem often determines the level of accuracy for measurements.

When students are given opportunities to explain and justify their mathematical ideas they become engaged in the Mathematical Practice of attending to precision. Similarly, you should expect your students to include appropriate units with quantities when sharing solutions to problems involving length, area, surface area, and volume measurements as well as other solutions to problems provided in context.

Finally, you should give students regular, consistent feedback about the precision of their peer-to-peer communication in class—vocabulary, notation, use of symbols, calculations, and descriptions of their procedures and problem-solving processes.

Mathematical Practices 1 and 6 should cross all middle school or junior high school courses as an integral part of student learning of mathematics on a unit-by-unit basis. Sharing ideas for how to develop the overarching habits of mind should be an ongoing part of discussions and planning with the members of your collaborative team—as part of the PLC process every day.

Reasoning and Explaining

Mathematical Practices 2 and 3 are about how students reason mathematically and communicate their mathematical reasoning and sense making to you and to other students. These Mathematical Practices emphasize the need for students to quantify, contextualize, and decontextualize mathematics. As they do so, students learn to make and justify mathematical arguments, justify their reasoning, and critique others' mathematical justifications as they learn the content together.

Mathematical Practice 2: Reason Abstractly and Quantitatively

In mathematics, you want students to be able to take specific situations and learn to make them more generalized or abstract so that they can reason about the mathematical properties and ideas and compute as needed, without the details of the situation. You also want them to interpret the results of their reasoning or computations in the original context, to see if they make sense. The goal is fluidity in this bidirectional reasoning, moving from concrete situations to abstract mathematical representations and the reverse. Students who are able to reason abstractly and quantitatively view mathematics as a way to make sense of the world around them and are able to reason with peers as well as you as the teacher.

What Is the Intent of Mathematical Practice 2, and Why Is It Important?

Reasoning in mathematics is the means by which students try to make sense (by thinking through ideas carefully, considering examples and alternatives, asking questions, hypothesizing, pondering, and so on) of mathematics so it is usable and useful (NCTM, 2000). Hence, the role of Mathematical Practice 2, "Reason abstractly and quantitatively," is critical to students' engagement in every area and at every level of the mathematics curriculum (NGA & CCSSO, 2010a, p. 6).

According to Ball and Bass (2003), "mathematical reasoning is something that students can learn to do" (p. 33). In fact, these authors suggest two very important benefits of reasoning: (1) it aids students' mathematical understanding and ability to use concepts and procedures in meaningful ways, and (2) it helps students reconstruct *faded knowledge*, that is, knowledge that is forgotten by your students, but can be restored through reasoning with the current content.

Expected student proficiencies in this practice are the ability to *decontextualize*—to create and work with an abstract representation of a given situation—partnered with the ability to *contextualize*—to interpret the abstract representations in context, both during the solution process if needed and after the solution has been obtained.

What Teacher Actions Develop Mathematical Practice 2?

Classroom discourse that promotes reasoning abstractly and quantitatively is talk that involves teacher-to-student communication as well as a significant amount of student-to-student communication as essential elements of your daily classroom lesson planning. Your teacher-to-student communication includes questions you pose that probe students' thinking beyond their suggestions of an answer. You consider students' answers, whether right or wrong, so that opportunities to stretch their thinking beyond the answer are realized. In addition, teacher-to-student communication that promotes reasoning abstractly and quantitatively should involve discussions emerging from students' hypotheses about a mathematical concept or procedure and students' propositions on how mathematics works. Peer-to-peer explanations and debates support student-to-student communication when students are required to provide justification and reasoning for their thinking.

These statements are examples that help elicit and promote discourse in the mathematics classroom.

- "Explain to a partner how Lindsay's and Brandon's strategies are similar and different."

- "Consider what questions might you ask Kevin about his strategy and why he chose it for these types of problems."

- "Create a problem and a rubric for scoring the problem that could be used on a quiz or test for this Mathematical Practice."

Additionally, you can do the following to promote discourse.

- Give students a solved problem representing student work containing errors. Ask students to identify the errors and indicate how to correct accordingly.

- Provide students a problem from prior experience, and then expand the problem to include new discoveries or extensions of the mathematical structures involved.

In addition, students working collaboratively to engage in mathematics can fuel student-to-student discourse about reasoning by sharing their mathematical thought and making decisions about routes for their thinking in order to arrive at sensible conclusions. Inferences about students' ability to reason can also be determined through carefully analyzing student work, discussions with peers, and performance on rigorous in-class and shared mathematical tasks.

When your students are engaged in Mathematical Practice 2, they are sharing and justifying their mathematical conceptions and adjusting their thinking based on mathematical information gathered through discussions and responses to questions. Mathematical reasoning must be a continuous expectation for students as they learn to *do* mathematics on their own or together, whether while working in groups or during whole-class discussion or after school working on homework. To facilitate discourse well takes advanced planning and intentional lesson design work by your collaborative team.

Additionally, students must consider the units involved in a problem and the meaning of those units in context, not just be able to compute with them. For students to learn to decontextualize and contextualize requires that students have regular opportunities to solve real-world or application problems that require those processes.

Figure 2.6 shows a sample problem to illustrate these ideas.

Verizon Wireless Problem

Does $0.002 = 0.002¢?

Diane called Verizon's customer service to question a charge on her bill. She was charged $71.79 for using 35,896 kilobytes of data. The posted rate was 0.002 cents per kilobyte, so she thought this charge must be wrong or that the rate had changed. When she called, the representative said, "Our rate is still 0.002 cents per kilobyte. That is the rate you were charged. When you multiply the number of kilobytes that you used—35,896—by the rate of 0.002, the answer is 71.792. So, the $71.79 on your bill is correct." Diane replied, "If the rate is 0.002 cents per kilobyte, my bill is wrong. It should be only $0.72."

Explain who is correct, Diane or the Verizon representative, and explain to the person who is wrong the error in his or her reasoning.

Figure 2.6: Sample problem for Mathematical Practice 2—Verizon Wireless.

Visit **go.solution-tree.com/commoncore** for a reproducible version of this figure.

Representing the situation as the multiplication problem $35,896 \times 0.002$ involves decontextualizing. Interpreting the result of the computation—71.792—in the original problem situation is contextualizing. In this problem, contextualizing 71.792 correctly as 71.792 cents or $0.72 instead of $71.79 requires attention to and understanding of the units in the problem. You can hear the customer's actual call to Verizon and his conversation with customer service representatives on YouTube (www.youtube.com /watch?v=ANDk0SWzplo). Visit **go.solution-tree.com/commoncore** for links to the resources in this book.

Typically, we provide more opportunities for students to engage in decontextualizing, representing real-world situations with mathematics, with less emphasis on contextualizing. Yet, as figure 2.6 illustrates, contextualizing is a critical aspect of solving real-world problems and should always be part of the solution process. To develop the contextualizing aspect of this practice, you should consistently ask students to interpret their solutions in the context of the original problem, and encourage them to ask themselves whether or not their answer makes sense.

In addition, asking students to create their own contextualization of mathematical expressions, equations, or relationships can be a valuable instructional and assessment technique. For example, asking students to create situations that can be represented by $3 \div \frac{1}{2}$ and $3 \times \frac{1}{2}$ forces them to think about the difference in meaning between those two expressions. It also provides valuable information about their understanding of the meaning of fraction multiplication and division.

Mathematical Practice 3: Construct Viable Arguments and Critique the Reasoning of Others

In order for students to authentically engage in the learning of mathematics, it is imperative they articulate their reasoning through the use of logical reasoning and argumentation. In their communication of ideas to others, students develop the ability to construct justifications based on mathematical definitions, properties, and conceptual understandings. As they listen to one another, students can distinguish between well-thought out explanations from arguments that lack specificity or accuracy. This practice involves both these deductive aspects of doing mathematics and the inductive aspect of doing mathematics—making conjectures. It also includes communicating and evaluating logical arguments, justifications, and solution processes.

What Is the Intent of Mathematical Practice 3, and Why Is It Important?

Students engaged in Mathematical Practice 3, "Construct viable arguments and critique the reasoning of others," are making conjectures based on their analysis of given situations (NGA & CCSSO, 2010a, pp. 6–7). Students make, explain, and justify their mathematical arguments and thinking as they communicate to other classmates and to you. Classmates listen to explanations and justifications, ask questions to clarify their understanding of the steps used to solve a problem, and judge the reasonableness of the claims.

The successful facilitation of this standard is based on the social learning environment of the classroom. As Rasmussen, Yackel, and King (2003) state:

> Every class, from the most traditional to the most reform-oriented, has social norms that are operative for that particular class. What distinguishes one class from another is not the presence or absence of social norms but, rather, the nature of the norms that differ from class to class. (pp. 147–148)

When students justify their arguments and critique the mathematical arguments of other students, they are making sense of the mathematics in meaningful ways. Students no longer view the teacher as the sole authority of mathematical knowledge, but rather the teacher facilitates student, and often peer-to-peer, construction of knowledge.

This practice extends beyond students explaining their solutions to the problem to include the provision of arguments about why particular strategies work and beyond being able to read, listen to, evaluate, and respond to the reasoning of their peers and others. As discussed in the next section, the problem in figure 2.7 (page 45) is one example of this; students are to analyze the solution presented in the problem and then create and explain their own solution to one another and to the class. Analyses and explanations can be oral or written.

What Teacher Actions Develop Mathematical Practice 3?

Developing students' proficiency in this practice requires that you establish a social learning environment in your classroom that values explanations and makes it safe for students to critique each other's reasoning. In a middle school classroom in which students are expected to construct arguments and critique others' reasoning, students should:

- Provide explanations and justifications to one another as part of their solution processes

- Attempt to make sense of their classmates' solutions by asking questions for clarification

- Communicate when they don't understand or don't agree with solutions others present by spurring discourse between and among students

- Respect all ideas and be open to challenge them, including the teacher's ideas

Eventually, these discussions become a natural part of the classroom discourse and can occur in an organized way without your direction. However, this type of student discourse will require well-established norms through a process of negotiation in which you make your expectations clear but involve students in the process of implementing the norms (Yackel & Cobb, 1996). These sorts of expectations help to support communication of what effective mathematics learners *do*. Mathematics learners make conjectures, test those conjectures, and discuss their implications within a community that is receptive to such discussions.

Your role as the teacher is to establish a classroom environment in which students are safe to present and challenge ideas without ridicule. Your lesson plan must also require you to read and address the sometime subtle signals of tone and body language between peers. Following are some possible classroom norms that support and encourage students to engage in discourse involving constructing viable arguments and critiquing the reasoning of others:

- Every student is responsible for sharing ideas about the lesson.

- Students respectfully listen to one another.

- Students ask another student a question before asking the teacher.

- Students understand that mistakes are opportunities and part of the process of learning.

- Students understand that sharing and discussing reasoning and justification are critical components and expectations of learning in the mathematics classroom.

Having common social norms for all middle school mathematics classrooms helps students learn structure and eliminates the need to re-establish norms from scratch when students change classes or progress to the next grade. These norms can become part of the school culture.

Such an environment includes regular student-to-student communication, rather than only the student-teacher-student communication that is typical of most classrooms. One of the most difficult parts of establishing such an environment is learning when you should be quiet and let the students do the talking.

As you plan your lesson, include opportunities for students to make and evaluate conjectures within meaningful mathematics discussions. Use your content knowledge to support the use of tasks that elicit conjectures and arguments and guide discussions around important mathematical ideas. The collective content knowledge and experiences of your collaborative team can be a great asset to create or identify such tasks.

For example, a key element of Mathematical Practice 3 is the ability of your students to distinguish correct logic from incorrect logic in both teacher and student arguments. In middle school, students also develop their understanding of mathematical proof, recognizing that counterexamples can be used to establish that conjectures are false, but that no amount of examples is sufficient to prove that conjectures are true. For example, consider the sample integers task in figure 2.7.

Integers

Decide if the following statements are true or false. Then, justify your answer mathematically; that is, explain your reasoning in a way that will convince someone else that you are correct.

1. The sum of a negative integer and a positive integer is always positive.

2. The sum of two negative integers is always negative.

3. The difference between two negative integers is always positive.

Figure 2.7: Sample integers task.

Visit **go.solution-tree.com/commoncore** for a reproducible version of this figure.

Students should be able to: (1) determine that statements one and three are false, construct a counterexample for each to illustrate that the sum or difference can be negative or 0, and recognize that a single counterexample for each is sufficient to establish that the statements are false; and (2) determine that statement two is true and construct a valid argument that demonstrates that this is always true, such as, "A negative integer is to the left of 0 on the number line. To add a negative integer, n, to it, you move n units to the left, so the sum is more negative. There is no way to get a sum that is 0 or positive, because those values are at or to the right of 0 on the number line, which is to the right of your original number on the number line." Furthermore, students should realize that providing examples of sums of different negative numbers is *not* sufficient to establish that statement two is always true.

To ensure that students have daily opportunities to explain their reasoning and critique the reasoning of others, you should explicitly build such opportunities into each lesson as part of your daily planning. Develop a core set of statements that you can use regularly to prompt such discussions, such as those listed for teacher actions to develop Mathematical Practice 2 (pages 40–43).

Other strategies that support Mathematical Practice 3 include:

- Students make conjectures then construct a logical argument to establish whether their conjecture is always true.

- Students solve a problem that is either correct or contains errors. Ask students to determine whether the reasoning in the problem is correct. If it is not correct, ask them to identify the errors, explain why it is an error, and indicate how to correct the solution accordingly.

- Students formulate conjectures and evaluate them. The middle grades geometry standards are a particularly rich context for this, since the standards call for students to develop formulas for finding area and volume of geometric figures and describe relationships between geometric figures (6.G.1, see appendix B, page 191).

In planning lessons for these content standards, look for opportunities for students to explore and make their own conjectures, instead of simply providing them with formulas or describing relationships to them.

Modeling and Using Tools

Mathematical Practices 4 and 5 combine to capture the essence of how students use and represent mathematics with appropriate and varied tools in order to reason and make sense of the content.

Mathematical Practice 4: Model With Mathematics

Just as students need to be able to generalize or reason abstractly, mathematically proficient students are able to use their knowledge of mathematics to model various phenomena or mathematical ideas. Modeling involves the ability to see mathematics as a way to make sense of the world around us as well as the world of mathematics.

What Is the Intent of Mathematical Practice 4, and Why Is It Important?

Students engaged in CCSS Mathematical Practice 4, "Model with mathematics," solve real-world problems by applying known mathematics (NGA & CCSSO, 2010a, p. 7). Because of the word *model*, this practice is often misinterpreted as representing mathematical concepts by using manipulatives. While manipulatives and other representations can be used as instructional tools to make sense of real-world problems, that is just one element of this mathematical practice. In this practice students also represent real-world situations with mathematics by using mathematical tools such as symbols, equations, diagrams, tables, graphs, graphing calculators, and formulas. Students move fluidly between different mathematical representations based on what questions they are trying to answer and also move between the real-world situation and the mathematical representation of it. The ways students model and represent situations will evolve as students learn more complex mathematics content in grades 6–8. The basic modeling process presented in figure 2.8 involves:

> (1) identifying variables in the situation and selecting those that represent essential features, (2) formulating a model by creating and selecting geometric, graphical, tabular, algebraic, or statistical representations that describe relationships between the variables, (3) analyzing and performing operations on these relationships to draw conclusions, (4) interpreting the results of the mathematics in terms of the original situation, (5) validating the conclusions by comparing them with the situation, and then either improving the model or, if it is acceptable, (6) reporting on the conclusions and the reasoning behind them. Choices, assumptions, and approximations are present throughout this cycle. (NGA & CCSSO, 2010a, pp. 72–73)

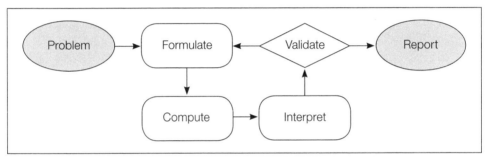

Source: NGA & CCSSO, 2010a, p. 72. © Copyright 2010. National Governors Association Center for Best Practices and Council of Chief State School Officers. All rights reserved.

Figure 2.8: The Common Core mathematics modeling cycle.

Typically, *model* can also mean using visual diagrams to represent a mathematical idea; for example, showing how to multiply two fractions using a rectangular area model. However, that definition is too limiting and is not the intended use of the term in Mathematical Practice 4. Model as used in this practice is "the process of choosing and using appropriate mathematics and statistics to analyze empirical situations, to understand them better, and to improve decisions" (NGA & CCSSO, 2010a, p. 72).

What Teacher Actions Develop Mathematical Practice 4?

This standard builds on and extends CCSS Mathematical Practices 1 and 2, with their focus on mathematizing real-world problems. Your students must first be given the opportunity to explore real-world problems or situations and then encouraged to represent those problems mathematically. Once students represent the problems with mathematics, they solve the problems and interpret their results within the context of the problem. All of this depends on middle school students being provided the chance to solve problems that arise from everyday life. In short, part of your role is to provide opportunities for students to explore and share solutions to real-world situations that present themselves in and out of daily school life. These sorts of experiences will prepare students for expectations related to reasoning mathematically in high school (NCTM, 2009).

The following sample problems both engage students in mathematical modeling but illustrate two different aspects of this mathematical practice. Figure 2.9 calls for students to represent the different video rental plans mathematically—perhaps creating a table or graph or using equations—then using their representation to determine when the three plans would cost the same. In solving this problem, students are creating an explicit model then using their model to draw a conclusion.

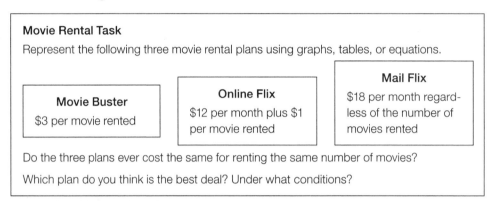

Movie Rental Task

Represent the following three movie rental plans using graphs, tables, or equations.

Movie Buster

$3 per movie rented

Online Flix

$12 per month plus $1 per movie rented

Mail Flix

$18 per month regardless of the number of movies rented

Do the three plans ever cost the same for renting the same number of movies?

Which plan do you think is the best deal? Under what conditions?

Source: Adapted from Inside Mathematics, 2010a.

Figure 2.9: Sample middle school mathematical modeling problem—movie rental plans.

The Wikipedia claim problem in figure 2.10 highlights a different aspect of mathematical modeling—making assumptions and approximations to simplify a situation, realizing these may need revision later. Typically, students do not construct an explicit mathematical representation of the situation, such as a single equation, table, or graph. Instead, they engage in a series of computations to answer questions like, How many people eat at McDonald's on average? How many people per hour are served? The students continue to make and refine assumptions about the real-world situation and use those to determine further calculations, and how to interpret the results of their computations. Questions that arise typically include, What does it mean to eat at McDonald's? Does going through the drive-through window count? How about people who only purchase coffee? What about people who are purchasing meals for others as well, not just themselves? This ongoing movement between the real-world situation and the mathematical calculations is at the heart of modeling complex phenomena. Although students don't create a single mathematical representation of the situation, they are still engaged in mathematical modeling.

Your role is to provide students opportunities to engage in varied types of modeling problems, and to support them as they try to make sense of the situation. In selecting tasks that will develop student proficiency in this mathematical practice consider how much structure students will need to be able to engage in the problem. While the

Wikipedia reports that 8 percent of all Americans eat at McDonald's every day. Data reveal approximately 311 million Americans in 2012 and 12,800 McDonald's restaurants in the United States.

Make a conjecture as to whether or not you believe the web release to be true, and then create a mathematical argument that justifies your conclusion.

Figure 2.10: Sample middle school mathematical modeling problem—Wikipedia claim.

Visit **go.solution-tree.com/commoncore** for a reproducible version of this figure.

Wikipedia claim problem is valuable, it may be too open for students who have never previously engaged in such a problem. Instead, you might want to use a problem with more structure, such as the one in figure 2.11.

Having Kittens

Cats can't add but they do multiply! In just eighteen months, a female cat can have 2,000 descendants. Figure out whether this number of descendants is realistic. Here are some facts that you will need.

- **Length of pregnancy:** About two months
- **Age at which a female cat can first get pregnant:** About four months
- **Number of kittens in a litter:** Usually four to six
- **Average number of litters a female cat can have in one year:** Three
- **Age at which a female cat no longer has kittens**: About ten years

Source: Adapted from Bowland Charitable Trust, 2010.
Figure 2.11: Sample middle school modeling problem—having kittens.

Modeling problems typically engage students in other Mathematical Practices as they explain why their models make sense and justify their assumptions to others. The examples in figures 2.9, 2.10, and 2.11 explicitly engage students in Mathematical Practices 1, 2, and 3. As your team develops or identifies problems that require students to model contextual problems and construct viable arguments to support their reasoning, you work together to anticipate what students will do, to determine what constitutes a viable argument, and to teach students how to use tools (such as a graphing and statistics tool) strategically.

Mathematical Practice 5: Use Appropriate Tools Strategically

Mathematical tools come in all shapes, sizes, and varieties, ranging from pencil and paper to the latest technology; they are available to help students solve problems and make sense of mathematical ideas. Using technology effectively requires making strategic choices about how and when to use these tools. Regardless of the tool, what is important is the way in which students use these tools to reason, solve problems, and learn mathematics.

What Is the Intent of Mathematical Practice 5, and Why Is It Important?

Mathematically proficient students have sufficient experience with a variety of tools to make appropriate decisions and strategic choices about when particular tools will be useful, recognizing both benefits and limitations of the tools. The tools referred to in this Mathematical Practice include pencil and paper, concrete models, rulers, protractors, and representational models (graphs, equations, tables, and so on), as well as various technology tools, including calculators, spreadsheets, dynamic geometry software, computer algebra systems, and web-based resources.

Mathematically proficient students use this practice to make thoughtful decisions about which tools to use in specific situations. For example, figure 2.12 illustrates how proficient students might select an appropriate computational tool or approach for a given problem (Kanold et al., 2012).

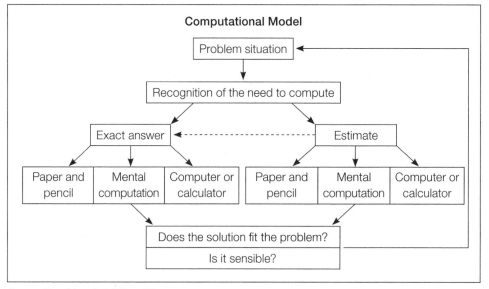

Source: Kanold et al., 2012, p. 35.

Figure 2.12: Student computational options model.

Visit **go.solution-tree.cm/commoncore** for a reproducible version of this figure.

Selection of an appropriate tool depends on the specific context and goal. For example, for the Wikipedia claim problem (see figure 2.10), one might decide that an estimate is good enough and that doing approximated pencil-and-paper calculations is sufficient. However, for the Verizon Wireless problem (see figure 2.6, page 42), a calculator may be the most efficient computational tool since the problem requires an exact answer and the computation involves multidigit numbers.

Tools in this standard include various mathematical representations and models in addition to physical tools like protractors, compasses, and calculators. Consider the expectations for students as they solve problems in the grade 8 domain Expressions and Equations for the content standard cluster *Analyze and solve linear equations and pairs of simultaneous linear equations* and the Functions domain and cluster *Use functions to model relationships between quantities* (see appendix D, page 205). In solving these problems, students proficient in Mathematical Practice 5 will not only be able to model functions and solve problems using equations, tables, and graphs but will also recognize the benefits and limitations of each representation so that they can make informed choices about when to use each representation and which technology to use—pencil and paper or graphing calculator—to construct their representation.

Similarly, the standards in the grade 7 Statistics and Probability domain (7.SP, see appendix C, page 198) call for students to learn different models for determining probabilities, such as organized lists, tables, tree diagrams, and simulation. Applying this Mathematical Practice in the study of probability means that students will not only learn to make and use these various models but also learn when each might be most helpful and learn the limitations of each one.

Regardless of the nature of the tool, mathematically proficient students will understand how to use the tool, when to use it, and the benefits or limitations that a particular tool offers in a specific situation. For this practice, it's the students who are selecting and using the tools, not the teacher. While teachers' use of technology as an instructional tool is important, the focus of this Mathematical Practice is on students' use of tools to solve problems and explore and understand mathematical ideas.

What Teacher Actions Develop Mathematical Practice 5?

For students to develop proficiency in this practice, they must (1) have a range of tools available to them on a regular basis, (2) have sufficient opportunities with the various tools to learn about their limitations and benefits in a particular situation, (3) have the opportunity to choose the tools they will use, and (4) have the opportunity to engage in explicit discussions about the benefits and limitations of specific tools in particular situations. Your role is to ensure that such opportunities occur in productive ways on a regular basis.

First, on a unit-by-unit basis, you and your collaborative team need to develop a plan for acquiring or providing access to tools and a system for students to use those tools. This includes decisions about which tools all students need access to every day so every classroom is equipped with them, and which are needed most during particular instructional units so that all students have access when needed and the tools can be shared effectively. Second, you and your team must collaboratively plan lessons that explicitly provide students opportunities to learn how to use specific tools, to learn about their benefits and limitations, and to have opportunities to make strategic choices. A key component of that planning is determining what tasks to use for each of these purposes.

To help students learn to use graphs, tables, diagrams, equations, and other models to solve problems, you need to provide students sufficient experience with each method (either by hand or using technology) so that they develop sufficient skills to be able to use the methods effectively. For example, a tree diagram is an effective model for the basketball problem in figure 2.5 (page 39). However, for situations in which the probability of making or missing a free throw is not the same (for example, the shooter has a 60 percent average), an area model might provide greater clarity to the solution. Or for a situation with more than two events, such as tossing a coin five times, a tree diagram may be unwieldy, so a frequency table showing the distribution of outcomes may be a more useful model. See figure 2.13 for examples.

Michael, who has a 60 percent free throw average, is attempting two free throws. A free throw is worth one point. Is he most likely to score zero points, one point, or two points? Explain.

	Makes First Shot 60 percent	Misses First Shot 40 percent
Makes Second Shot 60 percent	36 percent	24 percent
Misses Second Shot 40 percent	24 percent	16 percent

P(0 points) = 16 percent

P(1 point) = 48 percent

P(2 points) = 36 percent

Sam tosses four coins. What are the possible outcomes? How likely is he to toss all heads or all tails?

Possible Outcomes

0	1	2	3	4
TTTT	HTTT	HHTT	HHHT	HHHH
	THTT	HTHT	HHTH	
	TTHT	HTTH	HTHH	
	TTTH	THHT	THHH	
		THTH		
		TTHH		

16 possible outcomes

P(all heads or tails) = $\frac{2}{16} = \frac{1}{8}$

Figure 2.13: Sample probability models.

Visit **go.solution-tree.com/commoncore** for a reproducible version of this figure.

Your collaborative team should also discuss how to engage students in tasks specifically designed to highlight the benefits and limitations of tables and graphs as solution methods; for example, tables and graphs are difficult or time consuming to use to obtain an exact answer when it is not an integer value. When students recognize the limitations of graphs and tables, they understand the need to solve equations algebraically. Debriefing discussions for such lessons should specifically engage students in describing the benefits and limitations that they discovered, as well as describing conditions under which each tool might be useful. Student proficiency in this practice also includes identifying "relevant external mathematical resources, such as digital content on websites, and using them to pose or solve problems" (NGA & CCSSO, 2010a, p. 7; see appendix A, page 183).

To develop this proficiency, you and your collaborative team need to create specific tasks or assignments that engage students in such inquiry and design specific lessons for them to learn how to do such explorations. For example, while learning the Pythagorean theorem (8.G.6–8, see appendix D, page 206), you might assign students to find a proof of the theorem different from ones discussed in class, and be prepared to explain *their* proof to the class. Such research assignments could be done in collaboration with other teachers outside the mathematics department, such as a technology teacher or librarian. Regularly engaging students in such explorations enables them to develop and demonstrate proficiency in Mathematical Practice 5.

Once your students have access and experience in using various tools, you can also engage them in tasks that require them to select appropriate tools for a particular mathematics activity. This will further develop their understanding of how tools differ in usefulness. You can use these four questions to help students select the most appropriate tool (technology or otherwise) to do the mathematics.

1. Is the tool necessary?

2. Is the tool easy to use?

3. Is the tool effective and efficient for the problem or task presented?

4. Does the tool provide a meaningful model to support the mathematics?

One of the most challenging aspects of helping students learn to make strategic tool choices is helping them learn when and when not to use a calculator. Teaching your students to make this choice is particularly important for you as a middle grades teacher. In these grades, students are expected to extend their knowledge of the basic operations from whole numbers to integers and to all rational numbers. Some students inappropriately rely on the calculator for even the most basic integer computations; for example, they might use a calculator for -3 + 7 or -7 – (-10), instead of developing proficiency with mental computation for such problems. Your role is to help students set appropriate expectations for making basic computations, to provide opportunities for them to develop strategies for mental computations, and to provide practice that demonstrates using calculators for such problems is actually less efficient than mental computation.

Discussing effective use of technology and other tools with your students as they reason mathematically is an integral part of your collaborative team's discussions and decisions about task selection during the unit. Using technology as a tool to support student development of Mathematical Practices 4 and 5 is a powerful teacher weapon for expanding students' learning experiences well beyond pencil and paper. Technology can be especially powerful in advancing student mathematical thinking, notably in helping students to develop conceptual understanding of abstract mathematical concepts. NCSM's (2011) position paper on technology in the mathematics classroom highlights several benefits of technology on student mathematics learning, including greater student participation and engagement. Teachers can use technology to:

- Display student solution strategies for discussion and validation

- Illustrate multiple mathematical samples—leading to efficient student discovery within a dynamic environment

- Highlight multiple representations for solution paths that will verify student results and develop deeper understanding

- Collect and disseminate formative assessment data from students and student teams, and use the data to make decisions about next steps in class

- Enhance student collaborative learning and discussions

Discussing effective technology and strategic tool use with your middle school students, as they reason mathematically, is an integral part of your collaborative team's discussions and decisions about task selection during each unit.

Seeing Structure and Generalizing

Mathematical Practices 7 and 8 are about the inherent beauty and power of mathematics. Students develop proficiency toward seeing the structure of mathematics—expecting patterns and regularities and actively looking for them—then use these structures to solve problems and learn new mathematics. This will increase their ability and disposition to do mathematics successfully.

Mathematical Practice 7: Look For and Make Use of Structure

A defining feature of mathematics is its structure. There is structure across all strands of mathematics. For example, there is structure in geometry (every square is a rhombus), basic operations (the sum of two even numbers is always an even number), and numerical patterns (linear and exponential functions have particular patterns in their rates of change). Looking for structure in mathematical situations and using that structure to identify similarities and differences across topics and problems facilitates solving problems and learning new mathematical ideas.

What Is the Intent of Mathematical Practice 7, and Why Is It Important?

When students are mathematically proficient, they seek to connect new ideas to prior learning and to other mathematical ideas. Structure helps students learn what to expect in mathematics. If middle school students learn how mathematics works and why it works the way it does, they then begin to notice, look for, and make use of structure to solve problems as they become engaged in what it means to do mathematics. Proficiency in this practice involves three related habits of mind: (1) looking for patterns and relationships; (2) being able to step back, change perspective, and look at the big picture; and (3) being able to "see complicated things . . . as single objects, or as composed of several objects" (NGA & CCSSO, 2010a, p. 8; see appendix A, page 183).

Looking for patterns has long been part of the mathematics curriculum; in fact, mathematics has been characterized as the study of patterns. A key feature of this practice is looking for patterns related to the structure of mathematics and relationships between mathematical ideas. Students can look for patterns when computing with positive and negative numbers. Similarly, students can identify patterns related to the distributive and other properties of the real number system as the number patterns reveal the existence of the structure being studied. An important feature of this Mathematical Practice is the student use of patterns to help develop understanding of the mathematical relationships and structures that exist, rather than recognizing, describing, and extending patterns just for the sake of looking at the pattern.

What Teacher Actions Develop Mathematical Practice 7?

There are several actions you can take to support students in their development of looking for and making use of structure in mathematics. Students may or may not recognize structure in mathematics. For your students who do not readily recognize structure in mathematics, it is important for you to encourage them to attend to structure. You can do this by engaging students in tasks that are conducive for exploring structure and then providing students opportunities to create examples of structure of their own to share and discuss with each other. Encourage students to wonder by asking questions: "If every square is a rhombus, is every rhombus a square?" or "If the sum of two even numbers is always even, does the same property hold true for multiplication?"

Alternatively, to help students' understanding of the structure that surrounds the definitions of negative and zero exponents (8.EE.1, see appendix D, page 203), you can create and extend number patterns that allow students to conjecture about the laws of exponents for a^0 or a^{-m}. Thus, since $3^4 = 81$, $3^3 = 27$, $3^2 = 9$, $3^1 = 3$, does the pattern support the definition of $a^0 = 1$ and $a^{-m} = \frac{1}{a^m}$?

Students can benefit from acknowledging structure as they move across grades in the middle school mathematics curriculum. Encourage students to habitually look for similarities and differences across topics (for example, "What patterns emerge for exponential expressions in which the exponents are fractions of the form $\frac{1}{a}$ where a is a positive integer?") and to use prior mathematical knowledge (such as the properties of exponents for integers) to make sense of new situations.

Mathematical Practice 8: Look For and Express Regularity in Repeated Reasoning

Mathematically proficient students recognize that looking for patterns is a way to reason about and make sense of the mathematics. Looking for and being able to express regularity in their reasoning processes is one way students use patterns to learn and generalize mathematical concepts.

What Is the Intent of Mathematical Practice 8, and Why Is It Important?

Like Mathematical Practice 7, Mathematical Practice 8 also involves patterns and structure. However, when engaged in Mathematical Practice 8, "Look for and express regularity in repeated reasoning," students move beyond solving individual problems to finding ways to generalize their procedures into *efficient methods* for solving such problems (NGA & CCSSO, 2010a, p. 8; see appendix A, page 183). With their desire to simplify students' learning pathways and minimize confusion (Stigler et al., 1999), middle school teachers are often tempted to provide students with efficient procedures for algebraic computations too early. When this occurs, students miss the opportunity to look for and express regularity in repeated reasoning. Instead, teachers should provide students with opportunities to make sense of problems and to look for the regularity in their calculations. This practice interacts with Mathematical Practice 1, as this kind of activity requires that students develop perseverance to make sense of the repeated reasoning.

What Teacher Actions Develop Mathematical Practice 8?

The tasks you provide and the questioning techniques you employ are critical actions to help students develop proficiency in this practice. Engaging your students in tasks that require repeated calculations, then asking them to describe the processes they use and to look for repetition in those processes provides the scaffolding necessary for them to begin to determine general methods for calculations. You will need to consider multiple examples—as well as their progression—to help students move from seeing the repeated reasoning of a single example to being able to build a general method.

A common middle grades task that engages students in expressing regularity in repeated reasoning is investigating sums of small positive and negative integers. In this task, students use models (number line or chip model) to find the sums of two positive numbers, two negative numbers, and positive and negative integers, when the positive number is greater than, less than, or equal to the negative integer. Students are asked to extend their computations with small numbers to describe how they could find the sums of larger positive and negative integers then generalize to all integers. In this task, the generalization is a description of how to find the sum for particular cases (such as, integers with the same sign and integers with different signs).

Figure 2.14 illustrates another example of expressing regularity in repeated reasoning. In this problem, students calculate the number of tiles that border a square pool of a particular size to create an expression they could use for the number of tiles around any size square pool. Students typically create different expressions for the border, which leads to a discussion of equivalent algebraic expressions (6.EE.3, see appendix B, page 190).

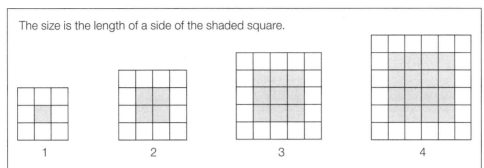

The size is the length of a side of the shaded square.

      1   2   3   4

1. How many tiles are around the first pool?

2. How many tiles are around the second pool? The third pool? The fourth pool? Figure this out without counting the tiles one by one.

3. How many tiles are around the tenth pool? Try to figure this out without drawing the pool.

4. How many tiles are around the one hundredth pool?

5. Find as many different ways as you can to compute the number of squares in the border of any square pool. Be prepared to justify each way.

6. Write an expression or describe how you could determine the number of tiles around any size square pool.

Figure 2.14: Sample problem for expressing regularity in repeated reasoning.

Another type of task that promotes student proficiency in expressing regularity in calculations is contextualized function problems, such as comparing CD prices. For example (Mark, Cuoco, Goldenberg, & Sword, 2010):

> Suppose you want to buy a music CD. A Web site offers a 28 percent discount on the list price. It also adds 5 percent for state sales tax and $3.50 for shipping. The local music store sells CDs for 10 percent off the list price, also charges a 5 percent sales tax, but has no shipping charge. Ignoring the convenience and driving time, is it less expensive to buy online or to buy from the local music store? (p. 506)

One way to help students develop skill in writing algebraic expressions to describe such situations is to have them compute a series of numerical examples for each plan ("How much will a $25 CD cost from the website versus the local music store? A $30 CD?" until they get the *rhythm* of the calculation and can describe a method that will work for any price CD. This general description then leads to writing an algebraic expression for each plan. Students can apply this process to any word problem. In so doing, they are developing and demonstrating their understanding of Mathematical Practice 8.

Once again, the classroom environment and expectations you establish related to social interactions in the classroom set the stage for students to engage in this practice. If there is an expectation that students will make conjectures related to what they notice in the pattern of calculations they complete and share them with their peers, students are more likely to look for and make sense of those generalizations. Your role is to create and maintain the social norms for this type of discovery to take place in your classroom. In classrooms with the expectation that students will create generalizations and then defend them to one another, as well as consider potential counterexamples, students have the opportunity to create general methods for repeated reasoning. Thus, Mathematical Practice 8 is closely linked to Mathematical Practice 3, Construct viable arguments and critique the reasoning of others.

As you consider the descriptions of the Mathematical Practices and the example tasks, the interrelationship among the practices should become apparent. Although some mathematical tasks or problems your team might use bring particular practices to the forefront, many tasks have the potential to engage students in multiple practices, depending on how you implement them in your classroom.

Lesson-Design Elements That Reflect the Common Core Mathematical Practices

In order for you and your team to begin a sustained effort to move toward the instructional vision of the CCSS Mathematical Practices, you should become intentional about using instructional practices and designing daily lessons that engage students in these practices on a unit-by-unit basis.

Mathematics learning has been characterized as an *active* process in which students build their own mathematical knowledge from experiences, coupled with feedback from peers, teachers and other adults, and themselves (Hiebert & Grouws, 2007). Thus, your instruction needs to be designed so that students are *doing* the mathematics—solving problems, analyzing solutions, explaining mathematical ideas. Watching you or other students solve problems, answer questions, or explain ideas and procedures during whole group discourse may be useful at times, but is insufficient for deep student learning and higher levels of student success.

Cognitive science and mathematics education researchers (Bransford, Brown, & Cocking, 2000; Bransford & Donovan, 2005; Donovan & Bransford, 2005; Hiebert & Grouws, 2007) identify the following instructional practices as effective in supporting mathematics learning:

- Engage students with challenging tasks that involve active meaning making
- Help students connect new learning with prior knowledge and address preconceptions and misconceptions
- Engage students in socially constructing knowledge through talk, activity, and interaction around meaningful problems
- Provide students timely feedback so they can revise their work, thinking, and understandings

- Develop students' metacognitive awareness of themselves as a learner, thinker, and problem solver and learn to monitor their learning and performance (Kanold et al., 2012)

Table 2.2 combines several research-informed instructional practices with essential elements of effective instruction (Marzano, 2007; Smith & Cartier, 2007, as cited in Smith & Stein, 2011; Stronge, 2007) and draws from the collective expectations of the CCSS Mathematical Practices. It provides general guidelines and questions that your collaborative teams can use as you work together to create unit and daily lessons that reflect the spirit and intent of the CCSS for mathematics.

Table 2.2: Elements of an Effective Middle School Mathematics Classroom Lesson Design

Lesson Components	Probing Questions for Effective Lesson Design	Reflection
1. Lesson Context: Identifying Learning Targets **Balancing Procedural Fluency *and* Conceptual Understanding**	What is the learning target for the lesson? How does it connect to the bigger focus of the unit?	
	What evidence will be used to determine the level of student readiness and prior knowledge for the learning target?	
	Are conceptual understanding and procedural fluency appropriately balanced in this lesson, given the unit goals?	
	Is the mathematics lesson primarily skill-based building and procedural-fluency building (a *how-to* lesson)?	
	Is the mathematics lesson concept or generalization based (a *what* lesson)?	
	How will you formatively assess students' conceptual understanding or procedural skills?	
	Which CCSS Mathematical Practices will students be engaged in during this lesson?	

continued →

Lesson Components	Probing Questions for Effective Lesson Design	Reflection
2. Lesson Process: Selecting and Using High-Cognitive-Demand Tasks **Planning and Implementing Student Discourse and Engagement** **Implementing Formative Assessment Through Small-Group Discourse**	What tasks will you use to engage students in the mathematics content of the lesson? What is the cognitive-demand level of the tasks?	
	How will you ensure the task is accessible and meaningful to all students while still maintaining a high level of cognitive demand for students?	
	What mathematical tools will be used during the lesson? How might technology play a useful role?	
	What student responses, solutions, and approaches do you anticipate? Where might students get stuck?	
	How will you sequence tasks to build mathematical reasoning and sense making, and connect new learning to student prior knowledge?	
	What are the assessing and advancing questions you might ask as students work on the tasks? What will you ask if students are stuck?	
	How will students be engaged in self-reflection and action about their own learning toward the learning targets?	
	What strategies will be used to collect data (formal or informal) about each student's progress toward the learning target and to provide students with formative feedback? What student misconceptions might need to be addressed?	

Lesson Components	Probing Questions for Effective Lesson Design	Reflection
2. Lesson Process (continued)	Which student solutions will you highlight in the closure discussion? In what sequence? What questions will you ask about each one?	
3. Introduction, Daily Review, and Closure	What activity will be used to immediately engage students at the beginning of the class period?	
	How will you provide brief, five-minute meaningful feedback on homework?	
	How will you structure the lesson summary? What questions will you ask? How will the students summarize their learning, including key vocabulary?	
4. Homework	How do the collaborative team–developed unit homework assignments provide variety and meaningful practice— including long-term review and questions—that promote procedural fluency, conceptual understanding, and development of the Mathematical Practices?	

Visit **go.solution-tree.com/commoncore** for a reproducible version of this table.

Table 2.2 highlights four essential lesson-design components for your team planning and discussion. These guidelines for effective mathematics lesson design are meant as a framework you can use with your collaborative team as you discuss how best to implement Common Core expectations in meaningful and enriching ways. The lesson-design elements are not intended for use as a checklist, nor is it practical to incorporate all the elements in every daily lesson. You can use the guiding questions to lead your collaborative team in a dialogue centered on the structure of critical lessons that support students' learning of particular standards or clusters of standards. The process of your collaborative team discussion and reflection on the lesson design for each unit— success and failure—are integral parts of the five-step teaching-assessing-learning cycle discussed in chapter 4.

Regardless of the textbook used, the lesson content, or unit goals to be addressed, this planning tool provides consistent focus on the *how to* of the lesson, including how to incorporate research-informed instructional practices into the lesson. The intention is not for this tool to replace any district or school lesson-planning tools but rather to guide your collaborative unit and lesson planning in the following areas: lesson context; lesson process; introduction, daily review, and closure; and homework.

Design Element One: Lesson Context

The lesson-design process begins with identifying the lesson context for the standards to be taught. Which standards will students be working toward? How does this lesson contribute to students' attainment of the unit's standards? What opportunities will there be for students to engage in the Mathematical Practices? Key elements of the standard should be established prior to delving into the intricacies of the actual classroom activities used to help students learn the standard. You should be explicit about the mathematical concepts and skills needed to guide the lesson.

Identifying Learning Targets

The context of the lesson is the driving force for the entire lesson-design process. The lesson context centers on clarity of the mathematical content (including the understanding of standards) and the skills students are to learn. The crux of the lesson rests on your collaborative team identifying and determining the learning targets that align with the content standard clusters for the unit. The learning target articulates for students what they are to learn and at the same time begins to give insight as to how students will be assessed. Although learning targets might be developed as part of curriculum writing or review, your collaborative team should take time during lesson design to make sure that the learning targets your collaborative team writes for the lesson clearly communicate to students the key content and level of reasoning on which they will be assessed (Stiggins, Arter, Chappuis, & Chappuis, 2007).

Balancing Procedural Fluency and Conceptual Understanding

A key consideration when identifying the learning target for a lesson is balancing students' acquisition of conceptual understanding and procedural fluency. CCSS call for a balance between these two goals, and research indicates that conceptual understanding promotes procedural fluency. That is, when procedures are learned in conjunction with the underlying concepts, students have better retention of procedures and are also better able to apply (transfer) the procedures in new situations (Bransford, Brown, & Cocking, 2000; Bransford & Donovan, 2005). The balance between developing concepts and procedures may occur within a particular lesson, or the balance may be achieved across lessons in a particular unit. Both must be present on a regular basis. Maintaining this balance must be an explicit focus of collaborative team planning.

In the United States, the mathematics primarily taught in middle school is focused on procedures and cursory knowledge of mathematical content (Hiebert et al., 2003).

Unless that balance is consciously attended to during your collaborative lesson planning, chances are your team will revert back to a disproportionate emphasis on procedural skills.

Before an architect can begin to draw out the specifics of a blueprint, he or she must have a vision of the end product. Similarly, Ainsworth (2007) asserts that to best impact instruction, your collaborative teams must design end-of-unit assessment instruments reflecting the intended outcomes of a unit of instruction prior to planning the details of each lesson. That is, as part of the initial stages of lesson design, your collaborative team has a vision of the assessment instruments that demonstrate learning of the outcomes. This process is part of step one in the teaching-assessing-learning cycle described in detail in chapter 4 (page 127).

Remember that in a professional learning community culture, your collaborative team must ask, "How will you know when students have achieved the learning target? What evidence will be used to determine what progress a student has made toward the intended learning? What probing questions will students be asked?" A shared understanding and agreement of what student learning looks like and sounds like leads to greater coherence in the instruction and expectations of mathematical learning by all students of the course as well as by every teacher for the course.

Design Element Two: Lesson Process

Once your team has decided on the learning targets and how they will be assessed at the end of the lesson, your team must have serious discussions about the common mathematical tasks you will use to develop student understanding and fluency for the learning target, the ways you will engage all students in learning during the lesson, and the overall sequence and flow of the lesson. Tasks need to highlight problem solving and mathematical reasoning in ways that "do not separate mathematical thinking from mathematical concepts and skills" (Martin, 2007, p. 33).

Selecting and Using Common High-Cognitive-Demand Tasks

The type of instructional tasks you and your collaborative team members select and use will determine students' opportunities to develop proficiency in the Mathematical Practices and develop conceptual understanding and procedural skills. As Lappan and Briars (1995) state:

> There is no decision that teachers make that has a greater impact on students' opportunities to learn and on their perceptions about what mathematics is than the selection or creation of the tasks with which the teacher engages students in studying mathematics. (p. 139)

Mathematical Practice 1, Make sense of problems and persevere in solving them, establishes the expectation for regularly engaging students in challenging, high-cognitive-demand tasks essential for their developing proficiency in the Mathematical Practices. Engagement in challenging tasks also promotes students' understanding of mathematics in general (Hiebert & Grouws, 2007). A growing body of research links students' engagement in high-cognitive-demand tasks to overall increases in mathematics learning, not just in the ability to solve problems (Resnick, 2006).

A key collaborative team decision is which tasks to use during key lessons for the unit. That is, every member of the team must use the agreed-on tasks with their students in the course as they help students successfully achieve the learning targets for the unit. If you include high-cognitive-demand tasks in your instructional materials, then selecting a task or tasks for a particular lesson is of less concern. However, if such tasks are not part of your materials, then your team either needs to select such tasks from other sources or create them yourselves. See the Online Resources (page 71) for several sources of effective tasks. Visit **go.solution-tree.com/commoncore** for links to those resources.

A critical step in selecting and planning to use a high-cognitive-demand task is for your collaborative team to work the task before giving it to students. Working the task together provides insight into the extent to which the task will engage students in the intended mathematics concepts, skills, and Mathematical Practices, and how students might struggle. Working the task with your team provides information about possible solution strategies or answers that students might obtain and your expectations for quality student work related to the problem.

Planning and Implementing Student Discourse and Engagement

Incorporating high-cognitive-demand tasks into lessons is not sufficient to ensure that students will engage in high-level thinking. How tasks are implemented influences what students learn from them (Stein, Grover, & Henningsen, 1996). The task setup, how students are supported as they work on the task, and how students work together on the task, all influence the extent to which students will benefit from using the task to successfully learn the intended learning target. Thus, another important component of lesson design is deciding how you and your collaborative team members will support student engagement in productive discourse.

Classroom discourse—how you and your students talk with one another in the classroom—influences both the mathematics that students learn and their understanding of what it means to do and learn mathematics (Franke, Kazemi, & Battey, 2007). Too often, discourse in mathematics primarily consists of teacher talk—you explaining, giving directions, or prompting students through procedures (Hiebert et al., 2003). The typical discourse pattern in U.S. classrooms is the IRE—the teacher *initiates* a question, a student *responds*, and the teacher *evaluates* the response. In *Looking Inside the Classroom*, an observational study of 364 mathematics and science classrooms, Weiss, Heck, and Shimbus (2004) identify the kinds of questions that teachers ask as key features in determining the extent to which lessons are likely to be effective in helping students learn mathematics and science concepts. Unfortunately, they saw effective questioning in only 16 percent of the lessons they observed. They note:

> Teachers can use questioning to monitor student understanding of new ideas and to encourage students to think more deeply, however, this

> kind of effective questioning is relatively rare in the nation's mathematics
> and science classes. More often, we saw questioning that was unlikely
> to deepen students' understanding, including teachers asking a series of
> questions too rapidly, and teachers asking questions focused only on a
> correct answer without checks for fuller understanding. . . . [For example]
> the teacher's questions in a 6th grade mathematics lesson were low-level,
> "micro-questions." As she worked the long division problem 4,879,000
> divided by 0.39 on the board, she called on students, by name, to give her
> each number to write down. (Weiss et al., 2004, p. 7)

Such discourse is unlikely to support students' development of either conceptual understanding or their proficiency in the Mathematical Practices. In contrast, classroom discourse that presses for justifications, explanations, or meaning is associated with effective implementation of higher-cognitive-demand tasks and increased conceptual understanding and problem solving (Stein et al., 2007).

Boaler and Brodie (2004) identify nine categories of questions based on their observations of both traditional mathematics classrooms and ones that are more student centered. Visit **go.solution-tree.com/commoncore** for an online reproducible of these types of teacher questions.

Smith and Stein (2011) identify five key actions to make discourse-focused instruction more manageable and effective by moderating the degree of improvisation teachers require. In particular, these practices support both effective work on the task and orchestrate effective summary discussions by students. You and your collaborative team members can use Smith and Stein's (2011) framework to develop deep discussions and classroom practices that support student discourse. The five actions are the following.

1. **Anticipating:** Once you have determined the instructional goal, selected an appropriate task, and worked the task with your colleagues, you can anticipate likely student responses. You should consider the various strategies—both correct and incorrect—that students might use to approach and solve the task, along with how those strategies relate to the learning target.

2. **Monitoring:** The practice of monitoring happens during the lesson as you observe how students are solving the problem. You take note of the students' particular strategies, representations, and other ideas that would be important to share during a whole-class discussion.

3. **Selecting:** From the array of strategies and solutions you observe, select specific students to share their work with the rest of the class in order to make particular mathematical ideas public, rather than asking volunteers to present. During your collaborative planning, you and your team should have discussed which anticipated responses will be most helpful to feature in the summary discussion to support student progress toward the lesson's learning target.

4. **Sequencing:** In this action, teachers determine how to sequence student responses in a particular way so as to maximize the chances that the mathematical goals for the discussion will be achieved. The learning target guides

the sequencing of responses or strategies. Although there is not one right way to sequence responses, sequencing should be part of your collaborative team planning discussion.

5. **Connecting:** The summary discussion should explicitly help students make connections among different responses that have emerged during the lesson so that students can understand how the same mathematical idea is embedded in different strategies. The key connections that you want to make, and the questions you will ask to do so, should also be part of your collaborative team planning discussion.

Using the Smith and Stein (2011) framework may not be feasible for every lesson. However, when your team uses the framework as an embedded part of your lesson planning, you will regularly anticipate student responses, sequence tasks and problems to intentionally build and connect, monitor student responses and work, and emphasize student voices in creating knowledge, reasoning, and making sense of the mathematical learning targets.

Figure 2.15 illustrates how you can utilize various strategies that support student involvement and engagement during small-group and whole-class discourse.

- Have a student paraphrase or summarize a student response or strategy and ask others to verify the first student's summary.

- Direct a student question to the class or another student to respond.

- Ask another student or team if they agree or disagree with the statement of a student or team and why.

- Ask a student or team to explain something in a different way and ask them to defend the response.

Figure 2.15: Strategies for student engagement during classroom discourse.

Implementing Formative Assessment Through Small-Group Discourse

As mentioned, students working in small groups or with peer partners are important formative assessment opportunities for you. As students work, you circulate the room, monitoring different students' solutions (for possible presentation during the debriefing discussion), and listening to students' discussions for evidence of their understanding or lack thereof. An important part of collaborative lesson design is planning the questions you will ask students as you're circulating. In particular, what questions will you ask individual students to *assess* what they understand or do not understand? In addition, you want to plan the questions you will ask to *advance* students' understanding and build on the work they have already done (see chapter 2, pages 64–65 and 69, and chapter 4, page 140, for examples).

Design Element Three: Introduction, Daily Review, and Closure

Middle school mathematics classes typically begin with a warm-up, an opener, or bell work. Important collaborative team planning questions for each lesson in the unit include, What is the goal of the opener or warm-up activity? How does the activity contribute to students' learning? While opening activities can be used as a quick practice of standardized testing strategies or problems, they also can be used to help students access prior knowledge for the day's lesson, or to assess what your students know about a previous learning target. The opening activity can also be a time for you to differentiate student practice to best meet their needs. Regardless of the goal of your opening or warm-up activity, the idea is to immediately engage students in *doing* mathematics—usually with other peers.

A common practice in U.S. classrooms is to spend a significant portion of the instructional period going over homework (Hiebert & Stigler, 1999). Usually at some point in the beginning of class, the teacher provides homework answers for students to check. Be sure to ask yourself, "Who is doing all of the work during the *going over* moments of class—going over homework, a test or quiz, a problem or task, or a key practice problem?" If you are the one doing all of the work while the students listen and watch, then you need to restructure the activity. For example, you could plan student-centered activities, such as working in pairs to go over homework, while you select a key problem for students to explain if necessary.

Whether the instructional period is thirty-two or ninety minutes, some type of *student-led* closing to the lesson is crucial to summarize and highlight key concepts or ideas from the lesson. The closing of class should be different from the task-debriefing activities during class. The bell is about to ring, and students are already thinking about meeting their friends in the hallway or already worrying about the test next period in science. The end of the period is a last opportunity for students to reflect on the key concepts and processes emphasized during the lesson, make connections to overarching themes, and reflect on their own learning.

The closure can be as simple as asking students to share their thoughts about new ideas or how the day's lesson connects to lessons previously taught. Whether the closure is a whole-class question, a group reflection, or an individual task, an end-of-lesson summary refocuses students on important conceptual understandings and Mathematical Practices. Teachers and students each need to reflect on whether students met the learning target that was set for that lesson. You might simply ask students what they learned in the lesson and what questions they have about the lesson's learning target. Asking students to solve a quick problem (or exit slip) that reflects the learning target enables them to receive immediate feedback about their progress toward the learning target. The exit slip also gives you valuable formative data about where student learning is at the end of the instructional period.

Design Element Four: Homework

To have a positive effect, homework should have a clear purpose that is communicated to students. The purpose of homework may be to deepen students' conceptual understanding, enhance procedural fluencies, or expose students to new content. Your collaborative team should intentionally consider and choose each homework problem set for the unit of study, based on the learning targets for that unit. Homework for the unit should be the same for all students in the course or grade level, and it should be given to the students and the parents in advance of teaching the unit with the understanding that your team may modify assignments during the unit in order to address specific student learning needs.

Well-designed homework also provides an opportunity for students to further develop their proficiency in the Mathematical Practices. For example, consider including correct or incorrectly worked examples which require students to evaluate, explain, or correct someone else's reasoning: for example, Joey claims, "A positive number subtracted from a positive number must always be positive. And 5 subtracted from 9 is 4, so it is true." Is Joey's reasoning correct? Such problems provide additional practice in Mathematical Practice 3, Construct viable arguments and critique the reasoning of others, as well as practice in the lesson's learning targets.

Finally, homework can be a valuable place to provide ongoing distributed practice of prior content, including that learned in previous school years, as well as practice on newly learned content.

The Mathematical Practices Lesson-Design Tool

Effective mathematics instruction rests in part on careful planning (Morris, Hiebert, & Spitzer, 2009). Ensuring that the CCSS Mathematical Practices are an important component of mathematics lessons will require significant and careful planning by your collaborative team. Collaborative teams are uniquely structured to provide the time and support they need to interpret the CCSS for mathematics, focus on the essence of these practices for students, embed the Mathematical Practices into daily mathematics lessons, and reflect together on the effectiveness of implementation. A lesson-planning tool, such as the one in figure 2.16, should support the vision of instruction for your school or district. You and your collaborative team can use this tool as you discuss daily lesson construction that will include the design elements described in table 2.2 (page 59).

The template provides an intentional focus on differentiated instructional planning, Mathematical Practice development, and the development of meaningful student tasks that are engaging and require student communication. The goal is to keep extending and moving students' thinking forward during the class. Regardless of the textbook or course materials, the lesson content, or unit standards, this template provides consistent planning for the teacher and student actions of the lesson. The intention is for this planning tool to be used in conjunction with your other lesson-planning tools within the instructional vision of your district as well.

Unit: Date: Lesson:		
Learning target: As a result of today's class, students will be able to _____.		
Formative assessment: How will students be expected to demonstrate mastery of the learning target during in-class checks for understanding?		
Probing Questions for Differentiation on Mathematical Tasks		

Assessing Questions	**Advancing Questions**
(Create questions to scaffold instruction for students who are "stuck" during the lesson or the lesson tasks.)	(Create questions to further learning for students who are ready to advance beyond the learning target.)

Targeted Standard for Mathematical Practice:

Which Mathematical Practice will be targeted for proficiency development during this lesson?

Tasks (Tasks can vary from lesson to lesson.)	**What Will the Teacher Be Doing?** (How will the teacher present and then monitor student response to the task?)	**What Will the Students Be Doing?** (How will students be actively engaged in each part of the lesson?)
Beginning-of-Class Routines How does the warm-up activity connect to students' prior knowledge?		
Task 1 How will the students be engaged in understanding the learning target?		
Task 2 How will the task develop student sense making and reasoning?		
Task 3 How will the task require student conjectures and communication?		
Closure How will student questions and reflections be elicited in the summary of the lesson? How will students' understanding of the learning target be determined?		

Figure 2.16: CCSS Mathematical Practices lesson-planning tool.

Visit **go.solution-tree.com/commoncore** for a reproducible version of this figure.

Reflecting on Lesson Design and Implementation

Collaborative planning is not the end to collaborative work on lesson design. An essential final step is collaboratively reflecting on the success of lessons as implemented in your collaborative team members' classrooms, and on what you can learn from each lesson to inform both upcoming lessons in future units as well as the design of a similar lesson for future implementation. Reflection questions to consider include:

- Were all students able to engage in the lesson tasks? Or is more direction, support, or scaffolding required?

- Did students produce a variety of solutions or use a variety of strategies? If not, was that because the tasks and examples were too scaffolded and should be more open in the future?

- Were there any unexpected or novel solutions that would be worth remembering and incorporating into future debriefing discussions?

- What student misconceptions became evident during the lesson?

- Which solutions were discussed and in what order? How did those choices support the debriefing discussion? Upon reflection, might other choices have been more productive?

Lesson reflections, including sample student solutions, should be added to each lesson plan for the unit and kept in the lesson plan file for each unit of the course. Using an electronic sharing folder such as Google Docs (https://docs.google.com) will make these lesson notes readily available for future lesson planning in following units and years. While this approach falls short of formal lesson study, such reflection provides ongoing opportunities for your team to continuously improve each lesson and learn from your experience.

Creating a repository of collaborative lessons, including plans, tasks and other materials, and reflections is an essential team activity for each team member to continue to improve and refine their professional practice and to increase the quality of your teams' instruction and your students' learning. If you have not yet established such a repository, doing so is an important component of collaborative planning.

Looking Ahead

Although the Standards for Mathematical Practice are not content but rather ways of interacting with the content, they exist as *habits of mind* that facilitate the learning of the CCSS content standards. They go hand-in-hand or they don't really go at all. Planning must therefore simultaneously involve careful consideration of the mathematical content goals of instruction and how the practices can be implemented during the lesson to aid students in developing deep understanding of the content standards. Chapter 3 will examine the unique characteristics and essential features of the Common Core mathematics content standards that you will need to understand, and chapter 4 will examine ways in which the CCSS content and the Mathematical Practices can be further assessed.

Chapter 2 Extending My Understanding

1. Examine the NCTM Process Standards (NCTM, 2000) and the Strands of Mathematical Proficiency from *Adding It Up* (NRC, 2001) in appendix E (**go.solution-tree.com/commoncore**). How are each foundational to the CCSS Mathematical Practices? How might you and your collaborative team explain these relationships to other stakeholders, including parents and guardians, in order to help them understand the CCSS connections to previous expectations in mathematics standards?

2. Design a plan for building student awareness (or deepening student understanding) of the Mathematical Practices. What initial tasks or activities will you use? How do you plan to continue to reinforce these practices? What is your plan for developing parent or guardian and family awareness of the practices? What tasks will you use initially? How will you provide ongoing reinforcement?

3. Develop a list of student behaviors as defined in the Mathematical Practices. Record the teacher actions that might promote student implementation of the practices. Then schedule informal peer observations or video mathematics classes in action. Spend time as a collaborative team debriefing these observations.

   ○ Did collaborative teams observe these dispositions? How, when, and under what conditions did they see students exhibit the Mathematical Practices?

   ○ What surprised you?

4. Analyze your current questioning. Video or audio record your questioning during an instructional segment, or ask another team member to scribe your questions. Then, categorize each of your questions using the Boaler and Brodie (2004) categories. (Visit **go.solution-tree.com/commoncore** for an online-only reproducible of these types of questions.)

   ○ What type of questions do you ask most often? What patterns do you notice? What types of responses are students giving? Numbers or single-word answers? Or are they giving explanations?

   ○ What would you do differently in future lessons?

Online Resources

Visit **go.solution-tree.com/commoncore** for links to these resources.

- **Common Core Implementation Video Series (NGA & CCSSO, 2011; www .ccsso.org/Resources/Digital_Resources/Common_Core_Implementation**

_Video_Series.html): To assist states with CCSS implementation, this series of video vignettes examines the standards in greater depth. Be sure to check out "Mathematical Practices, Focus and Coherence in the Classroom" and "The Importance of Mathematical Practices." You can also visit the Hunt Institute's YouTube channel (www.youtube.com/user/TheHuntInstitute#g/u) to access these videos.

- **Common Core Look-Fors (CCL4s; http://splaysoft.com/CCL4s/Welcome .html):** CCL4s is a comprehensive tool designed to help teacher learning teams deepen their awareness and understanding of the actions and conditions that promote student engagement with the CCSS Mathematical Practices, with connections to the content standards. These iPad and iPhone apps support purposeful classroom observation through effective staff collaboration.

- **Mathematical Practices Learning Community Templates (http://schools .utah.gov/CURR/mathsec/Common-Core/MathematicalPracticesLearning CommunityTemplates.aspx):** These resources include nine templates for teacher learning teams seeking to understand the Mathematical Practices and their connections to the NCTM Process Standards and Strands of Mathematical Proficiency.

- **Standards for Mathematical Practice (Common Core State Standards Initiative, 2011; www.corestandards.org/the-standards/mathematics /introduction/standards-for-mathematical-practice):** This site links the text of the eight Mathematical Practices and the selection on "Connecting the Standards for Mathematical Practice to the Standards for Mathematical Content."

- **Common Core State Standards Resources (NCSM, 2011; www.mathed leadership.org/ccss/materials.html):** These professional development files are ready to use and designed to help teachers understand how to implement the Mathematical Practices in their classrooms.

- **Illustrative Mathematics Project (http://illustrativemathematics.org):** The main goal for this project is to provide guidance to states, assessment consortia, testing companies, and curriculum developers by illustrating the range and types of mathematical work that students will experience in implementing the Common Core State Standards for mathematics.

- **Common Core Standards for Mathematical Practice (Inside Mathematics, 2010a; http://insidemathematics.org/index.php/common-core-standards):** This site provides classroom videos and lesson samples designed to illustrate the Mathematical Practices in action.

- **Doing What Works (http://www2.ed.gov/nclb/methods/whatworks /edpicks.jhtml):** Doing What Works provides videos, slideshows, and tools for using proven teaching practices based on findings from the What Works Clearinghouse.

CHAPTER 3

Implementing the Common Core Mathematics Content in Your Curriculum

The standards are meant to be a blueprint for math instruction that is more focused and coherent. The focus and coherence in this blueprint are largely in the way the standards progress from each other, coordinate with each other and most importantly cluster together into coherent bodies of knowledge. . . . Maintaining these progressions in the implementation of the standards will be important for helping all students learn mathematics at a higher level. . . . Fragmenting the Standards into individual standards, or individual bits of standards, erases all these relationships and produces a sum of parts that is decidedly less than the whole.

—Daro, McCallum, & Zimba

Chapter 2 addressed one of the two types of Common Core standards—the Standards for Mathematical Practice—and illustrated instructional practices that promote students' proficiency in these practices. This chapter analyzes the second type of standard—the Standards for Mathematical Content. As you read this chapter, keep in mind that the Standards for Mathematical Practice and the Standards for Mathematical Content *together* form the Common Core State Standards. Mathematical proficiency is defined both by the content and skills that students need to know and be able to use and the mathematical habits of mind they have acquired.

One implementation challenge you and your collaborative team face is how to design curriculum, instruction, and assessment that will develop students' proficiency in the content and practice standards simultaneously. This chapter focuses on the grades 6–8 content standards—what they are; how mathematical concepts and skills develop across grades; and what's familiar, new, and most challenging for each grade. It also provides tools to help your collaborative team understand essential changes in your curriculum, instruction, and assessment to implement Common Core mathematics.

Common Core Overview

The goal of the CCSS for mathematics is to ensure all students will be college and career ready—ready for success in college mathematics courses or technical training programs—when they complete their K–12 education. The Common Core expectations are based on research, expectations of other countries, and the most rigorous U.S. state standards. The Common Core State Standards "define what students understand and are able to do in their study of mathematics" (NGA & CCSSO, 2010a, p. 4). According to the Common Core, "Mathematical understanding and procedural skill are equally important, and both are assessable using mathematical tasks of sufficient richness" (NGA & CCSSO, 2010a, p. 4). This focus on conceptual understanding along with skill acquisition is a key aspect of the CCSS that your collaborative team must keep in mind as you analyze the implications for your mathematics curriculum, instruction, and assessment.

The research base for the Common Core for mathematics includes international comparison studies such as *Trends in International Mathematics and Science Study* (TIMSS) (Gonzales et al., 2008) and Programme for International Student Assessment (PISA) (Fleischman, Hopstock, Pelczar, & Shelley, 2010), of mathematics education in high-performing countries. These studies "have pointed to the conclusion that the mathematics curriculum in the United States must become substantially more focused and coherent in order to improve mathematics achievement in this country" (NGA & CCSSO, 2010a, p. 3). Consequently, the Common Core standards were explicitly designed to do the following.

- **Be focused:** Focus involves more than having fewer standards at a grade. In fact, in some cases, there may be more standards at a particular grade with the CCSS than previous standards. The difference is that the Common Core standards address fewer big ideas in each grade, so more time is available to support students' understanding of related concepts and skills. Three or four critical areas for instructional focus are clearly identified for each grade.

- **Be clear and coherent:** The CCSS have been carefully designed so that mathematical knowledge builds coherently over time. Coherence is achieved "not only by stressing conceptual understanding of key ideas, but also by continually returning to organizing principles such as place value or the properties of operations to structure those ideas" (NGA & CCSSO, 2010a, p. 4). For example—

  > The teaching of algebra in grade 8 actually starts in grade 1. This coherent stairway begins when students are asked to think algebraically about addition, subtraction, multiplication and division. It widens in grade 3 to include fractions and decimals, reaching, in grade 6, a solid platform of understanding on which to scaffold work with expressions and equations, culminating in the study of functions in grade 8. (McCallum, 2011, p. 3)

- **Reflect what is known about how students learn mathematics:** To the extent possible, the sequence of mathematical topics and the Mathematical Practices in the CCSS are consistent with what is known about how students develop mathematical knowledge, skill, and understanding over time (NGA & CCSSO, 2010a). Admittedly, much more is known about how young children learn mathematics concepts than is known about the mathematical development of students in middle and high school. So, while some sequences are based on research on learning, others are based on analysis of the mathematical ideas, informed by how high-achieving countries such as Singapore, Hong Kong, Korea, Japan, Finland, and the Netherlands, sequence instruction on these topics. (Ginsburg, Leinwand, & Decker, 2009; Mullis, Martin, & Foy, 2008).

The result is middle school standards that are rigorous, setting higher expectations for students in each grade. However, the increased focus, coherence, and attention to how students learn should make them more *teachable* and *learnable* within the typical time constraints of U.S. schools.

To make the focus and coherence more visible to readers, the Common Core standards are organized into content standard clusters within each domain. Figure 3.1 (page 78) illustrates this organization. The standards are the numbered and lettered statements that define what students should understand and be able to do. They frequently include specific examples; these examples are part of the standard. Related standards are organized into content standard clusters. Domains are larger groups of related standards. Standards from different domains and from different content standard clusters may be closely related, due to the relationships among mathematical ideas.

Notice the verbs used in the three standards in figure 3.1: *understand, compare*, and *interpret*. Each of these standards represents and expects students to be *doing* mathematics. Your team will need to have robust discussions about what it means to teach students to *understand that a function is a rule, compare properties*, or *interpret the equation* $y = mx + b$ as each learning target or standard surfaces during your grade-level or course-content scope and sequence of learning standards.

Table 3.1 (page 79) provides an overview of the grades 6–8 content standard domains and the progression of content domains by grade band—grades 3–5, grades 6–8, and high school.

Table 3.2 (page 80) provides more detail about the progression of content across grades K–8 and high school. It shows the content standard clusters associated with each domain; the content standard clusters summarize the content to be learned in each grade. It also shows the three to four *critical areas* for instructional focus for each grade. While the critical areas often address content from a single domain, they sometimes consist of related ideas that cut across domains. (See grade 7 for an example.) Table 3.2 includes specific information for grade 5 in addition to grades 6–8, to provide information about what students will be learning in grades K–5 as a basis for their middle school experiences. Since the high school standards are not organized into grade-level groups, the high school domains are not broken down by clusters (see NGA & CCSSO, 2010a, pp. 57–84, for the Mathematics Standards for High School). The CCSS Standards for Mathematical Content for grades 6–8 are listed in appendices B, C, and D, pages 185–206.

Standards define what students should understand and be able to do.

Clusters are groups of related standards. Note that standards from different clusters may sometimes be closely related because mathematics is a connected subject.

Domains are larger groups of related standards. Standards from different domains may sometimes be closely related. The domains for grades 6 to 8 are Ratios and Proportional Relationships (grades 6 and 7), the Number System, Expressions and Equations, Geometry, Statistics and Probability, and Functions (grade 8).

(**Conceptual categories** are the main topics of study for the high school mathematics standards, which are discussed in the sections "How Does This Domain Prepare Students for High School?" in this chapter.)

Domain

| Functions | 8.F |

Define, evaluate, and compare functions.

Standard

1. Understand that a function is a rule that assigns to each input exactly one output. The graph of a function is the set of ordered pairs consisting of an input and the corresponding output.*

2. Compare properties of two functions each represented in a different way (algebraically, graphically, numerically in tables, or by verbal descriptions). *For example, given a linear function represented by a table of values and a linear function represented by an algebraic expression, determine which function has the greater rate of change.*

Cluster

3. Interpret the equation $y = mx + b$ as defining a linear function, whose graph is a straight line; give examples of functions that are not linear. *For example, the function A = s^2 giving the area of a square as a function of its side length is not linear because its graph contains the points (1,1), (2,4) and (3,9), which are not on a straight line.*

* *Function notation is not required in grade 8.*

Source: Adapted from NGA & CCSSO, 2010a, p. 5.
Figure 3.1: How to read the grade-level standards.

Visit **go.solution-tree.com/commoncore** for a reproducible version of this figure.

Technically, the numbered statements in the Common Core standards are *the standards*. However, "'The Standards' refers to all elements of the design—the wording of the domain headings, cluster headings, and individual statements; the text of the grade level introductions and high school category descriptions; the placement of the Standards for Mathematical Practice at each grade level" (Daro, McCallum, & Zimba, 2012). Thus, your collaborative team needs to continuously analyze all of these components to truly understand the expectations of the CCSS for mathematics content standards and their impact of the standards for your unit-by-unit planning. As the epigraph opening this chapter indicates, analyzing the progression of standards across grades is essential to understanding the Common Core content standards.

Table 3.1: CCSS Content Domains by Grade Band

Grades 3–5	Grades 6 and 7	Grade 8	High School	
Number and Operations in Base Ten	The Number System		Number and Quantity	Modeling
Number and Operations—Fractions	Ratios and Proportional Relationships	Functions	Functions	Modeling
Operations and Algebraic Thinking	Expressions and Equations		Algebra	Modeling
Geometry	Geometry		Geometry	Modeling
Measurement and Data	Statistics and Probability		Statistics and Probability	Modeling

Visit **go.solution-tree.com/commoncore** for a reproducible version of this table.

Content Domain Analysis

As described in chapter 1, your collaborative team works together to develop a shared understanding of the content to be taught because, among other reasons, it develops consistent curricular expectations between you and your colleagues, serving equity goals for the course as well as creating ownership among all teachers (DuFour et al., 2008). As your team examines the content domains of the middle grades standards, you and your colleagues begin to develop this shared understanding that enables you to answer the critical question, "What is it we want all students to know and be able to do?"

Your collaborative team should use the following questions to guide your study of the CCSS content at the domain level.

1. Which standards are familiar in the content standard clusters for this domain?

2. Which standards appear to be new or challenging in the content standard clusters for this domain?

3. Which standards in the cluster need unpacking or emphasizing?

4. What opportunities exist for connections among the standards and clusters in this domain, other content domains, and the Standards for Mathematical Practice?

The following sections provide overviews of the grades 6–8 content standards by domain that begin to answer these questions. These overviews are intended as starting points, not replacements, for collaborative cross-grade analyses of content progressions within each domain and within-grade analyses of content standards for all the domains. In addition, to place the content of each domain into the larger K–12 context, the analyses include information about what students bring to this domain from their K–5 mathematics instruction, and how the content in this domain is extended and used in the high school standards.

Table 3.2: CCSS Content Domains and Clusters by Grade, With Emphasis on Grades 6–8

Grades K–4	Grade 5	Grade 6	Grade 7	Grade 8	High School
					Modeling
Number and Operations in Base Ten	**Number and Operations in Base Ten** Understand the place value system. Perform operations with multidigit whole numbers and with decimals to hundredths. *Critical area:* Extending division to two-digit divisors, integrating decimal fractions into the place value system and developing understanding of operations with decimals to hundredths, and developing fluency with whole number and decimal operations	**The Number System** Apply and extend previous understandings of multiplication and division to divide fractions by fractions. Compute fluently with multidigit numbers and find common factors and multiples. Apply and extend previous understandings of numbers to the system of rational numbers. *Critical area:* Completing understanding of division of fractions and extending the notion of number to the system of rational numbers, which includes negative numbers	**The Number System** Apply and extend previous understandings of operations with fractions to add, subtract, multiply, and divide rational numbers. *Critical area:* Developing understanding of operations with rational numbers and working with expressions and linear equations	**The Number System** Know that there are numbers that are not rational, and approximate them by rational numbers.	**Number and Quantity**

continued →

Grades K–4	Grade 5	Grade 6	Grade 7	Grade 8	High School
Number and Operations— Fractions (Grades 3–5 only)	**Number and Operations— Fractions** Use equivalent fractions as a strategy to add and subtract fractions. Apply and extend previous understandings of multiplication and division to multiply and divide fractions. ***Critical area:*** Developing fluency with addition and subtraction of fractions, and developing understanding of the multiplication of fractions and of division of fractions in limited cases (unit fractions divided by whole numbers, and whole numbers divided by unit fractions)	**Ratios and Proportional Relationships** Understand ratio concepts and use ratio reasoning to solve problems. ***Critical area:*** Connecting ratio and rate to whole number multiplication and division and using concepts of ratio and rate to solve problems	**Ratios and Proportional Relationships** Analyze proportional relationships and use them to solve real-world and mathematical problems. ***Critical area:*** Developing understanding of and applying proportional relationships	**Functions** Define, evaluate, and compare functions. Use functions to model relationships between quantities. ***Critical area:*** Grasping the concept of a function and using functions to describe quantitative relationships	**Modeling** **Functions**

Grades K–4	Grade 5	Grade 6	Grade 7	Grade 8	High School
Operations and Algebraic Thinking **Counting and Cardinality (Kindergarten only)**	**Operations and Algebraic Thinking** Write and interpret numerical expressions. Analyze patterns and relationships.	**Expressions and Equations** Apply and extend previous understandings of arithmetic to algebraic expressions. Reason about and solve one-variable equations and inequalities. Represent and analyze quantitative relationships between dependent and independent variables. ***Critical area:*** Writing, interpreting, and using expressions and equations	**Expressions and Equations** Use properties of operations to generate equivalent expressions. Solve real-life and mathematical problems using numerical and algebraic expressions and equations. ***Critical area:*** See the Number System	**Expressions and Equations** Work with radicals and integer exponents. Understand the connections between proportional relationships, lines, and linear equations. Analyze and solve linear equations and pairs of simultaneous linear equations. ***Critical area:*** Formulating and reasoning about expressions and equations, including modeling an association in bivariate data with a linear equation, and solving linear equations and systems of linear equations	**Modeling** **Algebra**

continued →

Grades K–4	Grade 5	Grade 6	Grade 7	Grade 8	High School
Geometry	**Geometry**	**Geometry**	**Geometry**	**Geometry**	**Modeling**
	Graph points on the coordinate plane to solve real-world and mathematical problems.	Solve real-world and mathematical problems involving area, surface area, and volume.	Draw, construct, and describe geometrical figures and describe the relationships between them.	Understand congruence and similarity using physical models, transparencies, or geometry software.	**Geometry**
	Classify two-dimensional figures into categories based on their properties.		Solve real-life and mathematical problems involving angle measure, area, surface area, and volume.	Understand and apply the Pythagorean theorem.	
			Critical area: Solving problems involving scale drawings and informal geometric constructions, and working with two- and three-dimensional shapes to solve problems involving area, surface area, and volume	Solve real-world and mathematical problems involving volume of cylinders, cones, and spheres.	
				Critical area: Analyzing two- and three-dimensional space and figures using distance, angle, similarity, and congruence, and understanding and applying the Pythagorean theorem.	

Grades K–4	Grade 5	Grade 6	Grade 7	Grade 8	High School
Measurement and Data	Measurement and Data	Statistics and Probability	Statistics and Probability	Statistics and Probability	Statistics and Probability
	Convert like measurement units within a given measurement system. Represent and interpret data. Geometric measurement: understand concepts of volume and relate volume to multiplication and to addition. *Critical area:* Developing understanding of volume	Develop understanding of statistical variability. Summarize and describe distributions. *Critical area:* Developing understanding of statistical thinking	Use random sampling to draw inferences about a population. Draw informal comparative inferences about two populations. Investigate chance processes and develop, use, and evaluate probability models. *Critical area:* Drawing inferences about populations based on samples	Investigate patterns of association in bivariate data. *Critical area:* See Expressions and Equations	

| | | | | | Modeling |

Visit **go.solution-tree.com/commoncore** for a reproducible version of this table.

Each domain begins with a reproducible table to support your collaborative team analyses. Table 3.3 is a completed example for Grade 7 Ratios and Proportional Relationships domain. Reproducible tables for all grades for each domain are available at **go.solution.tree.com/commoncore**, and the CCSS content standards for grades 6–8 are available in appendices B, C, and D, pages 185–206.

Table 3.3: Analysis Tool for Grade 7—Ratios and Proportional Relationships (7.RP) Domain

Content Standard Clusters	Which Standards in the Cluster Are Familiar?	What's New or Challenging in These Standards?	Which Standards in the Cluster Need Unpacking or Emphasizing?	How Is This Cluster Connected to the Other 6–8 Domains and Mathematical Practices?
Critical area: Developing understanding of and applying proportional relationships				
Analyze proportional relationships and use them to solve real-world and mathematical problems.	The cluster topic—using proportional relationships to solve problems—is familiar. It has been a seventh-grade emphasis as long as I've been teaching seventh-grade math. Almost all the types of multi-step problems are all familiar. Typically, I use problems about simple interest, tax, markups, markdowns, tips, commissions, fees, and percent increase and decrease. I also ask students to compute some common unit rates, like mph.	Although the topic is familiar, the approaches mentioned are not. I've taught students to set up and solve proportions using cross-multiplication. Graphing on a coordinate plane to determine whether two quantities are proportional is a new idea to me. While I've used multiple representations in my algebra 1 class, I haven't used them for proportional relationships in earlier grades. (7.RP.2.d) Also, I haven't used the vocabulary *constant of proportionality*. (7.RP.2.b)	This cluster is clearly an area of emphasis. I need to understand more about ways students might approach ratio and percent problems if I don't teach them cross-multiplication. Although standard 7.RP.2 is described in considerable detail, our current textbook doesn't approach proportional relationships in that way. I need to figure out how to use or adapt the problems in the book, or find/create problems to teach this new approach.	Geometry: Solving problems involving scale drawings and similar figures Statistics and Probability: Making inferences about a population from a sample or samples Work here is a context for developing many of the Standards for Mathematical Practice, especially Mathematical Practices 1, 2, 4 and 5.

Visit **go.solution-tree.com/commoncore** for a reproducible version of this table.

For each domain, your team should first read the standards including the introduction for your grade, then complete the table for your grade level, identifying the content that is familiar, new and challenging, or the content that you think will be challenging for your students or for you—content that you would like to study with your colleagues. After each member of your grade level *and* cross-grade-level collaborative teams completes the table, the cross-grade vertical team should engage in a discussion of the progression of the content standards across grades and the standards within each grade to identify common needs across the team and design a professional development plan to ensure that everyone is ready to teach the content at the required level. The check for consistency, patterns, and agreement across a team will provide a more equitable experience for all students in each grade. The first Common Core content domain for analysis by your team is the Number System.

The Number System Domain for Grades 6, 7, and 8 (6.NS, 7.NS, 8.NS)

Table 3.4 presents the grade 6 analysis tool for the Number System domain. Visit **go.solution-tree.com/commoncore** for the grades 7 and 8 counterparts of this analysis tool. After your grade-level and cross-grade middle school teams have discussed your individual analysis and understanding of this domain's expectations, use the analysis provided in this chapter for comparison and completion. For this domain in particular, what students bring from grades K–5 has significant implications for your instruction.

Common Core Grades K–5 Expectations

Some of the most significant new aspects of the Number System domain in grades 6, 7, and 8 are a result of differences in the knowledge and experiences that students bring to grades 6–8 from the CCSS K–5 domains of Numbers and Operations in Base Ten and Numbers and Operations—Fractions.

The K–5 Numbers and Operations in Base Ten domain features two advances that have direct implications for grades 6–8 content. First, instruction of computational algorithms has been extended to provide adequate time for students to develop understanding of the properties of operations and the structure of the number system; second, students then use those understandings to create and understand computational procedures. Instead of teachers presenting standard algorithms as sequences of steps for students to practice and memorize, the CCSS call for building a conceptual foundation for these procedural skills. Students first develop conceptual understanding based on their informal knowledge; then develop their own informal strategies to solve problems; and finally, refine their informal strategies to develop fluency with standard procedures (algorithms).

To provide adequate time for this development, expected fluency in standard algorithms has been pushed back to grade 4 for addition and subtraction, grade 5 for multiplication, and grade 6 for division. In grade 6, students are expected to fluently divide multidigit numbers using the standard algorithm (6.NS.2, see appendix B, page 188)

Table 3.4: Analysis Tool for Grade 6—The Number System (6.NS) Domain

Content Standard Clusters	Which Standards in the Cluster Are Familiar?	What's New or Challenging in These Standards?	Which Standards in the Cluster Need Unpacking or Emphasizing?	How Is This Cluster Connected to the Other 6–8 Domains and Mathematical Practices?
Critical area: Completing understanding of division of fractions and extending the notion of number to the system of rational numbers, which includes negative numbers				
Apply and extend previous understandings of multiplication and division to divide fractions by fractions.				
Compute fluently with multidigit numbers and find common factors and multiples.				
Apply and extend previous understandings of numbers to the system of rational numbers.				

Visit **go.solution-tree.com/commoncore** for a reproducible version of this table.

and fluently add, subtract, multiply, and divide multidigit decimals using the standard algorithm for each operation (6.NS.3, see appendix B, page 188). Progressions for the Common Core State Standards for mathematics (2011a) define fluency in this way:

> The word *fluent* is used in the Standards to mean fast and accurate. Fluency in each grade involves a mixture of just knowing some answers from patterns (e.g., "adding 0 yields the same number"), and knowing some answers from the use of strategies. (p. 18)

This fluency expectation does not mean that students will not have been exposed to or practiced the standard algorithm in previous grades. In fact, the grade 5 standard 5.NBT.6 expects students to "find whole-number quotients of whole numbers with up to four-digit dividends and two-digit divisors, using strategies based on place value, the properties of operations, and/or the relationship between multiplication and division" (NGA & CCSSO, 2010a, p. 35). However, students are not expected to be reasonably *fast and accurate* with the standard algorithm until grade 6.

Consequently, some of your students may be proficient with the standard division algo-rithm while others may still be transitioning from a more intuitive algorithm, such as partial quotients. Thus, an important grade 6 collaborative team activity is to commu-nicate with the students' grade 5 teachers about students' experiences with informal and standard division algorithms, so that you can best determine how to help students make the transition to the standard algorithm. While meeting with the fifth-grade teachers may be challenging when elementary and middle school and junior high schools are in separate school buildings or districts, the conversation is important to support students' success.

Second, the Common Core standards do not explicitly define *standard algorithm*. Figure 3.2 describes standard algorithms as algorithms "for base-ten computations [that] rely on decomposing numbers written in base-ten notation into base-ten units" (Progres-sions for the Common Core State Standards in Mathematics, 2011b, p. 3). The standard algorithm then, for multiplication of multidigit numbers involves: (1) decomposing the factors into their base-ten units—for example, thinking of 94 × 36 as (90 + 4) × (30 + 6); and (2) repeated application of the distributive property. However, the order of applying the distributive property or the way partial products or *regroupings* are recorded doesn't matter. Hence, any of the algorithms in figure 3.2 could be considered standard.

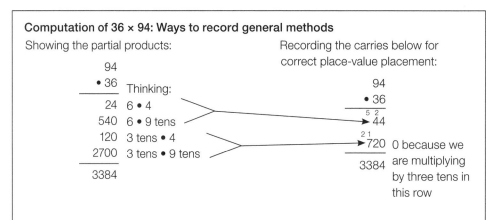

Computation of 36 × 94: Ways to record general methods

These proceed from right to left, but could go left to right. On the right, digits that repre-sent newly composed tens and hundreds are written below the line instead of above 94. The 1 from 30 × 4 = 120 is placed correctly in the hundreds place and the digit 2 from 30 × 90 = 2,700 is placed correctly in the thousands place. If these digits had been placed above 94, they would be in incorrect places. Note that the 0 in the ones place of the sec-ond line of the method on the right is there because the whole line of digits is produced by multiplying by 30 (not 3).

Source: Adapted from Progressions for the Common Core State Standards in Mathematics, 2011b, p. 3. Used with permission.

Figure 3.2: General multiplication algorithms.

As a result, your students may use forms of the *standard* algorithms different than those that you are most familiar with, especially for multiplication; for example, they might use partial products instead of the traditional *carry* algorithm, which is absolutely acceptable. However, you and your team must be aware of this so that you don't inadvertently cause confusion for students by either expecting them to use a different algorithm, or by consistently modeling problems using a version of the standard algorithm that is unfamiliar to them.

These same algorithms for multiplication of whole numbers can be extended to algorithms for multiplication of decimals, another important expectation for grade 6. Consequently, you want to take advantage of the algorithms students are already familiar with and help them extend the algorithms they understand to problems involving decimals.

Which Standards in the Cluster Are Familiar?

As you examine the content standards in this domain, many of the expectations should be familiar: extending previous understandings of multiplication and division to multiply and divide fractions in grade 6, extending operations with whole numbers and fractions to include negative numbers in grade 7, and introducing irrational numbers using square roots and π in grade 8.

Specifically, the following content standards should be familiar.

- Emphasize understanding numbers as points on the number line, absolute value of a number as its distance from 0, and use number line representations to solve problems.

- Expect students to extend representations and algorithms learned in previous grades to operations on rational numbers.

- Expect students to develop a "unified understanding" of number, "recognizing fractions, decimals (that have a finite or repeating decimal representation) and percents as different representations of rational numbers" (NGA & CCSSO, 2010a, p. 46).

What's New or Challenging in These Standards?

One new expectation is the conceptual understanding of these topics and their relationships to other concepts and skills. Another is that sixth graders will develop fluency with the standard algorithm for multidigit division. Although students will have considerable experience with various strategies and algorithms for multidigit division in grades 4 and 5, including partial quotients, it is not until grade 6 that they are expected to be fluent with the standard algorithm. Another new expectation is that when negative numbers are introduced in grade 6, they are defined using the concept of absolute value of a number as its distance from 0. This is a result of the emphasis on the number line as a foundational model throughout CCSS.

Two other aspects of these standards merit special attention:

1. The expectations are *bidirectional*, calling for students to be able to use rational number operations to solve problems as well as to create problems that can be

modeled by particular rational number operations. An example of bidirectionality is found in the standard 6.NS.1 (see appendix B, page 188), "Interpret and compute quotients of fractions, and solve word problems involving division of fractions by fractions, e.g., by using visual fraction models and equations to represent the problem" (NGA & CCSSO, 2010a, p. 42). This bidirectionality is a direct application of the contextualize and decontextualize process called for in Mathematical Practice 2, Reason abstractly and quantitatively.

2. The Number System standards contain explicit connections to mathematical properties to emphasize underlying structure of mathematics. An example is the standard 6.NS.4 (see appendix B, page 188), which calls for students to be able to find the greatest common factor of two numbers less than or equal to 100 and the least common multiple of two numbers less than or equal to 12. This standard also explicitly expects students to: "Use the distributive property to express a sum of two whole numbers 1–100 with a common factor as a multiple of a sum of two whole numbers with no common factor. *For example, express* 36 + 8 *as* 4 (9 + 2)" (NGA & CCSSO, 2010a, p. 42).

Finally, what's different about the standards in the Number System domain is what is *not* there. The Common Core standards make no mention of *simplifying* fractions or writing fractions in *lowest terms*. While it is certainly correct to rewrite fractions as an equivalent fraction with a smaller denominator, this is not a major focus of fraction computation. Instead, fractions should be expressed in the form that is most useful in the context in which they are being used.

Which Standards in the Cluster Need Unpacking or Emphasizing?

The Number System is a critical area in both grades 6 and 7, so merits significant instructional time. In grade 6, students extend their understanding of the number system in two ways. They extend their understanding of number and ordering of numbers to negative integers and then negative rational numbers, using the number line as a primary model. They also use their understanding of the meanings of multiplication and division and the relationship between multiplication and division to understand division of fractions. This understanding includes being able to explain why procedures for dividing fractions make sense. Students also are able to use these operations to solve problems.

In grade 7, students extend their understanding of rational numbers, "Recognizing fractions, decimals, and percents as different representations of rational numbers" (NGA & CCSSO, 2010a, p. 46). They rewrite numbers in different forms, depending on what is appropriate for a particular context. They also extend their understanding of operations to all rational numbers, using the meanings of negative numbers that they learned in grade 6, and properties of operations. In particular, students use their understanding of the relationship between multiplication and division to understand division involving zero (7.NS.2b, see appendix C, page 196). That is, they rewrite division problems involving zero as multiplication problems to show that while 0 divided by any nonzero number is 0, dividing by 0 is undefined. They also know that $0 \div 0$ is undefined for a different reason than $n \div 0$, in which $n \neq 0$.

Figure 3.3 illustrates student understanding of division by zero. The intent is to extend students' understanding by engaging them in investigating these ideas; not simply telling them. The work of your team is to plan such an investigation. Also, investigating division involving zero is a context for engaging students in "analyzing situations by breaking them into cases" (NGA & CCSSO, 2010a, p. 6) as called for by Mathematical Practice 3, Construct viable arguments and critique the reasoning of others.

Case One	Case Two	Case Three
$0 \div n, n \neq 0$	$n \div 0, n \neq 0$	$0 \div 0, n \neq 0$
For example, $0 \div 3 = a$	For example, $3 \div 0 = a$	$0 \div 0 = a$
Rewrite as equivalent multiplication equation and solve:	Rewrite as equivalent multiplication equation and solve:	Rewrite as equivalent multiplication equation and solve:
$3 \times a = 0$	$0 \times a = 3$	$0 \times a = 0$
Since any number multiplied by 0 is 0, $a = 0$.	Since any number multiplied by 0 is 0, there is no value for a that makes this equation true.	Since any number multiplied by 0 is 0, a can be any number! Because there is no unique value of a that makes this true, this quotient is undefined.
So, $0 \div 3 = 0$.	So, $3 \div 0$ is undefined.	So, $0 \div 0$ is undefined.

Figure 3.3: Understanding division involving zero.

Visit **go.solution-tree.com/commoncore** for a reproducible version of this figure.

How Is This Cluster Connected to the Other 6–8 Domains and Mathematical Practices?

The Number System standards, with their emphasis on understanding number, operations, and properties of operations, are the foundation for the Ratios and Proportional Relationships and Expressions and Equations standards. In addition, the understanding clusters and standards in this domain are excellent contexts for students to develop proficiency in the Standards for Mathematical Practice, as illustrated in figure 3.3 and the various examples in chapter 2.

How Does This Domain Prepare Students for High School?

The Number System domain is the foundation for the high school conceptual category, Number and Quantity. Students will extend their work with integer exponents and square and cube roots to define rational exponents. They will ultimately extend the number system to include complex numbers. Students will use their understanding of rational number computations and underlying properties as well.

Ratios and Proportional Relationships (6.RP and 7.RP) and Functions (8.F) Domains

This section addresses the grades 6 and 7 Ratios and Proportional Relationships domain and the grade 8 Functions domain. These domains are discussed together due to their close relationship. The concepts of rate, rate of change, and proportional relationships are foundational to students' work with linear functions in grade 8. This progression of the domains is illustrated in table 3.1 (page 79). These topics are critical areas for all three grades, so your team should plan to devote a significant amount of instructional time to them.

Table 3.5 contains the analysis tool for the Ratios and Proportional Relationships (grades 6 and 7) and Functions (grade 8) domains. Because these domains each have only one or two standard clusters, clusters for all three grades are included in the same table. After your cross-grade middle school team has discussed your individual analysis and understanding of this domain's expectations, use the analysis provided in this chapter for comparison and completion.

Table 3.5: Analysis Tool for Grades 6 and 7—Ratios and Proportional Relationships (6.RP and 7.RP) and Grade 8 Functions (8.F) Domains

Content Standard Clusters	Which Standards in the Cluster Are Familiar?	What's New or Challenging in These Standards?	Which Standards in the Cluster Need Unpacking or Emphasizing?	How Is This Cluster Connected to the Other 6–8 Domains and Mathematical Practices?
Grade 6 (6.RP) critical area: Connecting ratio and rate to whole number multiplication and division and using concepts of ratio and rate to solve problems				
Understand ratio concepts and use ratio reasoning to solve problems.				
Grade 7 (7.RP) critical area: Developing understanding of and applying proportional relationships				
Analyze proportional relationships and use them to solve real-world and mathematical problems.				

Content Standard Clusters	Which Standards in the Cluster Are Familiar?	What's New or Challenging in These Standards?	Which Standards in the Cluster Need Unpacking or Emphasizing?	How Is This Cluster Connected to the Other 6–8 Domains and Mathematical Practices?
Grade 8 (8.F) critical area: Grasping the concept of a function and using functions to describe quantitative relationships				
Define, evaluate, and compare functions.				
Use functions to model relationships between quantities.				

Visit **go.solution-tree.com/commoncore** for a reproducible version of this table.

Common Core Grades K–5 Expectations

As a foundation for the study of ratios and proportional relationships, grades 4 and 5 students have extensive experience with multiplication as scaling—that expressions such as 3 × 6 and ½ × 6 can be interpreted in terms of a quantity, 6, and a scale factor, 3 or ½. (5NF.5a). In grade 4, students solve multiplication problems involving whole numbers, such as "A blue hat costs $6. A red hat costs 3 times as much as the blue hat. How much does the red hat cost?" and "A red hat costs $18 and a blue hat costs $6. How many times as much does the red hat cost as the blue hat?" (4.OA.2) Later in grade 4 and in grade 5, students extend these ideas to solve real-world problems involving multiplication of fractions and mixed numbers using fraction models or equations to represent the problem (5.NF.6). This work with multiplication as scaling is a new emphasis in grades 4 and 5, with the intent of better preparing students for study of multiplicative relationships in grades 6 and 7.

Working with unit fractions and interpreting nonunit fractions as the accumulation of unit fractions (such as, ⅗ is 3 × ⅕, or ⅕ + ⅕ + ⅕ or 3 × ⅕) are the other foundational ideas established in grades 3–5. This emphasis on unit fractions sets the stage for work with unit rates and rates of change in grades 6 and 7, and consequently, for the concept of slope in grade 8.

Which Standards in the Cluster Are Familiar?

Focusing on understanding ratios and proportional relationships and using them to solve real-world mathematical problems in grades 6 and 7 should be familiar. This content has been part of the middle school curriculum, although sometimes introductory work with ratios and rates has been addressed in grade 7 instead of grade 6, as called for in the CCSS content standards.

What's New or Challenging in These Standards?

What is significantly different in this domain is the focus on understanding proportional relationships in multiple ways, then using those ways to support various methods of solving problems that involve proportional relationships. Specifically, the content standards:

- Emphasize understanding unit rates associated with ratios (for example, if it takes three cups of concentrate to make eight cups of juice, then there are three-eighths cups of concentrate for every cup of juice) and using unit rates to solve problems

- Expect students to represent proportional relationships with tables, equations, and graphs and to understand informally that the unit rate indicates the steepness of the graph of the line (informal introduction to slope)

- Expect students to solve problems involving proportional relationships using various methods, such as equivalent ratios and unit rates

The traditional method of creating and solving proportions by using cross-multiplication is *de-emphasized* (in fact, it is not mentioned in the CCSS) because it obscures the proportional relationship between quantities in a given problem situation. Figure 3.4 illustrates possible strategies for solving the proportion problem: "If 2 pounds of beans cost $5, how much will 15 pounds of beans cost?" The strategies in the figure progress from least to most sophisticated, illustrating the development in students' approaches to be expected over time (Progressions for the Common Core State Standards in Mathematics, 2011c, p. 7).

If 2 pounds of beans cost $5, how much will 15 pounds of beans cost?

Method One

Pounds	2	4	6	8	10	12	14	1	15
Dollars	5	10	15	20	25	30	35	2.50	37.50

"I found 14 pounds costs $35 and then 1 more pound is another $2.50, so that makes $37.50 in all."

Method Two

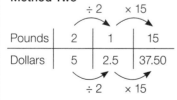

Pounds	2	1	15
Dollars	5	2.5	37.50

"I found 1 pound first because if I know how much it costs for each pound then I can find any number of pounds by multiplying."

Method Three

The previous method, done in one step.

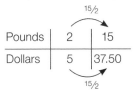

With this perspective, the second column is seen as the first column times a number. To solve the proportion one first finds this number.

Source: Progressions for the Common Core State Standards in Mathematics, 2011c, p. 7. Used with permission.
Figure 3.4: A progression of strategies for solving a proportion.

In grade 7, students use equations as well as tables and graphs to solve proportional relationship problems, and make connections among these different representations (Progressions for the Common Core State Standards in Mathematics, 2011c, p. 9). Figure 3.5 (page 96) illustrates how students connect their work with equations to their work with tables and diagrams. They also extend their understanding to solve multistep ratio and percent problems, including percent increase and decrease, and apply proportional relationships to geometry (similar figures and scale drawings) and statistics and probability (drawing inferences about a population from a random sample).

How Is This Cluster Connected to the Other 6–8 Domains and Mathematical Practices?

Students use ratios and proportional reasoning as they work with content in other domains. In grade 6, students use ratios and proportional relationships as they learn to construct and analyze tables and write equations to describe relationships between quantities (6.EE.9, see appendix B, page 190). In grade 7, students use ratios and proportional reasoning in geometry and statistics and probability. In geometry, students apply proportional reasoning to solve problems involving scale drawings (7.G.1, see appendix C, page 197). They learn to find missing side lengths either by calculating the scale factor that relates lengths in two different figures, or by using equivalent ratios of the corresponding sides in one of the figures. In grade 7, students also solve problems involving area, volume, and surface area of two and three-dimensional objects (7.G.6, see appendix C, page 198). As an outcome of working with areas, students should recognize that areas, surface areas, and volumes do not scale by the same factor as the one that relates side lengths. For example, if the side lengths of a rectangle are increased by a factor of 3, the area increases by a factor of 3^2, not 3.

Statistics provides another context for applying proportional relationships. In grade 7, students learn to draw inferences about a population from a random sample (7.SP.1 and 2, see appendix C, page 198). Because random samples are representative of the total population, the percentage of a sample having a particular characteristic should be approximately the same as that of the full population.

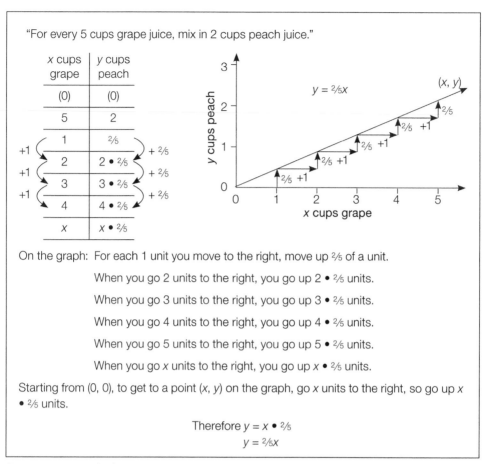

"For every 5 cups grape juice, mix in 2 cups peach juice."

On the graph: For each 1 unit you move to the right, move up $\frac{2}{5}$ of a unit.

When you go 2 units to the right, you go up $2 \cdot \frac{2}{5}$ units.

When you go 3 units to the right, you go up $3 \cdot \frac{2}{5}$ units.

When you go 4 units to the right, you go up $4 \cdot \frac{2}{5}$ units.

When you go 5 units to the right, you go up $5 \cdot \frac{2}{5}$ units.

When you go x units to the right, you go up $x \cdot \frac{2}{5}$ units.

Starting from (0, 0), to get to a point (x, y) on the graph, go x units to the right, so go up $x \cdot \frac{2}{5}$ units.

$$\text{Therefore } y = x \cdot \tfrac{2}{5}$$
$$y = \tfrac{2}{5}x$$

Source: Progressions for the Common Core State Standards in Mathematics, 2011c, p. 9. Used with permission.

Figure 3.5: Correspondence among a table, graph, and equation of a proportional relationship.

Functions Domain in Grade 8 (8.F)

The study of proportional relationships in grades 6 and 7 is the foundation for study of linear functions in grade 8. Linear functions are characterized by having a constant rate of change. Also, proportional relationships are a major type of linear function.

What's New or Challenging in These Standards?

The content standards for grade 8 have more new features than most other grades; most notable, the study of linear functions—defining, representing, and solving linear equations and systems of linear equations and using them to solve real-world problems—which typically is the content of algebra 1, integrated 1, is now a grade 8 expectation for all students.

The standards that define the expected proficiencies in these topics appear in the grade 8 standards for Functions (8.F, see appendix D, page 204) and Expressions and Equations (8.EE, see appendix D, page 203). The Functions domain standards describe expectations regarding functional relationships; the Expressions and Equations domain describes expectations for analyzing and solving linear equations. The study of linear functions in grade 8 does not mean that Algebra 1 has been moved to grade 8. The linear functions expectations are accompanied by expectations regarding number systems, geometry and statistics and probability. (See table 3.2, page 80.) Algebra 1 is still considered to be a high school course; however, CCSS expect that students will enter the study of algebra 1 with a basic understanding of and proficiency with linear functions.

Which Standards in the Cluster Need Unpacking or Emphasizing?

As table 3.5 (page 92) indicates, the Functions domain in grade 8 has two content standard clusters. *Define, evaluate, and compare functions*, the first content standard cluster, includes the definition of a function as "a rule that assigns to each input exactly one output," and that the graph of a function "is the set of ordered pairs consisting of an input and the corresponding output" (NGA & CCSSO, 2010a, p. 55). Function notation is not expected. It also includes comparing properties of two functions represented in different ways; for example, algebraically or graphically with a table or verbal descriptions. Students are expected to interpret the equation $y = mx + b$ as defining a linear function, to recognize that its graph is a straight line, and to give examples of functions that are not linear.

Use functions to model relationships between quantities, the second content standard cluster, addresses using functions to describe a relationship between two real-world quantities and solve real-world problems, determining and interpreting rate of change and the initial function value in terms of the situation being modeled. The expectation is that students will be able to flexibly use different representations of a function—verbal, numeric (table), graph, equation, or contextual structures—as needed to make sense of situations and solve problems. Figures 3.6 and 3.7 (page 98) show two example problems for the grade 8 Functions (8.F, see appendix D, page 204) domain. Both problems require students to use functions to model relationships between quantities. Figure 3.6 asks students to construct functions (that is, create a function rule) to model the relationships between quantities in the problem (8.F.4, see appendix D, page 205), while figure 3.7, Journey to the Bus Stop, requires students to analyze a graph to describe the relationship between the quantities (8.F.5, see appendix D, page 205). The expectation is that students will be able to start with any representation of a function, and use it, or re-represent it in another form, to make sense of a situation and solve problems. As John Van de Walle (2004) notes, there is a flexible interconnection among representations: language, tables, equations, graphs, and context.

The sample tasks in figures 3.6 and 3.7 also involve the use of selected Mathematical Practices. For example, the Baseball Jerseys problem engages students in Mathematical Practices 1, 2, and 4 (see appendix A, pages 181–182). Mathematical Practice 3 is excluded because this problem does not involve making a mathematical argument, even though it involves explaining one's process. This example illustrates the close connection between the Standards for Mathematical Content and Standards for Mathematical Practice, especially in content standards that address understanding.

Baseball Jerseys

Bill is going to order new jerseys for his baseball team.

The jerseys will have the team logo printed on the front.

Bill asks two local companies to give him a price.

1. Print It will charge $21.50 each for the jerseys.

   Using n for the number of jerseys ordered and c for the total cost in dollars, write an equation to show the total cost of jerseys from Print It.

2. Top Print has a one-time setting up cost of $70 and then charges $18 for each jersey.

   Using n to stand for the number of jerseys ordered and c for the total cost in dollars, write an equation to show the total cost of jerseys from Top Print.

3. Use the two equations from questions one and two to figure out how many jerseys Bill would need to order from Top Print to be less than from Print It.

   Explain how you figured it out.

4. Bill decides to order 30 jerseys from Top Print.

   How much would the jerseys cost if he had bought them from Print It? What's the difference between the two prices?

   Show all your calculations.

Source: Adapted from Mathematics Assessment Resource Service, 2012a.

Figure 3.6: Sample Functions problem—Constructing a function to model a linear relationship.

Journey to the Bus Stop

Every morning Tom walks along a straight road from his home to a bus stop, a distance of 160 meters. The graph shows his journey on one particular day.

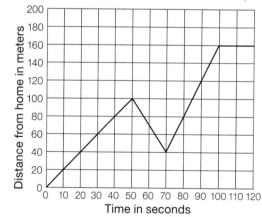

1. Describe what may have happened. You should include details like how fast he walked.

2. Are all the rates represented in the graph realistic? Fully explain your answer.

Source: Adapted from Mathematics Assessment Resource Service, 2012b.

Figure 3.7: Sample functions problem—Analyzing a graph.

How Is This Cluster Connected to the Other 6–8 Domains and Mathematical Practices?

The grade 8 Functions standards in general, and linear functions standards in particular, are directly connected to the Expressions and Equations (EE) domain. As will be described in detail in the next section, 8.EE (see appendix D, page 203) standards include expectations for students' work with linear equations that are an integral part of constructing and using linear functions. Specifically, 8.EE includes two clusters of standards that are directly related to the Functions domain: *Understand the connections between proportional relationships, lines, and linear equations* and *Analyze and solve linear equations and pairs of simultaneous linear equations.*

Finally, students apply their knowledge of linear functions in Statistics and Probability (8.SP, see appendix D, page 206). They informally construct lines of best fit to describe patterns of association in bivariate data (8.SP.1) and use the equation of a linear model to solve problems in the context of bivariate data (8.SP.3).

How Does This Domain Prepare Students for High School?

Students' work with functions in grade 8 is the foundation for their work in the Functions conceptual category in high school. In high school, students extend and formalize their understanding of functions, including the concepts of *domain* and *range* and using function notation. They describe functions using explicit and recursive expressions and extend their work with linear functions to other types of functions, including exponential, quadratic, trigonometric, and polynomial functions, and use these functions to solve a wide range of mathematical tasks and problems—including real-world applications represented by these functions.

Expressions and Equations Domain (6.EE, 7.EE, 8.EE)

Expressions and Equations is a critical area for grades 6, 7, and 8, and it requires substantial time and attention at each grade level. This domain is the bridge between students' work with numerical expressions in grades K–5 and their use of algebraic expressions and equations in high school. Table 3.6 (page 100) contains the grade 8 analysis tool for the Expressions and Equations domain. Visit **go.solution-tree.com /commoncore** for the grades 6 and 7 analysis tools. After your cross-grade middle school team has discussed your individual analysis and understanding of this domain's expectations, use the analysis provided in this chapter for comparison and completion.

Common Core Grades K–5 Expectations

The Operations and Algebraic Thinking domain in grades K–5 provides students a strong foundation for their work with expressions and equations in grades 6–8. Throughout the elementary grades, students have a variety of experiences with expressions and equations. They investigate different situations that operations model, learn to write equations, and solve problems with the unknown in different positions.

Table 3.6: Analysis Tool for Grade 8—Expressions and Equations (8.EE) Domain

Content Standard Clusters	Which Standards in the Cluster Are Familiar?	What's New or Challenging in These Standards?	Which Standards in the Cluster Need Unpacking or Emphasizing?	How Is This Cluster Connected to the Other 6–8 Domains and Mathematical Practices?
Critical area: Formulating and reasoning about expressions and equations, including modeling an association in bivariate data with a linear equation, and solving linear equations and systems of linear equations				
Work with radicals and integer exponents.				
Understand the connections between proportional relationships, lines, and linear equations.				
Analyze and solve linear equations and pairs of simultaneous linear equations.				

Visit **go.solution-tree.com/commoncore** for a reproducible version of this table.

Figure 3.8 shows examples of common addition and subtraction situations with the unknown in different positions.

	Result Unknown	Change Unknown	Start Unknown
Add to	Mike has eight pennies. Sam gives him two more. How many does Mike have now? 8 + 2 = ?	Mike has eight pennies. Sam gives him some more. Now he has ten. How many did he get from Sam? 8 + ? = 10	Mike has some pennies. Sam gives him two more. Now he has ten. How many did Mike have at the beginning? ? + 2 = 10
Take From	Mike has eight pennies. He loses two. How many does he have now? 8 − 2 = ?	Mike has ten pennies. He loses some. Now he has 8 pennies. How many did he lose? 10 − ? = 8	Mike has some pennies. He loses two. Now he has eight. How many did he have at the beginning? ? − 2 = 8

	Total Unknown	Addend Unknown	Both Addends Unknown
Put Together or Take Apart	Eight blue marbles and two red marbles are in a box. How many marbles are in the box? $8 + 2 = ?$	Ten marbles are in a box. Eight are blue; the rest are red. How many marbles are red? $8 + ? = 10$ $10 - 8 = ?$	Sam is making a box of ten marbles. Some are red and some are blue. How many of each color can he have? Find as many different ways as you can. $10 = 0 + 10$ $10 = 1 + 9$, and so on
	Difference Unknown	**Bigger Unknown**	**Smaller Unknown**
Compare	Mike has two pennies. Sam has ten pennies. How many more pennies does Sam have than Mike? $2 + ? = 10$ $10 - 2 = ?$	Sam has eight more pennies than Mike. Mike has two pennies. How many pennies does Sam have? $8 + 2 = ?$ $2 + 8 = ?$	Sam has eight more pennies than Mike. Sam has ten pennies. How many pennies does Mike have? $10 - 8 = ?$ $? + 8 = 10$

Figure 3.8: Common addition and subtraction situations.

Students also learn to write equations to represent such problems ($\square + 19 = 37$) using a symbol for the unknown (a situation equation). In K–2, unknowns are represented by blanks (_____), question marks, or other symbols (for example, $\square$). In grades 3 through 5, students use letters to represent the unknown. They also learn to write equivalent equations that are easier to solve for more difficult situation equations (a solution equation, such as, $37 - 19 = \square$). This informal work is a strong foundation for solving equations formally in middle grades. In particular, grade 5 students learn to "Use parentheses, brackets, or braces in numerical expressions, and evaluate expressions with these symbols" (5.OA.1) and to "Write simple expressions that record calculations with numbers, and interpret numerical expressions without evaluating them" (5.OA.2).

In addition, there is a strong emphasis on the relationships between operations in grades K–5, and use of the properties of operations to solve problems.

Which Standards in the Cluster Are Familiar?

Introducing the concept of *variable*, using variables to write expressions and equations to describe situations and mathematical relationships, and solving simple linear equations are standard parts of most current middle grades curricula. What is different in this domain are the grade levels for specific expectations and, most significantly, the grade 8 expectations. Specifically, in grade 8, *all* students are expected to (1) work with radicals and integer exponents; (2) understand the connections between proportional relationships, lines, and linear equations; and (3) analyze and solve linear equations and pairs of linear equations. Currently, these expectations typically are addressed in an algebra 1 course; however, as described previously for the Functions domain, the study of linear functions and equations is part of the CCSS grade 8 standards for all students.

What's New or Challenging in These Standards?

In grade 6, students make the transition from writing arithmetic expressions and equations to describing situations and solving problems to writing algebraic expressions and equations. In grade 6, students extend their grades 3–5 experiences representing word problems using equations with a letter to stand for the unknown quantity to writing expressions to describe general relationships. For example, students describe how much someone who makes $10 per hour would earn in (h) hours as $10h$ and express the amount earned (a) with an equation, $a = 10h$. Note that students use such expressions and equations as they are learning about proportional relationships. As part of this, sixth graders learn conventional algebraic notation for multiplication and division; for example, they use a dot (•) or juxtaposition for multiplication. In grade 6, students also learn to identify and generate equivalent algebraic expressions; solve simple equations of the form $x + p = q$ and $px = q$ for cases in which p, q, and x are all non-negative rational numbers; and write and evaluate numerical expressions involving whole number integers.

In grade 7, students extend these concepts and skills to expressions and equations involving negative rational numbers, consistent with their learning to compute with negative numbers. They also are expected to become fluent in solving equations of the form $px + q = r$ and extend this to equations involving the distributive property, $p(x + a) = r$, in which p, q, and r are specific rational numbers. This work with equations is also extended to include inequalities of the same form.

Formulating and reasoning about expressions and equations and solving linear equations and systems of linear equations are two foci of grade 8, along with learning about linear functions. Included in these expectations is using linear equations to model an association in bivariate data. An important expectation in this domain is that students will understand the connections between proportional relationships, lines, and linear equations. In addition, in grade 8, students extend the work they did in elementary grades with powers of ten to integer exponents and the properties of integer exponents. Eighth graders' work with square and cube roots lays the foundation for their work with rational exponents in high school.

How Is This Cluster Connected to the Other 6–8 Domains and Mathematical Practices?

Students' work in this domain is directly connected to other domains. In grades 6 and 7, expressions and equations are a direct extension of students' work in the Number System domain. In addition, students are expected to write expressions and equations to represent and solve problems in other domains. For example, in grade 7, angle measurement problems serve as a context for students to write and solve simple equations. In grade 8, work with expressions and equations is an integral part of students' work with functions. It is also directly connected to their work in Statistics and Probability, because students are expected to use linear equations to model associations in bivariate data and solve linear equations and systems of equations to answer questions about data.

How Does This Domain Prepare Students for High School?

Students' work with expressions and equations is the foundation for their work in the high school Number and Quantity and Algebra conceptual categories. In high school, students extend their work with radical and integer exponents to rational exponents (N-RN). They also extend their work with linear equations and systems of linear equations to quadratic, exponential, and polynomial equations and systems of equations. In addition, they work with inequalities as well as equations.

Geometry Domain (6.G, 7.G, 8.G)

The Geometry domain addresses three aspects of geometry: (1) solving real-world geometric measurement problems involving area, surface area, volume, and angle measure of various shapes and solids; (2) understanding and applying the Pythagorean theorem; and (3) understanding properties of geometric figures and relationships between them, including congruence and similarity (see table 3.2, page 80.). Geometry is a critical area in both grades 7 and 8.

Table 3.7 contains the analysis tools for the grade 8 Geometry domain. Visit **go.solution-tree.com/commoncore** for reproducibles of the analysis tools for grades 6 and 7. After your cross-grade middle school team has discussed your individual analysis and understanding of this domain's expectations, use the analysis provided in this chapter for comparison and completion.

Table 3.7: Analysis Tool for Grade 8—Geometry (8.G) Domain

Content Standard Clusters	Which Standards in the Cluster Are Familiar?	What's New or Challenging in These Standards?	Which Standards in the Cluster Need Unpacking or Emphasizing?	How Is This Cluster Connected to the Other 6–8 Domains and Mathematical Practices?
Critical area: Analyzing two- and three-dimensional space and figures using distance, angle, similarity, and congruence, and understanding and applying the Pythagorean theorem				
Understand congruence and similarity using physical models, transparencies, or geometry software.				

continued →

Content Standard Clusters	Which Standards in the Cluster Are Familiar?	What's New or Challenging in These Standards?	Which Standards in the Cluster Need Unpacking or Emphasizing?	How Is This Cluster Connected to the Other 6–8 Domains and Mathematical Practices?
Critical area: Analyzing two- and three-dimensional space and figures using distance, angle, similarity, and congruence, and understanding and applying the Pythagorean theorem				
Understand and apply the Pythagorean theorem.				
Solve real-world and mathematical problems involving volume of cylinders, cones, and spheres.				

Visit **go.solution-tree.com/commoncore** for a reproducible version of this table.

Common Core Grades K–5 Expectations

The elementary Geometry domain addresses three major goals: "(1) geometric shapes, their components (e.g., sides, angles, faces), their properties, and their categorization based on those properties; (2) composing and decomposing geometric shapes; and (3) spatial relations and spatial structuring" (Progressions for the Common Core State Standards in Mathematics, 2012, p. 2). In particular, elementary students learn to classify two- and three-dimensional shapes based on their properties, and organize two-dimensional figures into hierarchies as shown in figure 3.9.

Elementary students also learn the concepts of *area, perimeter,* and *volume* and the formulas for the area and perimeter of rectangles and volume of right rectangular prisms. They apply their knowledge of decomposing and recombining figures to calculate the areas of irregular regions composed of rectangles, which is an important foundation for developing area formulas for triangles and parallelograms and finding areas of complex shapes in grade 6.

Finally, fifth graders learn to graph points on the coordinate plane (using only the first quadrant) to solve real-world and mathematical problems.

Which Standards in the Cluster Are Familiar?

The expectations of the geometric measurement content standard cluster should be familiar, however, depending on your curriculum, particular expectations may shift

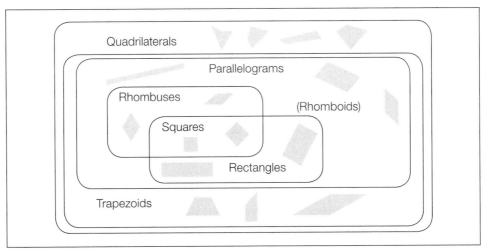

Rhomboids are parallelograms that are not rhombuses or rectangles. This example uses the inclusive definition of trapezoid that a trapezoid is a quadrilateral with at least one pair of parallel sides.

Source: Progressions for the Common Core State Standards in Mathematics, 2012, p. 17. Used with permission.

Figure 3.9: Venn diagram showing classification of quadrilaterals.

grades. Sixth graders build on the K–5 introductory work with perimeter, area, and volume and their experiences decomposing and recombining shapes to develop formulas for the area of triangles and special quadrilaterals; find volumes of right rectangular prisms with fractional-edge lengths; and apply these ideas to solve real-world and mathematical problems. Sixth graders also develop the concept of *surface area* using nets to represent three-dimensional figures with rectangular or triangular faces. In grade 7, students extend these geometric measurement ideas to include area and circumference of circles, then in grade 8, extend these ideas to find the volume and surface areas of cylinders, cones, and spheres.

In grade 7, students also learn facts about supplementary, complementary, adjacent, and vertical angles and use them to find the measure of unknown angles. In grade 8, students extend these ideas and use informal arguments to establish fundamental facts about angle measures, such as the interior angle sum and exterior angles of a triangle; the angles created when parallel lines are cut by a transversal; and the angle criterion for similar triangles. This is an application of Mathematical Practice 3, Construct viable arguments and critique the reasoning of others, and lays a foundation for more formal geometric proofs in high school.

The CCSS Geometry standards for grade 8 include a Pythagorean theorem cluster. Eighth-grade students are expected to understand and apply the Pythagorean theorem in real-world and mathematical problems in two and three dimensions. This is already an expectation in many grade 8 curricula. In addition, students are expected to explain a proof of the Pythagorean theorem and its converse.

What's New or Challenging in These Standards?

The most significant advance in the Geometry standards occurs in the grades 7 and 8 clusters involving properties of geometric figures and relationships, including similarity and congruence. In grade 7, students begin to explore similar and congruent figures. They solve problems involving scale drawings of geometric figures—an application of the grade 7 Ratios and Proportional Relationships standards (7.RP, see appendix C, page 194)—and explore which side lengths and angles of triangles determine a unique triangle, more than one triangle or no triangle.

Which Standards in the Cluster Need Unpacking or Emphasizing?

Understanding congruence and similarity is a major focus of grade 8 geometry. CCSS define similar and congruent figures using a transformation approach:

> A two-dimensional figure is congruent to another if the second can be obtained from the first by a sequence of rotations, reflections, and translations. . . . A two-dimensional figure is similar to another if the second can be obtained from the first by a sequence of rotations, reflections, translations, and dilations. (NGA & CCSSO, 2010a, pp. 55–56)

Defining congruence and similarity in terms of transformations is a significant change in how these terms are defined. The expectation is that not only will students understand congruence and similarity in terms of transformations but also describe a series of transformations to establish the congruence or similarity of two figures. Instruction about transformations should involve work within the coordinate plane as well. This transformational approach to congruence and similarity provides background for congruence and similarity in high school.

Because the transformation approach involves new content for you as well as the students, this should be a priority area for your collaborative team's professional learning. In particular, *dilations* may be new to you, since typically they have not been included in the transformations that middle school curricula address. Yet, dilations are essential for defining similar figures and determining whether two figures are similar. The Learning and Teaching Geometry Project (Seago, Jacobs, & Driscoll, 2010) at the Education Development Center is a good source of resources for your team's study of transformation geometry.

Another new expectation in grade 8 is that students apply the Pythagorean theorem to find the distance between two points in a coordinate plane. This expectation is part of students' work with linear functions and equations.

How Is This Cluster Connected to the Other 6–8 Domains and Mathematical Practices?

Geometric shapes, properties, and measurements are important contexts for applying concepts and skills from the Number System domain, Ratios and Proportional Relationships domain, and Functions domain. In grades 6 and 7, students apply the four operations with rational numbers to solve problems involving area, perimeter, volume, and surface of the two- and three-dimensional shapes appropriate for those grades. Also, in grade 7, angle measurement problems are a context for students to write and solve simple equations (7.EE, see appendix C, page 196).

The concepts and skills in the grade 8 congruence and similarity cluster are used extensively in the Expressions and Equations and Functions domains. In particular, 8.EE.6 calls for students to "use similar triangles to explain why the slope m is the same between any two distinct points on a non-vertical line in the coordinate plane" (see appendix D, page 204). In addition, geometric relationships are a context for exploring different types of functions; for example, area of a square as a function of side length is an example of a nonlinear function.

In addition, the Geometry standards provide a context for students to develop proficiency in the Standards for Mathematical Practice, especially Mathematical Practice 3, Construct viable arguments and critique the reasoning of others. In particular, 8.G.5 (see appendix D, page 205) explicitly calls for students to construct informal arguments to establish facts about specific angle relationships, and 8.G.6 (see appendix D, page 206) requires that students explain a proof of the Pythagorean theorem and its converse.

How Does This Domain Prepare Students for High School?

The geometry standards are an essential foundation for students' work in high school geometry and algebra. In high school geometry, students extend their use of transformations to use congruence and similarity to (1) derive the standard criteria for congruence and similarity of triangles and (2) to prove theorems about triangles, quadrilaterals, and other geometric figures. They extend the problem-solving strategy of decomposing regions to the strategy of drawing auxiliary lines. They use the Pythagorean theorem to establish facts about special right triangles, then generalize the theorem to the Law of Cosines. High school students connect their knowledge of geometry to algebra to develop new methods of analyzing and solving problems (analytical geometry). And, finally, high school students continue to develop proficiency in the Standards for Mathematical Practice; in particular, they extend their work constructing informal geometric arguments to creating and evaluating formal geometric proofs.

Statistics and Probability (6.SP, 7.SP, 8.SP)

The Statistics and Probability domain is a critical area for grades 6, 7, and 8. Middle-grades students use their knowledge of division, fractions and decimals, and patterns to develop fundamental concepts and skills in this domain. Specifically, the Statistics and Probability standards:

- Build on and emphasize understanding of the relationships between univariate and bivariate data

- Expect students to recognize the significance of a random sample and how the data can be used to generalize the conclusions to the larger population

- Expect students to solve real-world problems using a variety of displays of the distribution of data collected from relative frequency trials or simulations

Table 3.8 contains the grade 7 analysis tool for this domain. Visit **go.solution-tree .com/commoncore** for the grade 6 and grade 8 analysis tools. After your cross-grade middle school team has discussed your individual analysis and understanding of this domain's expectations, use the analysis provided in this chapter for comparison and completion.

Table 3.8: Analysis Tool for Grade 7—Statistics and Probability (7.SP) Domain

Content Standard Clusters	Which Standards in the Cluster Are Familiar?	What's New or Challenging in These Standards?	Which Standards in the Cluster Need Unpacking or Emphasizing?	How Is This Cluster Connected to the Other 6–8 Domains and Mathematical Practices?
Critical area: Drawing inferences about populations based on samples				
Use random sampling to draw inferences about a population.				
Draw informal comparative inferences about two populations.				
Investigate chance processes and develop, use, and evaluate probability models.				

Visit **go.solution-tree.com/commoncore** for a reproducible version of this table.

Common Core Grades K–5 Expectations

To provide sufficient instructional time for numbers, operations, and their properties, data play a supporting role in the K–5 curriculum. Data are addressed within the Measurement and Data domain and are never critical areas of focus. Students do work with both categorical and measurement data, representing the former with scaled bar graphs and picture graphs, and the latter with line plots (also called *dot plots*). They also use data as the context for real-world problems. While representing data distributions is a K–5 expectation, defining, computing, and using measures of center (mean, median, and mode) are not, nor is any extended formal work with probability expected in grades K–5.

Which Standards in the Cluster Are Familiar?

A major focus of this domain is summarizing and interpreting data distributions and making valid inferences from data. Students use familiar types of data displays to describe distributions: line plots, box plots, histograms, and, in grade 8, scatter plots. In grade 6, students apply the notion of symmetry to describe the distribution of data displays. Recognizing the shapes and patterns in data displays engages the use of Mathematical Practice 7, Look for and make use of structure. Specifically, sixth graders analyze dot plots and histograms then use box plots and the quartiles that they show to further analyze associations that become evident. Figure 3.10 illustrates the different data displays referred to in particular standards—6.SP.2 and 6.SP.4 (see appendix B, pages 191–192).

6.SP.2: Understand that a set of data collected to answer a statistical question has a distribution which can be described by its center, spread, and overall shape.

Box Plot

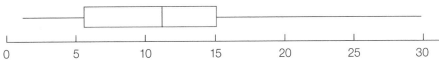

For the data set {1, 3, 6, 7, 10, 12, 14, 15, 22, 30}, the median is 11 (from the average of the two middle values 10 and 12), the interquartile range is 15 − 6 = 9, and the extreme values are 1 and 30.

6.SP.4: Display numerical data in plots on a number line, including dot plots, histograms, and box plots.

Comparing Distributions With Box Plots

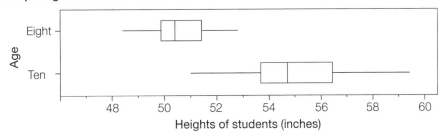

In grade 6, box plots can be used to analyze the data collected to answer the question: "How do heights of students change from age eight to ten?" Sixth graders can give more precise answers in terms of center and spread to questions asked at earlier grades. "Describe the key differences between the heights of these two age groups. What would you choose as the typical height of an eight-year-old? A ten-year-old? What would you say is the typical number of inches of growth from ages eight to ten?"

Figure 3.10: Data distribution displays.   continued →

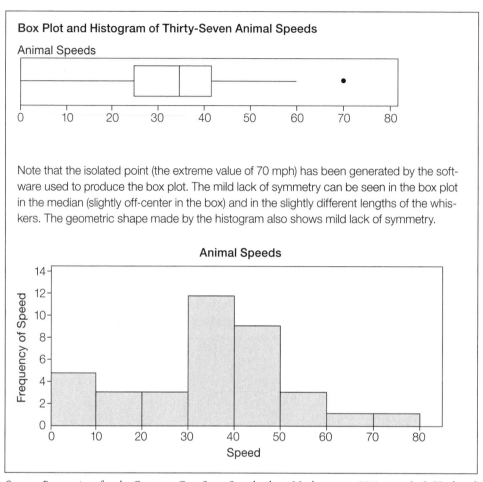

Box Plot and Histogram of Thirty-Seven Animal Speeds

Note that the isolated point (the extreme value of 70 mph) has been generated by the software used to produce the box plot. The mild lack of symmetry can be seen in the box plot in the median (slightly off-center in the box) and in the slightly different lengths of the whiskers. The geometric shape made by the histogram also shows mild lack of symmetry.

Source: Progressions for the Common Core State Standards in Mathematics, 2011c, pp. 4–6. Used with permission.

Another familiar expectation occurs in grades 6 and 7 as students learn to use different measures of center (mean, median, and mode) to describe and compare data sets.

The grade 7 standards also include a cluster focused on probability, which may or may not be familiar, depending on your current standards or curricula. Students learn basic concepts of probability—that the probability of a chance event is a number between 0 and 1 that expresses the likelihood of the event occurring. They collect data to approximate probability of a single event and learn to create sample spaces and probability models. They then extend these ideas to find probabilities of compound events using various models and methods; for example, organized lists, tree diagrams, tables, and simulations. Figure 3.11 shows different models of all the possible outcomes of the toss of two coins.

What's New or Challenging in These Standards?

One new aspect of this domain is the emphasis on *variability* as a key statistical idea throughout the middle grades. Another is that due to the focus on number and operations

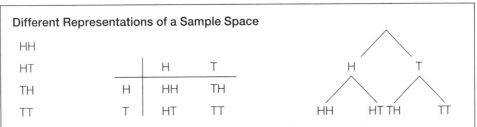

All the possible outcomes of the toss of two coins can be represented as an organized list, table, or tree diagram. The sample space becomes a probability model when a probability for each simple event is specified.

Source: Progressions for the Common Core State Standards in Mathematics, 2011c, p. 7. Used with permission.
Figure 3.11: Different representations of a sample space.

in grades K–5, students will be seeing many of the "familiar" concepts and skills for the first time in grade 6 (for example, *measures of center*) or grade 7 (for example, *probability*).

Which Standards in the Cluster Need Unpacking or Emphasizing?

In grade 6, the emphasis on variability leads to a focus on describing *data distributions* using both measures of center (for example, mean, median, and mode) and measures of spread (for example, quartiles and interquartile range), including the introduction of the *mean absolute deviation* (MAD)—finding the deviation from the mean in preparation for high school statistics. Students are expected to use geometric references—in particular, symmetry—to describe the shape of data displays. Although students will have used line plots to represent data in grades K–5, measures of center are now first introduced in grade 6. Consistent with CCSS emphasis on understanding, not just computation, students are expected to both calculate the mean for a data set and understand *mean* as "the value that each data point would take on if the total of the data values were redistributed equally" (NGA & CCSSO, 2010a, p. 39). That is, they see *mean* as *leveling out* the data or as the *balance point* of a data set. Students also learn to choose appropriate summary statistics to describe, compare, and answer questions about data sets.

Another new aspect of the grade 6 standards is de-emphasis on *mode* as a measure of center and instead focus on appropriate use of the other measures. CCSS also omit stem-and-leaf plots as data representation to be learned, instead emphasizing box plots, which clearly display information about both center and spread of data distributions.

The concept of a random sample is a critical area of focus in grade 7. Students learn that a random sample is a fair way to select a subset (sample) of the set of interest (the population) and use their understanding of proportional relationships to make inferences about a population based on a random sample from that population. A new standard in this domain involves studying the variability in samples from the same population, using the data-analysis tools that students learned in grade 6. Seventh graders also begin making informal comparative inferences between populations.

Figure 3.12 (page 112) illustrates how seventh-grade students might apply these ideas to address the questions "How many hours per week do middle school students typically spend on homework? Do males and females typically spend the same amount of time on homework?" Figure 3.12 also shows the results from a random sample of ten female students and ten male students from the same population.

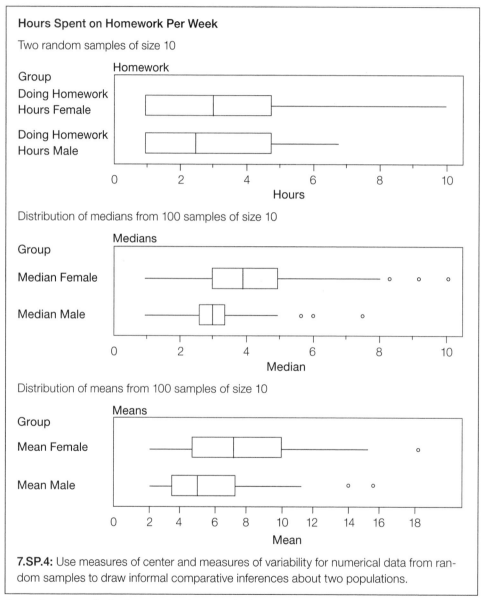

Source: Progressions for the Common Core State Standards in Mathematics, 2011c, p. 10. Used with permission.
Figure 3.12: Comparing data sets.

> Females have a slightly higher median, but students should realize that there is too much variation in the sample data to conclude that, in this population, females have a higher median homework time. An idea of how much variation to expect in samples of size 10 is needed. . . . [To determine

this] students can take multiple samples of size 10 . . . to see how much the sample *medians* themselves tend to vary.

The sample medians for 100 random samples of size 10 each, with 100 samples of males and 100 samples of females. . . . This plot shows that the sample medians vary much less than the homework hours themselves and provides more convincing evidence that the female median homework hours is larger than that for males. Half of the female sample medians are within one hour of 4 while half of the male sample medians are within half hour of 3, although there is still overlap between the two groups.

A similar analysis based on sample means gave the results seen in [the last set of box plots in figure 3.12]. Here, the overlap of the two distributions is more severe and the evidence weaker for declaring that the females have higher mean study hours than males. (Progressions for the Common Core State Standards in Mathematics, 2011d, p. 10)

Finally, seventh graders will formally learn probability for the first time. As your collaborative team creates instructional plans, be sure to allow adequate time for the probability cluster, given that students have little formal prior experiences to build on, and that most, if not all, of the probability concepts, skills, and vocabulary will be new to them.

The grade 8 Statistics and Probability standards are all new and reflect the Functions and Expressions and Equations domains' expectations related to linear functions and equations. Students extend their previous work with univariate data distributions to investigate patterns of association in bivariate data. They create scatterplots to represent bivariate data. For data showing a linear pattern, they informally determine a *line of best fit*, then apply their understanding of slope as rate of change and equations of lines to write an equation that models the relationship between the two quantities. Students use the terms *clustering*, *outliers*, *positive* or *negative association*, and *linear* or *nonlinear association* to describe the patterns created by the two quantities. Students also use relative frequencies and proportions to make comparisons or look for associations among the data. Figure 3.13 (page 114) shows the line of best fit for the scatterplot of scores earned on exam one and two, allowing students to make statements about the data shown.

How Is This Cluster Connected to the Other 6–8 Domains and Mathematical Practices?

Statistics and Probability is an important context for students to apply the concepts and skills from the other middle school domains. They use their knowledge of number and geometry to represent and describe data distributions. They use proportional reasoning to make inferences about populations from random samples. Lastly, they apply their understandings of functions and linear associations to analyze the relationship between two variables (bivariate data).

This domain also provides an important context for students to further develop proficiency in the Standards for Mathematical Practice. In particular, this domain provides regular opportunities for students to engage in Mathematical Practice 2, Reason abstractly and quantitatively, by moving between abstract representations and concrete situations. Mathematical Practice 4, Model with mathematics, is a central practice to all

8.SP.2

Scores on Exam One and Exam Two

Letters in First and Last Names of Students

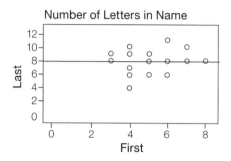

The least squares line fitted to the points has a positive slope and the points are closely clustered about the line, thus, the scores are said to show strong positive association. Students with high scores on one exam tend to have high scores on the other. Students with low scores on one exam tend to have low scores on the other.

The line fitted to the points is horizontal. The number of letters in a student's first name shows no association with the number of letters in a student's last name.

8.SP.3

High School Graduation and Poverty Percentages for States

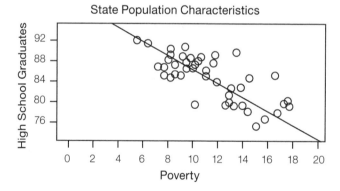

The line fitted to the data has a negative slope and data points are not all tightly clustered about the line. The percentage of a state's population in poverty shows a moderate negative association with the percentage of a state's high school graduates.

Source: Adapted from Progressions for the Common Core State Standards in Mathematics, 2011c, pp. 11–12. Used with permission.

Figure 3.13: Line of best fit for bivariate data.

the work in this domain. Finally, throughout their work in this domain, students make decisions about which tools to apply in particular contexts, where *tools* refers to both technology tools and representational tools (for example, box plot, line plot, and tree diagram).

How Does This Domain Prepare Students for High School?

In high school, students extend their analysis of univariate and bivariate data to more formal analysis of curves of best fit to model associations in data. They describe *spread* in terms of standard deviation, and express strong and weak association of bivariate data in terms of correlation coefficients. They also build an empirical understanding of the normal distribution, and use that to measure sampling error. Students extend their knowledge of probability to include conditional probability and expected value.

Collaborative Actions to Implement the CCSS Content Standards

The content standards involve considerable changes in grades 6–8. Clearly, making the transition to the CCSS is a multiyear endeavor. This section describes key issues and considerations for collaborative teamwork to support your transition to and ultimate implementation of the CCSS.

Collaborative Planning for Content Transitions

How to implement changes in curricula from current expectations to the CCSS expectations—content transitions—is a critical implementation question. The content changes called for in the Common Core involve *what* students should understand and be able to do regarding particular mathematical topics as well as *when* they should develop proficiency in particular content. Collaboratively developing a content transition plan is a necessary action that ensures your students are receiving the opportunities to learn newer content, yet are adequately prepared for current assessments. A coherent mathematics program provides opportunities for your students to learn the expected Common Core content and develop proficiency in the Standards for Mathematical Practice.

In some locations, developing such a plan might be a state- or district-level responsibility. In others, it could be a school responsibility. Even when your collaborative team is not directly involved in establishing such a plan, analyzing the plan in light of local needs is an important team activity. Key questions your collaborative team can use for this reflection include:

- What Common Core State Standards can we implement now?

- What current content can we eliminate or minimize to provide adequate instructional time for the CCSS content expectations?

- How can we most effectively use the time after our end-of-the year state test to support our content transition?

The grade 7 Ratios and Proportional Relationships standards (7.RP, see appendix C, page 194) are an example of standards that can be implemented immediately. These standards call for students to use proportional relationships to solve problems as did many previous state grade 7 standards. The difference is that the Common Core content standards emphasize representing such relationships using unit rates, scale factors, and equivalent ratios and using them as solution methods, instead of focusing on solving proportions using cross-multiplication. Because most test items assess problem solutions without specifying the solution methods, implementation of the CCSS ratio and proportional relationship expectations can begin immediately in place of current instruction in this area.

In contrast, the grade 6 Ratios and Proportional Relationships standards (6.RP, see appendix B, page 187) are an example of content that may be assigned to another grade. In many cases, ratio concepts and reasoning were introduced in grade 7, rather than grade 6, as part of the study of proportional relationships. A good transition strategy is to initially teach this new grade 6 content at the end of the school year. This strategy moves this content from grade 7 to grade 6 in a way that ensures that students have the opportunity to learn it. Teaching it at the end of the year does not take time away from instruction in grade 6 content. The additional time in the grade 7 curriculum provided by moving this content to grade 6 can then be used to teach new grade 7 Common Core content standards.

Collaborative Planning for Curriculum Design

Although the Common Core standards describe what students are expected to understand and be able to do at each grade, they are not a curriculum; that is, they are not organized and sequenced for instruction. Thus, a crucial implementation issue is organizing the standards for each grade into a curriculum. Most often, this is done at the state or district level. Though you and your collaborative team may not be designing curricula based on the CCSS, as implementers of such curricula, you need to be cognizant of key shifts in curriculum design required for faithful implementation of the CCSS. This should be part of your unit-by-unit team discussions.

Because the standards emphasize conceptual understanding as well as proficiency with skills, instruction in content of a particular standard will take more than a day. The grain size of instruction is no longer the typical *standard-a-day* level or pace. For the Common Core content standards, instructional planning needs to focus on sequences of lessons and the standards or clusters of standards which students are working toward in those lessons. With the CCSS, the idea is to zoom out and think of a grain size of learning built on a complete unit or chapter of study consisting of clusters of standards lasting three to four weeks.

Also, to maintain coherence of standards, particular units may involve content from more than one content cluster or domain. For example, the seventh-grade standard on solving problems involving scale drawings (7.G.1, see appendix C, page 197) could be taught in a unit addressing ratios and proportional relationships (7.RP, see appendix C, page 194) instead of in a geometry unit because the techniques are applications of proportional relationships. As your collaborative team examines curricular documents and the relevant content standards, be sure to look for opportunities for cross-domain connections, both for initial instruction on particular standards or clusters of standards, or to provide ongoing review and practice of particular standards.

Collaborative Planning for Pacing Instruction

Once the curriculum is in place, an important collaborative team activity is establishing a unit-by-unit pacing calendar for the year. How much time will you spend on each unit and on particular lessons with each unit? Key principles to attend to in designing your pacing calendar are:

- Allocating instructional time so that the majority of it is spent on the three to four critical areas for each grade (see table 3.2, page 80)

- Providing sufficient time for each unit to allow students to develop conceptual understanding and proficiency in the Standards for Mathematical Practice by engaging in solving challenging mathematical tasks, having mathematical discussions, and reflecting on and revising their work

- Providing sufficient time for assessments to be instructional activities—time for assessment revisions and for instructional interventions when needed (discussed in chapter 5)

Also, collaborative teams should set aside time periodically to re-evaluate their calendar. How much time did particular units actually take? What are the implications of that for scheduling and pacing of other units? Pacing calendars should be tools to keep learning moving forward, but not straightjackets to prevent additional time being spent on important topics if needed. A key message of the CCSS is that *less is more*. As you implement the CCSS, it will be necessary to monitor pacing on a regular basis to ensure that students have the opportunity to learn the critical content for each grade and have sufficient time to make sense of it and make connections among mathematical ideas.

Figure 3.14 (page 118) provides a sample middle school collaborative team's pacing calendar for a sixth-grade unit on ratios and proportional relationships. Notice that multiple lessons are devoted to each learning target, and that lessons often involve more than a single learning target. Although students use various Mathematical Practices in all lessons (like Mathematical Practice 1 and Mathematical Practice 6), particular lessons are designed to promote the use and development of specific Standards for Mathematical Practice.

Collaborative Planning for Instructional Practices

As described in chapter 2, implementation of the CCSS requires instruction in *both* the Standards for Mathematical Content and the Standards for Mathematical Practice. Instruction in the Mathematical Practices should be embedded in content instruction; that is, the Mathematical Practices are the means by which students learn mathematical content. The content standards that emphasize *understanding* are particularly good places to address the practices along with content.

November				
Monday	**Tuesday**	**Wednesday**	**Thursday**	**Friday**
		1 *3-1: Introducing Ratios* Learning Targets: 6.RP.1; Mathematical Practices 2, 4	2 *3-2: Reasoning About Ratios to Solve Problems* Learning Targets: 6.RP.1, 3a; Mathematical Practices 1, 4	3 *3-2: Reasoning About Ratios to Solve Problems, continued* Learning Targets: 6.RP.1, 3a; Mathematical Practices 1, 4
6 *3-3: Equivalent Ratios Using Tables* Learning Targets: 6.RP.3a; 6.EE.6, 9; Mathematical Practice 5	7 *3-4: Equivalent Ratios Using Tables and Graphs* Learning Targets: 6.RP.3a; Mathematical Practice 5	8 *3-5: Unit Rates and Ratios* Learning Targets: 6.RP.2, 3b; 6.EE.6, 9; Mathematical Practice 2	9 *3-6: Writing Equations for Equivalent Ratios* Learning Targets: 6.RP.3; 6.EE.6, 9; Mathematical Practices 7, 8	10 *Quiz: 3-1 to 3-5*
13 *3-7: Distance, Rate, and Time* Learning Targets: 6.RP.2, 3b; 6.EE.9; Mathematical Practice 4	14 *3-8: Other Rate Problems* Learning Targets: 6.RP.2, 3b; 6.EE.9; Mathematical Practice 4	15 *3-9: Solving Problems Using Ratios and Rates* Learning Targets: 6.RP.3d; Mathematical Practice 4	16 *3-9: Solving Problems Using Ratios and Rates, continued* Learning Targets: 6.RP.2, 3; Mathematical Practice 5	17 *Quiz: 3-6 to 3-9*
20 *3-10: Percent as a Rate Per 100 Investigation* Learning Targets: 6.RP.3c; Mathematical Practice 2	21 *3-11: Solving Percent Problems: Finding Percentages* Learning Targets: 6.RP.3c	22 *3-12: Solving Percent Problems— Finding the Total* Learning Targets: 6.RP.3c	23 *Thanksgiving Break*	24 *Thanksgiving Break*
27 *3-13: Solving Percent Problems— Putting It All Together* Learning Targets: 6.RP.3c; Mathematical Practice 4	28 *Unit 3 Preassessment*	29 *Unit 3 Review and Student Goal Setting*	30 *Unit 3 Test*	1 *Unit 3 Test Corrections Based on Comments*

Figure 3.14: Sample pacing calendar.

Visit **go.solution-tree.com/commoncore** for a reproducible version of this figure.

Chapter 2 (page 29) described research-informed instructional practices that promote both conceptual understanding and students' development of the Mathematical Practices, such as the following:

- Engage students in solving high-cognitive-demand tasks, using problem solving as a means of learning mathematics.

- Connect new learning with prior knowledge and, in the process, explicitly address preconceptions and misconceptions.

- Pose questions that challenge students to think and make sense of what they are doing, asking them to justify their conclusions, strategies, and procedures.

- Have students evaluate and explain the work of other students, and compare and contrast different solution methods for the same problem.

- Ask students to represent the same ideas in multiple ways (use multiple representations, such as using symbols, pictures, tables, graphs, or manipulatives).

- Provide ongoing review and practice of previously learned concepts and skills.

Working to implement these instructional practices on a unit-by-unit basis is a collaborative team activity. In many cases, these practices are a departure from current teaching. Common planning about task selection to support specific learning targets, how to best implement specific tasks in the classroom, and how to orchestrate productive discussions that support all students' learning of the learning target will increase the quality of the team's instruction and student learning.

Identify Common Instructional Tasks

The challenging tasks that students engage in provide the common experiences that can be drawn on to further learning at various points throughout the curriculum. Selecting appropriate tasks provides your collaborative team the opportunity for rich, engaging, and professional discussions regarding expectations and student performance. Thus, the critical questions for your collaborative team to consider are, What tasks should be used for each standard of the unit? What is the depth, rigor, order of presentation, and investigation that should be used to ensure student learning of the expected standards? For example, consider 7.RP.2 "Recognize and represent proportional relationships between quantities" (see appendix C, page 195). How does your collaborative team *choose* mathematical tasks that are best for the different components of this standard? Failure to choose tasks as a team can create gross inequities among student learning.

Determine Common Formative Assessments

In addition to identified core tasks, members of your collaborative team will actively seek data for agreed-on checkpoints of student learning on a unit-by-unit basis. As your collaborative team discusses the learning targets for an upcoming unit, you should also agree on how to assess that learning as a team. Then, as you and your team members design lessons for that unit, the common points of assessment are used to gather data to provide feedback to students and to the team. This process will be explored as part of the teaching-assessing-learning cycle in chapter 4.

These embedded assessments are a natural outgrowth of the discussions within your collaborative team and allow for immediate feedback to be provided to both students and teachers. Without these common formative moments, as implemented in tests, quizzes, or other opportunities, the members of your collaborative team do not have the information they need to ensure that all students are learning at the desired level. Therefore, the district's curriculum design team must support the work of the school site collaborative teams by providing guidance on what should be commonly assessed.

Provide Opportunities for Distributed Practice

The benefits of distributed or *spaced* practice with feedback are one of the most robust results from research on human learning (Pashler et al., 2007; Rohrer & Taylor, 2007). Distributed practice helps learners retain knowledge for a longer period of time, reinforces connections between key ideas, and promotes application of that knowledge to new situations. Such practice extends the idea of formative assessment within a unit of instruction to assessing previously taught concepts and skills, including those taught in previous grades or courses, across units of instruction on a regular basis.

Easy ways to provide such practice are to include four to six review problems in nightly homework or as warm-up problems at the start of each class period. Such practice is particularly effective when it includes problems that are prerequisites for upcoming lessons. For example, it would be helpful for sixth graders to review solving area problems involving decomposing rectangles (for example, see 3.MD.7d; NGA & CCSSO, 2010a) before they begin the lessons in which they decompose or compose shapes to develop area formulas for triangles and special quadrilaterals (6.G.1, see appendix B, page 191). Collaboratively creating sets of distributed practice problems, especially deciding when to include problems that address specific prerequisite concepts and skills, will increase the quality of the problem sets. It will also ensure that all the teachers on your team are providing review of prerequisite concepts and skills prior to new instruction, thus helping students connect their new learning with prior knowledge.

Analyze Instructional Materials

Another important foundation for your collaborative instructional planning is to analyze the instructional materials you currently use and determine the extent to which they support faithful implementation of the CCSS. Are the Common Core content standards for each grade addressed with relative emphases that reflect the critical areas specified in the CCSS? Do the materials present a balanced treatment of understanding and skill fluency? Do lessons regularly engage students in solving challenging mathematical tasks to promote conceptual understanding and proficiency in the Mathematical Practices? The CCSS Mathematics Curriculum Materials Analysis tools (Bush et al., 2011) provide valuable resources for such an analysis. They include rubrics to evaluate your current materials, as well as to select new materials in the future (see figure 3.15). Such rubrics are designed to engage cross-grade collaborative teams in rich discussions about the features, strengths, and weaknesses of specific instructional materials for a specific domain, and hence provide important information for your instructional planning.

Rubric One: Mathematics Content Analysis

Content Standards Alignment

1. Have you identified gaps within this domain? What are they? If so, can these gaps be realistically addressed through supplementation?

2. Within grade levels do the curriculum materials provide sufficient experiences to support student learning within this standard?

3. Within this domain is the treatment of the content across grade levels consistent with the progression within the standards?

Balance Between Mathematical Understanding and Procedural Skills

1. Do the curriculum materials support the development of students' mathematical understanding?

2. Do the curriculum materials support the development of students' proficiency with procedural skills?

3. Do the curriculum materials assist students in building connections between mathematical understanding and procedural skills?

4. To what extent do the curriculum materials provide a balanced focus on mathematical understanding and procedural skills?

5. Do student activities build on each other within and across grades in a logical way that supports mathematical understanding and procedural skills?

Rubric Two: Support for Mathematical Practices

Mathematical Practices → Content

- To what extent do the materials demand that students engage in the Standards for Mathematical Practice as the primary vehicle for learning the content standards?

Content → Mathematical Practices

- To what extent do the materials provide opportunities for students to develop the Standards for Mathematical Practice as habits of mind (ways of thinking about mathematics that are rich, challenging, and useful) throughout the development of the content standards?

Assessment

- To what extent do accompanying assessments of student learning (such as homework, observation checklists, portfolio recommendations, extended tasks, tests, and quizzes) provide evidence regarding students' proficiency with respect to the Standards for Mathematical Practice?

Support

- What is the quality of the instructional support for students' development of the Standards for Mathematical Practice as habits of mind?

Source: Adapted from CCSSO, the Brookhill Foundation, & Texas Instruments, 2011, pp. 71, 75.

Figure 3.15: Curriculum materials analysis rubrics.

Visit **go.solution-tree.com/commoncore** for a reproducible version of this figure.

Advanced Learners and Acceleration

A CCSS implementation issue of special concern to grades 6–8 teachers is how to meet the needs of more advanced learners—those students with particular interest in or talent for mathematics who are able to learn at a faster pace than their peers. This issue relates closely to the fourth question collaborative teams in a PLC culture must answer: How will we enrich the learning of students who are already proficient? Traditionally, these students have been placed into advanced classes in grades 6–8 so that they complete algebra 1 (or the equivalent) by the end of grade 8 and are able to take calculus in high school. In some school districts, this advancement is achieved by allowing students to skip a year of mathematics instruction (for example, skip grade 6 mathematics), or by allowing the curriculum to bifurcate at some point (more advanced students take algebra 1 in grade 8, while the majority of students take prealgebra in grade 8).

The CCSS complicate the issues of acceleration in two ways:

1. The CCSS have dramatically increased the content expectations for grade 8 mathematics and for algebra 1. Common Core grade 8 standards include expectations for linear functions and equations, which typically have been the focus of high school algebra 1. Consequently, students will now be expected to enter high school algebra 1 already proficient in this content. In essence, the CCSS for grade 8 are fairly similar to the first semester of many current high school algebra 1 courses.

2. Due to the increased rigor of the CCSS and the focused work within each grade, content is generally not repeated across grades. Consequently, skipping grades in mathematics is not a viable option. More able students need enriched, not reduced, curricula. Acceleration via skipping grades will create knowledge gaps—the exact opposite of what is desired.

How to best provide access to an honors-level mathematics curriculum is typically a district-level, or even a state-level, decision that involves a variety of stakeholders, including parents.

One option recommends creating a compacted course pathway in which more able students complete three years of mathematics instruction in two years (Achieve, 2010); for example, students complete grades 7 and 8 mathematics and a full year of high school algebra 1 in seventh and eighth grades. Students in such a pathway would enter high school having completed the more rigorous CCSS high school algebra 1 expectations, while still having had all the prior coursework. The rationale is that these students are able to learn mathematics more quickly and thus would be able to learn three years of content in two years.

Given the rigor of the CCSS, a better option would be to do four years of coursework in three years, beginning in sixth grade. One advantage of this approach is that accelerated students take algebra 1 in eighth grade, which is a familiar option in many communities. Only two course *pathways* or *sequences* are recommended for grades 6–8. (See figure 3.16.)

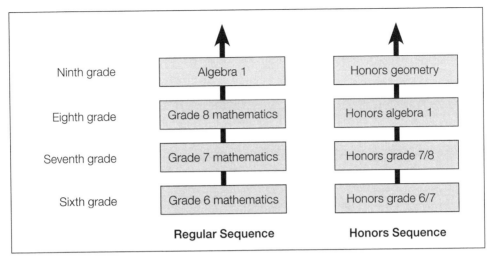

Figure 3.16: Recommended honors sequence.

Visit **go.solution-tree.com/commoncore** for a reproducible version of this figure.

Another option is to substantially increase the amount of instructional time for accelerated or honors students in grade 8 (for example, institute double period courses), so that their mathematics coursework experiences and access can address both the grade 8 and high school algebra 1 standards for your district. This, in essence, compacts two years of curriculum into a single year. Given the emphasis on functions in both courses, that may be a viable option, provided they have sufficient time. Increasing the length of class periods is one option; another is to address some of the eighth-grade standards in a required summer school class.

Yet a third option is to address accelerated or honors coursework in grade 8 as you work with your feeder high school to structure and schedule parallel middle school courses with high school courses such as geometry and algebra 2. In this case your collaborative team expands to include teachers from your middle school with teachers from the high school of the same courses, as you plan together on a unit-by-unit basis.

How to address an accelerated or honors-level curriculum is a local decision. The key issues to keep in mind are (1) the Standards for Mathematical Content have increased expectations for grade 8 and high school, so that grade 8 now includes a significant amount of traditional algebra 1 content, and (2) due to the increased rigor of the CCSS, students need to complete the content of all grades to be mathematically proficient. Whatever options are in place, it is important not to rush to accelerate students too soon—before sixth grade—so that they have the time to develop a sound conceptual foundation for their mathematics learning; to base acceleration decisions on sound evidence of students' learning; and to provide advanced movement options for students who may become interested in acceleration later in time (Achieve, 2010), such as after seventh or eighth grade.

Looking Ahead

This chapter was intended to help your collaborative team begin content discussions regarding the transition to the Common Core content standards expectations as part of the middle school curriculum redesign effort. You can then determine the depth desired for the analysis of the content and when and how your team will engage in the domain analysis (for example, see table 3.3, page 85). The ultimate goal will be for each member of your collaborative team to develop a clear understanding of the important mathematics impacting current grade levels and courses—to realize that what's provided within the CCSS content standards is somewhat different from what you have experienced, but to recognize that the content standards provide opportunities to dig deep and to make *less* (fewer expectations) become *more* (provide a depth of understanding).

Finally, several critical questions should be asked within your collaborative team. Your professional development efforts related to the mathematical domains and content standard clusters of the CCSS content could include, but are not necessarily limited to, the following:

1. How will you organize the domains and content standard clusters within each grade to maintain the within- and across-domain and cluster relationships and connections?

2. What is your collaborative team plan for the amount of time to dedicate for each cluster of standards in each unit each year? Does this plan provide sufficient instructional time for the critical content areas within each grade?

3. Do you have the instructional tools to accomplish your proposed content standards implementation plan? If not, what materials or tools do you need?

4. How will your students develop the Mathematical Practices through their learning experiences in the grades 6–8 domains: Ratios and Proportional Relationships (6.RP and 7.RP), the Number System (6.NS, 7.NS, and 8.NS), Expressions and Equations (6.EE, 7.EE, and 8.EE), Geometry (6.G, 7.G, and 8.G), Statistics and Probability (6.SP, 7.SP, and 8.SP), and Functions (8.F)?

This chapter has presented several resources to guide your school's professional development efforts in thinking about, analyzing, and unpacking the domains, clusters, and standards for grades 6–8. It will be the responsibility of your collaborative teams to implement the vision for Common Core mathematics and, as chapter 4 will suggest, the assessment of those standards.

Chapter 3 Extending My Understanding

1. Examine a specific Common Core content standard domain.

   ○ How do the standards and clusters within this specific domain develop over a student's middle school mathematics experience? How do the content standard clusters and standards within this domain relate to those in other domains?

○ Identify the familiar, new, or challenging content. How might this impact your implementation plan?

○ How do the grade K–5 standards and content standard clusters within the related domain provide a foundation for students' middle grades experience? How do the grades 6–8 standards and clusters provide a foundation for students' work in the related high school conceptual category?

2. Examine a specific content standard cluster.

○ What are the specific learning targets that are expected of students for each grade level of curriculum?

○ What mathematical tasks could be used to assess student understanding of the standards within this content cluster?

○ What Mathematical Practices can be developed within this specific content standard cluster?

3. Examine the instructional materials currently used to support your mathematics curriculum. Determine the extent to which these materials are aligned with the CCSS by using the Mathematics Curriculum Materials Analysis Project tools discussed in the Online Resources. How will you use this information to guide planning, delivery of instruction, and effective assessment?

Online Resources

Visit **go.solution-tree.com/commoncore** for links to these resources.

- **CCSS Mathematics Curriculum Materials Analysis Project (Bush et al., 2011; www.mathedleadership.org/docs/ccss/CCSSO%20Mathematics%20 Curriculum%20Analysis%20Project.Whole%20Document.6.1.11.Final .docx):** The CCSS Mathematics Curriculum Materials Analysis Project provides a set of tools to assist K–12 textbook selection committees, school administrators, and teachers in the analysis and selection of curriculum materials that support implementation of the CCSS for mathematics.

- **Illustrative Mathematics Project (http://illustrativemathematics.org):** The main goal for this project is to provide guidance to states, assessment consortia, testing companies, and curriculum developers by illustrating the range and types of mathematical work that students will experience in implementing the Common Core State Standards for mathematics.

- **National Council of Supervisors of Mathematics Great Tasks collection (mathedleadership.org):** This part of the NCSM website contains high-cognitive-demand tasks aligned to selected CCSS content and practice standards, along with student work and teachers' implementation guide.

- **National Council of Teachers of Mathematics Illuminations Resources (http://illuminations.nctm.org):** This part of the NCTM website contains ready-to-use lessons, including activity sheets, lesson plans, and online activities.

- **Progressions Documents for the Common Core Math Standards (Institute for Mathematics and Education, 2007; http://math.arizona.edu/~ime /progressions):** The CCSS for mathematics were built on progressions— narrative documents describing the progression of a topic across a number of grade levels informed by research on children's cognitive development and by the logical structure of mathematics. The progressions detail why standards are sequenced the way they are, point out cognitive difficulties and provide pedagogical solutions, and provide more detail on particularly difficult areas of mathematics. The progressions documents on this site are useful in teacher preparation, professional development, and curriculum organization, and they provide a link between mathematics education research and the standards.

CHAPTER 4

Implementing the Teaching-Assessing-Learning Cycle

An assessment functions formatively to the extent that evidence about student achievement is elicited, interpreted, and used by teachers, learners, or their peers to make decisions about the next steps in instruction that are likely to be better, or better founded, than the decisions they would have made in absence of that evidence.

—Dylan Wiliam

The focus of this chapter is to illustrate the appropriate use of ongoing student assessment as part of an interactive, cyclical, and systemic collaborative team *formative process* on a unit-by-unit basis. You and your collaborative team can use this chapter as the engine that will drive your systematic development and support for the student attainment of the Common Core mathematics content expectations as described in chapters 2 and 3.

When led well, ongoing unit-by-unit mathematics assessments—whether in-class, during the lesson checks or end-of-unit assessment instruments like tests, quizzes, or projects—serve as a feedback bridge within the teaching-assessing-learning cycle. The cycle requires your team to identify core learning targets or standards for the unit, create cognitively demanding common mathematics tasks that reflect the learning targets, create in-class formative assessments of those targets, and design common assessment instruments to be used during and at the end of a unit of instruction.

To embrace the student assessment and learning expectations within the Common Core, you and your students will constantly need to collect evidence of student learning and respond to that evidence (decide and *act* on what to do next) using rich, descriptive, and immediate corrective feedback as part of a formative decision-making process.

A Paradigm Shift in Middle School Mathematics Assessment Practices

Think about the current assessment practices and processes you, your team members, and others in your mathematics department use. What are they like? How would you know with any certainty if those assessment practices are of high quality and represent a process that will significantly impact student achievement?

Student assessment has largely been considered an isolated middle school teacher activity that served the primary summative purpose of grading. Thus, assessment instruments (mostly quizzes, tests, and projects) primarily serve as an *ends*, not a *means*, to support and advance student learning. Generally, when used as an end, assessment instruments do not result in student motivation to persevere (Mathematical Practice 1) and continue learning. If you use each quiz, test, or chapter assessment instrument only as a summative evaluation moment for the student, often there is little, if any, opportunity for the student to take action and respond to the evidence of learning the assessment provides. In this limited vision of how you and members of your team use assessment instruments (as ends), each teacher on your team would give a quiz or test to the students, privately grade the test questions right or wrong—based on a personal scoring rubric determined in isolation for colleagues—and then pass back student scores (grades) for the test and for the current class grade.

You return the assessment instrument to your students who in turn either file away the test or turn it back in to you. Typically, you file away the results and move on to the next chapter or unit of teaching—while also responding to the students who failed to take the test on time. For the most part, student learning on the previous unit stopped at this point, because the unit had ended. Do any of these isolated assessment practices seem familiar to you or your collaborative team members, either in the past or perhaps today?

With the Common Core mathematics, the fundamental purpose and process for the ongoing unit-by-unit student assessment in mathematics is undergoing a significant change. In a professional learning community, mathematics assessment functions as a multifaceted evidence-collecting process by which you gather information about student learning and your teacher practice *in order to* inform teacher and student daily decision making and to adjust the focus of instruction and re-engage in learning accordingly.

Your collaborative teams will use robust assessment processes grounded in the ongoing retrieval and analysis of information about the depth and rigor of student tasks, the effective learning of those mathematical tasks, and the creation of a learning environment in which "error is welcomed as a learning opportunity, where discarding incorrect knowledge and understandings is welcomed, and where participants [teachers and students] can feel safe to learn, re-learn and explore knowledge and understanding" (Hattie, 2009, p. 239). In this new paradigm, your appropriate use of ongoing student assessment becomes part of an interactive, cyclical, and systemic collaborative team *formative* process for both you and your students.

James Popham (2011b) states the case for a formative assessment process that gathers evidence in a variety of ways, moving from

> traditional written tests to a wide range of informal assessment procedures. Recent reviews of more than four thousand research investigations highlight that when the (formative assessment) process is well-implemented in the classroom, it can essentially double the speed of student learning producing large gains in students' achievement; at the same time, it is

sufficiently robust so different teachers can use it in diverse ways and still get great results with their students. (p. 36)

As a middle school teacher or teacher leader, one of your key collaborative responsibilities becomes ensuring that your collaborative team implements formative assessment processes into your unit-by-unit work. In this new paradigm, you understand that school mathematics assessments are no longer driven by and limited to the traditional *summative* function or purpose of unit or chapter tests and quizzes: assigning grades, scores, and rankings. Your collaborative team will use the assessment instruments and the information from them to make improvements and adjustments to your instruction and to the techniques you use for student learning. Essentially, any traditional school assessment instrument used for a grading purpose is only one part of a much bigger multistep formative process necessary for teacher learning and student learning (Popham, 2008).

Thus, an important distinction is that formative assessment is not a type of unit or benchmark test students take. Formative assessment processes are different from the assessment instruments used as part of the formative process. Popham (2011b) provides an analogy that describes the difference between summative assessment *instruments* and formative assessment *processes*. He describes the difference between a surfboard and surfing. While a surfboard represents an important tool in surfing, it is only that—a part of the surfing process. The entire process involves the surfer paddling out to an appropriate offshore location, selecting the right wave, choosing the most propitious moment to catch the chosen wave, standing upright on the surfboard, and staying upright while a curling wave rumbles toward shore. The surfboard is a key component of the surfing process, but it is not the entire process.

High-quality middle school assessment practices then function to integrate formative assessment processes into your decisive *actions* about shaping instruction to meet student needs, progress, pacing, and next steps. Similarly, these processes inform your students about their learning progress and direction, enabling them to become actively involved and to make decisions and take ownership of their work. You learn more about your instructional practice and students take ownership of their learning by:

1. Using unit-by-unit assessment instruments such as quizzes, projects, and tests as tools to support a formative learning process for students and teachers (steps one, four, and five of the teaching-assessing-learning cycle)

2. Designing and implementing formative assessment in-class strategies that check for student understanding during classroom instruction through student-engaged learning tasks (steps two and three of the teaching-assessing-learning cycle)

Note that teachers and students in conjunction with their peers must *act* on the evidence collected during the formative assessment process. Otherwise, as Wiliam (2011) describes, the formative process is empty in terms of impact on student learning.

Furthermore, Wiliam (2011) cites five elements that need to be in place, if the intent of your teaching and assessing during the lesson (your daily choice of mathematical tasks used for short-cycle assessments and checks for understanding) and unit (your weekly or monthly choice of assessment instruments, such as quizzes and tests) is to improve student learning. The five elements are:

1. The provision of effective feedback to students

2. The active involvement of students in their own learning

3. The adjustment of teaching to take into account the results of assessment

4. The recognition of the profound influence assessment has on the motivation and self-esteem of students, both of which are crucial to learning

5. The ability of students to assess themselves and understand how to improve

The teaching-assessing-learning cycle is built on the foundation of these essential assessment elements. The cycle is designed to develop a vision of effective high-quality assessment practice on a unit-by-unit basis for the teachers on your team and in your mathematics department. The process begins as your collaborative team designs mathematical tasks, formative in-class assessments for those tasks, lessons (and re-engagement lessons as needed) that allow for student engagement into those tasks, and assessment instruments (quizzes and tests) that align with the expected learning targets for a unit or chapter of content. Your team works together to determine how to provide students in the course with formative learning opportunities and strategies on those learning targets as you respond to evidence (or lack thereof) of student learning.

The PLC Teaching-Assessing-Learning Cycle

The PLC teaching-assessing-learning cycle in figure 4.1 provides a systemic collaborative team process that will recognize any assessment used—from the daily in-class informal checks for understanding with student feedback to the more formal unit assessment instruments—as formative, provided students and teachers use the assessments to make instructional and learning adjustments by students and teachers. Assessments—such as quizzes, tests, and projects—that your collaborative team uses strictly for the assignment of grades or mastery scores, not for authentic formative learning opportunities, fall far short of reaching the powerful impact assessment could have on improved student and teacher learning. However, when traditional assessment instruments are used as tools within a robust team assessment plan and process cycle, great things can happen. Great things happen too when in-class formative feedback is part of your team's lesson design and teaching becomes "*adaptive* to student learning needs" (Wiliam & Thompson, 2007, p. 64).

Moving clockwise in figure 4.1, your collaborative teacher team makes adjustments and moves back and forth in the cycle during a unit as needed, giving feedback to your students and to each other. In step one, you do the hard work of up-front planning and development for the unit: planning for the learning targets, planning the common and essential unit tasks and the formative assessment in-class responses to the tasks during instruction, and planning the common assessment instruments to be used throughout the unit.

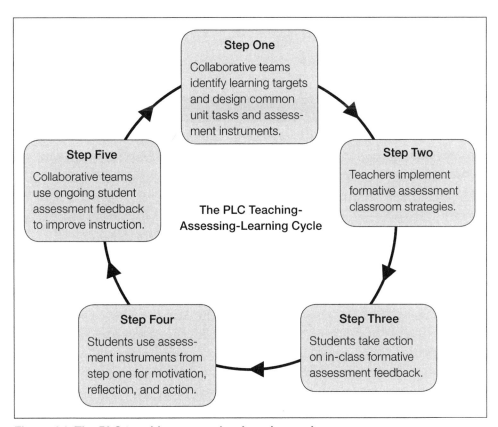

Figure 4.1: The PLC teaching-assessing-learning cycle.

Visit **go.solution-tree.com/commoncore** for a reproducible version of this figure.

In steps two and three, you use daily formative assessment classroom strategies around the team-designed mathematical tasks from step one and make adjustments as needed during the unit—including the use of re-engagement lessons if needed. In step four, students set goals and make adjustments to learning based on all unit or chapter assessment instrument results, at a developmentally appropriate level depending on the grade level (this might be different from the sixth grade to eighth grade middle school classes). Students reflect on successes and next-step actions based on evidence of areas of weakness, during and after the unit of study as the assessment instrument is used for formative learning.

Ultimately, in step five, you make adjustments to future lesson plans and unit assessment instruments due to individual differences in students and the success of students, as your team collects evidence and data at the end of the unit. At this step as you and your team members reflect on student performance during and after the unit of study, it is important for you to think about *all* students in the course, not just the ones you teach. You take notes and *share* with colleagues what went well, what changes to make, and so on, for the next unit of instruction.

The teaching-assessing-learning cycle enables you and your collaborative team to learn about and develop formative assessment practices designed to move learning forward.

Through your collaborative actions, you select and administer high-cognitive-demand tasks for all students, analyze the results, and discover important information that will drive student learning. These actions are central to the development of new lessons in the next unit that capitalize on the findings from formative assessments. The goal is to develop follow-up lessons—*re-engagement lessons*—that deepen student understanding of the mathematics standards and build a deep foundation of the conceptual knowledge to learn further mathematics. Such lessons overcome the diagnostic problems of merely directing students to "Try harder" or to complete more practice work that is the same as the original work on which they encountered difficulty. Later in the chapter you will find a more detailed discussion of a re-engagement lesson as a teaching and learning tool (page 145).

Step One: Collaborative Teams Identify Learning Targets and Design Common Unit Tasks and Assessment Instruments

In a professional learning community, before the first lesson of the next unit or cluster of mathematics instruction begins, your collaborative course-based team reaches agreement on the design and proper use of high-quality, rigorous common assessment tasks (for formative in-class feedback) and assessment instruments (unit quizzes and tests) for all students during the unit. However, to do so requires your collaborative team first reaches clarity on and understanding of the expected learning targets for the unit as you answer the first of three critical questions for step one.

What Are the Identified Learning Standards?

The grades 6–8 content standards define what students should *understand* as well as what skills they must be able to do in their study of mathematics. In figure 4.2, the very nature of the CCSS content domain Ratios and Proportional Relationships (7.RP, see appendix C, page 194) requires students to show how to recognize and represent proportional relationships as part of the learning target assessment.

Asking a student to understand something means you must formatively assess whether the student has understood it—and thus the tasks as well as the assessment of the tasks design must reflect your collective team effort to meet the vision of the CCSS *understanding* aspect of the learning target.

A collective team discussion on what is intended by the learning targets for the unit, as well as the progression of the learning targets in the unit and to other units, will help the team to better meet the vision of teaching to the CCSS understanding aspect of the standards. Although the specific number of total learning targets has been reduced per grade level in order to allow greater depth and less breadth, there is a greater expectation for the assessment of student understanding—the conceptual knowledge necessary for developing procedural fluency—which should be considered when developing the unit. As your collaborative team plans the unit calendar and pacing for the learning targets, adequate

---

Content standard cluster: Analyze proportional relationships and use them to solve real-world and mathematical problems.

2. Recognize and represent proportional relationships between quantities.

   a. Decide whether two quantities are in a proportional relationship, such as by testing for equivalent ratios in a table or graphing on a coordinate plane and observing whether the graph is a straight line through the origin.

   b. Identify the constant of proportionality (unit rate) in tables, graphs, equations, diagrams, and verbal descriptions of proportional relationships.

   c. Represent proportional relationships by equations. For example, if total cost t is proportional to the number n of items purchased at a constant price p, the relationship between the total cost and the number of items can be expressed as $t = pn$.

   d. Explain what a point (x, y) on the graph of a proportional relationship means in terms of the situation, with special attention to the points $(0, 0)$ and $(1, r)$ where r is the unit rate.

Source: NGA & CCSSO, 2010a.

Figure 4.2: Ratios and Proportional Relationships domain, grade 7 (7.RP.2).

---

time should be built in to allow for formative in-class assessment feedback, corresponding instructional adjustments, and the subsequent use of appropriate assessment instruments for student demonstration of understanding the learning targets.

Once your team understands the expected learning targets for the unit (your answer to the PLC question, What is it we want all students to know and be able to do in this unit?), you are ready for the next aspect of step one—identifying the common unit tasks that will be used to develop student understanding of the learning targets for the unit, which is the second critical focus necessary to be prepared for meaningful in-class formative assessment processes.

What Are the Identified Daily Formative Mathematical Tasks?

During step one, members of your collaborative team discuss the cognitive demand of the *mathematical tasks* that will be part of the daily lesson design and used in class as part of the formative feedback process to students (for more on cognitive demand, see chapter 2, page 37). Your lesson-design preparation should take into account both the skill- and understanding-level design of the mathematical tasks and problems presented to the students during the unit of mathematical study.

Without high-cognitive-demand tasks to be used throughout the unit (including on unit assessment instruments such as tests and quizzes), the feedback about student thinking will be limited. Merely knowing whether a student answered a question correctly provides limited information about what the student knows or can do or why the student struggled with the mathematics or answered incorrectly. Was it because the student misinterpreted or misread the problem? Was it because the student didn't know how to start the problem? Was it because the student could not reason through a process in order to solve the problem? Was it because the student could not accurately carry out calculations? Such questions about a student's performance are likely familiar to you.

Your collaborative team's preparation for the understanding aspects of the content standards is served through the lesson-design expectations of the CCSS Mathematical Practices as described in chapter 2 (see table 2.2, page 59). Common unit mathematical tasks need to be constructed so that Mathematical Practices, such as Construct viable arguments and critique the reasoning of others (Mathematical Practice 3) or Use appropriate tools strategically (Mathematical Practice 5), are part of the lesson design. The CCSS document states it like this:

> One hallmark of mathematical understanding is the ability to justify, in a way appropriate to the student's mathematical maturity, *why* a particular mathematical statement is true or where a mathematical rule comes from. Mathematical understanding and procedural skill are equally important, and both are assessable using mathematical tasks of sufficient richness. (NGA & CCSSO, 2010a, p. 4)

Consider figure 4.3 for examples of turning a low-cognitive-demand task into a high-cognitive-demand task.

Consider the following low-cognitive-demand task.

Evaluate: 2^{-3}

Imagine rewriting this task for a higher-cognitive-demand level:

$2^{-3} = \frac{1}{8}$

Provide a mathematical argument that verifies this statement is true and defend your argument to a student partner.

Figure 4.3: Sample low- and high-cognitive-demand tasks.

As your team determines which common tasks to use during the unit, step one is the critical place that potentially manufactures inequities in student mathematics learning. If your collaborative team fails to reach agreement on the use of various mathematical tasks or the rigor of other such tasks during the lessons for each unit, then the learning outcomes for students will vary according to the assigned teacher and his or her task selection—the implementation gap only widens. The same will be true if your collaborative team cannot reach agreement on the nature of viable student responses to such questions, and the advancing and assessing questions that help to scaffold the learning target expectations for your students.

An effective process of choosing a task starts with your team doing the task (as well as all types of assessments) as a learner would before the unit begins. In this manner, you are able to examine the core mathematical ideas embedded in the task, develop empathy for the mathematical thinking the students must engage in and the complexity of the steps and strategies students will encounter, and determine how you will assess quality student responses to the task. Teachers who are novice to worthwhile tasks are often concerned about the wording of the task and how it might be redesigned. Rather than focusing on modifying tasks, you should internalize the tension of understanding what the task requires of the learner. Focus on what mathematical ideas and thinking students will encounter, what is required to model the situation, and the appropriate productive struggle when engaging in a problem solution.

Figure 4.4 is a task-analysis tool that provides questions that will help you anticipate students' performances. The instrument features three sections: (1) where students will be successful, (2) where they will struggle, and (3) what the teacher's plan is for future instruction.

Task name: _____ Grade: _____ Year: _____ Total points: _____ Core points: _____	
In anticipating the student work, where will students show success?	
What parts of the task will students be successful with?	In terms of knowing and doing mathematics, what does this indicate?
In anticipating the student work, where will students struggle?	
What parts of the task will students be unsuccessful with?	In terms of knowing and doing mathematics, what does this indicate? What understandings or skills do the students need to learn?
Considering strengths and weaknesses from students, what are plans for future teaching?	
What are the implications for future instruction?	What specific instruction or lesson experiences will you design for students?

Source: Adapted from Foster & Poppers, 2009.

Figure 4.4: Task anticipation sheet.

Visit **go.solution-tree.com/commoncore** for a reproducible version of this figure.

You can use the answers to the questions in figure 4.3 (page 134) to select tasks that match the learning standards for the unit and the potential learning progressions for your students. The answers will frame both the direction of the mathematical ideas you present and processes to be learned and assessed as well as the attention to student thinking that will appear in students' work.

Consider the sample poster task in figure 4.5. You can use the task analysis tool provided in figure 4.3 to anticipate potential features that will prevail in student responses to the task. The poster problem is a task that would be used during a unit on Ratios and Proportional Relationships, *Analyze proportional relationships and use them to solve real-world and mathematical problems* (7.RP, see appendix C, page 194), which was highlighted in figure 4.2 (page 133).

The low-cognitive-demand task in question one (use a proportion) is transformed to a higher-cognitive-demand task in question two by asking students to use multiple steps, including a translation of units to determine whether or not a student's estimation about the building height is correct.

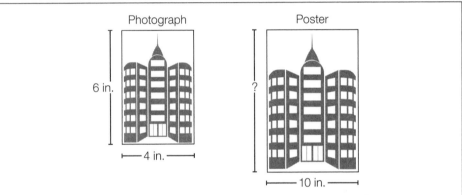

1. A photograph is enlarged to make a poster. The photograph is 4 in. wide and 6 in. high. The poster is 10 in. wide. How high is the poster?

2. On the poster, the building measures 12 in. tall. Samantha took the photograph and claims she measured the width of the actual landscape as 55 feet, and that in her estimation, the actual building is no taller than 60 feet. Is she right? How tall is the actual building shown in the photograph? Make a conjecture, and provide a mathematical argument to defend your answer.

Source: Adapted from Mathematics Assessment Collaborative, 2001.

Figure 4.5: Sample Ratios and Proportional Relationships problem.

It is your collaborative team's responsibility to ensure the fair implementation of daily mathematical tasks that teach and assess for student understanding. Equity in mathematics education requires your collaborative team to design instructional lessons that ensure the use of *common* mathematical tasks with sufficient richness to engage students in observable mathematical informal discussions that simultaneously serve as a form of ongoing formative assessment with feedback to you and your students (Kanold et al., 2012).

Once the team understands the expected learning targets for the unit and has identified the Common Core tasks that will be used to develop in-class student understanding of those learning targets for the unit, then the discussion and development of the common assessment instruments to be used is the third critical aspect of step one.

What Are the Identified Common Assessment Instruments?

When collaborative teams create and adapt unit-by-unit common assessment instruments together, they enhance the coherence, focus, and fidelity to student learning expectations across the school for all teachers. They also provide the hope of greater readiness and continuity for the mathematics the students will experience the following year. The wide variance in student task performance expectations (an inequity creator) from teacher to teacher is minimized when you work collaboratively with colleagues to design assessment instruments appropriate to the identified learning targets for the unit.

How do you decide if the unit-by-unit assessment instruments you use are of high quality? Figure 4.6 (page 138) provides an evaluation tool that your collaborative team can use to evaluate the quality of current assessment instruments, such as tests and quizzes, as well as build new assessment instruments for the course.

You and your collaborative team should rate and evaluate the quality of current unit or chapter assessment instruments (for example, tests, quizzes, or projects) using the evaluation tool in figure 4.6 (page 138). The goal is to write common assessment instruments that would score a four in all eight categories of the assessment evaluation rubric. The goal, as Popham (2011b) would say, is to create great surfboards for the students to use. Your collaborative team could also create your own agreed-on "Criteria for Assessment Instrument Quality" using figure 4.6 as a starting point based on your local vision for high-quality assessment.

The value of any collaborative team–driven assessment depends on the extent to which the assessment instrument reflects the learning targets, can be used for a student formative process in the aftermath of the assessment, provides valid evidence of student learning, and results in a positive impact on student *motivation and learning*. It is your responsibility to ensure your collaborative team implements this vision for the use of high-quality assessment processes.

As you and your team complete these three critical planning tasks from step one, you are ready to teach the unit of instruction over the next twelve to sixteen days and move on to step two of the teaching-assessing-learning cycle. You use formative assessment strategies in class to advance and assess observable and formative student discussions and experiences for the unit's learning targets.

Assessment Indicators	Description of Level 1	Requirements of the Indicator Are Not Present	Limited Requirements of This Indicator Are Present	Substantially Meets the Requirements of the Indicator	Fully Achieves the Requirements of the Indicator	Description of Level 4
Identification and emphasis on learning targets	Learning targets are unclear and absent from the assessment instrument. Too much attention is on one target.	1	2	3	4	Learning targets are clear, included on the assessment, and connected to the assessment questions.
Visual presentation	Assessment is sloppy, disorganized, difficult to read, and offers no room for work.	1	2	3	4	Assessment is neat, organized, easy to read, and well-spaced with room for teacher feedback.
Time allotment	Few students can complete the assessment in the time allowed.	1	2	3	4	Test can be successfully completed in time allowed.
Clarity of directions	Directions are missing and unclear.	1	2	3	4	Directions are appropriate and clear.
Clear and appropriate scoring rubrics	The scoring rubric is not evident or appropriate for the assessment task.	1	2	3	4	Scoring rubric is clearly stated and appropriate for each problem.
Variety of assessment task formats	Assessment contains only one type of questioning strategy and no multiple choice. Calculator usage is not clear.	1	2	3	4	Assessment includes a variety of question types and assesses different formats, including calculator usage.
Question phrasing (precision)	Wording is vague or misleading. Vocabulary and precision of language are struggles for student understanding.	1	2	3	4	Vocabulary is direct, fair, and clearly understood. Students are expected to attend to precision in responses.
Balance of procedural fluency and demonstration of understanding	Test is not rigor balanced. Emphasis is on procedural knowledge and minimal cognitive demand for demonstration of understanding.	1	2	3	4	Test is balanced with product- and process-level questions. High-cognitive-demand and understanding tasks are present.

Figure 4.6: Assessment instrument quality—evaluation tool.

Visit **go.solution-tree.com/commoncore** for a reproducible version of this figure.

Step Two: Teachers Implement Formative Assessment Classroom Strategies

Step two of the teaching-assessing-learning cycle occurs as part of your team members' daily assessment actions during a mathematics unit of study. You intentionally plan for and implement both formal and informal learning structures and design tasks as outlined in chapters 2 and 3 that will provide ongoing student engagement and descriptive feedback around the elements of the learning targets as well as the CCSS Mathematical Practices.

This step highlights the team's work to design and present the daily common mathematical tasks (designed in step one) in an engaging and formative learning environment and then use appropriate formative assessment feedback strategies to determine student understanding of the intended learning targets.

According to Wiliam (2011):

> When formative assessment practices are integrated into the minute-to-minute and day-by-day classroom activities of teachers, substantial increases in student achievement—of the order of a 70 to 80% increase in the speed of learning are possible. . . . Moreover, these changes are not expensive to produce. . . . The currently available evidence suggests that there is nothing else remotely affordable that is likely to have such a large effect. (p. 161)

You and your team should not ignore this wise advice.

Ginsburg and Dolan (2011) suggest several "informal" strategies of assessment *for* learning and checks for understanding that can provide you valuable insight into the level of student understanding as a lesson unfolds. Some of these strategies are included in figure 4.7 (page 140). An additional advantage of these formative assessment strategies is that they increase the level of student engagement, a key characteristic of classroom environments that promote high student achievement (Wiliam, 2011). You can use these strategies as implementation structures or boundary markers for team discussion regarding the use of the Mathematical Practices (student practices) as part of your lesson design.

Your collaborative team should discuss how to build in a formative process for observing evidence of student learning and providing in-class formative feedback to student peers by how you break down mathematics tasks and problems into parts. Consider a problem as part of an extended process for strategy five in figure 4.7, as your collaborative team seeks to design mathematics tasks that provide evidence of answers to the following formative assessment feedback questions.

1. How do we expect students will express their ideas, questions, insights, and difficulties?

2. Where and when will and should the most significant conversations be taking place (student to teacher, student to student, teacher to student)?

3. How approachable and encouraging should we be as students explore? Do students use and value each other as reliable and valuable learning resources?

Strategy One: Key Questioning During Whole-Class Discussion

You use preplanned questions during critical points of the lesson to assess student understanding. "These pivotal adjustment-influencing questions must be carefully conceptualized before the class session in which the discussion will take place. . . . Teachers can't expect to come up with excellent adjustment-influencing questions on the spur of the moment" (Popham, 2008, p. 60). The mathematical task should be designed to promote student demonstration of understanding.

Strategy Two: Mini or Large Whiteboard Responses

Supply every student with a mini or a large whiteboard. You ask a preplanned question or provide the students with a critical problem to solve. The students then hold up their responses on whiteboards, and you scan the responses to make a decision concerning the students' mastery levels and needed instructional modifications. Students can also rotate to new groups and use the whiteboard to explain their conjecture or solution to others.

Strategy Three: Traffic Lights or Red and Green Disks

You supply students with colored plastic cups—green, yellow, and red—or a CD-sized disk that is red on one side and green on the other. At critical points during the lesson, ask students to display the color of cup or disk that corresponds to their level of understanding (green means that the student understands, while the red—or yellow—cup indicates the student does not understand and instructional adjustments are necessary).

Strategy Four: All-Student Response Systems

If you have access to SMART Boards and clicker systems in your classroom, you can design key multiple-choice or open-ended questions that students can work on at critical points in the lesson and send their answers to you using the clickers. This displays a real-time public chart indicating the class's response to the question and immediately lets you know the level of the class's understanding or common misconceptions (if the multiple-choice options are keyed to common misconceptions).

Strategy Five: Diagnostic Interview Questions

Ask individual students questions to reflect on, articulate, and uncover how they are thinking while working individually or in small groups of two to four. The key is for you to engage in evaluative listening—listening to assess the student's or the student team's understanding in order to modify instruction and provide feedback.

Figure 4.7: Formative assessment strategies for student action.

Visit **go.solution-tree.com/commoncore** for a reproducible version of this figure.

By reaching agreement on the types of mathematical tasks and formative questions to use in class, there will be better in-class teacher adjustments to instruction. Daily demonstrations of student learning will be based on a more coherent *team-based* practice. However, this will not be sufficient. If during the best teacher-designed moments of classroom formative assessment students fail to *take action* on evidence of continued areas of difficulty (step three), then the teaching-assessing-learning cycle is stopped for the student.

Step Three: Students Take Action on In-Class Formative Assessment Feedback

Do your students learn to take more responsibility for their learning by reflecting long enough on their class work, including various in-class tasks and assessments for learning in order to view mistakes as learning opportunities? This is the goal of step three in the teaching-assessing-learning cycle. Students then view assessment as something they *do* in order to focus their energy and effort for future work and study. A great time for this type of student reflection is during small-group discourse as your students work together on various problems or tasks as you check for student understanding. This will also occur during the advancing and assessing moments that are part of lesson design or during the student-led closure activities at the end of the class period.

As Wiliam (2007b) indicates, in order to "improve the quality of learning within the system, to be formative, feedback needs to contain an implicit or explicit recipe for future action" (p. 1062). This requires you to think about how daily and weekly feedback from peers or from you as the teacher can be used for student-initiated action and engagement with the feedback.

Thus, students and teachers share the responsibility for successful implementation of the in-class formative assessment practices. Students who can demonstrate *understanding* connect to the learning targets for a unit and can reflect on their individual progress toward that target. Students can establish learning goals and actions they will take in order to reach the targets, and you support students' progress by using immediate and effective feedback not only during the daily classroom conversations but, importantly, as part of the common assessment instrument feedback process used in step four.

Step Four: Students Use Assessment Instruments From Step One for Motivation, Reflection, and Action

It is very rare to find middle school mathematics teachers or collaborative teams that use common assessment instruments such as quizzes and tests as part of a formative process for learning. In step four, the old paradigm of testing for grading purposes (an end goal) fades and the new paradigm of using assessment instruments and tools for formative assessment purposes (a means goal) emerges.

Wiliam (2007b) makes the distinction between using *assessment* instruments for the purposes of (1) monitoring, (2) diagnosing, or (3) formatively assessing. He states:

> An assessment *monitors* learning to the extent it provides information about whether the student, class, school or system is learning or not; it is *diagnostic* to the extent it provides information about what is going wrong, and it is *formative* to the extent it provides information about what to do about it. (p. 1062)

Furthermore, of the three purposes, simply monitoring or assessment progress, or providing diagnostic performance (your grade is a C) on an assessment instrument is the *least useful* for improving and motivating student thinking and achievement toward the identified learning targets for the unit-by-unit standards.

As Wiliam (2011) describes:

> [Effective feedback] should cause thinking. It should be focused; it should be related to the learning goals that have been shared with students; and it should be more work for the recipient than the donor. Indeed, the whole purpose of feedback should be to increase the extent to which students are owners of their own learning. (p. 132)

A *diagnostic* assessment, while necessary, is rarely sufficient for the student. Diagnostic assessments do not tell the student what he or she needs to do differently, nor do they indicate any expectation that the student is to take any action on errors. The frequent admonition to "Try harder" or the tendency to assign more practice problems is not likely to support the student in making progress. All too often, the teacher's solution when a student has not demonstrated mastery is to assign more practice. However, the primary function of practice is to solidify a student's current level of understanding. If the student does not understand the concept and continues to practice what he does not understand, then additional practice only results in the student solidifying his or her lack of understanding and increases frustration.

When you and your students take action to provide additional instruction, such as in a re-engagement lesson used in the next unit, then the summative assessment instrument becomes formative—part of a formative process of learning for the student—and has the potential to advance his or her learning. The important point is that any form of assessment becomes an opportunity to provide students with feedback, both with respect to their procedural fluency *and* conceptual understanding, to improve learning. When the student uses specific teacher *or* peer feedback, the assessment result has the potential to be *formative* for the student and improve performance on this learning target that is necessary to master the selected standards.

In one such class, students complete a self-evaluation form to identify which problems they did right or wrong in class over the past few days, what type of error was made and which questions were aligned with each learning target, and which learning targets were weakest or strongest for them. This helps the students focus on the specific learning targets necessary for preparation action and review before the final summative assessment (V. Keift, personal communication, June 27, 2011). As part of this student-led analysis, students complete the information provided in figure 4.8.

Bennett (2009) notes, "It is an oversimplification to say that formative assessment is *only* a matter of process or *only* a matter of instrumentation. Good processes require good instruments and good instruments are useless unless they are used intelligently" (as cited in Wiliam, 2011, p. 40). Your collaborative team will be wise to spend a lot of time designing common unit assessment instruments that can be used intelligently—ensuring all students in a course benefit from both good tasks (instruments) and good

My learning targets of strength are: _____

My learning targets of weakness are: _____

To prepare for the chapter test, I will commit to the following actions: _____

_____

Ideas:

- Redo my notes which cover my learning target areas of weakness.
- Retry book examples which cover my areas of weakness.
- Seek help at the learning center.
- Meet with my teacher or peers for help.
- Learn the vocabulary.
- Eliminate simple mistakes.

Figure 4.8: Student action and commitment for focused improvement.

Visit **go.solution-tree.com/commoncore** for a reproducible version of this figure.

formative processes that promote student action on the assessment instrument results and feedback. However, the assessment cycle is not complete until you and your colleagues work in your collaborative team during (and at the end of) the unit of instruction to discuss and decide how to respond to the student assessment evidence you have collected during the unit.

Step Five: Collaborative Teams Use Ongoing Student Assessment Feedback to Improve Instruction

In step five, you and your colleagues use students' assessment results to change your instruction for the next instructional cluster or unit. This allows the test or quiz assessment instruments to become formative for your collaborative team as well. Successes in step five depend on step one—writing and designing common assessment instruments in advance of teaching the next unit of instruction. The collaborative team's assessment has its greatest payoff in this final collaborative step, using the student performance results to make future instructional decisions together.

It will also allow your collaborative team, in hindsight, to evaluate the quality of the assessment questions; indicate improvements for next year; and discuss the quality of the descriptive student feedback, the accuracy of the predetermined student scoring rubrics, and the fidelity of students' grades for the unit. You and your collaborative team can also use the results to identify potential learning targets and assessment questions that may need to be repeated as part of your re-engagement and teaching plans in the next unit of study. Recall Wiliam's (2011) definition of formative assessment presented in the epigraph at the beginning of this chapter.

> An assessment functions formatively to the extent that evidence about student achievement is elicited, interpreted, and used by teachers, learners, or their peers to make decisions about the next steps in instruction that are likely to be better, or better founded, than the decisions they would have made in absence of that evidence. (p. 43)

Notice that assessment, then, is in the middle of the PLC assessment cycle, not the end. This is a fundamental shift for middle school mathematics teachers. Student learning becomes a result of your in-class daily formative assessment work around the mathematical tasks you chose for students, as well as the assessment instruments, such as tests and quizzes the team uses, not the other way around. Your team takes future actions that improve teaching, instruction, and learning based on the latest assessment evidence.

In steps two, three, and five of the teaching-assessing-learning cycle, you and members of your team collaborate to analyze student work to identify trends in student performance. In seeking trends, you can observe common errors in students' answers or flaws in students' problem-solving processes. Equally important is to find common student methods that produced successful solutions. Occasionally, you will observe unique, interesting, or unusual solutions. In some cases, student work shows the right answers, but the process is incomplete, flawed, or unclear.

With practice, your collaborative team can become skilled at looking at student work. Initially, a good starting point is to sort student work into piles of successful, partially successful, and not as successful. At this point, resist the temptation to assign grades to the student work. Instead, focus on analyzing the results. The goal is to diagnose what students thought, what they could do, and where they had errors or incomplete understanding. A class set of student work always has a story. Finding and documenting the trends and ranges of student performance goes a long way in informing instruction. Visit **go.solution-tree.com/commoncore** for an online-only story of a class set of student work.

Your collaborative team may engage in two major activities during steps two, three, or five of the teaching-assessing-learning cycle: (1) jointly scoring students' work (and thus calibrating your scores) and (2) analyzing the work for trends. In order to find interesting trends, your team must develop a process to skillfully look at student work. This process begins with jointly scoring the students' papers, not merely to determine a score or give a grade, but rather to look very closely at the student work and analyze the students' thinking. The act of scoring the assessments together raises the level of accuracy as you examine student work.

It is only after scoring that the students' papers are analyzed for trends. This examination seeks to determine successful approaches and solutions as well as common error or misconceptions. Dividing the papers by scores helps the analysis. You then can focus on specific mathematics of the task and determine how well the students understood the concepts. Helpful tools enhance these analyses. Calculating measures of proficiency by standard can illuminate performances.

A second outcome of analyzing student work is recording general findings. The analysis of these findings builds your team's collective knowledge of student performance. This analysis of student work involves selecting examples that illustrate various aspects of student performance. These papers could include examples of well-conceived and communicated solutions, as well as examples of common errors or invalid reasoning that resulted in unsuccessful attempts at solving the problems. The findings might also feature unique or unusual approaches that show interesting mathematical thinking and attacks on the problem. The analysis might include graphs that show the overall student performance and descriptions that explain the data distribution across the continuum of performances. After a thorough analysis, your collaborative team uses its collective mathematics and pedagogical knowledge to consider where the students are and what future learning is required either during the unit if this is done as a stage three activity or at the end of the unit if the analysis is done in response to the final unit assessment.

Using Re-Engagement Lessons in the Teaching-Assessing-Learning Cycle

One tool you can use to accomplish successful student learning experiences during the PLC teaching-assessing-learning cycle is to develop a team-designed follow-up—or *re-engagement*—lesson based on evidence of student learning needs either during or at the end of a unit of study. This would become either a stage three or stage five team activity. During collaborative team discussions about necessary re-engagement lessons, you and your colleagues try out and compare findings and ideas that arise from reflecting on actual student work.

Your team considers various learning dilemmas and how to compare different instructional strategies demonstrated by the students. You investigate teaching challenges, identifying interesting student work, and you examine students' responses and successes as well as the challenges or dilemmas revealed. Through this collaborative experience, you and your colleagues become miniresearchers and learn to rely on the evidence from your students as a primary source to make instructional decisions.

The purpose of a re-engagement lesson tool is to deepen students' understanding of the core mathematics standards involved and to help them build a deeper foundation of the conceptual knowledge to learn further mathematics.

A re-engagement lesson will address students' knowledge and skills across a learning continuum of success. The lesson provides access into the mathematics of the content standard and develops a conceptual foundation for all students to build further understanding regardless of their level of performance on the assessment. The lesson will focus on the mathematical arguments of the task so that students know how to approach similar problems in the future. For even the most successful student in class, a re-engagement lesson will deepen their understanding by asking students to critique others' work, apply the mathematics learned, and generalize or justify the mathematics.

Reteaching Versus Re-Engagement

In response to information about student performance, teachers often reteach a lesson, especially when they are uncomfortable with the class's overall performance on the assessment instrument. Often with reteaching, the teacher goes over similar material a second time with a minor change in emphasis, instead of using the assessment results to define what experiences would further students' learning. Thus, the approach of reteaching a lesson differs from that of a re-engagement lesson.

A *reteaching lesson* usually focuses on procedural knowledge that struggling students appear to lack. Repeating the lesson is usually unsuccessful because it seldom focuses on deep conceptual understanding and raising the cognitive demand on the student. If students cannot connect the mathematics and develop an understanding of the concepts underlying the problem, they will not have fully learned what they need for the future.

A *re-engagement lesson* requires students to learn the concept in a manner whereby they make connections and see the relationships necessary for learning. This is done as students re-engage in the most challenging aspects of the task. When students examine and critique other students' solution paths and reasoning, they make connections and reason at high-cognitive levels. A well-designed re-engagement lesson often requires students to analyze one another's work.

Table 4.1 illustrates the difference between lessons designed to reteach and lessons designed for re-engagement.

Table 4.1: Reteaching Versus Re-Engagement Lessons

Reteaching	Re-Engagement
Teach standards in the unit again, the same way as the original presentation.	Revisit student thinking using focused tasks that represent content standards for the unit.
Address basic skills that are missing.	Address conceptual understanding that is missing.
Do the same or similar problems over.	Examine the same or new tasks or from different perspectives.
Practice more to make sure students learn the procedures.	Critique student approaches and solutions to make connections to the tasks.
Focus mostly on students in need of additional support.	Focus on engaging both students in need of support and students in need of enrichment.
Lower the cognitive-demand expectations of the students.	Raise the cognitive-demand expectations of the students.

Visit **go.solution-tree.com/commoncore** for a reproducible version of this table.

The PLC teaching-assessing-learning cycle described in this chapter is designed to foster your collaborative team actions toward formative assessment practices that will enhance student learning. A re-engagement lesson then requires your team to:

- Develop and use assessment tasks and instruments (step one of the cycle)

- Examine and analyze student work on the assessment tasks or instruments (step three or five of the cycle)

- Use the findings to inform your understanding of student learning (steps three or five of the cycle)

- Design and use lessons that re-engage students for successful learning (step three or five of the cycle)

Visit **go.solution-tree.com/commoncore** for links to selected re-engagement lessons and for a story of a class set of student work.

In a re-engagement lesson you ask the students to examine student work and describe how another *anonymous* student approached the task. The students critique the work, trying to make sense of the student's reasoning, and judge why a method works or where the student's reasoning broke down.

Creating a follow-up student learning experience is essential in stage four of the PLC teaching-assessing-learning cycle, if students are to learn and *take action* from the assessments and task they are given. A re-engagement lesson is one tool for helping students to take action. The challenge is how to use the assessment information to create a positive learning experience for your students. Your formative goal is to design a lesson informed from the assessment findings. The lesson may take on different forms and target a range of mathematical aspects and students' learning needs.

Students need to establish a conceptual foundation of the mathematics. A worthwhile re-engagement lesson and learning task will allow this foundation to surface. The re-engagement lesson will revisit important mathematical ideas relevant to the content standard, allowing students to cement understanding to build a deeper knowledge.

To make the work anonymous, your collaborative team should re-transcribe it to focus in on a specific aspect of a performance. The work may contain inaccuracies or invalid assumptions. In the re-engagement lesson, the students examine the work and determine whether it is mathematically sound and to either justify the findings or show where the work lacked mathematical accuracy or logic. Critiquing other students' thoughts, discoveries, and misconceptions is a high-cognitive task—exactly what is expected in Mathematical Practice 3, Construct viable arguments and critique the reasoning of others.

Presenting student solutions and asking why and if an approach, explanation, or justification makes sense helps students deepen their understanding. It also provides models from which other classmates can learn. Identifying unusual approaches that show interesting mathematical thinking helps to extend the students' learning. Such solutions can be important tools for future instruction to highlight and encourage multiple solution strategies. A final tool used in the student work analysis is the task analysis tool (figure 4.9, page 148). Similar to the anticipation sheet (figure 4.4, page 135), the analysis tool focuses on three topics: (1) where students showed success, (2) where they struggled, and (3) plans for future teaching based on evidence of students' strengths or weaknesses.

Task name: _____ Grade: _____ Year: _____
Total points: _____ Core points: _____

In analyzing the student work, where did students show success?	
What parts of the task did students demonstrate success with?	In terms of knowing and doing mathematics, what does this indicate?

In analyzing the student work, where did students struggle?	
What parts of the task were students being unsuccessful with?	In terms of knowing and doing mathematics, what does this indicate? What understandings or skills do the students need to learn?

Considering strengths and weaknesses from students, what are plans for future teaching?	
What are the implications for future instruction?	What specific instruction or lesson experiences will you design for students?

Source: Adapted from Foster & Poppers, 2009.

Figure 4.9: Task analysis sheet.

Visit **go.solution-tree.com/commoncore** for a reproducible version of this figure.

After completing the analysis tool, compare your actual findings with the completed anticipation tool. This reflective lens helps you understand how your thinking is changed and informed from looking at actual student work. Your reflection on the analysis of student work is the foundation to inform future instruction and design learning experiences that move students forward.

This collaborative work during the unit is generative. You get better at the process, and the conversations among your team members are richer and centered squarely on teaching and learning using assessment in the middle—as a *means* intentionally. This is the core work of getting better at your craft and raising the expertise of everyone in the collaborative team. Using the teaching-assessing-learning cycle on a unit-by-unit basis can and should be the core work of your collaborative team.

Summative Grading in the Formative Feedback Paradigm

Using grades as a form of feedback to motivate student learning and effort is one of your most powerful assessment weapons. Your collaborative teams can overcome the great de-motivator that results in using common assessment tools such as tests and quizzes primarily for the purpose of assigning grades (or even assigning a mastery score such as a 1 through 4). The hope lies squarely in the team's ability to shift to a new assessment paradigm about grading: grades should serve primarily as a form of effective formative feedback to students and serve to enhance the teaching-assessing-learning cycle.

Reeves (2011) in *Elements of Grading*, establishes this primary purpose of grading, as a form of feedback provided to students in order to improve their performance. Reeves cites Thomas R. Guskey (2000): "In fact, when students are rewarded only with feedback on their [assessment instrument] performance and are not subjected to a grade, their performance is better than when they are graded" (p. 105).

Thus, collaborative teams must discuss whether their *collective* grading practices act as feedback to students in such a way that motivates continued and improved effort (Mathematical Practice 1) and performance. Can your teams develop students' mathematical *habits of mind* in which every assessment opportunity is viewed as a formative learning moment?

Reeves (2011) provides four boundary markers as a basis to measure your teams' current grading practices. In a PLC approach, grading is viewed as a form of effective feedback to students, based on the following four characteristics.

1. **Grades must be accurate**: Do grades on homework, tests, and quiz instruments reflect actual student knowledge and performance on the expected learning targets?

2. **Grades must be specific**: Do grades provide sufficiently specific information to help parents and students identify areas for improvement (formative and not just diagnostic) with student action long before the final summative grade is assigned?

3. **Grades must be timely**: Do grades on homework, tests, and quizzes provide a steady stream of immediate and corrective teacher feedback to students?

4. **Grades must be fair:** Do grades on tests and quizzes reflect solely on the student's work and not other characteristics of the student? Or some form of student comparison, such as assigning grades on a curve, based on other students' performance in the class?

Equity and Effective Summative Grading Practices

To clearly establish a relationship between a student's grade and his or her demonstration of mathematical understanding, your collaborative teams should engage in honest conversations about their beliefs related to grading. Figure 4.10 (page 150) provides an activity to use with your teams as you help them investigate potential areas for grading inequity and bias.

In your collaborative team, complete the following, and describe your practices during a grading period.

1. List all components used to determine a student's grade in your course, such as tests, quizzes, homework, projects, and so on. Are the components and the percentages assigned to each component the same for every teacher on your team? Do the percentages align with the actual percentage of total points?

2. What is the grading scale your team uses? Is it the same for every member? How does your team address the issue of the "really bad" F, such as a 39 percent that distorts a student's overall grade performance?

3. What position does your team follow for assigning zeros to students? If teachers assign zeros, how does your team address the elimination of those zeros before the summative grade is assigned (the goal is not to assign students a zero—in a PLC, the goal is to motivate every student to do his or her mathematics homework, prepare for tests, complete assignments, and so on)? Do you:

   • Drop one homework grade from the grading period?

   • Drop one quiz or test score per grading period?

   • Allow for student makeup or retesting on weak performing learning targets?

4. What is your collaborative team's position on makeup work for class? Is your makeup policy fair for students, and do all members apply it equitably? Does your makeup policy encourage and motivate all students to keep trying?

5. How does your collaborative team prepare students for a major unit exam or quiz? Do all team members provide students with the same formative opportunities for preparing for the learning targets?

6. How does your team provide for the immediate and corrective feedback on major quiz and test instruments? Do all students receive results, identify areas of weakness, and then act on those results within two to three days?

7. Does your collaborative team average letter grades or use total points throughout the grading period? Explain your current grading system. How does your team address the inequity caused by total points as part of a summative grade cause (in which it is impossible to offset zeros and one really bad F with enough good grades to accurately represent overall performance)?

8. How does your team provide for the strategic use of technology tools as an aspect of evaluating student performance during the unit?

Source: Adapted from Kanold, 2011.

Figure 4.10: A collaborative team analysis of grading practice.

Visit **go.solution-tree.com/commoncore** for a reproducible version of this figure.

You can use this activity to search for your own biases and to better understand whether or not their collaborative grading practices motivate or destroy student effort and learning.

By answering the questions in figure 4.10 your teams will discover built-in biases and issues relating to the accuracy, timeliness, specificity, and fairness of assigned grades. Before any form of a summative grade is assigned, students should be given the opportunity to re-engage in lessons that allow them to improve their learning.

Your Focus on Large-Scale Assessment Data

You may feel like many middle school mathematics teachers do—far removed from the decision-making realities of large-scale assessments and state assessment data, yet under pressure to respond. Under the curriculum guidelines of the CCSS expectations, a state assessment system must now provide a coherent and consistent formative system anchored in college- and career-ready expectations. Two state consortia, the Partnership for Assessment of Readiness for College and Careers (PARCC) and the SMARTER Balanced Assessment Consortium (SBAC), are designing state-level common assessments for the middle school standards. These common assessments will reflect the middle school expectations for the Mathematical Practices' content with large-scale assessments that measure beyond the traditional multiple-choice, bubble-in answer sheets. As Achieve (2010) notes, it is the hope and the expectation that these new exams will:

> Improve the quality and types of items included in on-demand tests to create more cognitively-challenging tasks that measure higher-order thinking and analytic skills, such as reasoning and problem solving; move beyond a single, end-of-year test to open the door for performance measures and extended tasks that do a better job of measuring important college and career ready skills and model exemplary forms of classroom instruction. (p. 1)

Implementing Common Core mathematics is not likely to alter the scrutiny and pressure you will face as a middle school mathematics teacher from large-scale assessments. Both consortia intend to implement their state-level common assessments for middle school during the 2014–2015 school year.

PARCC and SBAC also intend to provide adaptive online tests that will include a mix of constructed-response items, performance-based tasks, and computer-enhanced items that require the application of knowledge and skills. (You should check your state website or visit www.parcconline.org/about-parcc or www.smarterbalanced.org for the latest information about the assessment consortia progress.) It will be imperative that you and your team monitor the PARCC and SBAC assessment progress for interpretation of assessment items that will be used to establish the operational definitions of the standards.

Regardless of the opportunity for the PARCC and SBAC assessments to provide school districts formative assessment information on the state assessment instruments, what will make the most difference in terms of student learning is the shorter cycle, unit-by-unit classroom-based formative assessment described in this chapter. As Wiliam (2007a) writes, "If students have left the classroom before teachers have made adjustments to their teaching on the basis of what they have learned about students' achievement, then they are already playing catch-up" (p. 191).

Ultimately, any assessment your team uses can be formative if it is used to make decisions and take future action for improvement on learning target success and improve a student's summative grade. Your collaborative team is empowered to carry out this vision of assessment as an ongoing *cycle of formative learning* throughout each unit—for both the students and each team member.

Looking Ahead

The questions every middle school teacher must then ask are, "What is the vision of our assessment policies and practices in our department or math program?" "How will we work together so that assessment can become a motivational student bridge in the assessment cycle in our school?" As you develop your response, you must ask, "Will student motivation and the level of student learning in our course and in our mathematics program be improved?"

The five-step assessment cycle has a powerful impact on student achievement and learning. More than just becoming a master of teaching content, you also become a master at using varied assessment tasks and tools, including the formative classroom assessment strategies (listed in step three) for students to take greater ownership of their learning.

As the mathematics unit comes to an end, students who have received formative feedback (allowing them to correct errors *before and after* the final unit assessment on the cluster of learning targets) and a chance to re-engage in elements of the unit lessons, perform at significantly improved rates of learning (Wiliam, 2007b). After a unit's instruction is over, the teacher and the student must reflect on the results of their work and be willing to use the unit assessment instruments to serve a formative feedback purpose. For you, this means a commitment to understanding one of your most powerful assessment weapons—the use of re-engagement lessons *as a form of feedback to motivate student learning and effort.* In chapter 5, you will examine how an effective professional learning community team responds to various levels of intervention in mathematics.

Chapter 4 Extending My Understanding

1. Using the definition of formative assessment on page 141, describe how your current assessment practices either do or do not meet this standard.

2. High-quality middle school assessment practices function to integrate formative assessment processes for adult and student learning by:

   a. Implementing formative assessment classroom strategies and advancing and assessing questions that check for student understanding during the classroom period

   b. Using assessment instruments such as quizzes and tests as tools to support a formative learning process for teachers and students to take action

   How can your middle school mathematics department and collaborative team use common classroom assessment instruments, along with other formative assessment information sources collected each day, to advance student learning and support students' active involvement in taking ownership of their own learning?

3. Examine the assessment cycle in figure 4.1 (page 131). For the following five steps, rate your current level of implementation, and explain what your team can do to improve in this assessment practice during the school year. Note there are two different step-one paths.

○ **Step one (in-class formative assessment processes):** How well do we understand and develop in advance of teaching the unit of study the student learning targets; the content standard clusters and domains; the common student tasks that will align with those targets; the use of technology to develop understanding of those targets; and the homework that will be assigned?

○ **Step one (common assessment instruments):** How well do we identify the agreed-on common assessment instruments, scoring rubrics for those instruments, and grading procedures that will accurately reflect student achievement of the learning targets for the unit?

○ **Step two:** How well do we use daily classroom assessments that are formative, build student confidence, and require student goal setting and reflection on the learning targets they know and don't know?

○ **Step three:** How well do we use diagnostic and formative assessment feedback that provides frequent, descriptive, timely, and accurate feedback for students during the unit—allowing members of our teacher team as well as our students to take action on specific insights regarding our strengths as well as how to improve?

○ **Step four:** How well do we, as a team, ask students to adjust and take action based on the results of the common assessment instruments (quizzes and tests) used during the unit of study? Do we allow that action to improve their grade?

○ **Step five:** How well do we, as a team, adjust and differentiate our instruction based on the results of formative assessment evidence as well as the common assessment instruments used during the unit of study? Do we use re-engagement lessons based on the results and analysis of student work?

4. As a team, review the five formative assessment strategies listed in figure 4.7, page 140. Discuss how you might implement each of these strategies or how you might adapt them for your students. Also, discuss and share additional in-class formative assessment strategies that work for you.

5. As a team, examine figure 4.10 (page 150). Discuss your current grading practices, and judge those practices on whether or not you believe current practices meet the standards for effective feedback and result in motivating student performance. Discuss how your current team grading practices could improve.

Online Resources

Visit **go.solution-tree.com/commoncore** for links to these resources.

• **Math Common Core Coalition (www.nctm.org/standards/math commoncore):** This site includes materials and links to information and resources that the organizations of the coalition provide to the public and the education community about the CCSS for mathematics.

- **Mathematics Assessment Project (MAP; http://map.mathshell.org.uk /materials):** The Mathematics Assessment Project contains exemplar formative lessons, summative assessments, and rich mathematical tasks for grades 6–8 and high school CCSS.

- **Partnership for Assessment of Readiness for College and Careers (www .parcconline.org):** This site provides content frameworks, sample instructional units, sample assessment tasks, professional development assessment modules, and more.

- **SMARTER Balanced Assessment Consortium (www.smarterbalanced.org):** This site provides content frameworks, sample instructional units, sample assessment tasks, professional development modules, and more.

- **Public Lessons Numerical Patterning (www.insidemathematics.org/index .php/classroom-video-visits/public-lessons-numerical-patterning):** This resource provides a re-engagement lesson for learners to revisit a problem-solving task.

- **The Silicon Valley Mathematics Initiative (www.svmimac.org):** This site provides tools on formative assessment, high-cognitive performance assessment tasks and rubrics, and re-engagement lessons.

- **Re-Engagement Protocol (Inside Mathematics; http://insidemathematics.org /pdfs/tools-for-principals/MACtookitMtg102108.pdf):** This tool describes a three-step protocol for designing re-engagement lessons.

- **Classroom Video Visits (Inside Mathematics; www.insidemathematics.org /index.php/classroom-video-visits):** These videos feature a variety of lessons for mathematics teaching and learning. "Public Lessons" are field-tested lessons that are presented to an audience of participating students and observing teachers. "Number Talks" feature examples of lessons for teachers to engage students in mental math problems.

CHAPTER 5

Implementing Required Response to Intervention

Ultimately there are two kinds of schools: learning enriched schools and learning impoverished schools. I have yet to see a school where the learning curves . . . of the adults were steep upward and those of the students were not. Teachers and students go hand in hand as learners . . . or they don't go at all.

—Roland Barth

As the curriculum is written, the learning targets are set, and your assessments are in place, your instructional processes need to meet the needs of *each* student in the courses you teach. As you read the grades 6–8 Common Core mathematics for the first time, what went through your mind? Were you thinking about the students in your class, your school, or part of your district and wondering, "Will they be able to respond positively to the expected complexity in each grade level?" Did you reflect on how you would be able to develop the CCSS Mathematical Practices in each student? How will *each* student be able to succeed with rich and rigorous mathematical tasks? Are there different learning opportunities for different groups of students, depending on their mathematics ability or diversity? How can you generate equitable learning experiences so that *each* student is prepared to meet the demands of the Common Core mathematics as described in this book? The key to answering these questions is part of the essential work of your collaborative team. To create an equitable mathematics program, you and your colleagues must ensure current structures for teaching and learning will generate greater access and opportunity to learn for each student.

In previous chapters, you read about how professional collaboration, the Common Core Standards for Mathematical Practice and Standards for Mathematical Content, and assessment work synergistically when a collaborative team connects them all in meaningful ways. Here, we add another dimension to your collaborative teamwork: attention to equity. Paying attention to equity in mathematics means finding ways to provide *all* students access and opportunity to wrestle with, make sense of, and communicate about important mathematics.

This chapter focuses on students who need help catching up and provides some guiding principles to your collaborative team for the selection or development of interventions that ensure equitable instructional practices—practices that provide those students the opportunities to learn necessary to meet the same high standards as everybody else.

In other words, practices that provide students access to the knowledge and skills they need to be successful in mathematics in school and beyond.

Vision of Equity

Two of the most relevant associations of mathematics educators, the National Council of Teachers of Mathematics (NCTM) and the National Council of Supervisors of Mathematics (NCSM), recognize that to ensure that all learners have the opportunity to learn important mathematics, a culture of equity in every classroom is necessary. This is only possible when inequities that hinder students' access to mathematical knowledge and access to the opportunity to learn this mathematics knowledge are addressed using a systematic and systemic approach. Both organizations present a framework to ensure equity. Creating and sustaining a culture of equity is developed through a common effort by all learning participants, including teachers, administrators, students, and the community (NCTM, 2008a). The NCTM (2008a) position statement on equity provides a definition and a rationale for a systemic approach:

> Excellence in mathematics education rests on equity—high expectations, respect, understanding, and strong support for all students. Policies, practices, attitudes, and beliefs related to mathematics teaching and learning must be assessed continually to ensure that all students have equal access to the resources with the greatest potential to promote learning.

Similarly, NCSM (2008a) in its *PRIME Leadership Framework* describes, "A vision for equity begins with understanding your responsibility to seek out and erase biases and inequities that exist in student learning and assessment experiences" (p. 10). NCSM's position statement on equity—*Improving Student Achievement by Leading the Pursuit of a Vision for Equity*—advises addressing equity with the same rigor and intensity as curriculum, instruction, and assessment. Further, this position statement (NCSM, 2008b, p. 1) describes four actions your collaborative team should use to ensure you are paying attention to equity:

- Respond to equity as a meaningful process to address social justice issues of race, language, gender, and class bias.

- Embrace a mindset shift from a student deficit perspective of equity to a focus on creating opportunities for equal access to meaningful mathematics.

- Respond to equity being less about equality and more about the need for political and social policy changes.

- Recognize underachievement not as a result of group membership but more likely a symptom of varying beliefs, opportunities, and experiences to learn mathematics.

To ensure equity—access to important mathematics for *all* students—your collaborative team must work toward identifying the causes of potential inequities in your system and finding ways to erase them; developing a common vision for equity; ensuring you have shared values and beliefs; and taking actions and making decisions that build a school culture that guarantees *all* students the opportunity to learn important mathematics. Then, and only then, can your collaborative team make decisions about the kinds of interventions needed for students who are struggling. In fact, your collaborative team must ensure support for each and every student, orchestrating strong interventions for those who need them. For students who need to catch up, interventions cannot be optional. This requires your team to monitor students' progress constantly and to move students in and out of the intervention as quickly as possible. It is the team's responsibility to ensure that this is the case for every student.

Sources That Inform Equity in Mathematics

Despite the evidence collected over the years about the detrimental effect of tracking practices, it is likely that inequities still exist in your school and in every school's mathematics classes and programs. Erasing inequities is a forever pursuit of your collaborative team. Far too frequently, adults in the systems hold very low expectations for students who are economically disadvantaged, minorities, or English learners or who have special needs. Such expectations lead to tracking students by placing them into remedial mathematics classes, which are viewed as having less status with lower expectations for learning than the rest of the mathematics classes. Others (Boaler, Wiliam, & Brown, 2000; Stiff, Johnson, & Akos, 2011; Tate & Rousseau, 2002) find that in these classes, students repeat basic skills year after year, fall further and further behind their peers, and do not experience significant mathematical substance.

Further, studies show that remedial courses more often than not are focused on procedural skills, reducing students' opportunities to learn rigorous, engaging, and meaningful mathematics (Darling-Hammond, 2010). Wilkins and the Education Trust Staff (2006) find that less than one-third of African American high school students are exposed to college-preparatory mathematics classes, and students of color—including African American, Latino, and Native Americans—are twice as likely to be taught by inexperienced teachers. Haycock's (Peske & Haycock, 2006) review on teacher effectiveness finds that schools with high-poverty or high-minority students were twice as likely to have mathematics teachers who were not mathematics majors. This might be the case in your school, too.

The CCSS require *all* students be held accountable to and supported in meeting the same rigorous standards in order to be college and career ready. If this vision is to be accomplished, students must be provided a middle school education focused on critical thinking and reasoning about the mathematics they are learning from knowledgeable teachers. This sense-making focus of mathematics instruction is particularly important for students historically identified as underperformers.

You can use the equity questions in figure 5.1 (page 158) in your collaborative team to reflect on the degree to which all students are provided access to a rigorous mathematics curriculum based on grade-level CCSS. When using these questions, you should think about the evidence you use to support your responses. For example, if the least-experienced teachers on your team are teaching the most-challenged students, is it reasonable to argue that all students are receiving equitable instruction? Some of these team or school decisions are made in an effort to reward teacher seniority, but may inadvertently be contributing to inequitable learning opportunities and outcomes (Lubienski, 2007).

1. Do all students receive the same high-quality common instructional tasks by each teacher on our team?

2. Do all students receive equally rigorous instruction, balancing conceptual and procedural development and mathematical practices?

3. Do all students receive the same amount of teaching and learning time for mathematics each day?

4. Who teaches the most-struggling students—the most experienced or the least experienced teachers?

5. Do all students receive rich, compelling lessons with a focus on student understanding and learning?

6. Do all students receive grade-level (or above) mathematics instruction on the CCSS?

7. Are there any students identified as low achieving, and what is the team's intentional response for intervention and support?

Figure 5.1: Equity reflection questions.

Visit **go.solution-tree.com/commoncore** for a reproducible version of this figure.

If your collaborative team is ready for a deeper reflection on equity and would like a more detailed tool to conduct such reflection, consider using the tool in table 5.1. Complete the equity reflection activity in table 5.1 both individually and as a team, and then use it as a focus for future improvement. This exercise should help you and your team find balance between holding high standards and finding ways to support struggling students.

Table 5.1: Equity Reflection Activity

Focus Area	Reflection Questions	Comments
Access	What process is used for mathematics placement into the freshman-level mathematics courses?	
	Do students have opportunities to advance through the mathematics matriculation, and how does this get demonstrated or decided?	
	What percentage of students are enrolled in college-preparatory mathematics courses?	
Grading	Is every team member's definition of an A, B, C, D, or F the same?	
	Does the team grade the assessments together to ensure equitable grading?	
	What feedback is provided to students?	

Focus Area	Reflection Questions	Comments
Data-Driven Practices	Are data broken down by subpopulations to ensure the needs of each learner are met? Are data reviewed to inform instructional practices? Are data collected on specific interventions and support to track and monitor effectiveness?	
Task Selection	When planning a unit of instruction, do teacher teams develop common artifacts to meet the learning needs of every student? Does the team select or develop rich mathematical tasks for each student to use? Does the team identify essential skills needed for an upcoming unit of instruction?	
Assessments	Does the team use common scoring rubrics on formative assessments? Are assessments high quality and representative of the Common Core mathematics? How are students involved in the assessment cycle?	
Interventions and Support	Do teachers have time within the school day to collaborate on issues specific to student learning, students with special needs, or English learners? What interventions are currently being offered? Are students required to attend intervention if deemed not meeting the standards?	

Visit **go.solution-tree.com/commoncore** for a reproducible version of this table.

Student Learning Needs for Success

Interventions, if needed, must be focused on developing the same level of understanding expected of all students. The Common Core State Standards (NGA & CCSSO, 2010a) define understanding mathematics:

> One hallmark of mathematical understanding is the ability to justify, in a way appropriate to the student's mathematical maturity, why a particular mathematical statement is true or where a mathematical rule comes from. There is a world of difference between a student who can summon a mnemonic device to expand a product such as $(a + b)(x + y)$ and a student who can explain where the mnemonic comes from. The student who can explain the rule understands the mathematics, and may have a better chance to succeed at a less familiar task such as expanding $(a + b + c)(x$

+ *y*). Mathematical understanding and procedural skill are equally important, and both are assessable using mathematical tasks of sufficient richness. (p. 4)

With any intervention program your collaborative team selects or develops, you must take into account the balance between mathematical understanding and procedural knowledge. Both your regular instruction and the instruction used in intervention must create such a balance. Furthermore, a focused and coherent instructional program, as defined by the CCSS, should prevent and clear student misconceptions to begin with, and if necessary, interventions must be provided as soon as students show evidence of not learning what they are expected to learn. However, the most effective teachers should teach the most intensive level of intervention, to students with the greatest needs, for the shortest time required for students to be back on level in the course.

This type of intervention requires a diagnostic assessment process that identifies students' needs as early as possible, matches the right intervention with the right student need, and makes sure students leave the intervention as soon as their identified need has been met. A combination of formative and summative assessment instruments that track students' progress through the intervention and determine when students no longer need the intervention is essential. An effective assessment system—both formative and summative—is needed to determine that students are showing success and are learning the mathematics we expect them to learn. That is, they can keep up with the assignments in their regular classroom and continue to learn with minimal support.

Your collaborative team should use the PLC teaching-assessing-learning cycle (figure 4.1, page 131) to guide your activities and decisions. One of the products of step two of the cycle will be diagnostic data on the mathematical understandings of each student. Those should be the basis for identifying which students should be targeted for short-term intervention. This will then lead to steps three and four, as students take action on the feedback they receive from you and from their peers, either in their regular class or in their intervention, to move their learning forward. Then, in step five, your collaborative team takes stock of each student's progress, both in the regular classroom and in the interventions, and adjusts instruction accordingly.

Your collaborative team should closely monitor students' progress toward the learning targets identified in step one of the cycle. To do that, your collaborative team should review specific data on a weekly basis. But, the actual frequency with which you meet will depend on the questions your team is trying to answer and the data you decide to collect and analyze. Table 5.2 provides a checklist your collaborative team can use to ensure you are looking at the right data.

In a PLC, your collaborative team will decide what data to analyze to assess students' knowledge. (Visit www.allthingsplc.info and search the Tools & Resources for more information about specific data and dialogue prompts to ask while reviewing data.)

Table 5.2: High-Quality Data Checklist

Data Type	Essential Questions	What Data Can Answer This Question?	How Are Data Monitored? How Often?
Collaborative Teacher Teams			
Formative Data	What assessment tools are used to determine student learning?		
	Can we identify students (by name and need) who are not proficient?		
	How is feedback provided to students?		
	How are students expected to take action on the feedback?		
	Are rubrics given to students to assist with self-assessment?		
Tasks	What are the common student misconceptions for this learning target?		
	Is this a trend for all or just a specific subpopulation?		
	What are the literacy demands of the student mathematical tasks?		
Intervention	What interventions are provided in the class as well as outside the class?		
	How many students are attending the required intervention?		
	How frequent is the intervention?		
	How is the intervention deemed to be successful for students?		
Schoolwide or Districtwide Teams			
Summative Data	What percent of our students are achieving As, Bs, and Cs?		
	What percent of students are receiving Ds and Fs?		
	What percent of students are not proficient on the assessment instruments we use?		
	Are there defined benchmark assessments that are not being met by the students?		

continued →

Data Type	Essential Questions	What Data Can Answer This Question?	How Are Data Monitored? How Often?
Schoolwide or Districtwide Teams			
Accessibility	What is the student participation rate in each course by subgroup? What percent of students at each grade level are enrolled in college-readiness courses?		
Attendance	Do varying levels of attendance effect grade-distribution rates? How do you know?		

Visit **go.solution-tree.com/commoncore** for a reproducible version of this table.

Middle school collaborative teams will be required to come together and embrace an intentional plan to support learning for each student. The plan must include (Knight, 2011):

- Research-informed practices for instruction

- High-quality assessments that provide meaningful feedback for action to students and teachers

- Cognitively demanding instructional tasks

- A strong behavioral expectation for teachers and students

Recall that when collaborative teams reflect on the four critical questions of a PLC, the answers drive the work of the collaborative teams in PLCs (DuFour et al., 2008). The four questions are:

1. What are the knowledge, skills, and dispositions we want all students to acquire as a result of their experience in our course?

2. How will we know each student has acquired the intended knowledge, skills, and dispositions? What is our process for gathering information on each student's proficiency?

3. How will our team and school respond to students who experience difficulty in acquiring the intended knowledge and skills? How will we provide them with additional time and support for learning in a way that is timely, directive, precise, and systematic?

4. How will our team and school provide additional enrichment for students who are already proficient?

To meet the demands of the CCSS, create equity, and provide access and opportunities to learn rich mathematics, collaborative teams must be especially attentive to address and answer these last two questions through their understanding of the paradigm shift in mathematics intervention.

A Major Paradigm Shift in Middle School Mathematics Intervention Practices

The Common Core will require a shift in how your collaborative team responds to learning by making student participation in interventions required, not optional. Buffum, Mattos, and Weber (2009) say, "As adults, we understand the long-term consequences of educational failure far better than our students do. We should never allow them to embark upon that path" (p. 62). To guarantee equity for each student and to implement an effective response to intervention framework, your collaborative team's and PLC's efforts should focus on how to require participation in interventions at every tier, hence R²TI.

If students are able to demonstrate proficiency on the learning targets in class and in the homework assignments and make sense of the mathematics they are learning, they do not need intervention.

A system of interventions is necessary *as soon as* students are struggling with more than a few assignments, are not learning the intended learning targets, or are falling behind in the curriculum unit they are studying. The interventions consist of a schoolwide system to monitor students' progress toward clear and specific learning goals that identify extra time and support needed for those students who are struggling and provides help in an increasingly intensive way; for example, more intensive support for students with bigger needs.

Selecting the right interventions requires careful consideration of key questions and making decisions collaboratively. Kanold et al. (2012) have proposed a list of questions a collaborative team must answer when considering interventions:

> The teachers as a team, must answer questions such as: What will we re-teach? How will we re-teach it? How will we intervene and expect students to learn what they yet don't know? What required interventions will we develop in class and outside of class to support student learning in and out of the classroom? How will our team address the needs of English language learners—such as effective comprehension strategies? How will we adjust lesson plans and design meaningful instructional support to struggling students? (p. 59)

Answers to all these questions will result in strong and effective interventions. But, they must be answered within an equity framework, one that is built on key beliefs about students:

- Being mathematically proficient—in and outside of school—means being able to apply the eight Mathematical Practices as outlined in chapter 2 and listed in appendix A (page 181).

- Academic success must not be predictable on the basis of their skin color, gender, socioeconomic status, language, religion, sexual orientation, or ethnic and cultural affiliation.

- All deserve opportunities to make sense of the mathematics they are learning—they wrestle with key concepts, become mathematically proficient, and build on their prior knowledge and experiences.

- Equity in mathematics takes into account how students perceive themselves, the messages they get from their school environment, and how these factors have an impact on students' and teachers' beliefs, goals, and relationships with each other.

Collaborative teams are the ideal context in which teachers, in partnership with other school-based instructional leaders, can examine, make agreements about, and use these beliefs as design principles that keep students' sense-making opportunities at the heart of learning.

Thompson and Wiliam (2007) argue that collaborative teams in a PLC are not only appropriate but are a necessary learning structure for educators to develop the collective expertise needed to establish a continuous improvement process that result in better learning. The task of your collaborative team members is to become experts at implementing the strategies, routines, and interventions that will result in improved student learning. Since this requires the team's development of expertise, working together to develop such expertise is vital and best accomplished through sustained, extended practice. That is, practicing much like an expert pianist or master chess player would. Practice involves not mindlessly repeating actions but, rather, systematically practicing improvements to their craft and analyzing the results of their practice to make further adjustments.

The PLC collaborative team structure embodies what you should model for students in the classroom: learning is a dynamic, socially negotiated, sense-making process and is supported by the kind of creation of knowledge described by Nonaka and Takeuchi (1995). These authors use a taxonomy of *explicit* and *implicit* knowledge. They describe implicit knowledge as *inherited practices* for knowledge, or knowledge passed via apprenticeship through observation and guidance of a master. Implicit knowledge includes the beliefs, assumptions, and experiences that are shared within a cultural group (nation, company, family, collaborative team, and so on) and are not commonly articulated as they are assumed to be familiar to all (for example, all word processor users know what this symbol ¶ stands for).

Explicit knowledge refers to books, manuals, printed procedures, and guides that express information clearly through language, images, sounds, or other means of communication. Understanding this explicit-implicit knowledge contrast is essential in generating new knowledge and making commitments to actions. The purpose of collaborative teams should be to generate new knowledge paying attention to that contrast. Thus, learning to improve students' understanding requires the collaborative team to develop collective, common principles, and expertise, not to merely recall facts or partake in rote application.

An effective collaborative team implements a process for analyzing and meeting struggling students' needs in four steps that build on and support the PLC teaching-assessing-learning cycle described earlier (see figure 4.1, page 131). Figure 5.2 illustrates the

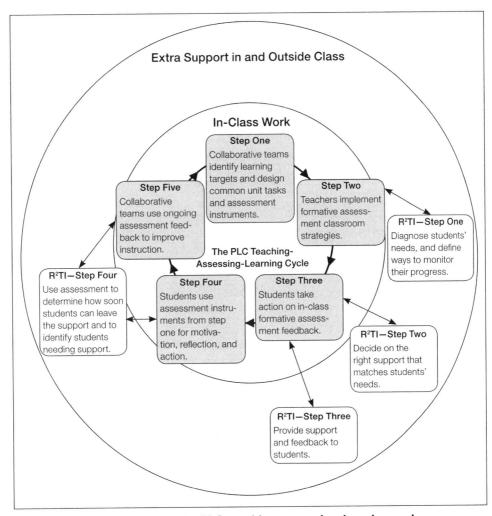

Figure 5.2: R²TI in support of the PLC teaching-assessing-learning cycle.

Visit **go.solution-tree.com/commoncore** for a reproducible version of this figure.

four steps in this process: (1) diagnosing why your students are struggling and monitoring their performance on the CCSS for mathematics; (2) evaluating, selecting, or creating support when students struggle; (3) planning your R²TI—clear, concrete instruction and feedback on how to improve based on students' needs, backgrounds, and interests; and (4) using follow-up assessment to determine next steps. A discussion of the implications of each of these for the intervention work of your collaborative team follows.

Diagnosing Why Your Students Are Struggling and Monitoring Their Performance

It is essential to diagnose the factors that cause middle school students to struggle and to understand how those factors affect their disposition, belief, and motivation toward learning mathematics. Some of the most common reasons include the following.

- Students have partial conceptions or misconceptions about the mathematics they are expected to learn.

- School mathematics doesn't seem relevant.

- School mathematics doesn't seem coherent—in many instances it is reduced to merely a set of unrelated skills and procedures to memorize and practice.

- Students have incomplete or immature procedural knowledge.

- The system tells them they are not good at mathematics.

- They struggle learning the language of mathematics.

- They have ineffective metacognitive strategies.

Some of those reasons are easier to diagnose than others. For example, unearthing students' perceptions about mathematics and the message they are getting from school may require an interview with the student. Therefore, the first step in considering an intervention program or creating a system of interventions is to make sure that it includes a good diagnostic tool. The tool should be sensitive enough to identify the specific reasons why students are struggling. You must keep in mind that even though your classrooms may include several struggling students, not all of the students are struggling and that students may struggle for different reasons. In many instances, they may be struggling for more than one reason. Therefore, the most important first step is to diagnose what is causing different students to struggle. This requires a diagnostic tool that identifies each struggling student's needs. (For examples of such tools, see Online Resources at the end of this chapter.) Once you have a clear picture of each struggling student's needs, then you can collectively make the next set of decisions.

Evaluating, Selecting, or Creating Support

Many resources exist to guide the selection of appropriate interventions. Figure 5.3 shows guiding questions for evaluating potential supports for your team to use (NCTM, 2007, p. 2). Selecting the right support requires a clear picture of an effective system of interventions.

Creating or Selecting an Intervention Program

Teachers and administrators should consider the following questions in the process of creating or selecting an intervention program.

1. **Diagnostic assessment:**

   a. Does the intervention program include diagnostic assessments that identify students' specific strengths and weaknesses with respect to both conceptual understanding and procedures?

   b. Do the assessments investigate students' knowledge of fundamental mathematics concepts that are grade appropriate?

    c. Does the content that is assessed align with the school's prescribed curriculum?

    d. Do the assessments communicate students' strengths and weaknesses in ways that teachers and parents can understand?

2. **Instructional activities:**

    a. Does the intervention program include a series of instructional activities that are carefully linked with the diagnostic assessments?

    b. Do the program's instructional activities support and enhance, but not supplant or duplicate, regular classroom instruction?

    c. Are tools for ongoing, formative assessment embedded in the instructional activities?

    d. Is the mathematics in the instructional activities correct?

    e. Do the instructional activities advance the school's curriculum and promote reasoning and conceptual understanding?

    f. Do the instructional activities contain challenging tasks that are appropriate for students' interests and backgrounds?

3. **Postassessment:**

    a. Does the intervention program contain postassessments that indicate whether the instructional activities have been effective?

    b. Are follow-up assessments administered in a timely fashion?

    c. Do the assessments communicate students' growth or need for further instruction in ways that teachers and parents can understand?

4. **Organizational structure of the intervention:**

    a. Is the structure of the intervention program feasible given the organizational structure of the school?

    b. Does the school have the necessary resources to implement the intervention program as designed?

    c. Does the intervention program include adequate and ongoing professional development to ensure effective implementation?

5. **Research supporting the intervention:**

    a. Have rigorous and appropriate methods been used to evaluate the intervention program and determined it to be successful?

    b. Does theoretical and empirical evidence support the efficacy of the intervention program in a setting that is similar to your school?

Source: Adapted from NCTM, 2007.

Figure 5.3: Creating or selecting an intervention program.

Imagine you're a collaborative team member in a school that takes responsibility for the instruction of the students in its classrooms. That means you and your colleagues focus on every student's education as you work and learn together. As a team, you monitor each student's progress toward the agreed-on learning outcomes for a curriculum unit. As students do not learn what you expected them to learn, you identify the specific skills or concepts necessary to support their learning.

You and your team collect and analyze the evidence of the progress students are making and make instructional decisions to adjust the way you are delivering mathematics instruction throughout the unit. As part of steps two and three of the teaching-assessing-learning cycle shows, you do this continually, providing students opportunities to perform and feedback on how they can improve.

For further illustrations of how specific schools have implemented an effective system of interventions as part of becoming PLCs, we recommend *Revisiting Professional Learning Communities at Work: New Insights for Improving Schools* (DuFour et al., 2008). In this book, DuFour et al. (2008) describe how the superintendent at a school district provided each school the flexibility to create its own plan for intervention but required the plans to be consistent with the SPEED criteria of implementation, which are the following (visit **go.solution-tree.com/commoncore** for a link to an online version of the SPEED criteria).

- **Systematic:** The intervention plan is schoolwide, independent of the individual teacher, and communicated in writing (who, why, how, where, and when) to everyone, including staff, parents, and students.

- **Practical:** The intervention plan is affordable within the school's available resources (time, space, staff, and materials). The plan must be sustainable and replicable so that its programs and strategies can be used in other schools.

- **Effective:** The intervention plan must be effective, available, and operational early enough in the school year to make a difference for students. Collaborative teams should design flexible entrance and exit criteria to respond to the ever-changing needs of students.

- **Essential:** The intervention plan should focus on agreed-on standards and the essential outcomes of the district's curriculum and be targeted to a student's specific learning needs per his or her formative and summative assessments.

- **Directive:** The intervention plan should be directive. It should be mandatory—not invitational—and a part of students' regular school day. Students cannot opt out, and parents and teachers cannot waive the student's participation in the intervention program.

With the SPEED criteria in mind, your team should analyze current targeted intervention programs for effectiveness and make the decisions about future interventions based on these criteria. For an example of how a district created a system of interventions, visit **go.solution-tree.com/commoncore** for a link to an online version of the West Bend Middle Level Pyramid of Interventions.

Planning Your R²TI

Your planning for intervention is based on clear, concrete instruction and feedback on how to improve based on students' needs, backgrounds, and interests. The challenge of providing extra time and the right support for struggling students is a team's and a school's challenge, not an individual teacher's problem. Far too often the question of what to do when students are not learning is left to the classroom teacher to answer. If every teacher implemented his or her way of solving that problem, the result would be an inconsistent approach to a schoolwide need. In fact, the school as a whole must create a culture of high expectations and hold those high expectations for all students. To do so, DuFour et al. (2008) argue that schools need to respond collectively by doing the following:

- Ensuring students who experience difficulty are given extra time and additional support for learning
- Providing timely intervention at the first indication of difficulty in a way that does not remove students from the classroom during new direct instruction
- Becoming increasingly directive, requiring rather than inviting students to continue working until they are successful
- Being fluid, moving students in and out of various levels of intervention depending on their demonstrated proficiency
- Most importantly, being *systematic*—*ensuring* students receive support regardless of the individual teacher to whom they are assigned because procedures are in place to guarantee the *school* responds (p. 255)

The implementation of your system of intervention, should meet several criteria. First, the intervention should match the purpose of the core instructional program and ensure that the instruction during the intervention moves students toward a balance of mathematical understanding and procedural skill. Instruction on procedural knowledge should be explicit and systematic. This includes providing students clear opportunities to practice the procedures they need to learn, ensuring they aren't missing steps in the procedure, supporting them with guided practice, and frequent review of their learning.

Second, your intervention programs should include instruction on solving word problems based on common underlying structures. The Mathematical Practices (see appendix A, page 181) must be at the core of the instructional activities that students engage in during the intervention to develop the habits of mind to understand the mathematical structure of problems they solve and support students' mathematical reasoning. Students need practice in identifying the mathematical structure of word problems. When students learn to identify the underlying structure of a word problem, they become better problem solvers and have access to the mathematical concepts and relationships in the problem. It is particularly important that the intervention materials push students to generalize from familiar to new problems. In other words, students seeing the structure in one problem should be able to generalize what they know to new problems with similar structures.

Third, intervention content materials should include opportunities for students to work with multimodal communication, in particular with visual representations of mathematical ideas. As students make different representations of the mathematical structure of a problem, they need to learn to make connections among them. That is, connections among the words in the problem, visual representation of the structure of the problem, and symbolic representation of the same. Intervention activities must help students become adept at using key representations, such as equations, number lines, graphs, sketches that represent mathematical structure, equivalent fractions, and so on. A key goal of any intervention has to be to help students move from the more concrete visual representations to the symbolic representation of the mathematics they are working with.

Students' motivation to learn mathematics will increase when they begin to experience success and the deficit messages they get from the system are replaced by experiences that support their understanding that effort pays off. It is essential that the intervention program and materials address the *stereotype threat* many students perceive by bringing them experiences that help them change their belief from intelligence as fixed to an understanding of intelligence as malleable. This change has positive effects in student learning as documented by relevant research on this topic (Aronson, Fried, & Good, 2002; Blackwell, Trzesniewski, & Dweck, 2007; Dweck, 2002; Good, Aronson, & Inzlicht, 2003).

Remember the intervention content you decide to use must be flexible enough to accommodate the adjustments your team will make as a result of the close monitoring and data analysis your team will perform on the students' evidence of their progress.

Using Follow-Up Assessment to Determine Next Steps

Frequent formative assessments are needed to make sure that students are progressing through the interventions and learning the skills and concepts they need per the diagnostic assessment instruments used to place them in the intervention. Thompson and Wiliam (2007) provide three guiding questions: (1) Where is the learner going? (2) Where is the learner right now? (3) How do you help the learner get there? Any assessment instrument used in the intervention program must provide the answer to these key questions for each student.

Where is the learner going?

- Are the learning goals of the intervention clear to the students?
- Is the student learning the skills the collaborative team identified as important?
- Is the student deepening her or his understanding of the concepts the collaborative team identified for him or her?
- Is the student identifying the mathematical structure of the word problems presented to him or her in the interventions and generalizing from them?

Where is the learner right now?

- Has the student reached the learning goals the team set?

- Are there new or different skills or concepts the student needs to learn?

- What evidence do we have of where the student is now?

How do we help the learner get there?

- Are we there yet? Is the student ready to leave the intervention?

- What feedback are we providing the student? How are we helping the student implement the feedback we are giving him or her?

- Are the interventions supporting students' learning as the team expected?

- Are there better ways to implement the interventions?

This analysis should be the work of your collaborative team: making agreements about what students should learn, continually monitoring students' progress both in the core program and in the interventions, and gathering and analyzing the evidence of students' performance. Once you determine the need for interventions, you should decide on what your team's response to learning is inside a framework of intensified help for students who are struggling. Response to intervention is a model for schoolwide instructional design that ensures all students' learning needs are met and enables all students to be successful. According to the National Center on Response to Intervention (NCRTI, 2010):

> Response to intervention integrates assessment and intervention within a multi-level prevention system to maximize student achievement and to reduce behavioral problems. With RTI, schools use data to identify students at risk for poor learning outcomes, monitor student progress, provide evidence-based interventions and adjust the intensity and nature of those interventions depending on a student's responsiveness, and identify students with learning disabilities or other disabilities. (p. 2)

For the purpose of this book, we present a framework with three tiers, based on the principles of RTI: Tier 1 is differentiated response to learning, Tier 2 is targeted response to learning, and Tier 3 is intensive response to learning.

Tier 1: What Is Your Differentiated Response to Learning?

Tier 1 instruction, research-informed practices designed to meet the needs of each learner, is the core of the RTI model and addresses the expected student outcomes. During this first stage of RTI, supports are provided to every student. Fisher, Frey, and Rothenberg (2011) suggest that "interventions are an element of good teaching" (p. 2), and these interventions begin in the classroom. Therefore, it is imperative you and your collaborative team focus your work on meaningful and rigorous mathematical tasks delivered with high-quality instruction.

If students are struggling with a few assignments, they just need extra attention from their classroom teacher. Students often need you to ask them guiding and scaffolding questions to help them make sense of the tasks and the assignment as you provide meaningful feedback on how they can move their learning forward. Students may benefit from study groups designed as part of your class instruction—peers that help them make sense of the learning target assignments. Tier 1 instruction is the first line of defense for students struggling to achieve the learning targets for the unit of study and can include but is not limited to:

- High-quality, researched-based instructional practices

- Differentiated instruction

- Screening and use of multiple assessment measures to monitor students' progress (Bender & Crane, 2011)

- Guided instruction with scaffolding and modeling that integrates listening, speaking, writing, and reading for ELs

- Language-acquisition instruction that supports learning of both content and language (Fisher et al., 2011)

During Tier 1 support, you use in-class formative assessments to diagnose why your students are struggling and require students to act on the differentiated instruction you provide according to the teaching-assessing-learning cycle.

Your collaborative team needs to find tasks that allow students multiple points of entry and to plan for differentiation. How you and your team address students' misconceptions or challenge students to think deeper about the content is one way to begin planning for differentiation. With your team, reflect on the prompts in table 5.3. Use the tool to analyze tasks to ensure your collaborative team is planning for differentiation.

Table 5.3: Tool for Your Differentiated Response to Learning

Questions to Consider	Reflection
What is the learning target for all, for some, or for few? What is the expected level of mastery for the standard?	
Does this task provide opportunities for different student readiness levels?	
Are there multiple ways to make sense of the mathematics for this standard?	
How can the task be adjusted to challenge students more deeply?	
Can the task be adjusted to increase access to students who are still struggling with background or prior knowledge?	

Visit **go.solution-tree.com/commoncore** for a reproducible version of this table.

Tier 2: What Is Your Targeted Response to Learning?

Tier 2 interventions are not for every student. These interventions are directed more toward Common Core mathematics skills or understandings of learning targets and will include academic and behavioral interventions. These interventions are more intensive and intended for students for whom Tier 1 differentiated instruction inside their classroom is not enough to meet their learning needs. Tier 2 interventions will be based on the criteria described in table 5.3.

Tier 2 interventions should include those that focus on clearing specific misconceptions. Malcolm Swan's (2005) observations in his book *Improving Learning in Mathematics: Challenges and Strategies* illustrate what many students experience in their mathematics classrooms.

> In our own survey of about 750 learners of mathematics from over 30 FE and sixth-form colleges, learners described their most frequent behaviours in the following ways:
>
> "I listen while the teacher explains."
>
> "I copy down the method from the board or textbook."
>
> "I only do questions I am told to do."
>
> "I work on my own."
>
> "I try to follow all the steps of a lesson."
>
> "I do easy problems first to increase my confidence."
>
> "I copy out questions before doing them."
>
> "I practise the same method repeatedly on many questions."
>
> For these learners, mathematics is something that is 'done to them,' rather than being a creative, stimulating subject to explore. It has become a collection of isolated procedures and techniques to learn by rote, rather than an interconnected network of interesting and powerful ideas to actively explore, discuss, debate and gradually come to understand. (p. 3)

Swan (2005) states, "There is now a vast body of research literature documenting learners' mistakes in mathematics. This work shows that mistakes are often the result of consistent, alternative interpretations of mathematical ideas" (p. 34). It is that consistency of interpretation that makes it possible to address those misconceptions in a systematic way. Alan Bell and the Toolkit Team (2005) write in support of that argument that "without exposure of pupils' misconceptions and their resolution through conflict discussion, students may not know why a mistake occurred" (p. 2). Therefore, any intervention teachers use in mathematics should be designed to help students explore their mistakes and misconceptions and discuss errors with others to unearth the source of their mistakes to make sense of the underlying concepts (Bell & the Toolkit Team, 2005; Fuson, Kalchman, & Bransford, 2005).

Further, students' misconceptions should not be conceived as wrong thinking but instead as *stages of development* (Swan, 2005). Some generalizations that lead to mathematical misconceptions include:

- "You can't divide smaller numbers by larger ones"
- "Division always makes numbers smaller"
- "The more digits a number has, then the larger is its value"
- "Shapes with bigger areas have bigger perimeters"
- "Letters represent particular numbers"
- "'Equals' means 'makes'" (Swan, 2005, p. 34)

Interventions can be targeted at these misconceptions and their related concepts, and in order to engage students in misconceptions, students must be active rather than passive learners (Swan, 2005).

An example includes students asked to evaluate statements about length and area written on cards. They are asked to decide whether the statements are always, never, or sometimes true. If students are having trouble with the statement cards, they can be given the hint cards to probe their thinking. Their justifications about their choices will uncover misconceptions they may have, and the discussion about the task will help clear those misconceptions and solidify the understanding of the concepts underlying the activity.

As discussed throughout this book, when students work on high-cognitive-demand tasks, they will be able to explore the connected concepts and discuss related misconceptions. Doing this will result in more durable learning with understanding, and students will be ready to leave the intervention sooner. High-cognitive-demand tasks can focus students' attention on the process rather than the solution only and will give them the opportunity to develop stronger ways to reason and to generalize.

With Tier 2 interventions, teachers find a way to provide every targeted student required access to the important mathematics for the learning standard in ways that the regular class instruction could not. Be sure that your intervention resources are not just more of the same materials and experiences with which students were not successful. Also, the targeted interventions should provide students clear, actionable feedback on how to improve their understanding of the mathematics in which they have gaps.

Tier 3: What Is Your Intensive Response to Learning?

Tier 3 interventions are intensive in nature and are intended for students who are behind in understanding the grade-level standards and learning targets for the standards. These students usually have multiple needs. This intensive additional support must not replace the instruction of the regular classroom, but should be provided in addition to it. Interventions at this stage can include, but are not limited to, placement into inclusion classrooms, one-on-one tutoring, or specific learning and behavioral interventions (Johnson, Smith, & Harris, 2009). Your collaborative team's role in Tier 3 interventions is to monitor closely the progress students are making and adjust the instruction if students are not progressing as expected. Your *intensive* response to learning should be individualized and based on addressing multiple academic and behavioral needs in conjunction with the support of learning and behavioral specialists.

English Learners

Among all the factors in Tiers 1, 2, and 3, the conditions for students' success also require strong mathematics instruction that integrates literacy and academic language development. ELs need to learn the language of mathematics. Mathematics teachers need to teach explicitly and deliberately the academic language needed for students to be successful in doing mathematics, without interrupting students' reasoning. Mathematics teachers must provide ELs opportunities to develop the language of the discipline in authentic and meaningful ways. Even more, teachers need to help students understand that language is more than a communication tool: it is a thinking tool. The clearer and more complete our sentences are, the clearer our thinking is about those ideas. Driscoll, Heck, and Malzahn (2012) identify three principles to guide the instruction of English learners.

1. No matter what category ELs fit into—from students newly arrived in the country and just beginning to learn English to those who have advanced to *former* limited English proficient—it is both possible and important to engage all these students in regular mathematical work that challenges them to reason, solve problems, conjecture, and convince.

2. Classroom environments that make ample use of multimodal communication—pictures, diagrams, presentations, written explanations, and gestures—afford ELs the means to express the thinking behind their reasoning and problem solving.

3. In the mathematics classroom, ELs can learn to express their mathematical thinking and reasoning in precise academic language, provided mathematics teachers work to understand and apply the ways in which language is implicated in the learning of mathematics. In brief, mathematics teachers of ELs need to recognize that they also are language teachers.

Using these as design principles, your team can provide opportunities to learn that will ensure ELs access to important mathematics and opportunities to produce language to communicate their reasoning. In addition to having clear goals of content and mathematical practices, tasks and activities should be looked through the lens of receptive and productive language issues. Receptive language demands are those that may prevent ELs access to important mathematics. Productive language opportunities are those scaffolds that will support students in producing the language to communicate their thinking. All these are essential in ensuring that all students, but particularly ELs, make sense of the mathematics they are learning.

Looking Ahead

Once your collaborative team has designed an intervention program, you should communicate that design to every stakeholder interested in the success of the students. That communication should include your plans for monitoring students' placement into, progress through, and exit from the intervention for each of the tiers.

Always remember that your teacher content knowledge influences how you engage students with the subject matter. You need strong content knowledge to interpret the students' ideas and understandings of the mathematics they are learning, to orchestrate discussions that advance students' learning, to adjust their instruction, and to provide specific feedback on how to improve. Hill et al. (2005) finds that a one standard deviation increase in teachers' mathematical knowledge for teaching was associated with a 4 percent increase in the rate of student learning. The logic is that the more the teacher knows the more successful students will be.

In mathematics, the more knowledgeable you are the more likely you are to present high-cognitive-demand tasks in contexts that are familiar to the students and to link those tasks to what students have already learned. If you understand multiple representations of mathematics concepts, you are more able to use these representations to further students' understanding. In contrast, colleagues with less mathematics knowledge tend to focus on algorithms rather than on the underlying mathematics concepts.

As you provide students opportunities to learn that ensure a balance between understanding and procedural knowledge, you must also understand how the culture of the classroom and the students' home culture affect their learning; and similarly, understand how their own and their students' mathematical identity affect their teaching-learning relationship. Several researchers (Cobb & Hodge, 2002; Lubienski & Gutiérrez, 2008; Martin, 2003, 2006) note that teachers' beliefs drive instructional decisions and that those instructional decisions readily impact whether students—particularly those from traditionally underserved groups—are participating in and getting access to a challenging mathematics program.

Thus, you must reflect on your own beliefs about students' potential and how those beliefs affect your instructional decisions. Moreover, you and your colleagues need to reflect (usually at the end of each unit of study) on whether the decisions you are making increase or diminish students' access to important mathematics. Creating the right conditions for learning requires that you are able to collectively reflect on your practice.

A hallmark of expert teachers is the willingness to learn through sustained, reflective student practice (Ross, 2006). This willingness, in turn, requires inquiry-based learning for the value of using formative assessment for instruction (Foster & Poppers, 2009). You know your students best—what motivates them, worries them, and shapes their realities. You are able to develop students' trust, a relationship building block essential for learning to occur. All these efforts, when collaboratively developed and implemented, will work synergistically to improve the experiences, learning, and achievement of your students and should guide not only the implementation of your core curriculum but also any interventions you decide to use.

Chapter 5 Extending My Understanding

1. Refer to your reflections with figure 5.1 (page 158) and table 5.1 (page 158). What is your current reality regarding equitable learning experiences for all students? How can you pursue and erase inequities that exist?

2. Refer to table 5.2 (page 161). What data do you have or what data do you need to effectively monitor students' CCSS learning?

3. What is your differentiated response to learning? How are you and your collaborative team making content accessible for each student?

4. As you develop your R²TI framework, what are your next steps for ensuring it is implemented with fidelity? What are your current strengths? What will be your challenges? What additional support or professional development will be needed to solidify you and your collaborative team's response to learning?

5. Considering your collaborative team's responses to the previous questions, how does the intervention reflect CCSS mathematics content and Mathematical Practices?

Online Resources

Visit **go.solution-tree.com/commoncore** for links to these resources.

- **West Bend Middle Level Pyramid of Interventions (www.allthingsplc.info /pdf/links/POImiddlelevelexample.pdf):** The West Bend Middle Level Pyramid of Interventions is a systematic intervention plan to increase student success in grades 6–8. The plan was a collaborative effort between community members, teachers, guidance counselors, administrators, and more, who are constantly improving it as new needs emerge.

- **Classroom-Focused Improvement Process (http://mdk12.org/process /cfip):** The Classroom-Focused Improvement Process is a six-step process for increasing student achievement that teachers plan and carry out during grade-level or cross-level team meetings as a part of their regular lesson-planning cycle.

- **Mathematics Assessment Resource Service (MARS; http://map.mathshell .org/materials/tests.php):** This website offers exams and tasks that can be used both as formative and diagnostic assessments. The purpose of these tests is to provide examples of the type of tests students should be able to tackle, if the aspirations of the Common Core State Standards are to be realized.

- **Mathematics Leadership Program (www.mathedleadership.org):** The National Council of Supervisors of Mathematics is an organization that assists mathematics educators in interpreting and understanding the CCSS to support the development and implementation of comprehensive, coherent instruction and assessment systems.

- **Math Reasoning Inventory (MRI; https://mathreasoninginventory.com):** The Math Reasoning Inventory is an online formative assessment tool designed to make teachers' classroom instruction more effective. The MRI questions focus on number and operations and are based on content from the Common Core State Standards for mathematics prior to sixth grade. The questions are those we can expect all middle school students to answer successfully.

- **National Center on Response to Intervention (www.rti4success.org):** This site provides a wealth of resources to plan, implement, and screen RTI, including professional development modules that teacher learning teams can use to initiate or improve an RTI program in schools, districts, or states.

- **RTI Action Network Middle School Resources (www.rtinetwork.org/middle -school):** The RTI Action Network is dedicated to the effective implementation of RTI in U.S. school districts. This website offers specific middle school research, strategies for tiered interventions, and tools for implementation.

- **RTI books and reproducibles (go.solution-tree.com/rti):** This site offers free reproducibles and numerous resources on RTI, including *Simplifying Response to Intervention: Four Essential Guiding Principles* (Buffum et al., 2012).

- **TODOS: Mathematics for ALL (www.todos-math.org):** TODOS is an affiliate of NCTM whose mission is to advocate for an equitable and high-quality mathematics education for all students— in particular, Hispanic and Latino students —by increasing the equity awareness of educators and their ability to foster students' proficiency in rigorous and coherent mathematics.

- **Understanding Language (http://ell.stanford.edu):** Understanding Language aims to heighten educator awareness of the critical role that language plays in the new Common Core State Standards and Next Generation Science Standards. The long-term goal of the initiative is to increase recognition that learning the language of each academic discipline is essential to learning content. Obtaining, evaluating, and communicating information; articulating and building on ideas; constructing explanations; engaging in argument from evidence—such language-rich performance expectations permeate the new standards.

EPILOGUE

Your Mathematics Professional Development Model

Implementing the Common Core State Standards for mathematics presents you with both new challenges and new opportunities. The unprecedented adoption of a common set of mathematics standards by nearly every state provides the opportunity for U.S. educators to press the reset button on mathematics education (Larson, 2011). Collectively, you and your colleagues have the opportunity to rededicate yourselves to ensuring all students are provided with exemplary teaching and learning experiences, and you have access to the supports necessary to guarantee all students the opportunity to develop mathematical proficiency.

The CCSS college and career aspirations and vision for teaching, learning, and assessing students usher in an opportunity for unprecedented implementation of research-informed practices in your school or district's mathematics program. In order to meet the expectations of the five fundamental paradigm shifts described in this book, you will want to assess your current practice and reality as a school against the roadmap to implementation described in figure E.1 (page 180).

Figure E.1 describes the essential paradigm shifts for your collaborative team (chapter 1) focus in the four critical areas of instruction (chapter 2), content (chapter 3), assessment (chapter 4), and intervention (chapter 5) in your mathematics program. As you professionally develop through your interaction and work as members of a collaborative team, your students will not only be better prepared for the Common Core mathematics assessment expectations but also for the college and career readiness that is an expectation for all students K–12—whether your state is part of the CCSS or not. Each sector in figure E.1 (page 180) describes three vital collaborative team behaviors for that area of change. If you hope to break through any current areas of student stagnation in your mathematics program and achieve greater student success than ever before, then these paradigms provide part of your mindset for never-ending change, growth, and improvement within the reasoning and sense-making focus of the mathematics instruction your students receive in your school.

Working collaboratively in a grade-level team will make the CCSS attainable not only for you but ultimately for your students. Working within a PLC culture is the best vehicle available to support you and your colleagues as you work together to interpret the Common Core State Standards, develop new pedagogical approaches through intensive collaborative planning, engage students in their progress toward meeting the standards, and provide the targeted supports necessary to ensure that all students meet mathematical

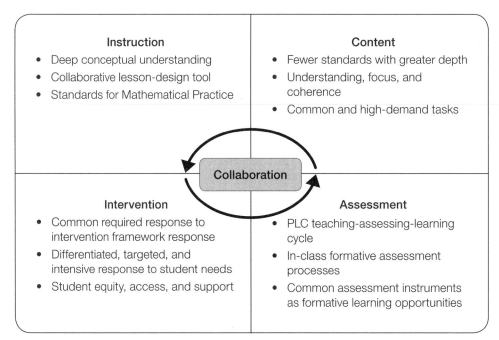

Figure E.1: PLCs at Work implementing Common Core mathematics.

Visit **go.solution-tree.com/commoncore** for a reproducible version of this figure.

opportunities of the Common Core mathematics. But perhaps most significantly, collaborative learning teams in a PLC can foster an environment in which you work to support one another and develop a culture that is fun for you, your colleagues, and the students in each course you teach. Middle school mathematics, as described in the Common Core, is intended to be rigorous, engaging, and focused on improved student learning for college and career readiness. Working together, you and your colleagues can accomplish great things.

APPENDIX A

Standards for Mathematical Practice

Source: NGA & CCSSO, 2010a, pp. 6–8. © Copyright 2010. National Governors Association Center for Best Practices and Council of Chief State School Officers. All rights reserved. Used with permission.

The Standards for Mathematical Practice describe varieties of expertise that mathematics educators at all levels should seek to develop in their students. These practices rest on important "processes and proficiencies" with longstanding importance in mathematics education. The first of these are the NCTM process standards of problem solving, reasoning and proof, communication, representation, and connections. The second are the strands of mathematical proficiency specified in the National Research Council's report *Adding It Up*: adaptive reasoning, strategic competence, conceptual understanding (comprehension of mathematical concepts, operations and relations), procedural fluency (skill in carrying out procedures flexibly, accurately, efficiently and appropriately), and productive disposition (habitual inclination to see mathematics as sensible, useful, and worthwhile, coupled with a belief in diligence and one's own efficacy).

1. **Make sense of problems and persevere in solving them**. Mathematically proficient students start by explaining to themselves the meaning of a problem and looking for entry points to its solution. They analyze givens, constraints, relationships, and goals. They make conjectures about the form and meaning of the solution and plan a solution pathway rather than simply jumping into a solution attempt. They consider analogous problems, and try special cases and simpler forms of the original problem in order to gain insight into its solution. They monitor and evaluate their progress and change course if necessary. Older students might, depending on the context of the problem, transform algebraic expressions or change the viewing window on their graphing calculator to get the information they need. Mathematically proficient students can explain correspondences between equations, verbal descriptions, tables, and graphs or draw diagrams of important features and relationships, graph data, and search for regularity or trends. Younger students might rely on using concrete objects or pictures to help conceptualize and solve a problem. Mathematically proficient students check their answers to problems using a different method, and they continually ask themselves, "Does this make sense?" They can understand the approaches of others to solving complex problems and identify correspondences between different approaches.

2. **Reason abstractly and quantitatively**. Mathematically proficient students make sense of quantities and their relationships in problem situations. They bring two complementary abilities to bear on problems involving quantitative relationships: the ability to decontextualize—to abstract a given situation and represent it symbolically and manipulate the representing symbols as if they have a life of their own, without necessarily attending to their referents—and the ability to contextualize, to pause as needed

during the manipulation process in order to probe into the referents for the symbols involved. Quantitative reasoning entails habits of creating a coherent representation of the problem at hand; considering the units involved; attending to the meaning of quantities, not just how to compute them; and knowing and flexibly using different properties of operations and objects.

3. **Construct viable arguments and critique the reasoning of others**. Mathematically proficient students understand and use stated assumptions, definitions, and previously established results in constructing arguments. They make conjectures and build a logical progression of statements to explore the truth of their conjectures. They are able to analyze situations by breaking them into cases, and can recognize and use counterexamples. They justify their conclusions, communicate them to others, and respond to the arguments of others. They reason inductively about data, making plausible arguments that take into account the context from which the data arose. Mathematically proficient students are also able to compare the effectiveness of two plausible arguments, distinguish correct logic or reasoning from that which is flawed, and—if there is a flaw in an argument—explain what it is. Elementary students can construct arguments using concrete referents such as objects, drawings, diagrams, and actions. Such arguments can make sense and be correct, even though they are not generalized or made formal until later grades. Later, students learn to determine domains to which an argument applies. Students at all grades can listen or read the arguments of others, decide whether they make sense, and ask useful questions to clarify or improve the arguments.

4. **Model with mathematics**. Mathematically proficient students can apply the mathematics they know to solve problems arising in everyday life, society, and the workplace. In early grades, this might be as simple as writing an addition equation to describe a situation. In middle grades, a student might apply proportional reasoning to plan a school event or analyze a problem in the community. By high school, a student might use geometry to solve a design problem or use a function to describe how one quantity of interest depends on another. Mathematically proficient students who can apply what they know are comfortable making assumptions and approximations to simplify a complicated situation, realizing that these may need revision later. They are able to identify important quantities in a practical situation and map their relationships using such tools as diagrams, two-way tables, graphs, flowcharts and formulas. They can analyze those relationships mathematically to draw conclusions. They routinely interpret their mathematical results in the context of the situation and reflect on whether the results make sense, possibly improving the model if it has not served its purpose.

5. **Use appropriate tools strategically**. Mathematically proficient students consider the available tools when solving a mathematical problem. These tools might include pencil and paper, concrete models, a ruler, a protractor, a calculator, a spreadsheet, a computer algebra system, a statistical package, or dynamic geometry software. Proficient students are sufficiently familiar with tools appropriate for their grade or course to make sound decisions about when each of these tools might be helpful, recognizing both the insight

to be gained and their limitations. For example, mathematically proficient high school students analyze graphs of functions and solutions generated using a graphing calculator. They detect possible errors by strategically using estimation and other mathematical knowledge. When making mathematical models, they know that technology can enable them to visualize the results of varying assumptions, explore consequences, and compare predictions with data. Mathematically proficient students at various grade levels are able to identify relevant external mathematical resources, such as digital content located on a website, and use them to pose or solve problems. They are able to use technological tools to explore and deepen their understanding of concepts.

6. **Attend to precision.** Mathematically proficient students try to communicate precisely to others. They try to use clear definitions in discussion with others and in their own reasoning. They state the meaning of the symbols they choose, including using the equal sign consistently and appropriately. They are careful about specifying units of measure, and labeling axes to clarify the correspondence with quantities in a problem. They calculate accurately and efficiently, express numerical answers with a degree of precision appropriate for the problem context. In the elementary grades, students give carefully formulated explanations to each other. By the time they reach high school they have learned to examine claims and make explicit use of definitions.

7. **Look for and make use of structure.** Mathematically proficient students look closely to discern a pattern or structure. Young students, for example, might notice that three and seven more is the same amount as seven and three more, or they may sort a collection of shapes according to how many sides the shapes have. Later, students will see 7×8 equals the well remembered $7 \times 5 + 7 \times 3$, in preparation for learning about the distributive property. In the expression $x^2 + 9x + 14$, older students can see the 14 as 2×7 and the 9 as $2 + 7$. They recognize the significance of an existing line in a geometric figure and can use the strategy of drawing an auxiliary line for solving problems. They also can step back for an overview and shift perspective. They can see complicated things, such as some algebraic expressions, as single objects or as being composed of several objects. For example, they can see $5 - 3(x - y)2$ as 5 minus a positive number times a square and use that to realize that its value cannot be more than 5 for any real numbers x and y.

8. **Look for and express regularity in repeated reasoning.** Mathematically proficient students notice if calculations are repeated, and look both for general methods and for shortcuts. Upper elementary students might notice when dividing 25 by 11 that they are repeating the same calculations over and over again, and conclude they have a repeating decimal. By paying attention to the calculation of slope as they repeatedly check whether points are on the line through (1, 2) with slope 3, middle school students might abstract the equation $(y - 2)/(x - 1) = 3$. Noticing the regularity in the way terms cancel when expanding $(x - 1)(x + 1)$, $(x - 1)(x^2 + x + 1)$, and $(x - 1)(x^3 + x^2 + x + 1)$ might lead them to the general formula for the sum of a geometric series. As they work to solve a problem, mathematically proficient students maintain oversight of the process, while attending to the details. They continually evaluate the reasonableness of their intermediate results.

Connecting the Standards for Mathematical Practice to the Standards for Mathematical Content

The Standards for Mathematical Practice describe ways in which developing student practitioners of the discipline of mathematics increasingly ought to engage with the subject matter as they grow in mathematical maturity and expertise throughout the elementary, middle and high school years. Designers of curricula, assessments, and professional development should all attend to the need to connect the mathematical practices to mathematical content in mathematics instruction.

The Standards for Mathematical Content are a balanced combination of procedure and understanding. Expectations that begin with the word "understand" are often especially good opportunities to connect the practices to the content. Students who lack understanding of a topic may rely on procedures too heavily. Without a flexible base from which to work, they may be less likely to consider analogous problems, represent problems coherently, justify conclusions, apply the mathematics to practical situations, use technology mindfully to work with the mathematics, explain the mathematics accurately to other students, step back for an overview, or deviate from a known procedure to find a shortcut. In short, a lack of understanding effectively prevents a student from engaging in the mathematical practices.

In this respect, those content standards which set an expectation of understanding are potential "points of intersection" between the Standards for Mathematical Content and the Standards for Mathematical Practice. These points of intersection are intended to be weighted toward central and generative concepts in the school mathematics curriculum that most merit the time, resources, innovative energies, and focus necessary to qualitatively improve the curriculum, instruction, assessment, professional development, and student achievement in mathematics.

APPENDIX B

Standards for Mathematical Content, Grade 6

Source: NGA & CCSSO, 2010a, pp. 39–45. © Copyright 2010. National Governors Association Center for Best Practices and Council of Chief State School Officers. All rights reserved. Used with permission.

In Grade 6, instructional time should focus on four critical areas: (1) connecting ratio and rate to whole number multiplication and division and using concepts of ratio and rate to solve problems; (2) completing understanding of division of fractions and extending the notion of number to the system of rational numbers, which includes negative numbers; (3) writing, interpreting, and using expressions and equations; and (4) developing understanding of statistical thinking.

(1) Students use reasoning about multiplication and division to solve ratio and rate problems about quantities. By viewing equivalent ratios and rates as deriving from, and extending, pairs of rows (or columns) in the multiplication table, and by analyzing simple drawings that indicate the relative size of quantities, students connect their understanding of multiplication and division with ratios and rates. Thus students expand the scope of problems for which they can use multiplication and division to solve problems, and they connect ratios and fractions. Students solve a wide variety of problems involving ratios and rates.

(2) Students use the meaning of fractions, the meanings of multiplication and division, and the relationship between multiplication and division to understand and explain why the procedures for dividing fractions make sense. Students use these operations to solve problems. Students extend their previous understandings of number and the ordering of numbers to the full system of rational numbers, which includes negative rational numbers, and in particular negative integers. They reason about the order and absolute value of rational numbers and about the location of points in all four quadrants of the coordinate plane.

(3) Students understand the use of variables in mathematical expressions. They write expressions and equations that correspond to given situations, evaluate expressions, and use expressions and formulas to solve problems. Students understand that expressions in different forms can be equivalent, and they use the properties of operations to rewrite expressions in equivalent forms. Students know that the solutions of an equation are the values of the variables that make the equation true. Students use properties of operations and the idea of maintaining the equality of both sides of an equation to solve simple one-step

equations. Students construct and analyze tables, such as tables of quantities that are in equivalent ratios, and they use equations (such as $3x = y$) to describe relationships between quantities.

(4) Building on and reinforcing their understanding of number, students begin to develop their ability to think statistically. Students recognize that a data distribution may not have a definite center and that different ways to measure center yield different values. The median measures center in the sense that it is roughly the middle value. The mean measures center in the sense that it is the value that each data point would take on if the total of the data values were redistributed equally, and also in the sense that it is a balance point. Students recognize that a measure of variability (interquartile range or mean absolute deviation) can also be useful for summarizing data because two very different sets of data can have the same mean and median yet be distinguished by their variability. Students learn to describe and summarize numerical data sets, identifying clusters, peaks, gaps, and symmetry, considering the context in which the data were collected.

Students in Grade 6 also build on their work with area in elementary school by reasoning about relationships among shapes to determine area, surface area, and volume. They find areas of right triangles, other triangles, and special quadrilaterals by decomposing these shapes, rearranging or removing pieces, and relating the shapes to rectangles. Using these methods, students discuss, develop, and justify formulas for areas of triangles and parallelograms. Students find areas of polygons and surface areas of prisms and pyramids by decomposing them into pieces whose area they can determine. They reason about right rectangular prisms with fractional side lengths to extend formulas for the volume of a right rectangular prism to fractional side lengths. They prepare for work on scale drawings and constructions in Grade 7 by drawing polygons in the coordinate plane.

Grade 6 Overview

Ratios and Proportional Relationships

- Understand ratio concepts and use ratio reasoning to solve problems.

The Number System

- Apply and extend previous understandings of multiplication and division to divide fractions by fractions.

- Compute fluently with multi-digit numbers and find common factors and multiples.

- Apply and extend previous understandings of numbers to the system of rational numbers.

Expressions and Equations

- Apply and extend previous understandings of arithmetic to algebraic expressions.

- Reason about and solve one-variable equations and inequalities.

- Represent and analyze quantitative relationships between dependent and independent variables.

Geometry

- Solve real-world and mathematical problems involving area, surface area, and volume.

Statistics and Probability

- Develop understanding of statistical variability.

- Summarize and describe distributions.

Ratios and Proportional Relationships 6.RP

Understand ratio concepts and use ratio reasoning to solve problems.

1. Understand the concept of a ratio and use ratio language to describe a ratio relationship between two quantities. For example, "The ratio of wings to beaks in the bird house at the zoo was 2:1, because for every 2 wings there was 1 beak." "For every vote candidate A received, candidate C received nearly three votes."

2. Understand the concept of a unit rate a/b associated with a ratio $a:b$ with $b \neq 0$, and use rate language in the context of a ratio relationship. For example, "This recipe has a ratio of 3 cups of flour to 4 cups of sugar, so there is ¾ cup of flour for each cup of sugar." "We paid $75 for 15 hamburgers, which is a rate of $5 per hamburger."[1]

3. Use ratio and rate reasoning to solve real-world and mathematical problems, e.g., by reasoning about tables of equivalent ratios, tape diagrams, double number line diagrams, or equations.

   a. Make tables of equivalent ratios relating quantities with whole number measurements, find missing values in the tables, and plot the pairs of values on the coordinate plane. Use tables to compare ratios.

   b. Solve unit rate problems including those involving unit pricing and constant speed. For example, if it took 7 hours to mow 4 lawns, then at that rate, how many lawns could be mowed in 35 hours? At what rate were lawns being mowed?

   c. Find a percent of a quantity as a rate per 100 (e.g., 30% of a quantity means 30/100 times the quantity); solve problems involving finding the whole, given a part and the percent.

---

[1] *Expectations for unit rates in this grade are limited to non-complex fractions.*

d. Use ratio reasoning to convert measurement units; manipulate and transform units appropriately when multiplying or dividing quantities.

The Number System 6.NS

Apply and extend previous understandings of multiplication and division to divide fractions by fractions.

1. Interpret and compute quotients of fractions, and solve word problems involving division of fractions by fractions, e.g., by using visual fraction models and equations to represent the problem. For example, create a story context for ($\frac{2}{3}$) ÷ ($\frac{3}{4}$) and use a visual fraction model to show the quotient; use the relationship between multiplication and division to explain that ($\frac{2}{3}$) ÷ ($\frac{3}{4}$) = $\frac{8}{9}$ because $\frac{3}{4}$ of $\frac{8}{9}$ is $\frac{2}{3}$. (In general, ($\frac{a}{b}$) ÷ ($\frac{c}{d}$) = $\frac{ad}{bc}$.) How much chocolate will each person get if 3 people share $\frac{1}{2}$ lb of chocolate equally? How many $\frac{3}{4}$-cup servings are in $\frac{2}{3}$ of a cup of yogurt? How wide is a rectangular strip of land with length $\frac{3}{4}$ mi and area $\frac{1}{2}$ square mi?

Compute fluently with multi-digit numbers and find common factors and multiples.

2. Fluently divide multi-digit numbers using the standard algorithm.

3. Fluently add, subtract, multiply, and divide multi-digit decimals using the standard algorithm for each operation.

4. Find the greatest common factor of two whole numbers less than or equal to 100 and the least common multiple of two whole numbers less than or equal to 12. Use the distributive property to express a sum of two whole numbers 1–100 with a common factor as a multiple of a sum of two whole numbers with no common factor. For example, express 36 + 8 as 4 (9 + 2).

Apply and extend previous understandings of numbers to the system of rational numbers.

5. Understand that positive and negative numbers are used together to describe quantities having opposite directions or values (e.g., temperature above/below zero, elevation above/below sea level, credits/debits, positive/negative electric charge); use positive and negative numbers to represent quantities in real-world contexts, explaining the meaning of 0 in each situation.

6. Understand a rational number as a point on the number line. Extend number line diagrams and coordinate axes familiar from previous grades to represent points on the line and in the plane with negative number coordinates.

   a. Recognize opposite signs of numbers as indicating locations on opposite sides of 0 on the number line; recognize that the opposite of the opposite of a number is the number itself, e.g., -(-3) = 3, and that 0 is its own opposite.

b. Understand signs of numbers in ordered pairs as indicating locations in quadrants of the coordinate plane; recognize that when two ordered pairs differ only by signs, the locations of the points are related by reflections across one or both axes.

c. Find and position integers and other rational numbers on a horizontal or vertical number line diagram; find and position pairs of integers and other rational numbers on a coordinate plane.

7. Understand ordering and absolute value of rational numbers.

a. Interpret statements of inequality as statements about the relative position of two numbers on a number line diagram. For example, interpret -3 > -7 as a statement that -3 is located to the right of -7 on a number line oriented from left to right.

b. Write, interpret, and explain statements of order for rational numbers in real-world contexts. For example, write -3° C > -7° C to express the fact that -3° C is warmer than -7° C.

c. Understand the absolute value of a rational number as its distance from 0 on the number line; interpret absolute value as magnitude for a positive or negative quantity in a real-world situation. For example, for an account balance of -30 dollars, write $|-30| = 30$ to describe the size of the debt in dollars.

d. Distinguish comparisons of absolute value from statements about order. For example, recognize that an account balance less than -30 dollars represents a debt greater than 30 dollars.

8. Solve real-world and mathematical problems by graphing points in all four quadrants of the coordinate plane. Include use of coordinates and absolute value to find distances between points with the same first coordinate or the same second coordinate.

Expressions and Equations 6.EE

Apply and extend previous understandings of arithmetic to algebraic expressions.

1. Write and evaluate numerical expressions involving whole-number exponents.

2. Write, read, and evaluate expressions in which letters stand for numbers.

a. Write expressions that record operations with numbers and with letters standing for numbers. For example, express the calculation "Subtract y from 5" as $5 - y$.

b. Identify parts of an expression using mathematical terms (sum, term, product, factor, quotient, coefficient); view one or more parts of an expression as a single entity. For example, describe the expression 2 (8 +

7) as a product of two factors; view (8 + 7) as both a single entity and a sum of two terms.

    c. Evaluate expressions at specific values of their variables. Include expressions that arise from formulas used in real-world problems. Perform arithmetic operations, including those involving whole number exponents, in the conventional order when there are no parentheses to specify a particular order (Order of Operations). For example, use the formulas $V = s^3$ and $A = 6 s^2$ to find the volume and surface area of a cube with sides of length $s = ½$.

3. Apply the properties of operations to generate equivalent expressions. For example, apply the distributive property to the expression $3 (2 + x)$ to produce the equivalent expression $6 + 3x$; apply the distributive property to the expression $24x + 18y$ to produce the equivalent expression $6 (4x + 3y)$; apply properties of operations to $y + y + y$ to produce the equivalent expression $3y$.

4. Identify when two expressions are equivalent (i.e., when the two expressions name the same number regardless of which value is substituted into them). For example, the expressions $y + y + y$ and $3y$ are equivalent because they name the same number regardless of which number y stands for.

Reason about and solve one-variable equations and inequalities.

5. Understand solving an equation or inequality as a process of answering a question: which values from a specified set, if any, make the equation or inequality true? Use substitution to determine whether a given number in a specified set makes an equation or inequality true.

6. Use variables to represent numbers and write expressions when solving a real-world or mathematical problem; understand that a variable can represent an unknown number, or, depending on the purpose at hand, any number in a specified set.

7. Solve real-world and mathematical problems by writing and solving equations of the form $x + p = q$ and $px = q$ for cases in which p, q and x are all nonnegative rational numbers.

8. Write an inequality of the form $x > c$ or $x < c$ to represent a constraint or condition in a real-world or mathematical problem. Recognize that inequalities of the form $x > c$ or $x < c$ have infinitely many solutions; represent solutions of such inequalities on number line diagrams.

Represent and analyze quantitative relationships between dependent and independent variables.

9. Use variables to represent two quantities in a real-world problem that change in relationship to one another; write an equation to express one quantity, thought of as the dependent variable, in terms of the other quantity, thought of as the

independent variable. Analyze the relationship between the dependent and independent variables using graphs and tables, and relate these to the equation. For example, in a problem involving motion at constant speed, list and graph ordered pairs of distances and times, and write the equation $d = 65t$ to represent the relationship between distance and time.

Geometry 6.G

Solve real-world and mathematical problems involving area, surface area, and volume.

1. Find the area of right triangles, other triangles, special quadrilaterals, and polygons by composing into rectangles or decomposing into triangles and other shapes; apply these techniques in the context of solving real-world and mathematical problems.

2. Find the volume of a right rectangular prism with fractional edge lengths by packing it with unit cubes of the appropriate unit fraction edge lengths, and show that the volume is the same as would be found by multiplying the edge lengths of the prism. Apply the formulas $V = l\, w\, h$ and $V = b\, h$ to find volumes of right rectangular prisms with fractional edge lengths in the context of solving real-world and mathematical problems.

3. Draw polygons in the coordinate plane given coordinates for the vertices; use coordinates to find the length of a side joining points with the same first coordinate or the same second coordinate. Apply these techniques in the context of solving real-world and mathematical problems.

4. Represent three-dimensional figures using nets made up of rectangles and triangles, and use the nets to find the surface area of these figures. Apply these techniques in the context of solving real-world and mathematical problems.

Statistics and Probability 6.SP

Develop understanding of statistical variability.

1. Recognize a statistical question as one that anticipates variability in the data related to the question and accounts for it in the answers. For example, "How old am I?" is not a statistical question, but "How old are the students in my school?" is a statistical question because one anticipates variability in students' ages.

2. Understand that a set of data collected to answer a statistical question has a distribution which can be described by its center, spread, and overall shape.

3. Recognize that a measure of center for a numerical data set summarizes all of its values with a single number, while a measure of variation describes how its values vary with a single number.

Summarize and describe distributions.

4. Display numerical data in plots on a number line, including dot plots, histograms, and box plots.

5. Summarize numerical data sets in relation to their context, such as by:

   a. Reporting the number of observations.

   b. Describing the nature of the attribute under investigation, including how it was measured and its units of measurement.

   c. Giving quantitative measures of center (median and/or mean) and variability (interquartile range and/or mean absolute deviation), as well as describing any overall pattern and any striking deviations from the overall pattern with reference to the context in which the data were gathered.

   d. Relating the choice of measures of center and variability to the shape of the data distribution and the context in which the data were gathered.

APPENDIX C

Standards for Mathematical Content, Grade 7

In Grade 7, instructional time should focus on four critical areas: (1) developing understanding of and applying proportional relationships; (2) developing understanding of operations with rational numbers and working with expressions and linear equations; (3) solving problems involving scale drawings and informal geometric constructions, and working with two- and three-dimensional shapes to solve problems involving area, surface area, and volume; and (4) drawing inferences about populations based on samples.

(1) Students extend their understanding of ratios and develop understanding of proportionality to solve single- and multi-step problems. Students use their understanding of ratios and proportionality to solve a wide variety of percent problems, including those involving discounts, interest, taxes, tips, and percent increase or decrease. Students solve problems about scale drawings by relating corresponding lengths between the objects or by using the fact that relationships of lengths within an object are preserved in similar objects. Students graph proportional relationships and understand the unit rate informally as a measure of the steepness of the related line, called the slope. They distinguish proportional relationships from other relationships.

(2) Students develop a unified understanding of number, recognizing fractions, decimals (that have a finite or a repeating decimal representation), and percents as different representations of rational numbers. Students extend addition, subtraction, multiplication, and division to all rational numbers, maintaining the properties of operations and the relationships between addition and subtraction, and multiplication and division. By applying these properties, and by viewing negative numbers in terms of everyday contexts (e.g., amounts owed or temperatures below zero), students explain and interpret the rules for adding, subtracting, multiplying, and dividing with negative numbers. They use the arithmetic of rational numbers as they formulate expressions and equations in one variable and use these equations to solve problems.

(3) Students continue their work with area from Grade 6, solving problems involving the area and circumference of a circle and surface area of three-dimensional objects. In preparation for work on congruence and similarity in Grade 8 they reason about relationships among two-dimensional figures using scale

drawings and informal geometric constructions, and they gain familiarity with the relationships between angles formed by intersecting lines. Students work with three-dimensional figures, relating them to two-dimensional figures by examining cross-sections. They solve real-world and mathematical problems involving area, surface area, and volume of two- and three-dimensional objects composed of triangles, quadrilaterals, polygons, cubes and right prisms.

(4) Students build on their previous work with single data distributions to compare two data distributions and address questions about differences between populations. They begin informal work with random sampling to generate data sets and learn about the importance of representative samples for drawing inferences.

Grade 7 Overview

Ratios and Proportional Relationships

- Analyze proportional relationships and use them to solve real-world and mathematical problems.

The Number System

- Apply and extend previous understandings of operations with fractions to add, subtract, multiply, and divide rational numbers.

Expressions and Equations

- Use properties of operations to generate equivalent expressions.
- Solve real-life and mathematical problems using numerical and algebraic expressions and equations.

Geometry

- Draw, construct and describe geometrical figures and describe the relationships between them.
- Solve real-life and mathematical problems involving angle measure, area, surface area, and volume.

Statistics and Probability

- Use random sampling to draw inferences about a population.
- Draw informal comparative inferences about two populations.
- Investigate chance processes and develop, use, and evaluate probability models.

Ratios and Proportional Relationships 7.RP

Analyze proportional relationships and use them to solve real-world and mathematical problems.

1. Compute unit rates associated with ratios of fractions, including ratios of lengths, areas and other quantities measured in like or different units. For example, if a person walks ½ mile in each ¼ hour, compute the unit rate as the complex fraction ½/¼ miles per hour, equivalently 2 miles per hour.

2. Recognize and represent proportional relationships between quantities.

   a. Decide whether two quantities are in a proportional relationship, e.g., by testing for equivalent ratios in a table or graphing on a coordinate plane and observing whether the graph is a straight line through the origin.

   b. Identify the constant of proportionality (unit rate) in tables, graphs, equations, diagrams, and verbal descriptions of proportional relationships.

   c. Represent proportional relationships by equations. For example, if total cost t is proportional to the number n of items purchased at a constant price p, the relationship between the total cost and the number of items can be expressed as $t = pn$.

   d. Explain what a point (x, y) on the graph of a proportional relationship means in terms of the situation, with special attention to the points $(0, 0)$ and $(1, r)$ where r is the unit rate.

3. Use proportional relationships to solve multistep ratio and percent problems. Examples: simple interest, tax, markups and markdowns, gratuities and commissions, fees, percent increase and decrease, percent error.

The Number System 7.NS

Apply and extend previous understandings of operations with fractions to add, subtract, multiply, and divide rational numbers.

1. Apply and extend previous understandings of addition and subtraction to add and subtract rational numbers; represent addition and subtraction on a horizontal or vertical number line diagram.

   a. Describe situations in which opposite quantities combine to make 0. For example, a hydrogen atom has 0 charge because its two constituents are oppositely charged.

   b. Understand $p + q$ as the number located a distance $|q|$ from p, in the positive or negative direction depending on whether q is positive or negative. Show that a number and its opposite have a sum of 0 (are additive inverses). Interpret sums of rational numbers by describing real-world contexts.

   c. Understand subtraction of rational numbers as adding the additive inverse, $p - q = p + (-q)$. Show that the distance between two rational numbers on the number line is the absolute value of their difference, and apply this principle in real-world contexts.

    d. Apply properties of operations as strategies to add and subtract rational numbers.

2. Apply and extend previous understandings of multiplication and division and of fractions to multiply and divide rational numbers.

    a. Understand that multiplication is extended from fractions to rational numbers by requiring that operations continue to satisfy the properties of operations, particularly the distributive property, leading to products such as (-1)(-1) = 1 and the rules for multiplying signed numbers. Interpret products of rational numbers by describing real-world contexts.

    b. Understand that integers can be divided, provided that the divisor is not zero, and every quotient of integers (with a non-zero divisor) is a rational number. If p and q are integers, then $-(p/q) = (-p)/q = p/(-q)$. Interpret quotients of rational numbers by describing real-world contexts.

    c. Apply properties of operations as strategies to multiply and divide rational numbers.

    d. Convert a rational number to a decimal using long division; know that the decimal form of a rational number terminates in 0s or eventually repeats.

3. Solve real-world and mathematical problems involving the four operations with rational numbers.[1]

Expressions and Equations 7.EE

Use properties of operations to generate equivalent expressions.

1. Apply properties of operations as strategies to add, subtract, factor, and expand linear expressions with rational coefficients.

2. Understand that rewriting an expression in different forms in a problem context can shed light on the problem and how the quantities in it are related. For example, $a + 0.05a = 1.05a$ means that "increase by 5%" is the same as "multiply by 1.05."

Solve real-life and mathematical problems using numerical and algebraic expressions and equations.

3. Solve multi-step real-life and mathematical problems posed with positive and negative rational numbers in any form (whole numbers, fractions, and decimals), using tools strategically. Apply properties of operations to calculate with numbers in any form; convert between forms as appropriate; and assess the reasonableness of answers using mental computation and estimation strategies. For

---

[1] *Computations with rational numbers extend the rules for manipulating fractions to complex fractions.*

example: If a woman making $25 an hour gets a 10% raise, she will make an additional ⅒ of her salary an hour, or $2.50, for a new salary of $27.50. If you want to place a towel bar 9 ¾ inches long in the center of a door that is 27 ½ inches wide, you will need to place the bar about 9 inches from each edge; this estimate can be used as a check on the exact computation.

4. Use variables to represent quantities in a real-world or mathematical problem, and construct simple equations and inequalities to solve problems by reasoning about the quantities.

   a. Solve word problems leading to equations of the form $px + q = r$ and $p(x + q) = r$, where p, q, and r are specific rational numbers. Solve equations of these forms fluently. Compare an algebraic solution to an arithmetic solution, identifying the sequence of the operations used in each approach. For example, the perimeter of a rectangle is 54 cm. Its length is 6 cm. What is its width?

   b. Solve word problems leading to inequalities of the form $px + q > r$ or $px + q < r$, where p, q, and r are specific rational numbers. Graph the solution set of the inequality and interpret it in the context of the problem. For example: As a salesperson, you are paid $50 per week plus $3 per sale. This week you want your pay to be at least $100. Write an inequality for the number of sales you need to make, and describe the solutions.

Geometry 7.G

Draw, construct, and describe geometrical figures and describe the relationships between them.

1. Solve problems involving scale drawings of geometric figures, including computing actual lengths and areas from a scale drawing and reproducing a scale drawing at a different scale.

2. Draw (freehand, with ruler and protractor, and with technology) geometric shapes with given conditions. Focus on constructing triangles from three measures of angles or sides, noticing when the conditions determine a unique triangle, more than one triangle, or no triangle.

3. Describe the two-dimensional figures that result from slicing three-dimensional figures, as in plane sections of right rectangular prisms and right rectangular pyramids.

Solve real-life and mathematical problems involving angle measure, area, surface area, and volume.

4. Know the formulas for the area and circumference of a circle and use them to solve problems; give an informal derivation of the relationship between the circumference and area of a circle.

5. Use facts about supplementary, complementary, vertical, and adjacent angles in a multi-step problem to write and solve simple equations for an unknown angle in a figure.

6. Solve real-world and mathematical problems involving area, volume and surface area of two- and three-dimensional objects composed of triangles, quadrilaterals, polygons, cubes, and right prisms.

Statistics and Probability 7.SP

Use random sampling to draw inferences about a population.

1. Understand that statistics can be used to gain information about a population by examining a sample of the population; generalizations about a population from a sample are valid only if the sample is representative of that population. Understand that random sampling tends to produce representative samples and support valid inferences.

2. Use data from a random sample to draw inferences about a population with an unknown characteristic of interest. Generate multiple samples (or simulated samples) of the same size to gauge the variation in estimates or predictions. For example, estimate the mean word length in a book by randomly sampling words from the book; predict the winner of a school election based on randomly sampled survey data. Gauge how far off the estimate or prediction might be.

Draw informal comparative inferences about two populations.

3. Informally assess the degree of visual overlap of two numerical data distributions with similar variabilities, measuring the difference between the centers by expressing it as a multiple of a measure of variability. For example, the mean height of players on the basketball team is 10 cm greater than the mean height of players on the soccer team, about twice the variability (mean absolute deviation) on either team; on a dot plot, the separation between the two distributions of heights is noticeable.

4. Use measures of center and measures of variability for numerical data from random samples to draw informal comparative inferences about two populations. For example, decide whether the words in a chapter of a seventh-grade science book are generally longer than the words in a chapter of a fourth-grade science book.

Investigate chance processes and develop, use, and evaluate probability models.

5. Understand that the probability of a chance event is a number between 0 and 1 that expresses the likelihood of the event occurring. Larger numbers indicate greater likelihood. A probability near 0 indicates an unlikely event, a probability around ½ indicates an event that is neither unlikely nor likely, and a probability near 1 indicates a likely event.

6. Approximate the probability of a chance event by collecting data on the chance process that produces it and observing its long-run relative frequency, and predict the approximate relative frequency given the probability. For example, when rolling a number cube 600 times, predict that a 3 or 6 would be rolled roughly 200 times, but probably not exactly 200 times.

7. Develop a probability model and use it to find probabilities of events. Compare probabilities from a model to observed frequencies; if the agreement is not good, explain possible sources of the discrepancy.

   a. Develop a uniform probability model by assigning equal probability to all outcomes, and use the model to determine probabilities of events. For example, if a student is selected at random from a class, find the probability that Jane will be selected and the probability that a girl will be selected.

   b. Develop a probability model (which may not be uniform) by observing frequencies in data generated from a chance process. For example, find the approximate probability that a spinning penny will land heads up or that a tossed paper cup will land open-end down. Do the outcomes for the spinning penny appear to be equally likely based on the observed frequencies?

8. Find probabilities of compound events using organized lists, tables, tree diagrams, and simulation.

   a. Understand that, just as with simple events, the probability of a compound event is the fraction of outcomes in the sample space for which the compound event occurs.

   b. Represent sample spaces for compound events using methods such as organized lists, tables and tree diagrams. For an event described in everyday language (e.g., "rolling double sixes"), identify the outcomes in the sample space which compose the event.

   c. Design and use a simulation to generate frequencies for compound events. For example, use random digits as a simulation tool to approximate the answer to the question: If 40% of donors have type A blood, what is the probability that it will take at least 4 donors to find one with type A blood?

Standards for Mathematical Content, Grade 8

Source: NGA & CCSSO, 2010a, pp. 52–56. © Copyright 2010. National Governors Association Center for Best Practices and Council of Chief State School Officers. All rights reserved. Used with permission.

In Grade 8, instructional time should focus on three critical areas: (1) formulating and reasoning about expressions and equations, including modeling an association in bivariate data with a linear equation, and solving linear equations and systems of linear equations; (2) grasping the concept of a function and using functions to describe quantitative relationships; (3) analyzing two- and three-dimensional space and figures using distance, angle, similarity, and congruence, and understanding and applying the Pythagorean Theorem.

(1) Students use linear equations and systems of linear equations to represent, analyze, and solve a variety of problems. Students recognize equations for proportions ($y/x = m$ or $y = mx$) as special linear equations ($y = mx + b$), understanding that the constant of proportionality (m) is the slope, and the graphs are lines through the origin. They understand that the slope (m) of a line is a constant rate of change, so that if the input or x-coordinate changes by an amount A, the output or y-coordinate changes by the amount m·A. Students also use a linear equation to describe the association between two quantities in bivariate data (such as arm span vs. height for students in a classroom). At this grade, fitting the model, and assessing its fit to the data are done informally. Interpreting the model in the context of the data requires students to express a relationship between the two quantities in question and to interpret components of the relationship (such as slope and y-intercept) in terms of the situation.

Students strategically choose and efficiently implement procedures to solve linear equations in one variable, understanding that when they use the properties of equality and the concept of logical equivalence, they maintain the solutions of the original equation. Students solve systems of two linear equations in two variables and relate the systems to pairs of lines in the plane; these intersect, are parallel, or are the same line. Students use linear equations, systems of linear equations, linear functions, and their understanding of slope of a line to analyze situations and solve problems.

(2) Students grasp the concept of a function as a rule that assigns to each input exactly one output. They understand that functions describe situations where one quantity determines another. They can translate among representations

and partial representations of functions (noting that tabular and graphical representations may be partial representations), and they describe how aspects of the function are reflected in the different representations.

(3) Students use ideas about distance and angles, how they behave under translations, rotations, reflections, and dilations, and ideas about congruence and similarity to describe and analyze two-dimensional figures and to solve problems.

Students show that the sum of the angles in a triangle is the angle formed by a straight line, and that various configurations of lines give rise to similar triangles because of the angles created when a transversal cuts parallel lines. Students understand the statement of the Pythagorean Theorem and its converse, and can explain why the Pythagorean Theorem holds, for example, by decomposing a square in two different ways. They apply the Pythagorean Theorem to find distances between points on the coordinate plane, to find lengths, and to analyze polygons. Students complete their work on volume by solving problems involving cones, cylinders, and spheres.

Grade 8 Overview

The Number System

- Know that there are numbers that are not rational, and approximate them by rational numbers.

Expressions and Equations

- Work with radicals and integer exponents.
- Understand the connections between proportional relationships, lines, and linear equations.
- Analyze and solve linear equations and pairs of simultaneous linear equations.

Functions

- Define, evaluate, and compare functions.
- Use functions to model relationships between quantities.

Geometry

- Understand congruence and similarity using physical models, transparencies, or geometry software.
- Understand and apply the Pythagorean Theorem.
- Solve real-world and mathematical problems involving volume of cylinders, cones and spheres.

Statistics and Probability

- Investigate patterns of association in bivariate data.

The Number System 8.NS

Know that there are numbers that are not rational, and approximate them by rational numbers.

1. Know that numbers that are not rational are called irrational. Understand informally that every number has a decimal expansion; for rational numbers show that the decimal expansion repeats eventually, and convert a decimal expansion which repeats eventually into a rational number.

2. Use rational approximations of irrational numbers to compare the size of irrational numbers, locate them approximately on a number line diagram, and estimate the value of expressions (e.g., π^2). For example, by truncating the decimal expansion of $\sqrt{2}$, show that $\sqrt{2}$ is between 1 and 2, then between 1.4 and 1.5, and explain how to continue on to get better approximations.

Expressions and Equations 8.EE

Work with radicals and integer exponents.

1. Know and apply the properties of integer exponents to generate equivalent numerical expressions. For example, $3^2 \times 3^{-5} = 3^{-3} = 1/3^3 = 1/27$.

2. Use square root and cube root symbols to represent solutions to equations of the form $x^2 = p$ and $x^3 = p$, where p is a positive rational number. Evaluate square roots of small perfect squares and cube roots of small perfect cubes. Know that $\sqrt{2}$ is irrational.

3. Use numbers expressed in the form of a single digit times an integer power of 10 to estimate very large or very small quantities, and to express how many times as much one is than the other. For example, estimate the population of the United States as 3×10^8 and the population of the world as 7×10^9, and determine that the world population is more than 20 times larger.

4. Perform operations with numbers expressed in scientific notation, including problems where both decimal and scientific notation are used. Use scientific notation and choose units of appropriate size for measurements of very large or very small quantities (e.g., use millimeters per year for seafloor spreading). Interpret scientific notation that has been generated by technology.

Understand the connections between proportional relationships, lines, and linear equations.

5. Graph proportional relationships, interpreting the unit rate as the slope of the graph. Compare two different proportional relationships represented in different ways. For example, compare a distance-time graph to a distance-time equation to determine which of two moving objects has greater speed.

6. Use similar triangles to explain why the slope m is the same between any two distinct points on a non-vertical line in the coordinate plane; derive the

equation $y = mx$ for a line through the origin and the equation $y = mx + b$ for a line intercepting the vertical axis at b.

Analyze and solve linear equations and pairs of simultaneous linear equations.

7. Solve linear equations in one variable.

   a. Give examples of linear equations in one variable with one solution, infinitely many solutions, or no solutions. Show which of these possibilities is the case by successively transforming the given equation into simpler forms, until an equivalent equation of the form $x = a$, $a = a$, or $a = b$ results (where a and b are different numbers).

   b. Solve linear equations with rational number coefficients, including equations whose solutions require expanding expressions using the distributive property and collecting like terms.

8. Analyze and solve pairs of simultaneous linear equations.

   a. Understand that solutions to a system of two linear equations in two variables correspond to points of intersection of their graphs, because points of intersection satisfy both equations simultaneously.

   b. Solve systems of two linear equations in two variables algebraically, and estimate solutions by graphing the equations. Solve simple cases by inspection. For example, $3x + 2y = 5$ and $3x + 2y = 6$ have no solution because $3x + 2y$ cannot simultaneously be 5 and 6.

   c. Solve real-world and mathematical problems leading to two linear equations in two variables. For example, given coordinates for two pairs of points, determine whether the line through the first pair of points intersects the line through the second pair.

Functions 8.F

Define, evaluate, and compare functions.

1. Understand that a function is a rule that assigns to each input exactly one output. The graph of a function is the set of ordered pairs consisting of an input and the corresponding output.[1]

2. Compare properties of two functions each represented in a different way (algebraically, graphically, numerically in tables, or by verbal descriptions). For example, given a linear function represented by a table of values and a linear function represented by an algebraic expression, determine which function has the greater rate of change.

3. Interpret the equation $y = mx + b$ as defining a linear function, whose graph is a straight line; give examples of functions that are not linear. For example, the

---

[1] *Function notation is not required in Grade 8.*

function A = s^2 giving the area of a square as a function of its side length is not linear because its graph contains the points (1,1), (2,4) and (3,9), which are not on a straight line.

Use functions to model relationships between quantities.

4. Construct a function to model a linear relationship between two quantities. Determine the rate of change and initial value of the function from a description of a relationship or from two (x, y) values, including reading these from a table or from a graph. Interpret the rate of change and initial value of a linear function in terms of the situation it models, and in terms of its graph or a table of values.

5. Describe qualitatively the functional relationship between two quantities by analyzing a graph (e.g., where the function is increasing or decreasing, linear or nonlinear). Sketch a graph that exhibits the qualitative features of a function that has been described verbally.

Geometry 8.G

Understand congruence and similarity using physical models, transparencies, or geometry software.

1. Verify experimentally the properties of rotations, reflections, and translations:

    a. Lines are taken to lines, and line segments to line segments of the same length.

    b. Angles are taken to angles of the same measure.

    c. Parallel lines are taken to parallel lines.

2. Understand that a two-dimensional figure is congruent to another if the second can be obtained from the first by a sequence of rotations, reflections, and translations; given two congruent figures, describe a sequence that exhibits the congruence between them.

3. Describe the effect of dilations, translations, rotations, and reflections on two-dimensional figures using coordinates.

4. Understand that a two-dimensional figure is similar to another if the second can be obtained from the first by a sequence of rotations, reflections, translations, and dilations; given two similar two-dimensional figures, describe a sequence that exhibits the similarity between them.

5. Use informal arguments to establish facts about the angle sum and exterior angle of triangles, about the angles created when parallel lines are cut by a transversal, and the angle-angle criterion for similarity of triangles. For example, arrange three copies of the same triangle so that the sum of the three angles appears to form a line, and give an argument in terms of transversals why this is so.

Understand and apply the Pythagorean Theorem.

6. Explain a proof of the Pythagorean Theorem and its converse.

7. Apply the Pythagorean Theorem to determine unknown side lengths in right triangles in real-world and mathematical problems in two and three dimensions.

8. Apply the Pythagorean Theorem to find the distance between two points in a coordinate system.

Solve real-world and mathematical problems involving volume of cylinders, cones, and spheres.

9. Know the formulas for the volumes of cones, cylinders, and spheres and use them to solve real-world and mathematical problems.

Statistics and Probability 8.SP

Investigate patterns of association in bivariate data.

1. Construct and interpret scatter plots for bivariate measurement data to investigate patterns of association between two quantities. Describe patterns such as clustering, outliers, positive or negative association, linear association, and non-linear association.

2. Know that straight lines are widely used to model relationships between two quantitative variables. For scatter plots that suggest a linear association, informally fit a straight line, and informally assess the model fit by judging the closeness of the data points to the line.

3. Use the equation of a linear model to solve problems in the context of bivariate measurement data, interpreting the slope and intercept. For example, in a linear model for a biology experiment, interpret a slope of 1.5 cm/hr as meaning that an additional hour of sunlight each day is associated with an additional 1.5 cm in mature plant height.

4. Understand that patterns of association can also be seen in bivariate categorical data by displaying frequencies and relative frequencies in a two-way table. Construct and interpret a two-way table summarizing data on two categorical variables collected from the same subjects. Use relative frequencies calculated for rows or columns to describe possible association between the two variables. For example, collect data from students in your class on whether or not they have a curfew on school nights and whether or not they have assigned chores at home. Is there evidence that those who have a curfew also tend to have chores?

References and Resources

Achieve. (2010). *On the road to implementation*. Accessed at www.achieve.org/files/CCSS Comm&Outreach.pdf on December 19, 2011.

Ainsworth, L. (2007). Common formative assessments: The centerpiece of an integrated standards-based assessment system. In D. Reeves (Ed.), *Ahead of the curve: The power of assessment to transform teaching and learning* (pp. 79–101). Bloomington, IN: Solution Tree Press.

Aronson, J., Fried, C. B., & Good, C. (2002). Reducing the effects of stereotype threat on African American college students by shaping theories of intelligence. *Journal of Experimental Social Psychology, 38*(2), 113–125.

Baccellieri, P. (2010). *Professional learning communities: Using data in decision making to improve student learning*. Huntington Beach, CA: Shell Education.

Baker, S., Gersten, R., & Lee, D. (2002). A synthesis of empirical research on teaching mathematics to low-achieving students. *Elementary School Journal, 103*(1), 51–73.

Balanced Assessment Program. (2000). *Assessment task m014tr.doc*. Cambridge, MA: President and Fellows of Harvard College. Accessed at http://balancedassessment .concord.org/docs/m014tr.pdf on March 10, 2012.

Ball, D. L., & Bass, H. (2003). Making mathematics reasonable in school. In J. Kilpatrick, W. G. Martin, & D. Schifter (Eds.), *A research companion to principles and standards for school mathematics* (pp. 27–44). Reston, VA: National Council of Teachers of Mathematics.

Barber, M., & Mourshed, M. (2007). *How the world's best-performing school systems come out on top*. Accessed at http://mckinseyonsociety.com/downloads/reports/Education/Worlds _School_Systems_Final.pdf on December 19, 2011.

Bell, A., & the Toolkit Team. (2005). *Introduce diagnostic teaching*. East Lansing: Mathematics Assessment Resource Service, Michigan State University.

Bender, W. N., & Crane, D. (2011). *RTI in math: Practical guidelines for elementary teachers*. Bloomington, IN: Solution Tree Press.

Bennett, R. E. (2009). *A critical look at the meaning and basis of formative assessment* (ETS Research Report RM-09-06). Princeton, NJ: Educational Testing Service.

Black, P., & Wiliam, D. (1998). Assessment and classroom learning. *Assessment in Education, 5*(1), 7–74.

Blackwell, L. S., Trzesniewski, K. H., & Dweck, C. S. (2007). Implicit theories of intelligence predict achievement across an adolescent transition: A longitudinal study and an intervention. *Child Development, 78*(1), 246–263.

Boaler, J., & Brodie, K. (2004, October). *The importance of depth and breadth in the analysis of teaching: A framework for analyzing teacher questions*. Paper presented at the twenty-sixth meeting of the North American Chapter of the International Group for the Psychology of Mathematics Education, Toronto.

Boaler, J., Wiliam, D., & Brown, M. (2000). Students' experiences of ability grouping—disaffection, polarisation, and the construction of failure. *British Educational Research Journal*, *26*(5), 631–648.

Bowland Charitable Trust. (2010). *Cats and kittens*. Accessed at www.bowland.org.uk /assessment/tasks/pdf/cats_and_kittens_v3_1.pdf on August 3, 2012.

Bransford, J. D., Brown, A. L., & Cocking, T. (Eds.). (2000). *How people learn: Brain, mind, experience, and school* (Expanded ed.). Washington, DC: National Academies Press.

Bransford, J. D., & Donovan, M. S. (2005). Scientific inquiry and how people learn. In M. S. Donovan & J. D. Bransford (Eds.), *How students learn history, mathematics, and science* (pp. 397–419). Washington, DC: National Academies Press.

Buffum, A., Mattos, M., & Weber, C. (2009). *Pyramid response to intervention: RTI, professional learning communities, and how to respond when kids don't learn*. Bloomington, IN: Solution Tree Press.

Bush, W. S., Briars, D. J., Confrey, J., Cramer, K., Lee, C., Martin, W. G., et al. (2011). *Common Core State Standards (CCSS) Mathematics Curriculum Materials Analysis Project*. Accessed at www.mathedleadership.org/docs/ccss/CCSSO%20Mathematics%20 Curriculum%20Analysis%20Project.Whole%20Document.6.1.11.Final.docx on November 15, 2011.

Cobb, P., & Hodge, L. (2002, July). Learning, identity, and statistical data analysis. In B. Phillips (Ed.), *Developing a statistically literate society*. Paper presented at the Sixth International Conference on Teaching Statistics, Cape Town, South Africa. Accessed at www.stat.auckland.ac.nz/~iase/publications/1/2e1_cobb.pdf on April 25, 2012.

Cohen, D. K., & Hill, H. C. (2001). *Learning policy: When state education reform works*. New Haven, CT: Yale University Press.

Collins, J., & Hansen, M. T. (2011). *Great by choice: Uncertainty, chaos, and luck—why some thrive despite them all*. New York: HarperCollins.

Common Core State Standards Initiative. (2011). *Mathematics: Introduction—Standards for mathematical practice*. Accessed at www.corestandards.org/the-standards/mathematics /introduction/standards-for-mathematical-practice on November 15, 2011.

Conley, D. T., Drummond, K. V., de Gonzalez, A., Rooseboom, J., & Stout, O. (2011). *Reaching the goal: The applicability and importance of the Common Core State Standards to college and career readiness*. Eugene, OR: Educational Policy Improvement Center. Accessed at www.epiconline.org/files/pdf/ReachingtheGoal-FullReport.pdf on December 20, 2011.

Corcoran, T. B., Shields, P. M., & Zucker, A. A. (1998). *Evaluation of NSF's Statewide Systemic Initiatives (SSI) program: The SSIs and professional development for teachers*. Menlo Park, CA: SRI International.

Council of Chief State School Officers, Brookhill Foundation, & Texas Instruments. (2011). *Common Core State Standards (CCSS) Mathematics Curriculum Materials Analysis Project*. Accessed at www.k12.wa.us/CoreStandards/pubdocs/CCSSOMath AnalysisProj.pdf on August 8, 2012.

Daro, P., McCallum, B., & Zimba, J. (2012, February 16). The structure is the standards [Web log post]. Accessed at http://commoncoretools.me/2012/02/16/the-structure-is-the -standards on March 11, 2012.

Darling-Hammond, L. (2010). *The flat world and education: How America's commitment to equity will determine our future.* New York: Teachers College Press.

Darling-Hammond, L., Wei, R. C., Andree, A., Richardson, N., & Orphanos, S. (2009). *Professional learning in the learning profession: A status report on teacher development in the United States and abroad.* Dallas, TX: National Staff Development Council.

Donovan, M. S., & Bransford, J. D. (Eds.). *How students learn history, mathematics, and science.* Washington, DC: National Academies Press.

Driscoll, M., Heck, D., & Malzahn, K. (2012). Knowledge for teaching English language learners mathematics: A dilemma. In N. Ramirez & S. Celedon-Pattichis (Eds.), *Beyond good teaching: Advancing mathematics education for ELLs* (pp. 163–182). Reston, VA: National Council of Teachers of Mathematics.

DuFour, R., DuFour, R., & Eaker, R. (2008). *Revisiting professional learning communities at work: New insights for improving schools.* Bloomington, IN: Solution Tree Press.

DuFour, R., DuFour, R., Eaker, R., & Many, T. (2006). *Learning by doing: A handbook for professional learning communities at work.* Bloomington, IN: Solution Tree Press.

DuFour, R., DuFour, R., Eaker, R., & Many, T. (2010). *Learning by doing: A handbook for professional learning communities at work* (2nd ed.). Bloomington, IN: Solution Tree Press.

Dweck, C. S. (2002). Messages that motivate: How praise molds students' beliefs, motivation, and performance (in surprising ways). In J. Aronson (Ed.), *Improving academic achievement: Impact of psychological factors on education* (pp. 37–60). Boston: Academic Press.

Dweck, C. S. (2006). *Mindset: The new psychology of success.* New York: Random House.

Easton, L. B. (2008). *Powerful designs for professional learning* (2nd ed.). Oxford, OH: Learning Forward.

Education Trust. (2005). *Gaining traction, gaining ground: How some high schools accelerate learning for struggling students.* Washington, DC: Author.

Ferrini-Mundy, J., Graham, K., Johnson, L., & Mills, G. (Eds.). (1998). *Making change in mathematics education: Learning from the field.* Reston, VA: National Council of Teachers of Mathematics.

Fisher, D., Frey, N., & Rothenberg, C. (2011). *Implementing RTI with English learners.* Bloomington, IN: Solution Tree Press.

Fisher, L. (2007). *Mathematics assessment collaborative final report.* Palo Alto, CA: Noyce Foundation.

Fleischman, H. L., Hopstock, P. J., Pelczar, M. P., & Shelley, B. E. (2010). *Highlights from PISA 2009: Performance of U.S. 15-year-old students in reading, mathematics, and science literacy in an international context* (NCES 2011-004). Washington, DC: U.S. Government Printing Office.

Foster, D., & Noyce, P. (2004). The Mathematics Assessment Collaborative: Performance testing to improve instruction. *Phi Delta Kappan, 85*(5), 367–374.

Foster, D., Noyce, P., & Spiegel, S. (2007). When assessment guides instruction: Silicon Valley's Mathematics Assessment Collaborative. In A. H. Schoenfeld (Ed.), *Assessing mathematical proficiency* (pp. 137–154). New York: Cambridge University Press.

Foster, D., & Poppers, A. (2009). *Using formative assessment to drive learning: The Silicon Valley Mathematics Initiative: A twelve-year research and development project.* Accessed at www .svmimac.org/images/Using_Formative_Assessment_to_Drive_Learning_Reduced .pdf on August 3, 2012.

Franke, M. L., Kazemi, E., & Battey, D. (2007). Mathematics teaching and classroom practice. In F. K. Lester (Ed.), *Second handbook of research on mathematics teaching and learning* (pp. 225–256). Charlotte, NC: Information Age.

Fullan, M. (2008). *The six secrets of change: What the best leaders do to help their organizations survive and thrive.* San Francisco: Jossey-Bass.

Fuson, K. C., Kalchman, M., & Bransford, J. D. (2005). Mathematical understanding: An introduction. In M. S. Donovan & J. D. Bransford (Eds.), *How students learn: History, mathematics, and science in the classroom* (pp. 217–256). Washington, DC: National Academies Press.

Garet, M. S., Wayne, A. J., Stancavage, F., Taylor, J., Walters, K., Song, M., et al. (2010). *Middle school mathematics professional development impact study: Findings after the first year of implementation* (NCEE 2010–4009). Washington, DC: National Center for Education Evaluation and Regional Assistance.

Garmston, R. J., & Wellman, B. M. (2009). *The adaptive school: A sourcebook for developing collaborative groups* (2nd ed.). Norwood, MA: Christopher-Gordon.

Ginsburg, A., Leinwand, S., & Decker, K. (2009). *Informing grades 1–6 standards development: What can be learned from high-performing Hong Kong, Korea, and Singapore?* Washington, DC: American Institutes for Research.

Ginsburg, H., & Dolan, A. (2011). Assessment. In F. Fennell (Ed.), *Achieving fluency: Special education and mathematics* (pp. 85–103). Reston, VA: National Council of Teachers of Mathematics.

Gonzales, P., Williams, T., Jocelyn, L., Roey, S., Kastberg, D., & Brenwald, S. (2008). *Highlights from TIMSS 2007: Mathematics and science achievement of U.S. fourth- and eighth-grade students in an international context* (NCES 2009–001, Revised). Washington, DC: National Center for Education Statistics, Institute of Education Sciences, U.S. Department of Education.

Good, C., Aronson, J., & Inzlicht, M. (2003). Improving adolescents' standardized test performance: An intervention to reduce the effects of stereotype threat. *Journal of Applied Developmental Psychology, 24,* 645–662.

Graham, P., & Ferriter, B. (2008). One step at a time. *Journal of Staff Development, 29*(3), 38–42.

Grover, R. (Ed.). (1996). *Collaboration: Lessons learned series.* Chicago: American Association of School Librarians.

Hanley, T. V. (2005). Commentary on early identification and intervention for students with mathematical difficulties: Make sense—do the math. *Journal of Learning Disabilities, 38*(4), 346–349.

Hatfield, M. M., Edwards, N. T., Bitter, G. G., & Morrow, J. (2008). *Mathematics methods for elementary and middle school teachers.* Hoboken, NJ: Wiley.

Hattie, J. A. C. (2009). *Visible learning: A synthesis of over 800 meta-analyses relating to achievement*. New York: Routledge.

Hiebert, J., Gallimore, R., Garnier, H., Givvin, K. B., Hollingsworth, H., Jacobs, J., et al. (2003). *Teaching mathematics in seven countries: Results from the TIMSS 1999 video study* (NCES 2003–013). Washington, DC: National Center for Education Statistics. Accessed at http://nces.ed.gov/pubs2003/2003013.pdf on April 23, 2012.

Hiebert, J., Gallimore, R., & Stigler, J. W. (2002). A knowledge base for the teaching profession: What would it look like and how can we get one? *Educational Researcher, 31*(5), 3–15.

Hiebert, J., & Grouws, D. A. (2007). The effects of classroom mathematics teaching on students' learning. In F. K. Lester (Ed.), *Second handbook of research on mathematics teaching and learning: A project of the National Council of Teachers of Mathematics* (pp. 371–404). Charlotte, NC: Information Age.

Hiebert, J., & Stigler, J. W. (1999). *The teaching gap: Best ideas from the world's teachers for improving education in the classroom*. New York: Free Press.

Hiebert, J., & Stigler, J. W. (2004). A world of difference: Classrooms abroad provide lessons in teaching math and science. *Journal of Staff Development, 25*(4), 10–15.

Hill, H. C., Rowan, B., & Ball, D. L. (2005). Effects of teachers' mathematical knowledge for teaching on student achievement. *American Educational Research Journal, 42*(2), 371–406.

Horn, I. S. (2010). Teaching replays, teaching rehearsals, and re-visions of practice: Learning from colleagues in a mathematics teacher community. *Teachers College Record, 112*(1), 225–259.

Inside Mathematics. (2010a). *Common Core standards for mathematical practice*. Accessed at http://insidemathematics.org/index.php/common-core-standards on November 15, 2011.

Inside Mathematics. (2010b). *Tools for coaches*. Accessed at www.insidemathematics.org/index php/tools-for-teachers/tools-for-coaches on April 23, 2012.

Inside Mathematics. (2010c). *Tools for principals and administrators*. Accessed at www.inside mathematics.org/index.php/tools-for-teachers/tools-for-principals-and-administrators on November 15, 2011.

Institute for Mathematics and Education. (2007). *Progressions documents for the Common Core math standards*. Accessed at http://ime.math.arizona.edu/progressions on November 15, 2011.

Johnson, E. S., Smith, L., & Harris, M. L. (2009). *How RTI works in secondary schools*. Thousand Oaks, CA: Corwin Press.

Kanold, T. D. (2006). The flywheel effect: Educators gain momentum from a model for continuous improvement. *Journal of Staff Development, 27*(2), 16–21.

Kanold, T. D. (2011). *The five disciplines of PLC leaders*. Bloomington, IN: Solution Tree Press.

Kanold, T. D., Briars, D. J., & Fennell, F. (2012). *What principals need to know about teaching and learning mathematics*. Bloomington, IN: Solution Tree Press.

Kantowski, M. G. (1980). Some thoughts on teaching for problem solving. In S. Krulik & R. Reys (Eds.), *Problem solving in school mathematics: 1980 yearbook* (pp. 195–203). Reston, VA: National Council of Teachers of Mathematics.

Kersaint, G. (2007). The learning environment: Its influence on what is learned. In W. G. Martin, M. E. Strutchens, & P. C. Elliot (Eds.), *The learning of mathematics: 69th yearbook* (pp. 83–96). Reston, VA: National Council of Teachers of Mathematics.

Knight, J. (2011). *Unmistakable impact: A partnership approach for dramatically improving instruction*. Thousand Oaks, CA: Corwin Press.

Lappan, G., & Briars, D. J. (1995). How should mathematics be taught? In I. M. Carl (Ed.), *75 years of progress: Prospects for school mathematics* (pp. 131–156). Reston, VA: National Council of Teachers of Mathematics.

Larson, M. R. (2011). *Administrator's guide: Interpreting the Common Core State Standards to improve mathematics education*. Reston, VA: National Council of Teachers of Mathematics.

Learning Forward. (2011). *Standards for professional learning*. Oxford, OH: Author. Accessed at www.learningforward.org/standards/standards.cfm on November 15, 2011.

Leithwood, K., & Seashore Louis, K. (Eds.). (1998). *Organizational learning in schools*. Lisse, the Netherlands: Swets & Zeitlinger.

Lewis, C. (2002). *Lesson study: A handbook of teacher-led instructional change*. Philadelphia: Research for Better Schools.

Loucks-Horsley, S., Stiles, K., Mundry, S., Love, N., & Hewson, P. (2009). *Designing professional development for teachers of science and mathematics* (3rd ed.). Thousand Oaks, CA: Corwin Press.

Lubienski, S. T. (2007). What can we do about achievement disparities? *Educational Leadership, 65*(3), 54–59.

Lubienski, S. T., & Gutiérrez, R. (2008). Research commentary: Bridging the gaps in perspectives on equity in mathematics education. *Journal for Research in Mathematics Education, 39*(4), 365–371.

Mark, J., Cuoco A. E., Goldenberg, E. P., & Sword, S. (2010). Developing mathematical habits of mind. *Mathematics Teaching in the Middle School, 15*(9), 505–509.

Martin, D. B. (2003). Hidden assumptions and unaddressed questions in mathematics for all rhetoric. *The Mathematics Educator, 13*(2), 7–21.

Martin, D. B. (2006). Mathematics learning and participation as racialized forms of experience: African American parents speak on the struggle for mathematics literacy. *Mathematical Thinking and Learning, 8*(3), 197–229.

Martin, T. S. (Ed.). (2007). *Mathematics teaching today: Improving practice, improving student learning* (2nd ed.). Reston, VA: National Council of Teachers of Mathematics.

Marzano, R. (2007). *The art and science of teaching: A comprehensive framework for effective instruction*. Alexandria, VA: Association for Supervision and Curriculum Development.

Maryland State Department of Education. (2010). *Introduction to the classroom-focused improvement process.* Accessed at http://mdk12.org/process/cfip on September 17, 2012.

Mathematics Assessment Collaborative. (2001). *The poster.* Morgan Hill, CA: Silicon Valley Mathematics Initiative.

Mathematics Assessment Resource Service. (2012a). *A05: Baseball jerseys.* Accessed at http://map.mathshell.org/materials/tasks.php?taskid=362&subpage=apprentice on August 8, 2012.

Mathematics Assessment Resource Service. (2012b). *Interpreting distance-time graphs.* Accessed at http://map.mathshell.org/materials/download.php?fileid=667 on August 8, 2012.

McCall, M. S., Hauser, C., Cronin, J., Gage Kingsbury, G., & Houser, R. (2006). *Achievement gaps: An examination of differences in student achievement and growth—Research brief.* Lake Oswego, OR: Northwest Evaluation Association.

McCallum, W. G. (2011). The Common Core State Standards for mathematics. In the Center for K–12 Assessment & Performance Management at ETS, *Coming together to raise achievement: New assessments for the Common Core State Standards* (pp. 3–4). Austin, TX: Author.

McCallum, W. G., Black, A., Umland, K., & Whitesides, E. (n.d.). [Common Core Mathematical Practices model]. *Tools for the Common Core standards.* Accessed at http://commoncoretools.files.wordpress.com/2011/03/practices.pdf on March 7, 2012.

Morris, A. K., & Hiebert, J. (2011). Creating shared instructional products: An alternative approach to improving teaching. *Educational Researcher, 40*(1), 5–14.

Morris, A. K., Hiebert, J., & Spitzer, S. M. (2009). Mathematical knowledge for teaching in planning and evaluating instruction: What can preservice teachers learn? *Journal for Research in Mathematics Education, 40*(5), 491–529.

Mueller, C. M., & Dweck, C. S. (1998). Praise for intelligence can undermine children's motivation and performance. *Journal of Personality and Social Psychology, 75*(1), 33–52.

Mullis, I. V. S., Martin, M. O., & Foy, P. (2008). *TIMSS 2007 international mathematics report: Findings from IEA's Trends in International Mathematics and Science Study at the fourth and eighth grades.* Chestnut Hill, MA: TIMSS & PIRLS International Study Center, Boston College.

National Board for Professional Teaching Standards. (2010). *National board certification for teachers: Mathematics standards for teachers of students ages 11–18+.* Arlington, VA: Author.

National Center on Response to Intervention. (2010). *Essential components of RTI: A closer look at response to intervention.* Washington, DC: U.S. Department of Education, Office of Special Education Programs, National Center on Response to Intervention.

National Center on Response to Intervention. (n.d.). *Monitoring progress.* Accessed at www.rti4success.org on June 15, 2011.

National Commission on Teaching and America's Future & WestEd. (2010). *STEM teachers in professional learning communities: A knowledge synthesis.* Washington, DC: Author. Accessed at www.nctaf.org/wp-content/uploads/STEMTeachersinProfessionalLearningCommunities.AKnowledgeSynthesis.pdf on October 1, 2012.

National Council of Supervisors of Mathematics. (2007). *Improving student achievement by leading effective and collaborative teams of mathematics teachers*. Denver, CO: Author.

National Council of Supervisors of Mathematics. (2008a). *The PRIME leadership framework: Principles and indicators for mathematics education leaders*. Bloomington, IN: Solution Tree Press.

National Council of Supervisors of Mathematics. (2008b). *Improving student achievement by leading the pursuit of a vision for equity*. Denver, CO: Author.

National Council of Supervisors of Mathematics. (2010). *Improving student achievement in mathematics by promoting positive self-beliefs*. Denver, CO: Author.

National Council of Supervisors of Mathematics. (2011). *Improving student achievement in mathematics by systematically integrating effective technology*. Denver, CO: Author.

National Council of Teachers of Mathematics. (1989). *Curriculum and evaluation standards for school mathematics*. Reston, VA: Author.

National Council of Teachers of Mathematics. (1991). *Professional standards for teaching mathematics*. Reston, VA: Author.

National Council of Teachers of Mathematics. (1995). *Assessment standards for school mathematics*. Reston, VA: Author.

National Council of Teachers of Mathematics. (2000). *Principles and standards for school mathematics: An overview*. Reston, VA: Author.

National Council of Teachers of Mathematics. (2006). *Curriculum focal points for prekindergarten through grade 8 mathematics: A quest for coherence*. Reston, VA: Author.

National Council of Teachers of Mathematics. (2007). *Creating or selecting intervention programs*. Accessed at www.nctm.org/uploadedFiles/Lessons_and_Resources/Intervention_Resources/Intervention%20Programs%20%28NCTM,%20Nov%202007%29.pdf on April 16, 2012.

National Council of Teachers of Mathematics. (2008a). *Equity in mathematics education: A position of the National Council of Teachers of Mathematics*. Accessed at www.nctm.org/about/content.aspx?id=13490 on October 15, 2011.

National Council of Teachers of Mathematics. (2008b). *Intervention. A position of the National Council of Teachers of Mathematics*. Accessed at www.nctm.org/about/content.aspx?id=30506 on October 15, 2011.

National Council of Teachers of Mathematics. (2009). *Focus in high school mathematics: Reasoning and sense making*. Reston, VA: Author.

National Governors Association Center for Best Practices & Council of Chief State School Officers. (2010a). *Common Core State Standards for mathematics*. Washington, DC: Authors. Accessed at www.corestandards.org/assets/CCSSI_Math%20Standards.pdf on November 22, 2010.

National Governors Association Center for Best Practices & Council of Chief State School Officers. (2010b). *Common Core State Standards for mathematics: Appendix A—Designing high school mathematics courses based on the Common Core State Standards*. Washington,

DC: Authors. Accessed at www.achieve.org/files/CCSSI_Mathematics%20Appendix%20A_101110.pdf on April 19, 2012.

National Governors Association Center for Best Practices & Council of Chief State School Officers. (2011). *Resources: Common Core implementation video series.* Accessed at www.ccsso.org/Resources/Digital_Resources/Common_Core_Implementation_Video_Series.html on November 15, 2011.

National Research Council. (2001). *Adding it up: Helping children learn mathematics.* Washington, DC: National Academies Press.

Nonaka, I., & Takeuchi, H. (1995). *The knowledge-creating company: How Japanese companies create the dynamics of innovation.* New York: Oxford University Press.

O'Neill, J., & Conzemius, A. (2006). *The power of SMART goals: Using goals to improve student learning.* Bloomington, IN: Solution Tree Press.

Pashler, H., Bain, P., Bottge, B., Graesser, A., Koedinger, K., McDaniel, M., et al. (2007). *Organizing instruction and study to improve student learning* (NCER 2007–2004). Washington, DC: National Center for Education Research, Institute of Education Sciences, U.S. Department of Education. Accessed at http://ncer.ed.gov on April 5, 2011.

Penuel, W. R., Fishman, B. J., Yamaguchi, R., & Gallagher, L. P. (2007). What makes professional development effective? Strategies that foster curriculum implementation. *American Educational Research Journal, 44*(4), 921–958.

Peske, H. G., & Haycock, K. (2006). *Teaching inequality: How poor and minority students are shortchanged on teacher quality—A report and recommendations by the Education Trust.* Washington, DC: Education Trust. Accessed at www.edtrust.org/sites/edtrust.org/files/publications/files/TQReportJune2006.pdf on July 21, 2011.

Pölya, G. (1957). *How to solve it: A new aspect of mathematical method* (2nd ed.). Garden City, NY: Doubleday.

Popham, W. J. (2008). *Transformative assessment.* Alexandria, VA: Association for Supervision and Curriculum Development.

Popham, W. J. (2011a). *Transformative assessment in action: An inside look at applying the process.* Alexandria, VA: Association for Supervision and Curriculum Development.

Popham, W. J. (2011b). Formative assessment—A process and not a test. *Education Week, 30*(21), 35–37.

Progressions for the Common Core State Standards in Mathematics. (2011a). *K, counting and cardinality; K–5, operations and algebraic thinking* (Draft, May 29, 2011). Tucson: Institute for Mathematics and Education, University of Arizona. Accessed at http://math.arizona.edu/~ime/progressions on May 15, 2012.

Progressions for the Common Core State Standards in Mathematics. (2011b). *K–5, numbers and operations in base ten* (Draft, April 21, 2012). Tucson: Institute for Mathematics and Education, University of Arizona. Accessed at http://math.arizona.edu/~ime/progressions on May 15, 2012.

Progressions for the Common Core State Standards in Mathematics. (2011c). *6–7 ratios and proportional relationships* (Draft, December 26, 2011). Tucson: Institute for

Mathematics and Education, University of Arizona. Accessed at http://math.arizona .edu/~ime/progressions on May 15, 2012.

Progressions for the Common Core State Standards in Mathematics. (2011d). *6–8 statistics and probability* (Draft, December 26, 2011). Tucson: Institute for Mathematics and Education, University of Arizona. Accessed at http://math.arizona.edu/~ime /progressions on May 15, 2012.

Progressions for the Common Core State Standards in Mathematics. (2011e). *K–3, categorical data*; *grades 2–5, measurement data* (Draft, June 20, 2011). Tucson: Institute for Mathematics and Education, University of Arizona. Accessed at http://math.arizona .edu/~ime/progressions on May 15, 2012.

Progressions for the Common Core State Standards in Mathematics. (2012). *K–6, geometry* (Draft, June 23, 2012). Tucson: Institute for Mathematics and Education, University of Arizona. Accessed at http://math.arizona.edu/~ime/progressions on May 15, 2012.

Rasmussen, C., Yackel, E., & King, K. (2003). Social and sociomathematical norms in the mathematics classroom. In H. L. Schoen & R. I. Charles (Eds.), *Teaching mathematics through problem solving: Grades 6–12* (pp. 143–154). Reston, VA: National Council of Teachers of Mathematics.

Reeves, D. B. (2010). *Transforming professional development into student results*. Alexandria, VA: Association for Supervision and Curriculum Development.

Reeves, D. B. (2011). *Elements of grading: A guide to effective practice*. Bloomington, IN: Solution Tree Press.

Reinhart, S. C. (2000). Never say anything a kid can say! *Mathematics Teaching in the Middle School, 5*(8), 478–483.

Resnick, L. (Ed.). (2006). Do the math: Cognitive demand makes a difference. *American Educational Research Association, 4*(2), 1–4. Accessed at www.eric.ed.gov/PDFS /ED497645.pdf on August 3, 2012.

Reys, R., Lindquist, M. M., Lambdin, D. V., & Smith, N. L. (2009). *Helping children learn mathematics* (9th ed.). Hoboken, NJ: Wiley.

Rohrer, D., & Taylor, K. (2007). The shuffling of mathematics problems improves learning. *Instructional Science, 35*, 481–498.

Ross, P. E. (2006). The expert mind. *Scientific American, 295*(2), 64–71.

Saunders, W. M., Goldenberg, C. N., & Gallimore, R. (2009). Increasing achievement by focusing grade-level teams on improving classroom learning: A prospective, quasi-experimental study of Title I schools. *American Educational Research Journal, 46*(4), 1006–1033.

Seago, N., Jacobs, J., & Driscoll, M. (2010). Transforming middle school geometry: Designing professional development materials that support the teaching and learning of similarity. *Middle Grades Research Journal, 5*(4), 199–211.

Seeley, C. L. (2009). *Faster isn't smarter: Messages about math, teaching and learning in the 21st century*. Sausalito, CA: Math Solutions.

SMARTER Balanced Assessment Consortium. (n.d.). *Consortium governance.* Olympia: State of Washington Office of Superintendent of Public Instruction. Accessed at www .smarterbalanced.org on December 20, 2011.

Smith, M. S., & Stein, M. K. (2011). *5 practices for orchestrating productive mathematics discussions.* Thousand Oaks, CA: Corwin Press.

St. John, M., Houghton, N., & Tambe, P. (2000). *A study of the MARS project: The contributions to clients.* Inverness, CA: Inverness Research Associates. Accessed at www .inverness-research.org/reports/2000-12-Rpt-MARS-ContributionToClients.pdf on April 23, 2012.

Stein, M. K., Grover, B. W., & Henningsen, M. (1996). Building student capacity for mathematical thinking and reasoning: An analysis of mathematical tasks used in reform classrooms. *American Educational Research Journal, 33*(2), 455–488.

Stein, M. K., Remillard, J., & Smith, M. S. (2007). How curriculum influences student learning. In F. K. Lester (Ed.), *Second handbook of research on mathematics teaching and learning* (pp. 319–370). Charlotte, NC: Information Age.

Stein, M. K., & Smith, M. S. (1998). Mathematical tasks as a framework for reflection: From research to practice. *Mathematics Teaching in the Middle School, 3*(4), 268–275.

Stein, M. K., Smith, M. S., Henningsen, M., & Silver, E. A. (2000). *Implementing standards-based mathematics instruction: A casebook for professional development.* New York: Teachers College Press.

Stepanek, J., Appel, G., Leong, M., Managan, M. T., & Mitchell, M. (2007). *Leading lesson study: A practical guide for teachers and facilitators.* Thousand Oaks, CA: Corwin Press.

Stiff, L. V., Johnson, J. L., & Akos, P. (2011). Examining what we know for sure: Tracking in middle grades mathematics. In W. F. Tate, K. D. King, & C. R. Anderson (Eds.), *Disrupting tradition: Research and practice pathways in mathematics education* (pp. 63–75). Reston, VA: National Council of Teachers of Mathematics.

Stiggins, R. J., Arter, J. A., Chappuis, J., & Chappuis, S. (2007). *Classroom assessment for student learning: Doing it right—using it well.* Upper Saddle River, NJ: Pearson Education.

Stigler, J., Gonzales, P., Kawanka, T., Knoll, S., & Serrano, A. (1999). *The TIMSS videotape classroom study: Methods and findings from an exploratory research project on eighth-grade mathematics instruction in Germany, Japan, and the United States.* Washington, DC: U.S. Department of Education, Office of Educational Research and Improvement.

Stigler, J. W., & Hiebert, J. (1999). *The teaching gap: Best ideas from the world's teachers for improving education in the classroom.* New York: Free Press.

Stronge, J. H. (2007). *Qualities of effective teachers* (2nd ed.). Alexandria, VA: Association for Supervision and Curriculum Development.

Swan, M. (2005). *Standards unit: Improving learning in mathematics—Challenges and strategies.* Nottingham, England: University of Nottingham, Department for Education and Skills Standards Unit.

Tate, W., & Rousseau, C. (2002). Access and opportunity: The political and social context of mathematics education. In L. D. English (Ed.), *Handbook of international research in mathematics education* (pp. 271–300). Mahwah, NJ: Erlbaum.

Thompson, M., & Wiliam, D. (2007). *Tight but loose: A conceptual framework for scaling up school reforms.* Washington, DC: American Educational Research Association.

Ushomirsky, N., & Hall, D. (2010). *Stuck schools: A framework for identifying schools where students need change—now!* Washington, DC: Education Trust. Accessed at www.edtrust .org/sites/edtrust.org/files/publications/files/StuckSchools.pdf on February 26, 2012.

Van de Walle, J. A. (2004). *Elementary and middle school mathematics: Teaching developmentally* (5th ed.). Boston: Allyn & Bacon.

Waters, T., Marzano, R., & McNulty, B. (2003). *Balanced leadership: What 30 years of research tells us about the effect of leadership on student achievement.* Denver, CO: McREL.

Wayne, A. J., Yoon, K. S., Zhu, P., Cronen, S., & Garet, M. S. (2008). Experimenting with teacher professional development: Motives and methods. *Educational Researcher, 37*(8), 469–479.

Weiss, I. R., Heck, D. J., & Shimbus, E. S. (2004). Looking inside the classroom: Mathematics teaching in the United States. *NCSM Journal of Mathematics Education Leadership, 7*(1), 23–32.

Wellman, B., & Lipton, L. (2004). *Data-driven dialogue: A facilitator's guide to collaborative inquiry.* Sherman, CT: MiraVia.

Wheatley, C. L., & Wheatley, G. H. (1984). Problem solving in the primary grades. *Arithmetic Teacher, 31*(8), 42–44.

Wiliam, D. (2007a). Content then process: Teacher learning communities in the service of formative assessment. In D. Reeves (Ed.), *Ahead of the curve: The power of assessment to transform teaching and learning* (pp. 183–205). Bloomington, IN: Solution Tree Press.

Wiliam, D. (2007b). Keeping learning on track: Classroom assessment and the regulation of learning. In F. K. Lester (Ed.), *Second handbook of research on mathematics teaching and learning* (pp. 1053–1098). Charlotte, NC: Information Age.

Wiliam, D. (2011). *Embedded formative assessment.* Bloomington, IN: Solution Tree Press.

Wiliam, D., & Thompson, M. (2007). Integrating assessment with instruction: What will it take to make it work? In C. A. Dwyer (Ed.), *The future of assessment: Shaping teaching and learning* (pp. 53–82). Mahwah, NJ: Erlbaum.

Wilkins, A., & Education Trust Staff. (2006). *Yes we can: Telling truths and dispelling myths about race and education in America.* Washington, DC: Education Trust. Accessed at www .edtrust.org/sites/edtrust.org/files/publications/files/YesWeCan.pdf on June 5, 2011.

Williams, B. (2003). Reframing the reform agenda. In B. Williams (Ed.), *Closing the achievement gap: A vision for changing beliefs and practices* (2nd ed., pp. 178–196). Alexandria, VA: Association for Supervision and Curriculum Development.

Yackel, E., & Cobb, P. (1996). Sociomathematical norms, argumentation, and autonomy in mathematics. *Journal for Research in Mathematics Education, 27*(4), 458–477.

Index

A

Achieve, 151

Adding It Up, 2, 29, 71

advanced learners, meeting the needs of, 122–123

Ainsworth, L., 63

AllThingsPLC, 26

anticipating, 65

assessments

    data, focus on large-scale, 151

    diagnostic, 142

    follow-up, 170–171

    instruments, identifying, 137–138

    instruments, reasons for using, 141–143

    role of, 4

    See also formative assessments; teaching-assessing-learning cycle

B

Ball, D. L., 1, 40

Barth, R., 155

Bass, H., 40

Bell, A., 173

Bennett, R. E., 142

Boaler, J., 65

book study, 23

Briars, D. J., 63

Brodie, K., 65

Buffum, A., 163

C

case study, 23

CCL4s (Common Core Look-Fors), 32, 72

CCSS (Common Core State Standards)

    key terms used in, 20–22

    overview of, 75–79

    purpose of, 76–77

CCSS for Mathematical Practice

    advances in, 8

    description of, 29, 31–58

    key questions used to understand, 30, 31, 32

    lesson-design elements, 58–68

    lesson-design tool, 68–69

    organization model, 32

    resources, 71–73, 125–126, 153–154, 177–178

    See also individual Mathematical Practices

Center for Comprehensive School Reform and Improvement, The, 26

change

    first-order, 2

    grain size of, 3

    second-order, 2–3, 4

    without difference, xvi

Chicago Lesson Study Group, 27

Classroom-Focused Improvement Process (CFIP), 177

clusters, use of term, 78

collaboration

    role of, 3, 7–8

    versus cooperation or coordination, 11–14

collaborative grading, 23

collaborative teams

    agendas and meeting minutes, 17–18

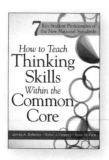

How to Teach Thinking Skills Within the Common Core
7 Key Student Proficiencies of the New National Standards
James A. Bellanca, Robin J. Fogarty, and Brian M. Pete
Empower your students to thrive across the curriculum. Packed with examples and tools, this practical guide prepares teachers across all grade levels and content areas to teach the most critical cognitive skills from the Common Core State Standards.
BKF576

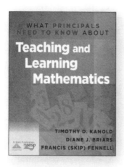

What Principals Need to Know About Teaching and Learning Mathematics
Timothy D. Kanold, Diane J. Briars, and Francis (Skip) Fennell
This must-have resource offers support and encouragement for improved mathematics achievement across every grade level. With an emphasis on Principles and Standards for School Mathematics and Common Core State Standards, this book covers the importance of mathematics content, learning and instruction, and mathematics assessment.
BKF501

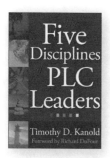

The Five Disciplines of PLC Leaders
Timothy D. Kanold
Foreword by Richard DuFour
Effective leadership in a professional learning community requires practice, patience, and skill. Through engaging examples and accessible language, this book offers a focused framework that will help educators maintain balance and consistent vision as they strengthen the skills of PLC leadership.
BKF495

Learning by Doing
A Handbook for Professional Learning Communities at Work™
Richard DuFour, Rebecca DuFour, Robert Eaker, and Thomas Many
Learning by Doing is an action guide for closing the knowing-doing gap and transforming schools into PLCs. It also includes seven major additions that equip educators with essential tools for confronting challenges.
BKF416

Wait! Your professional development journey doesn't have to end with the last pages of this book.

We realize improving student learning doesn't happen overnight. And your school or district shouldn't be left to puzzle out all the details of this process alone.

No matter where you are on the journey, we're committed to helping you get to the next stage.

Take advantage of everything from **custom workshops** to **keynote presentations** and **interactive web and video conferencing**. We can even help you develop an action plan tailored to fit your specific needs.

Let's get the conversation started.

Call 888.763.9045 today.

solution-tree.com

Solution Tree

Solution Tree's mission is to advance the work of our authors. By working with the best researchers and educators worldwide, we strive to be the premier provider of innovative publishing, in-demand events, and inspired professional development designed to transform education to ensure that all students learn.

NATIONAL COUNCIL OF
TEACHERS OF MATHEMATICS

The National Council of Teachers of Mathematics is a public voice of mathematics education, supporting teachers to ensure equitable mathematics learning of the highest quality for all students through vision, leadership, professional development, and research.